THE FUTURE OF THE MUSIC BUSINESS

THIRD EDITION

music **PRO**
guides

THE FUTURE OF THE MUSIC BUSINESS

THIRD EDITION

HOW TO SUCCEED WITH THE NEW DIGITAL TECHNOLOGIES

A Guide for Artists and Entrepreneurs

STEVE GORDON

Hal Leonard Books
An Imprint of Hal Leonard Corporation

Hal Leonard Books
An Imprint of Hal Leonard Corporation
7777 West Bluemound Road
Milwaukee, WI 53213

Trade Book Division Editorial Offices
33 Plymouth St., Montclair, NJ 07042

Third edition published in 2011 by Hal Leonard Books

Second edition published in 2008 by Hal Leonard Books; first edition published in 2005 by Backbeat Books

Cover design: Patrick Devine
Front cover photos: Powell Burns (top), Comstock Images © Getty Images (bottom)

Printed in the United States of America

The Library of Congress has cataloged the Backbeat Books edition as follows:

Gordon, Steve.
The future of the music business : how to succeed with the new digital technologies / by Steve Gordon
        p. cm.
Includes index.
    1. Music trade—Vocational guidance. 2. Sound—Recording and reproducing—Digital techniques. I. Title.
ML3790.G67 2005
780'.68—dc22   2005007155

ISBN 978-1-4234-9969-5

www.halleonardbooks.com

This book is dedicated to my father, Harry, 1922–2010,
a good man who lived a good life.

Contents

Special Acknowledgments.. xiii

Foreword to the Third Edition by Tom Silverman, CEO of Tommy Boy Records
    and Cofounder of the New Music Seminar xv

Foreword to the Second Edition by Derek Sivers, Founder
    and Former President of CD Baby...xviii

Foreword to the First Edition by John Simson, Executive Director of SoundExchange................xix

Preface xxi

Introduction xxv

Part I: The Law
An overview of the rules that apply to the music business and the new rules that apply to digital music.

Chapter 1: Music Law and Business Primer...5
    Copyright Law: The Foundation of the Music Publishing and Recording Business................ 5
    Songwriters and Music Publishers: Rules and Business Practices 7
    Artists and Labels: Rules and Business Practices 15
    The "360" Deal...18
    Copyright Registration: Why Do It, and How? 19
    Duration of Copyright 21
    Fair Use 24
    Creative Commons: An Alternative to Copyright 27

Chapter 2: Practical Advice in Response to Clients' Most-Asked Questions.....................34
    Somebody Stole My Song! What Can I Do? How Much Can I Get?
        When Can I Get It, and How Much Will It Cost? 34

How Can I Protect My Name, the Name of My Band, or the Name of My Company?
Should I Register with the Trademark Office, and How Much Will It Cost? 40
How Can a Music Lawyer Help Me? Will They Shop My Music,
and How Much Will It Cost?... 51

Chapter 3: Overview of Digital Music Law...**55**
Statutes Applicable to Digital Music: AHRA, DPRSRA, and DMCA 55
Webcasting, Tethered Downloading, Interactive Streaming, and Downloading.................... 57

Chapter 4: Focus on Webcasting...**60**
What Is Webcasting? 60
Why Is Webcasting Important? 62
Compulsory License for Recorded Music: What Is It, and How Do I Get One? 66
The Role of SoundExchange... 68
Current Rates Payable by Webcasters to SoundExchange for Recorded Music..................... 69
Current Rates Payable by Webcasters to ASCAP, BMI, and SESAC for Songs 74

Chapter 5: Focus on Tethered Downloading, Interactive Streaming, and Downloading **76**
How Much Do the Digital Music Services Pay the Labels? 77
How Much Do the Labels Pay the Artists?... 79
Eminem's Lawsuit Against Universal Music 79
How Much Do the Digital Music Services Pay the Publishers? 81
How Much Do the Publishers Pay the Writers? 84

Chapter 6: Music-Licensing Fundamentals...**85**
Audio Compilations... 85
Home Video 86
Television Programs... 90
Motion Pictures 93
Advertising 94
Musical Theater... 100
Practical Tips for Music Licensing 101
Billboard Commentary: Music Documentary Filmmakers
Deserve a Break on Licensing Fees 106

Chapter 7: Licensing Music for New Media...**107**
Websites 107
Ringtones.. 108
Video Games 111

Part II: Crisis and Solutions—The Recording Industry in Transition

A look at the recording industry's tumultuous struggle to come to grips with the digital age, proposed solutions to the crisis, and a summary of the most recent legal cases and legislative initiatives.

Chapter 8: A Brief History of the Digital Music Business 119

Labels vs. the Consumer Electronics Industry
and the Failure of the Secure Digital Music Initiative (SDMI) 120

Labels vs. Technology: The Rootkit Disaster 121

Labels vs. P2P: Napster and Grokster Cases 121

Labels vs. Fans: RIAA's Lawsuits 124

Labels Enter the Digital Music Business: MusicNet and Pressplay 125

Labels Give Away the Store: The Birth of iTunes 126

Chapter 9: Proposed Solutions 127

Legalize File Sharing in Exchange for a Levy Payable to the Labels,
Music Publishers, Artists, and Songwriters 128

Other Solutions 132

Chapter 10: Latest Cases and Legislative Initiatives 135

Viacom vs. YouTube 135

Universal vs. Grooveshark 136

Network Neutrality: The Battle over the Future of the Internet 138

Public Performance Rights Act: Will the Labels Finally Get Radio to Pay Up? 140

Labels vs. LimeWire: The End of P2P? 143

Update on the RIAA's Lawsuits 144

RIAA's Latest Tactics 148

France's Three-Strikes Law 148

Part III: How to Succeed in the New Music Business

Chapter 11 provides strategies for using the power of the Internet to succeed in the music business as an independent artist. Chapter 12 provides tips for online marketing by an industry expert. Chapter 13 discusses more traditional models of success that still dominate the pop, R&B, and hip-hop worlds.

Chapter 11: How Artists Can Use New Technologies to Succeed 153

Social Networks: How to Get the Most from Them 153

How to Create a Strong Online Presence Through Facebook and Twitter 155

Is Myspace Dead? 160

How to Go Viral on YouTube and How to Use Ustream 162

The Justin Bieber Story 163

OK Go Becomes a Household Name from Making a $20 Video 164

How to Broadcast Yourself on Ustream 164

Music Blogs: The New Tastemakers 165
An Overview of Music Blogs 166
How to Attract Bloggers to Your Music 167
Aggregators 168
Your Website: How to Make It Great 168
Why Your Own Website Is Essential in Crafting an Online Presence 168
Methods to Easily Create Your Own Website 169
What to Include on Your Website and Why 170
Apps for Artists 172
How They Work 172
Should You Get One, and How Much Will It Cost? 172
Other Music Sites to Utilize 174
SoundCloud, Last.fm, and Bandcamp 174
How to Sell Your Music Online 176
TuneCore and CD Baby 176
How to Sell Music from Your Website for Almost Nothing and Keep All the Money 179

Chapter 12: Insights from an Online Marketing Guru **181**
Online Marketing Manual by Jason Spiewak, President of Rock Ridge Music 181

Chapter 13: Big Money and Mainstream Success: Major Labels and New Business Models **186**
Big-Label Deals: Who Gets Them, How, and How Many Are Left? 186
Interview with Craig Kallman, Chairman and CEO of Atlantic Records 187
Interview with Jason Jordan, VP of A&R at Disney's Hollywood Music 191
Facing Extinction, the Major Labels Adapt: EMI Label Services
and an Interview with Its Chief, Michael Harris 194

Part IV: Interviews with Artists and Music Industry Leaders

The following discussions are drawn from my podcast "The Future of the Music Business" and include new Q&A never before published that address a wide array of issues in today's music business.

Chapter 14: Artists Adapting to a Digital World **201**
How to Raise $80,000 in Two Months: Interview with Singer,
Songwriter, and Recording Artist Jill Sobule 201

Chapter 15: Are Indie Labels Better for Artists than Majors? **209**
Interview with Musician, Composer, and Recording Artist Moby 209

Chapter 16: A Digital Artist: DJ Spooky, aka That Subliminal Kid **216**
Interview with Paul Miller 216

Chapter 17: How to Measure Success in a Digital World 220
Interview with Eric Garland, Cofounder and CEO of BigChampagne..........................220

**Chapter 18: The True Story of Napster and the Labels: How Shawn Fanning
Made the Labels an Offer They *Had* to Refuse** 227
Interview with Ted Cohen, Managing Partner of TAG Strategic
and Former Senior VP at EMI Music 227

Chapter 19: How to Make a Hit Song in the Digital Age..235
Interview with Jay Frank, Senior VP of Country Music Television...............................235

Chapter 20: How to Distribute Music in the Digital Age 244
Interview with Jason Pascal, Vice President and Senior Counsel at The Orchard................244

Chapter 21: How a Music Publisher and Indie Label Adapt to a Digital World 246
Interview with Alisa Coleman, Senior VP of ABKCO Music and Records.........................246

Chapter 22: The Changing Role of the Manager in Today's Music Business...................251
Interview with Ari Martin, Nettwerk Management..251

Chapter 23: The Changing Role of the Manager in Today's Music Business, Part 2 255
Interview with Ed Arrendell, Manager of Wynton Marsalis 255

Chapter 24: The Changing Role of A&R..259
Interview with Michael Caplan, CEO of One Haven Music
and Former Senior VP at Epic 259

Chapter 25: How to Make It in Today's Music Business...266
Interview with Don Passman, Author of
All You Need to Know About the Music Business...266

Chapter 26: Indie-Label Perspective...273
Interview with Rich Bengloff, President of A2IM:
American Association of Independent Music 273

Chapter 27: Are Record Labels Still Necessary?..277
Interview with Bruce Iglauer, President and Founder, Alligator Records 277

Chapter 28: Are Record Labels Still Necessary? (A Futurist's POV) 287
Interview with Greg Kot, Music Critic at the *Chicago Tribune*
and Author of *Ripped: How the Wired Generation Revolutionized Music* 287

Chapter 29: New Business Models **296**
    Interview with John Buckman, President and Founder of Magnatune.com 296

Chapter 30: Music Videos in Today's Music Business...**300**
    Interview with Camille Yorrick, Former VP of Video Sony Music 300

Chapter 31: Challenges Facing Digital Music Entrepreneurs **304**
    Interview with Steve Masur, Digital Media Attorney,
        and Moses Avalon, Author of *Confessions of a Music Producer* 304

Acknowledgments **317**

Index...**319**

Special Acknowledgments

The author gratefully expresses his appreciation to

Laurel Chartow
&
Nari Roye, Esq.,

for their valuable assistance in research pertaining to many issues discussed in this book.

Foreword
to the third edition

In my board positions at American Association of Independent Music (A2IM), Merlin, Recording Industry Association of America (RIAA), and SoundExchange, I am able to get a good pulse on the vision and direction of the music business. Recently it occurred to me that the record business was probably not going to come back, yet the major industry trade bodies continued their exclusively protectionist direction. I did some music-sales calculations using generally available SoundScan and RIAA data, and it became clear that it is time to shift our energy to building a new sustainable music business. Around the same time, Dave Lory, a former staff member of the original New Music Seminar, approached me about starting the New Music Seminar again. It had been seventeen years since I bowed out of the original New Music Seminar, of which I was one of the founding partners. The idea felt really good. The world needs a forum to discuss and create that new sustainable music business. Two factors convinced me to say yes to Dave and the New Music Seminar.

1. The original promise of the Internet and digital technology was to democratize music and allow more music and artists to break than ever before. Now, fifteen years later, we have the proof that fewer new artists are breaking than ever before. The predicted golden age looks more like the dark ages. Artists will need to adopt new definitions of success, and the old arbiters of success will be replaced by new ones.
2. A music business based on album sales was no longer sustainable. A new paradigm would have to be adopted to allow for more investment in new artists and music. My passion is looking for new ways of addressing these issues so that all artists will achieve their maximum potential.

As a student of the music business or an aspiring artist, understanding of the future of the music business has always been an important factor in setting your sails for success. Whether it is a career in the business or as an artist, knowing "the rules" helps you win at the game.

Today's music-business scenario sets quite a different stage than seen in prior issues of this book. Everything we thought was true may no longer be true. The things we thought would be good have not been good, and the things we thought would be bad might not have been bad. The industry leaders and professional prognosticators have made absolute declarations of the future that have been declared false within as little as eighteen months.

In Steve Gordon's last introduction, he referred to the shrinkage of the value of music sales in America from $15 billion in 1999 to $11.5 billion in 2006. That $11.5 billion has continued to shrink to just over $6 billion and continues to fall.

This chart was created by RIAA to show the actual inflation-adjusted value of the music business from 1961 to 2009. The value of the business in 2009 was roughly equivalent to the music business in 1967. As of this writing in 2010, album sales (including digital albums) have fallen another 16 percent, while the growth in single sales (track downloads) has peaked and begun to fall on catalog titles and overall sales.

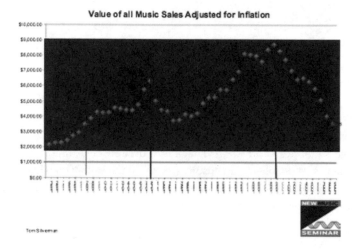

"The cloud" of inexpensive access to music is about to rear its head. As music acquisition evolves to music access, it is highly likely that the value of music will take an even sharper dive.

There is no absolute value. Value equals perception. The consumer's perception of the value of music has fallen since 2000 and keeps falling. The value of the recorded-music business today is roughly 20 percent of what it was ten years ago when you adjust for inflation, and it continues to drop.

It is important to understand this scenario to identify the unprecedented opportunities that now exist for music entrepreneurs as well as artists. But in order to grasp these opportunities, we must remove our "record business" glasses and see the music business a brand-new way.

Here the story splits. If you are an artist, you must see your career one way. If you are in the music business, you must see it another. Artists want to expose their art and maximize revenues from their art. The music business wants to maximize the return on its investment in artists and their art.

Labels are like venture capitalists. They would like to get a ten-to-one return on their investment on a real hit. But unlike venture capitalists, labels also are operating partners in the venture, providing A&R, promo and marketing, international, distribution, legal, accounting, and many other services. So the artist has it much better than the entrepreneur who goes to a VC (venture capitalist) for funding. And with all the extra services and overhead that the labels shoulder, they still deliver a much lower return on a hit than the VC expects.

We are in a period of rapid adjustment by those who invest in music and artists (labels). They are reducing risk as their reward decreases, and they are increasing their potential reward by expanding their rights beyond just master exploitation.

In hindsight, the old business model was great for artists. Labels funded A&R, marketing and promotion, and artist development and laid claim only to the masters. This agreement left the artist free to make separate, non-cross-collateralized deals on publishing, merchandising, touring, and ancillary revenues. These five silos may not have maximized the overall revenues that an artist was capable of creating, but they did maximize the revenues kept by the artist.

In the new world these silos merge, maximizing the value of the portfolio of rights, but now the investor/label shares in all revenues, not only music sales. In addition, the labels are much more risk averse and are taking fewer shots (maybe 90 percent fewer) and spending far less on each of those shots than they had in the past.

The reduced risk means that almost no new artists are being signed from scratch. Most artists are expected to get their careers started and up to speed on their own. In the past, labels may have signed brand-new artists based solely on their music and look, but now they want that artist to be going 30 to 50 mph already.

Today, artists must kick-start their own careers, and, like the New Music Seminar, this book gives artists many tips on how to get their careers up to speed inexpensively and strategically.

However, does the new music business favor web-savvy artists over talented and original artists? Web-savvy artists will certainly be able to have an edge in exposing themselves and their music, but will that edge beat artists with amazing vision and talent? It is still unclear.

My illustrious predecessor in writing this book's foreword, Derek Sivers, pointed beyond data analysis and technological aptitude to the heart of creation. He said, whatever excites you, do it. Whatever drains you, don't do it. His words were aimed at artists but absolutely valid for all of us.

The new world demands that artists see themselves as businesses and learn to use the new technologies to help expose and monetize their music and message. However, it is important to note that the creators who have most changed the world were rarely those who used technologies and played by the rules. Indeed, the real change makers were the ones who abused technology and broke the rules.

This book gives you a primer on the latest new rule set that is emerging for the "next" music business, and this information is critical. One must learn the techniques in order to abuse them. One must learn the rules in order to break them.

While you read this book, try to think of ways that you can become the creative disruptor, the rule breaker. Try to think of how to use technology in ways that it was not designed for.

This is an amazing time. There are no rules. All bets are off. Don't look for new rules; look for new ways to do something that no one has ever done. It is my hope that some of you reading this book have the insight and the balls to blaze a new path that will not only lead you to legendary success and fortune, but also lead the rest of us to that elusive new profitable and sustainable music business.

Tom Silverman, CEO of Tommy Boy Records
and Cofounder of the New Music Seminar
October 17, 2010

Foreword
to the second edition

I'm already impressed that you're reading the foreword to *The Future of the Music Business*. It means you're ahead of most of your fellow musicians, who make no attempt to learn. Once you read the whole book, you will literally be an expert on the digital music business, incredibly prepared to take advantage of this new, exciting industry.

It used to be that, as a musician, only 10 percent of your career was up to you. "Getting discovered" was about all you could do. A few gatekeepers controlled ALL outlets. You had to impress one of these magic few people to be allowed to present your music to the world. (Even then, they assigned you a manager, stylist, producer, band, et cetera.)

As of the last few years, 90 percent of your career is now up to you. You have all the tools to make it happen.

Record labels aren't guessing anymore. They're only signing artists that have made a success on their own. As Alan Elliott says, "A record label used to be able to look at a tree and say, 'That would make a great table.' Now all they can do is take a finished table and sell it at Wal-Mart."

You have to make a great recording, a great show, a great image. You have to come up with a plan and make it happen, too. You have to make thousands of people want your music so much they pay good money for it. You have to make things happen on your own. Even if a record label puts it in the stores for you, it's still up to your own hard work to make people buy it.

The only thing stopping you from great success is yourself. This is both scary and exciting. At least you're in control.

That being said, please remember there's a compass in your gut that points two directions: EXCITING and DRAINING.

No matter what advice anyone gives you—no matter how smart the person telling you what to do—you need to let this compass override your other decisions. Whatever excites you, go do it. Whatever drains you, stop doing it. If it doesn't excite you, don't do it.

There's almost nothing that you M.U.S.T. do. Someone else somewhere else is excited to do the things that drain you. Find them and let them do it.

Work toward this ideal, and soon you'll be doing only what excites you the most, all day. Then you'll find that doors open for you, opportunities come your way, life seems to go easier, because you're doing what you're meant to do. Welcome to the future of the music business!

Derek Sivers, Founder and Former President of CD Baby
July 2008

Foreword
to the first edition

On November 14, 1971, I opened for Jethro Tull at the Albany Palace Theatre. It was an incredible evening for a young singer-songwriter opening his first big show. The sound of three-thousand-odd people chanting, "You suck, we want Tull," brought me back to reality and taught me the humbling lessons of being the opening act. Once again, I'm in the unenviable position of being the opening act. Fortunately, this time I can't hear the chanting!

Steve Gordon and I shared a common experience: he was an attorney at Sony Music at the same time I managed one of their artists. We have both witnessed the cosmic change that our industry has seen since the mid-1990s, and while some like to complain that the labels stuck their heads in the sand and tried to ignore the coming digital-music landslide, those closer to the action knew it was more of a mixed bag.

Sony Music Nashville broke new ground when they released an "interactive" press kit for Mary Chapin Carpenter's *Stones in the Road* album in 1994. The kit was released on discs for both Mac and Windows and allowed a user to click on a bio, a discography, some photos, and other features. No one was thinking about the Internet, but PC-related interactive products were the rage. Would we like to create a screensaver? Some CD-ROM specials for an enhanced CD? We participated in a Microsoft interactive sampler with other artists. But few in the industry were preparing for the onslaught just around the corner.

RIAA (Recording Industry Association of America) president and CEO Jay Berman, on behalf of his members, was looking down the road and, along with members of AFTRA, the AFofM, and other artists' groups, went to Congress in 1995 to obtain the first performance right in U.S. history for performers and sound-recording copyright owners. On behalf of the industry, Berman warned that a performance right was essential to the protection of copyright, as digital services would soon be capable of making available perfect copies to consumers. Clearly, some in the industry were looking toward the future and how digital music would transform things.

Internally, record companies were trying to gauge what this digitization would mean for their businesses. Promotion departments, for example, were excited by the cost savings of no longer having to mail promo copies to radio stations. They could deliver new music via satellite or some other digital means for all stations to use at a specified time. Other departments were similarly studying how they could benefit from digital music distribution.

We are now looking back at the revolution in technology that has dramatically transformed our industry. Steve Gordon, who worked at one of the major labels and then transitioned into private practice during this tumultuous time, was perfectly positioned to see the impact of this technology shift on the industry's business practices. He tackles some very tough issues and reflects on the conflicting perspectives that have fashioned the debate over peer-to-peer, webcasting, and other new technologies.

Gordon has done a very fine job of explaining the statutory licensing regime put in place by Congress when they created the Digital Performance Right in Sound Recordings Act of 1995 and the Digital Millennium Copyright Act of 1998.

The book also helps artists take advantage of the new technologies by detailing the steps for building websites, online music stores, Internet music broadcasts, blogs, and more. The interviews with artists and entrepreneurs offer fascinating insights into new business models that did not even exist a few years ago. Gordon shows that the future of the music business is indeed full of new opportunities for those who have the imagination and energy to take advantage of them.

John Simson, Executive Director of SoundExchange
July 2005

Preface

As I write this, it is late December 2010, and at this moment in time, these are two of the most interesting developments in the music business:

▶ Google's proposed music service
▶ The Combating Online Infringement and Counterfeits Act (COICA)

Although these may be two of the most important developments now, by the time you read this, they may not be. In the last ten years, the music business has undergone constant change. As new technologies have revolutionized the way music is produced, distributed, and consumed, an ever-changing array of business models, business practices, statutes, laws, and judicial decisions have arisen in order to attempt to impose order on the chaos. Therefore, to stay current with these changes I will periodically update this book in my blog, www.futureofthemusicbusiness.biz.

Please take advantage of the blog. I would appreciate any comments you have on the posts. In effect, we will be writing the next edition of *The Future of the Music Business* together!

Google's New Service and COICA

Before delving into the details, I would first like to point out why these developments are significant. Both the Google music service and COICA seek to address two of the key issues facing the record business at this time: the need for a new business model to revive an industry on the verge of collapse, and a partnership with government to control rampant piracy.

Google's move to develop a music service reflects the continuing search for the "silver bullet"—that is, the one business model that will reverse the dramatically declining fortunes of recorded music. As discussed by Tommy Silverman in his foreword to this edition, the recording industry has suffered a devastating decline in income, adjusted for inflation, of approximately 80 percent in the last ten years. The industry has been unable to find a business model to compete with free music available on peer-to-peer BitTorrent sites and private networks.

The new federal anti-piracy legislation Combating Online Infringement and Counterfeits Act (COICA) addresses the most dire issue that the record business has faced since Shawn Fanning introduced Napster—online piracy. It also represents a partnership between the music business and government to control piracy. In the late 1990s, rights holders argued that Internet Service Providers (ISPs) should be held liable for the infringing acts of their customers who were downloading music illegally. Everyone who operates on the Internet must utilize ISPs for access to the web—you need high-speed Internet access in order to obtain free music. In response to the charges that ISPs contributed to the infringement ("contributory infringement") or supervised and profited from the infringement ("vicarious infringement") of their customers, the ISPs argued that they are simply passive carriers of information that should not have to police content, even though people use their service to trade billions of music files each year without paying a cent to the copyright owners, that is, the labels and music publishers, or the artists and songwriters. The ISPs successfully lobbied Congress to insulate themselves from liability for online piracy through the Digital Millennium Copyright Act of 1999 (DMCA). A provision of the act, known as the "safe harbor" provision, protects ISPs from any responsibility for illegal content. Under Title II of the DMCA (17 U.S.C. § 511, et seq.), an ISP can avoid financial liability by adhering to the "notice and takedown" provisions, should one of its subscribers offer an infringing copy online.

While the music industry was not strong enough to prevent the ISPs from escaping liability for their role in facilitating infringing behavior, in recent years Hollywood film studios have proven a valuable partner in the fight against online piracy. As bandwidth and high-speed Internet access have increased over the years, it is now possible to access and share movies, including Hollywood blockbusters, almost as fast as it is to share music. In response to this development, the industry got two of their top campaign-contribution recipients, Senators Patrick Leahy and Orrin Hatch, to push forward a bill that would allow the Department of Justice to censor or shut down certain websites deemed "dedicated to infringing activities." COICA is a signal that the federal government has now taken up the cause of the rights holders—the labels, music publishers, and the Hollywood studios—and is willing to take action on a macro level to address the problem of those who provide access to content without proper remuneration to the creators.

Will Google Give Us the "Silver Bullet"?

Google has announced that it plans to launch a music service that offers song downloads, streaming music, and a digital song locker. Although there is no firm launch date, Google is currently in discussions with music labels and publishers. From its search engine and YouTube, Google not only grants access to tens of millions of users, it also has a wealth of information on the kinds of music people want to hear. In addition, the new music service will be fully integrated with Google's Android mobile phones.

Importantly, Google has positioned its new venture to be a "cloud"-based music service. Users will be able to buy music, store it in a cloud-locker, and access it from any Internet-based device. Google already offers a digital locker box called Google Docs, which allows users to store digital files (including music) in the "cloud" and access them from any Internet-based device. The new service, however, will be solely dedicated to music and video. Google Docs already allows people to share their music playlists, but there is no record that Google ever received formal permission from the labels or publishers to do so. The labels still contend that digital locker boxes are illegal if not authorized. In its current lawsuit against Michael Robertson's MP3Tunes.com, EMI contends that digital locker boxes must receive permission from copyright owners before allowing people to store their music files, even if the service does not allow people to share playlists. It will be interesting to see if this becomes a point of negotiation in launching the new music service—that is, whether the labels and publishers will seek better terms to formally authorize Google to allow its users to share music.

Pricewise, Google has been circulating a proposal among record labels offering users a two-fold plan that includes, for $25 a year, a cloud-based locker where users can store their music, and a conventional digital music store to buy tracks from. As of December 2010, iTunes dominates the online music market with 66.2 percent of sales, with Amazon coming in second with 13.3 percent, followed by Walmart at 12 percent.[1]

Anti-Piracy Legislation: Combating Online Infringement and Counterfeits Act

A bipartisan group of senators has united to introduce legislation, known as COICA, designed to attack online piracy and protect U.S. intellectual property. The act would specifically target websites that the legislation deems are "dedicated to infringing activities." The bill is co-sponsored by the Senate Judiciary Committee's chairman, Senator Patrick Leahy (D-VT). Other committee members sponsoring the bill include Senators Orrin Hatch (R-Utah), Charles Schumer (D-New York), Dick Durban (D-Illinois), George Voinovich (R-Ohio), and Evan Bayh (D-Ind).

This new antipiracy initiative is perhaps the most important to date. COICA allows the attorney general of the U.S. Department of Justice to file for an injunction (a legal remedy that stops the wrongdoer's illegal acts) against any website that is "dedicated to infringing activities." The legislation defines a site that is "dedicated to infringing activities" as one that "is primarily designed, has no demonstrable, commercially significant purpose, or use, other than . . . to offer goods or services in violation of title 17, United States Code [i.e., the Copyright Act] or enable, or facilitate a violation of title 17."

Once the attorney general obtains a court-ordered injunction, he can do either of two things, depending on where the domain registrant is located. If the person or company who registered the domain name is located in the United States, the injunction would force that person or company to suspend the infringing domain. If the attorney general cannot get hold of the person or entity that registered the domain name, the order can be served on whoever the site is registered with, such as ICANN (Internet Corporation of Assigned Names and Numbers). ICANN will then suspend operation of the site, causing it to literally evaporate. In the event that the site operates outside of the United States, the attorney general can serve the order for injunction on: (1) the ISP that services U.S. users of the site; (2) credit card companies working with the infringing site (e.g., Visa or MasterCard); or (3) advertisers such as Google that advertise on the infringing site. If the ISP is served, it must extinguish access to the domain in the United States. If the credit card companies are served, they are required to stop processing purchases from the infringing website. If the advertisers are served, they must cease and desist from further advertising on the website.

---

1. "Apple Owns 66% of Online Music Market, Amazon Second at 13%," http://www.onenewspage.com/news/Technology/20101217/18009363/Apple-owns-66-of-online-music-market-Amazon.htm. Accessed April 21, 2011.

This legislation is geared toward attacking sites such as Pirate Bay, which is a popular BitTorrent file-sharing site where users can download free music, movies, books, and TV shows. The *Los Angeles Times* proclaimed Pirate Bay to be "the world's largest facilitator of illegal downloading." In response, Pirate Bay has publicly expressed its support for the dissemination of free culture and has aligned itself with the "copyleft" movement. Some commentators actually refer to COICA as the "Pirate Bay" Act, because, if enacted, it would allow the Department of Justice to go after all pirate sites—including those located in foreign countries—by preventing merchants such as PayPal, Visa, and American Express from processing transactions, and advertisers, such as Google, from placing ads on the site. The merchants and advertisers have no incentive to challenge or object to the attorney general's directives—so long as they comply with the order, they will not be held liable for the underlying infringing activities. The proposed law anticipates that the target sites will scramble for new identities; significantly, the law provides for modification of the injunctive order to target any new domain names that the miscreant website attempts to use. For example, if the DOJ shuts down the site name Pirate.com and the site reopens under Pirate.biz, the order could be easily expanded to include the Pirate.biz domain name.

COICA has the support of major entertainment-industry groups, record labels, and media companies, including Viacom, which owns MTV, VH1, BET, and CBS. President Obama's administration has also expressed support for the measure. On the other side of the debate, critics supportive of the "copyleft" movement posit that this type of law is "censorship" that poses a severe threat to the freedom of the Internet. On November 18, 2010, the Senate Judiciary Committee unanimously approved the bill.

Introduction

The Impact of Digital Technologies on the Recording Industry—Nightmares for Major Labels and Brilliant New Opportunities for Artists and Entrepreneurs

Digital technologies have created nightmares for the traditional recording business, particularly the major record labels. But the same technologies have created brilliant new opportunities for artists and entrepreneurs. This was the main thesis and inspiration for the original edition of this book, and it remains the central thesis of this third edition.

When I was a lawyer at Sony Music in 1998, we visited the Pitman plant in New Jersey. This was the factory in which Sony made CDs for the entire northeastern United States. From the outside, the factory looked as big as a football stadium. Inside, we looked down from the mezzanine to see the immense factory floor, where workers clad in white suits resembling astronaut uniforms tended to huge machines that spewed out tens of thousands of shiny little discs, which contained the music of Sony's biggest stars, including Mariah Carey, Celine Dion, Pearl Jam, Michael Jackson, and Bruce Springsteen. Outside the factory, dozens of massive trucks lined up to take all those shiny discs to warehouses, and then to stores throughout the Northeast. But, about a year later, for the price of creating a website, an artist could distribute his own music. He would not need that huge factory, tens of thousands of discs, big trucks, and warehouses, nor would he need the people who attended to the manufacture, shipping, and sales of those shiny discs. The artist could reach not only everyone in the northeastern United States, but everyone in the entire world! It is an amazing and incredible shift, and that's the world we live in today—an age of information when MP3 files can be exchanged as easily as e-mail attachments.

Not only have digital technologies created low-cost worldwide distribution, they have also drastically cut down the cost of recording. With the introduction of low-cost digital home recording studios, laptops that record and mix music, and software programs that make available all kinds of samples from drum beats to entire orchestras, an artist can produce a commercially acceptable record at a fraction of the price compared to just a generation ago.

Because digital technology provides almost free distribution and makes it possible to record music very inexpensively, it is now possible for an artist to bypass labels entirely. And many artists are doing just that.

The Suffering of Major Labels

The impact of digital technologies on the major record companies has been nothing short of disastrous. In 1999, income from recorded music was approximately $14.5 billion in the United States alone. By the end of 2009, that income plummeted to an astonishing $7.7 billion, an incredible decline that does not even account for inflation. Take a look at this graph from the RIAA showing units shipped from 1973 to 2008:

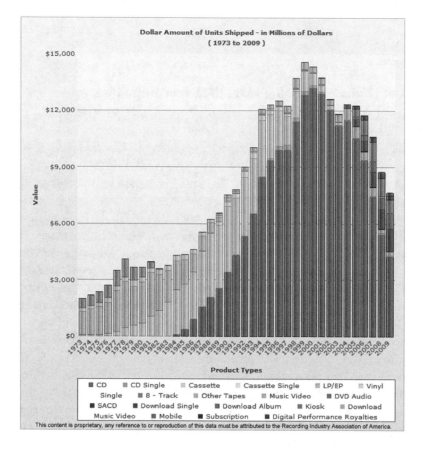

This grid shows that digital downloads, interactive streaming subscription services, and mobile delivery have not made up for the huge decline in CD sales in the United States. In 2009, digital sales increased nearly 20 percent, but total revenues fell by another 12 percent. Income has declined in every year except one since 1999.

The following chart illustrates the worldwide decline in income from recorded music. It shows a greater than 50 percent decline: from approximately $38.6 billion in 1999 to approximately $18.4 billion in 2008.

Year	Revenue – Physical Sales (in US$ millions)	Revenue – Digital Sales (in US$ millions)	TOTAL Revenue (in US$ millions)
1999	38671.2	—	38671.2
2000	36936.6	—	36936.6
2001	33655.4	—	33655.4
2002	32281.2	—	32281.2
2003	32012.2	—	32012.2
2004	33613.6	397	33613.6
2005	19652	1143	20795
2006	17432.43	2154.57	19587
2007	16494.25	2910.75	19405
2008	13829.3	3783.8	18415.2

Total global recorded music sales declined an additional 7.2 percent in 2009 to approximately $17 billion. Although worldwide income from digital music increased by $4.2 billion in 2009, an increase of 12 percent from the previous year, that increase was down from the 25 percent digital growth recorded in 2008.[1]

Over five years since 2004, digital sales grew by 940 percent, but the overall music market fell by 30 percent. In the decade from 1999 to—2009, the major players in the music industry underwent significant changes. In 2004, the merger of Sony and BMG resulted in thousands of layoffs and scores of dropped artists; BMG subsequently sold its interest to Sony at a considerable loss. That same year, Warner was sold to private investors and has been struggling ever since. As of December 2010, EMI is facing receivership and being taken over by Citibank. In 2007, retail chain Tower Records went out of business, and Virgin's New York City megastore closed in 2009.

Since its launch in 2003 through February 2010, iTunes has sold approximately 10 billion songs. However, this has not compensated for lost CD sales, especially since sales of songs on iTunes have slowed. In 2008, it took Apple five and half months to sell a billion songs, which was twice as long as it took to sell double that amount the year prior. Amazon MP3, which launched its download service in September 2007, sold only 27 million songs by July 2008.

Subscription services such as Rhapsody and Napster continue to struggle to win over new subscribers. Monies for subscription services actually decreased by 3.7 percent from 2008 to 2009. As the following grid indicates, total income from subscription services is only $213.1 million in the United States. Also, sales of music on mobile systems have not been as successful as many in the industry had hoped. Income from mobile music, including master ringtones, ringbacks, music videos, and full-length downloads, declined 25.4 percent from 2008 to 2009. The RIAA grid shows the continuing erosion of income from recorded music:

---

1. The source for worldwide stats is IFPI (International Federation of the Phonographic Industry).

2009 Year-End Shipment Statitics
Manufacturers' Unit Shipment and Retail Dollar Value
(In millions, net after returns)

Digital	2008	2009	% Change 2008–2009
(Units Shipped) (Dollar Value) **Download Single**	1,042.7 1,032.2	1,138.3 1,220.3	9.2% 18.2%
Download Album	63.6 635.3	76.4 763.4	20.2% 20.2%
Kiosk[a]	1.6 2.6	1.7 6.3	7.9% 147.1%
Music Video	20.8 41.3	20.4 40.6	-1.9% -1.9%
Total Units **Total Value**	**1,128.6** **1,711.5**	**1,236.8** **2030.7**	**9.6%** **18.7%**
Mobile[b]	405.1 977.1	305.8 728.8	-24.5% -25.4%
Subscription[c]	1.6 221.4	1.2 213.1	-25.5% -3.7%
Digital Performance Royalties[d]	100.0	155.5	55.5%

Source: This grid was prepared by RIAA. "Dollar Value" is value of shipments at recommended or estimated list prices.

[a]Includes singles and albums.

[b]Includes master ringtones, ringbacks, music videos, full length downloads, and other mobile.

[c]Weighted annual average.

[d]Estimated payments in dollars to performers and copyright holders distributed by SoundExchange.

Physical	2008	2009	% Change 2008–2009
CD	368.4	292.9	-20.5%
	5471.3	4272.1	-21.9%
CD Single	0.7	0.9	17.8%
	3.5	3.1	-12.5%
Cassette	0.1	0.0	-102.8%
	0.9	0.0	-104.9%
LP/EP	2.9	3.2	10.8%
	56.7	60.2	6.2%
Vinyl Single	0.4	0.3	-30.2%
	2.9	2.5	-15.3%
Music Video	12.8	12.1	-5.2%
	218.9	218.1	-0.4%
DVD Video[e]	12.3	11.5	-6.4%
	215.7	212.9	-1.3%
Total Units[f]	**385.5**	**309.5**	**-19.7%**
Total Value	**5,758.5**	**4,562.0**	**-20.8%**

Total Digital and Physical

	2008	2009	% Change
Total Units[g]	**1,919.2**	**1,852.1**	**-3.5%**
Total Value	**8,768.4**	**7,690.0**	**-12.3%**

% of Shipments		
Physical	66%	59%
Digital	34%	41%

[e]While broken out for this chart, "DVD video product" is included in the "music video" totals in the digital chart, so the 12.3 million is not included in the total value for physical sales.

[f]Both totals (units and value) include cassette single, DVD audio, and SACD shipments not broken out separately in this report.

[g]Units total includes both albums and singles, and does not include subscriptions or royalties.

Distributions for digital performance rights, which include payments to performers and copyright holders for webcasting, satellite radio, and other noninteractive digital-music services, increased 55 percent in 2009. While this seems great, total income was only a paltry $155 million. Overall income from recorded music in the United States fell 12 percent to $7.7 billion. Growth in digital formats only partially offset a decline of 21 percent in physical formats.

Perfect Storm

Although these figures include independent labels as well as majors, the majors have been hardest hit because they had the most to lose. Over 80 percent of recorded music is still distributed through the four majors. In large part, the labels cannot be blamed for their woes. The CD was introduced before the Internet, and personal computers became widely popular. The Internet converted CDs into unprotected digital copies of master recordings. The labels could not have known that, in effect, they were selling perfect copies of their masters. When personal computers and the Internet became popular, and after the development of the MP3 format, it became all too easy to rip all those CDs, convert them to MP3s, and upload almost perfect copies to everyone in the world. So it has been very difficult for the labels to compete with the web, which is, in effect, a perfect copying and distribution machine.

Another often overlooked reason for the plight of the labels is that "free music" is not free at all. You need to pay for a computer to consume all that free music, and unless you want to wait forever on a download, you need a broadband connection to get it swiftly. So you are paying a lot to the electronics business and the Internet service providers (ISPs) for so-called free music. In addition, if you want portability, you may buy blank optical discs, MP3 players, smart phones, and yes, even an iPad. Apple has reported selling more than 260 million iPods alone. So a fortune is paid for so-called free music, but the money is going into pockets other than those of the labels. This development has given the electronics business and the ISPs every incentive to encourage people to acquire "free" music. The electronics industry has steadfastly refused to place codes in their machines that would prevent sharing free content. The ISPs have successfully insulated themselves from liability by successfully pushing for legislation (see Chapter 3) that prevents them from being responsible for people sharing music through their networks.

Bad Choices

Because the record companies could not deter the electronics business or the ISPs from facilitating free music, they targeted the peer-to-peer (P2P) services, such as Napster, Grokster, Kazaa, and then LimeWire. Although they were able to shut all these services down through lawsuits, other services, such as BitTorrent, and other online file-sharing services like Mediafire, Rapidshare, and Dropbox, have replaced them. In the United States, the labels' trade organization, the Recording Industry Association of America (RIAA), also launched an estimated thirty thousand lawsuits against the labels' own customers for sharing music through P2P services. But these suits have not stemmed the tide of free music. Rather, the number of files traded on P2P has not declined, and more and more people are sharing music with their friends in private groups in order to avoid lawsuits. In fact, there may be more music sharing through private online file-sharing networks than on P2P networks, as this activity is almost impossible to monitor or legally attack.

DRM

The labels exacerbated their ordeal by being extremely slow to create new business models that would provide an attractive, reasonably priced alternative to free. Instead, they initially insisted on coding authorized music with forms of digital rights management (DRM) to prevent it from being shared with others. DRM operates by supplying a "lock" to prevent legally bought music from being illegally shared. In the last several years, however, DRM was largely abandoned due to the fact that it severely lacked "interoperability"-- the ability for different devices, such as MP3 players and mobile phones, to play the same audio files. By 2009, all of the servicing major labels (Warner, Sony, EMI, and Universal) ceased selling DRM-protected music.

New Opportunities for Artists and Entrepreneurs

As noted in Tom Silverman's foreword, beyond the suffering of the major labels and their flagging sales on iTunes, a growing group of forward-thinking artists and entrepreneurs are not-so-quietly creating a revolution. The Internet is teeming with new roadmaps for distributing and discovering music. For example, Internet radio (including Last.fm and Pandora) or social music-discovery sites such as iLike, where fans can create and make playlists of their latest obsessions, get personalized recommendations, and follow what their friends are listening to.

In addition, music itself is more abundant than ever. More music is being created and distributed now because: (1) the Internet offers infinite shelf space, not just room for the best sellers; (2) the web provides almost free distribution to anyone with a computer; (3) digital technology has drastically reduced the cost of recordings. The longtime goal for a lot of artists has been: How can I have a hit? How can I be a rock star? How can I get on MTV? Now the goal may be a long-term sustainable career: How can I leave my day job and make enough money as a niche artist? How do I navigate success as a do-it-yourself artist?

Digital Has Created the Tools for Success

Digital technology has drastically reduced the price of recording, so you can make a commercial record cheaply. And the web has made worldwide distribution almost free. Not only can you sell your records by download on your own website, you can also gain access to almost every digital music service or store by using an aggregator such as TuneCore or CD Baby (see Chapter 11 for details). Bandcamp, a new website hosting service for musicians, allow artists to create one-stop, easily customizable web pages with music players and online shopping carts. The website Kickstarter makes it possible to run online fund-raising campaigns, and many artists have already used it to raise money to record their albums or produce videos. Finally, social networks and blogs have made it that much easier for artists to post their music online and build an Internet fanbase.

Better Business Model for Artists

For artists who decide to take advantage of these new opportunities, the financial rewards can be much better than under the traditional business model. What's exciting is that if artists do it themselves (the "do-it-yourself" or so-called DIY approach), they can make much more money than they would if they had a traditional deal with a label. These are the economics: the usual artist recording royalty is 10 to 15 percent of retail. The record company also takes a number of deductions from that royalty, including packaging of 25 percent and net sales of 10 percent. The net sales deduction used to be justified, because in the early days of the record business, records were made of shellac and a percentage of them would break during shipment. Despite the fact that records were replaced by other formats that did not break, such as CDs and MP3s, the labels retained this deduction anyway. At the end of the day, the average per-unit rate for the artist is generally less than a dollar an album. Most record companies apply the same calculation to digital delivery. So from a 99-cent download on iTunes, although the labels receive around 70 cents, the artist's royalty will add up to only a few pennies. Compounding the problem of a low royalty is the principle of recoupment. Recording costs and other charges such as video production and independent marketing are deductible from the artists' recording royalties. That seems fair on the surface, as the record label has to pay itself back for expenses. But the way they do it makes sense only from the labels' point of view. In calculating recoupment, the label uses the artists' royalty rate—not how much the label receives from sales. For example, if recoupable expenses are $100,000, and the artist's royalty is $1, the labels have to sell 100,000 records in order for the artist to recoup. If the label sells 90,000 albums, the artist would not have earned any royalties. But if the label sold those 90,000 units at a suggested retail of $12 and the wholesale rate was $6, the label would have made more than a half a million dollars.

Ownership

Under standard recording contracts, the labels make the artist's recording services a "work for hire." This means the labels are considered the "author" of the master recordings and own all the copyrights. Even if artists recoup the recording costs and other expenses, they never get to own the masters. As my friend, noted radio personality and author Harry Allen points out, this is why labels are worse than banks. If you borrow money to buy a home and you pay off the mortgage, you get to own the house. But even if artists pay back the label, they never get to own their own recordings. The practical impact of this scenario is that they can never sell their own records and receive more than their royalty rate, even after recoupment. In addition, the record company reserves the right to license the recordings for movies, television shows, commercials, and so forth. Although the royalty for this licensing is usually 50 percent, the 50 percent is on "net receipts" subject to recoupment of production and marketing costs. And most artists never "recoup." If the artists retained the rights to their recordings, they would be in control of these deals and keep all the money.

Examples of Artists Doing It Themselves

I like to point to a Grammy award--winning jazz musician Jeff "Tain" Watts as an example of an artist who uses new technologies to take control of his career. He recently recorded an album, *Folk's Songs,* for only $15,000. He released the album through his website and sells it for ten dollars. You can download the album artwork for an additional dollar. He needs to make only 1,500 sales to recoup his investment. If he sells more, it's all profit.

Suppose Tain were still signed to a major label. In his case, that would have been Columbia Records. In this era of cutbacks, Sony Music, the owner, has shut down Columbia's jazz department to focus on bigger-selling records. Assuming Tain's royalty was approximately a dollar, if

Sony sold 1,500 albums, the label would credit his account only $1,500, that is, a dollar per album. In order to recoup his recording costs of $15,000, the label would have to sell 15,000 units. Suppose the label did sell 15,000. Tain's income would still equal zero, because he would not have recouped the recording costs. But if Tain sells 15,000 units on his own, that would amount to $150,000—a profit of $135,000. If Sony sold 15,000 units, he would have made nothing. But the label would have pocketed the wholesale price of the records and would have made good money.

The trick is that under standard recording contracts, as just discussed, production costs and other expenses are usually recouped at the artist's royalty rate. By doing it himself, Tain avoids the label's burdensome method of paying (or, more precisely, not paying) recording royalties. Also, because Tain retains his rights to the master recordings, he can license the recordings for film and TV himself and retain all the license fees.

The Radiohead Experiment

In 2007, Radiohead, following the expiration of their record deal with EMI, decided to offer their seventh album, *In Rainbows,* exclusively through their website as a digital download and let fans decide what they wanted to pay for it. Fans could obtain the download for free if they so desired. Radiohead wasn't the first artist to do this—Issa, formerly known as Jane Siberry, actually offered the "pay what you want" model a few years earlier. But Radiohead was definitely the highest-profile act to do this, and their experiment paid off. In addition to generating massive publicity, the band earned significant income. According to Internet information service comScore, in the first month after the release of the album, over one million fans downloaded *In Rainbows*. Roughly 40 percent of them paid an average of $6 each, netting the band nearly $3 million. "In terms of digital income," according to Radiohead front man Thom Yorke, "we've made more money out of this record than out of all the other Radiohead albums put together." Chris Anderson, editor of *Wired* magazine, points out, "the reason they made more is not that they sold more, but they got 100 percent of the revenues." Plus, since the band owns the masters, Radiohead was also able to subsequently license the album for distribution as a CD. This experiment proved that at least established artists are capable of releasing their music without the major labels and securing a great deal of financial success.

Other examples of major artists achieving success without traditional labels include Madonna, Trent Reznor, Paul McCartney, the Eagles, and Prince. A week after Radiohead released *In Rainbows,* Madonna announced that she was leaving her longtime record label Warner Brothers and teaming up with concert conglomerate Live Nation. She signed a ten-year deal worth $120 million. Live Nation estimated that during the life of her ten-year deal term, they will probably make a billion dollars. Most of the money will come from live performance and merchandise rather than record sales, although they did acquire the right to distribute three new albums.

The major-label mutiny didn't end there. Trent Reznor, founder and primary creative force behind the industrial rock band Nine Inch Nails, split his ties with Interscope Records and is now an independent, unsigned musician with plans to release music directly to fans.

So the late 2000s saw major artists coming to the end of their contracts thinking about whether they needed to go the traditional label route at all. During this time, artists also started forming alliances with non-music-specific retailers. Paul McCartney became the first major artist to sign with Starbucks' Hear Music. The Eagles gave Walmart exclusive rights to sell their first studio album since 1979; the result was over 700,000 in sales, beating out Britney Spears for the number-one album spot and forcing *Billboard* to change its album-charting policy.

As we discuss in Part III of this book, more recently bands such as Arcade Fire and OK Go have shown that worldwide success can be achieved without a major label and largely due to the power of the Internet.

The foregoing experiments by major artists, as well as the success of new artists that have largely done it on their own, demonstrate that the current state of the music business, although challenging, provides more opportunities for both established and new artists than they have had at any other time. They also show that the old rules don't apply anymore.

Disclaimer

The information in this book has been prepared for informational purposes only and does not constitute legal advice. This book should be used as a guide to understanding the law, not as a substitute for the advice of qualified counsel. You should consult an attorney before making any significant legal decisions.

DVD

The DVD included in this book, titled *How to Succeed in Today's (Digital) Music Business,* is a presentation delivered at NYU's Tisch School of the Arts. The DVD includes a PowerPoint presentation and lecture by Steve Gordon on the following issues:

▶ Opportunities and challenges facing new artists
▶ Whether an artist should sign with a label
▶ What record companies give to and take from artists
▶ What to avoid in signing with a label
▶ Advantages of doing it yourself (DIY)
▶ How new technologies have made it possible for new artists to succeed
▶ How artists should use online tools

This presentation is intended to be helpful not only to new artists, but to those people hoping to become music industry professionals and entrepreneurs. It is also available online at http://futureofthemusicbusiness.halleonardbooks.com.

Part I
The Law

Chapter 1
Music Law and Business Primer

This chapter is intended to provide a comprehensive overview of the rules and business practices pertaining to the music business. The next chapter addresses the questions most often asked of music lawyers. Chapters 3–5 examine the rules pertaining to digital music. Chapter 6 and 7 discuss licensing music in traditional media such as TV and movies, and new media such as websites and video games.

Copyright Law: The Foundation of the Music Publishing and Recording Business

Copyright is the basis of virtually every music business transaction. Without copyright, there would be no protection for musical compositions and recorded music. Without copyright, they would have no financial value.

What Is Copyright?

Copyright is a form of protection provided by the laws of the United States, that is, the Copyright Act (Title 17 of the U.S. Code), to the authors of "original works of authorship," including literary, dramatic, musical, artistic, and certain other intellectual works.

What Kind of Work Does Copyright Protect?

Copyright protects original works of authorship fixed in any tangible medium of expression, rather than mere ideas. Works of authorship include the following categories:

(1) Literary works
(2) **Musical works, including any accompanying words**
(3) Dramatic works, including any accompanying music
(4) Pantomimes and choreographic works
(5) Pictorial, graphic, and sculptural works
(6) Motion pictures and other audiovisual works
(7) **Sound recordings**
(8) Architectural works
Section 102 of the Copyright Act. (Emphasis added.)

Musical works are musical compositions including songs, as well as longer works such as a symphony or a movie score. *Sound recordings* are defined in the Copyright Act as "works that result from the fixation of a series of musical, spoken, or other sounds . . . regardless of the nature of the material objects, such as disks, tapes, or other phonorecords, in which they are embodied." The act further defines *phonorecords* as "material objects in which sounds, other than those accompanying a motion picture or other audiovisual work, are fixed by any method now known or later developed." The difference is that *sound recordings* refers to works that are subject to copyright, and *phonorecords* are physical embodiments of such works. In music-business parlance, though, the word *master* is used to refer to the copyright in a sound recording.

What Are the Rights That Copyright Protects?

Section 106 of the 1976 Copyright Act generally gives the owner of copyright the exclusive right to do, and to authorize others to do, any of the following:

(1) To reproduce the copyrighted work in copies or phonorecords
(2) To prepare derivative works based upon the copyrighted work
(3) To distribute copies or phonorecords of the copyrighted work to the public by sale or other transfer of ownership, or by rental, lease, or lending
(4) In the case of literary, musical, dramatic, and choreographic works; pantomimes; and motion pictures and other audiovisual works, to perform the copyrighted work publicly
(5) In the case of literary, musical, dramatic, and choreographic works; pantomimes; and pictorial, graphic, or sculptural works, including the individual images of a motion picture or other audiovisual work, to display the copyrighted work publicly
(6) In the case of sound recordings, to perform the copyrighted work publicly by means of a digital audio transmission

The origins of copyright law go back to the protection of books by the Statute of Queen Anne adopted by the British Parliament in 1710. The law provided protection for publishers against those who would make physical copies and sell them without permission. The United States continued this tradition by including a provision in our constitution that specifically protects "works of authorship." The copyright law was eventually expanded to protect other works, including songs, and then, with the invention of the phonograph record, to sound recordings. The rights of copyright owners were also expanded to include all the additional rights set forth here. The history of copyright is laid out in various sources.[1]

---

1. For instance, Professor Lawrence Lessig discusses the interesting history of the Statute of Queen Anne in the chapter titled "Property" in his book *Free Culture* (Penguin 2004). You can buy this book, but Professor Lessig has also made the book available for anyone to read for free at www.free-culture.cc/freeculture.pdf under a "Creative Commons" license. We discuss Creative Commons at the end of this chapter.

Why Is Copyright Important in the Music Business?

The Copyright Act specifically protects songs (musical works) and masters (sound recordings) by spelling out the precise rights reserved to the copyright owner. For example without item 3 listed earlier, anyone could record your song and sell copies without paying you. Without item 1, anyone could take your record and make copies without your permission and without paying you. Without item 4, anyone could publicly perform your song, on the radio, for instance, and not pay you. Copyright is the house in which the music business lives, and without it the business would be homeless and broke.

Note that the public performance right in item 6 applies to sound recordings, but only by means of digital distribution, not traditional "analog" methods of performance such as radio. We will discuss this critical distinction in Chapter 3 and examine the recording industry's attempt to change the law in Chapter 10.

Songwriters and Music Publishers: Rules and Business Practices

Now that we know what copyright is, the rights it protects, and the kinds of works to which it applies, we're ready to discuss how copyright law applies to the music business.

First, it's important to distinguish between rights in a song and rights in a master, that is, a sound recording embodying a musical composition. When we hear a song on the radio, two separate and distinct intellectual properties are involved. The first is the song or music composition—the words and music composed by the songwriter(s) or composer(s). There is also another copyright: the sound recording—the physical embodiment of sounds resulting from the recorded performance of that musical composition. Therefore, a CD or a digital music file is like a copyright sandwich: the songs embodied in the CD or digital file are protected by copyright as musical works, and the masters are protected by the copyright protection applicable to sound recordings.

Music Publishers

Rights in a song are generally controlled by the songwriters or their representatives, the music publishers. Major music publishing companies include EMI Music, Warner/Chappell, Sony/ATV, Universal Music, and BMG. These are major corporations that have worldwide operations and generate hundreds of millions of dollars each year. But there are thousands of other publishers throughout the world, ranging in size from big companies to one-person operations. The relationships between songwriters and music publishers vary, but historically the standard deal provides that the songwriters grant the publishers the exclusive right to exploit the songs that they write during the term of the agreement, and the writer and publisher share fees that are received from most uses on a fifty-fifty basis. The publisher's 50 percent is generally referred to as the "publisher's share." The other 50 percent is known as the "writer's share." The publisher earns its 50 percent by undertaking certain crucial functions, including negotiating and issuing licenses for use of the songs, collecting the money, registering copyrights in songs (see the discussion on registration below), and other administrative chores. The publisher is also supposed to promote the writer's songs and interest others, such as recording artists, record labels, and producers, and TV and movie music supervisors, in using them. Here is a list of additional services that publishers provide to their writers:

- ▶ Produce demos
- ▶ Secure record deals for writers who are also performers
- ▶ Secure covers by third-party artists
- ▶ Secure placements in advertising campaigns
- ▶ Register songs with collections agents, including PROs and mechanical societies
- ▶ Monitor payments and make sure royalties (from record companies, video distributors, ringtone companies, television and film producers, etc.) are paid on time
- ▶ Check royalty statements for accuracy and audit licensees in case of possible underpayment
- ▶ Litigate against licensees who fail to pay or against users who do not acquire licenses
- ▶ Promote interest in songs to representatives in foreign countries
- ▶ Lobby for legislation helpful to writers
- ▶ Negotiate blanket deals with services such as interactive streaming

A popular song can earn money in a remarkable number of ways. The majority of revenue comes from sales of records embodying the song (these are called *mechanical royalties,* or "mechanicals") and public performance on radio, TV, and now the Internet. Other sources of revenue include the "synchronization" licensing of the song in movies, TV programs, documentaries, video games, and TV commercials. Sales of printed music, including sheet music (printed music of single songs), used to be a principal source of income but has largely been supplanted by other uses. The publisher's primary responsibility, though, is to assure that all these uses are properly licensed and paid for. Subsequent sections of this chapter discuss mechanical, synchronization, and public-performance licenses in further detail.

Since publishers generally negotiate rights on behalf of the writer, if, for example, you were to seek a license to use Bob Dylan's "Blowin' in the Wind" in your movie, you would contact his publisher, Special Rider Music, rather than Dylan's manager, agent, or lawyer. If the writer has passed away, instead of contacting his estate, you would communicate with the publisher. For instance, you would contact Warner/Chappell Music instead of the estate of Cole Porter for a license to use "Night and Day." If a song has more than one writer, or if it contains a sample, you can expect that there will be more than one music publisher. The following databases are good sources of information for ownership of songs: www.ASCAP.com, www.BMI.com, and www.SESAC.com. Master recording rights, on the other hand, are generally controlled by record companies. When Norah Jones does another album for Blue Note, Blue Note Records, not Norah, will control the copyright in the master. Generally, the deal between an artist and a major record company requires the artist to agree that the record label acquire ownership in the copyright in any recording made under the agreement. Sometimes, if the artist is sufficiently powerful, he or she can negotiate that the record company does not own the copyright in the masters but merely has an exclusive license to sell those masters, and that the copyright in the sound recordings will revert to the artist after the termination of the recording agreement and after the label "recoups" its costs. (See section on recoupment below.) Generally, however, the record company will retain the copyright in the masters even after the recording agreement has terminated and the artist no longer records for the label. On the other hand, it is becoming more common for smaller, independent labels in today's music business to forgo this standard model and engage in a more progressive agreement with the artist, whereby the label secures the right to sell the masters under an exclusive license and either maintains the copyright only for the limited tenure of the agreement or completely keeps the copyright in the hands of the artist.

We discussed at the beginning of this section that publishers generally acquire control over the copyrights in a writer's songs and split the income from those songs on a fifty-fifty basis. Here are the three standard deals that publishers offer writers:

▶ Individual song deals
▶ Exclusive deals
▶ Admin and co-pub deals

The first type, the individual song deal, is perhaps the most flexible: in this deal, the publisher will provide the writer with an advance per song, and the writer is free to place other songs with any other publisher. This type of deal might be the most attractive for those seeking the freedom to work with others and to not have an entire catalog of songs stuck at one publisher.

The next type, the exclusive deal, is much less flexible. A writer will sign an agreement with the publisher, and the deal applies to any song written during the tenure of the agreement. The term for this type of deal is usually one year, with up to six options of one year each at the election of the publisher. Since the writer signs up for an extended relationship with the publisher, the publisher has a stronger financial interest in the writer, who receives advances on a periodic basis. But this type of deal is also risky, as a writer's songs could potentially end up "on the shelf" if the publisher loses interest in the work.

The third type, administrative and co-publishing deals, are perhaps the most attractive to songwriters: they enable the writer to retain copyright in the songs for the duration of the agreement term, so that at the end of the term the rights fully revert back to the writer. Administrative and co-publishing deals are also financially attractive, and they grant writers much larger shares of revenue accrued from their songs. For administrative deals, the publisher takes a small percentage of the total revenue (for example, 15 percent), and with co-publishing deals, the writer is entitled to 50 percent of the publisher's share in addition to his or her original 50 percent, for a total of 75 percent.

Mechanical, Synchronization, and Public-Performance Rights

As we discussed, the three most lucrative sources of revenue from songs are mechanicals, synchronization, and public performance.

Mechanical Rights

The right to reproduce and distribute to the public a copyrighted musical composition on audio "phonorecords" such as CDs, tapes, and vinyl is referred to as the "mechanical" right. This terminology dates back to the days of the player piano, when a mechanical object—a cylinder wrapped with perforated paper—was inserted into a piano, and the music was literally "mechanically" reproduced. Phonorecords, as we will discuss in subsequent chapters, also include MP3s and other formats by which recordings of music are distributed on the Internet.

Compulsory License for Mechanicals

Licenses to exploit mechanical rights are called *mechanical licenses*. The Copyright Act contains compulsory licensing provisions governing the making and distribution of phonorecords of musical compositions including songs, although "dramatic works" such as operas are excluded from the compulsory license (see the section on dramatic works below). Section 115 of the act provides that once phonorecords of a nondramatic musical work have been publicly distributed in the United States with the copyright owner's consent, anyone else may obtain a "compulsory" license to make and distribute phonorecords of the work without securing the owner's consent. For instance, once the Beatles recorded and released the record containing the song "Yesterday" by Lennon and McCartney, anyone else could rerecord "Yesterday" without having to obtain consent so long as they pay the compulsory mechanical license fee.

Anyone may use the compulsory licensing provisions of the Copyright Act to rerecord a previously released song by following the procedures established by the act. Those procedures require giving notice to the owner and paying a statutory royalty for each phonorecord manufactured and distributed. This is called a *statutory*, or "compulsory," license, because the copyright owner cannot deny permission. On the other hand, it assures that copyright owners will be paid for the use of their work. For the period from January 1, 2004, to December 31, 2005, the statutory mechanical royalty rate was 8.5 cents for songs five minutes or less. As of January 1, 2006, the statutory mechanical rate is 9.10 cents for songs five minutes or less, or 1.75 cents per minute or fraction thereof over five minutes. For example:

- ▶ 5:01 to 6:00 = \$.105 (6 x \$.0175 = \$.105)
- ▶ 6:01 to 7:00 = \$.1225 (7 x \$.0175 = \$.1225)
- ▶ 7:01 to 8:00 = \$.14 (8 x \$.0175 = \$.14)

This rate will remain in effect until the next schedule of mechanical licensing rates is determined. As we discuss in Chapter 3, these rates also apply to digital downloads of songs.

Harry Fox Agency

Publishers may, and usually do, issue voluntary mechanical licenses at the rates set forth above rather than depending on the compulsory rate provisions of the Copyright Act. For this purpose, most publishers utilize the Harry Fox Agency (also known as "HFA," the Fox Agency, or "Harry Fox") to handle mechanical licensing on their behalf. In 1927, the National Music Publishers' Association, an organization representing music publishers, established HFA to act as an information source, clearinghouse, and monitoring service for licensing musical copyrights. The Fox Agency acts as licensing agent for more than 27,000 music publishers, who in turn represent the interests of more than 160,000 songwriters. Although the rate is the same whether the licensee obtains a license directly from the owner or from the Fox Agency, the license issued by the Fox Agency is far simpler to comply with. For example, HFA requires quarterly accounting instead of monthly accounting required under the Copyright Act. Also, the Copyright Act requires filing with the copyright owner a detailed annual statement of account certified by a public accountant. Dealing with the Fox Agency is much easier, and many music publishers depend on Fox to handle mechanical licenses. If you are planning to release your own original recording of someone else's song and your arrangement of the song hasn't substantially altered it, the quickest and most efficient path is usually to contact Harry Fox.

Uses Not Covered by Compulsory Mechanical License

Now that we know what the compulsory license for mechanicals is, and how to secure such a license, and how much it costs, let's be clear about what it does not cover. The compulsory license is available only for musical works that have been previously authorized for release to the public. It does not extend to recordings of songs that have never been released to the public, such as private demos. Also, you cannot secure a compulsory mechanical license for the use of music in audiovisual works such as television programs or motion pictures (see discussion of synchronization rights in the next section). The technical reason for this is that the mechanical compulsory license only gives you the right to make and distribute "phonorecords" of a previously recorded song, and "phonorecords" do not include audiovisual works such as TV programs and movies. It also makes sense that the law limits the compulsory license to "phonorecords" because it would be unfair to the copyright owner of a song to be paid the same amount for different uses that may be radically unlike in terms of their financial character. For instance, think of the use of "New York, New York" by Fred Ebb and John Kander over the credits in the next Steven Spielberg blockbuster, compared to the use of the same song in an indie documentary film. It would be unreasonable to make the owner of that song accept the same compensation for both uses.

The compulsory mechanical license was intended to permit "covers," that is, new recordings of songs that are faithful to the original music. The compulsory license includes the privilege of making a musical arrangement of the work "to the extent necessary to conform it to the style or manner of interpretation of the performance involved." However, Section 115 of the act also provides that the arrangement "shall not change the basic melody or fundamental character of the work, and shall not be subject to protection as a derivative work . . . except with the express consent of the copyright owner." For instance, you cannot change the lyrics. If you do, you will need the consent of the copyright owner.

Synchronization Rights

The right to record a musical composition in synchronized relationship to the frames or pictures in an audiovisual production, such as a motion picture, television program, television commercial, video production, or website, is called the synchronization (or "synch") right. There is no compulsory license for this right; it is subject to the licensor and licensee negotiating an agreement. The Harry Fox Agency used to negotiate synch licenses for some of its publisher members but discontinued this service in June 2002. So you generally must secure synchronization rights by contacting the publisher. You can search for publisher information using the database of the Fox Agency, www.songfile.com, as well as the websites of the performing-rights organizations discussed below.

The fees for synch licenses can vary wildly depending on a variety of circumstances, including the popularity of the song and the nature of the audiovisual work. For instance, it will cost a great deal more to use an American standard such as "They Can't Take That Away from Me" by the Gershwins in a major motion picture than a song by an obscure garage band in a low-budget indie movie. We will revisit clearing music for TV programs and movies in more detail in Chapter 6, Music Licensing Fundamentals.

A television producer is generally required by the television service on which the program will air (including a TV network, pay cable service, or basic cable) to acquire synch rights for any copyrighted music that is included in the program. The television service, as we discuss below, generally handles the license of public-performance rights.

Public Performance Rights

Section 106(4) of the Copyright Act gives the copyright owners of musical compositions (songs), but not sound recordings (or, as they are referred to in the music business, *masters*), the exclusive right to "perform the copyrighted work publicly." The act first recognized the right of public performance in musical compositions approximately a hundred years ago. Today, public performance is the most lucrative source of income for many songwriters. What does "perform publicly" mean?

As the Copyright Act defines it, to perform or display a work "publicly" means:

(1) to perform or display it at a place open to the public or at any place where a substantial number of persons outside of a normal circle of a family and its social acquaintances is gathered; or

(2) to transmit or otherwise communicate a performance or display of the work to a place specified by clause (1) or to the public, by means of any device or process, whether the members of the public capable of receiving the performance or display receive it in the same place or in separate places and at the same time or at different times.

In the case of songs, public performances defined in subparagraph (1) include concerts and live performances (e.g., Bruce Springsteen performing at the Meadowlands or your gig at Mercury Lounge), a jukebox playing in a bar, background music at a bowling alley, or music playing at any other public venue. But public performances go well beyond performances at physical venues. Playing music on the radio and television also constitutes public performance, because these are "transmissions" to the public under subparagraph (2). Also, as we discuss in Chapter 3 and in more detail in Chapter 4, transmitting music on the Internet is a public performance and consequently a new and important source of income for songwriters.

ASCAP, BMI, and SESAC

Since copyright owners of songs enjoy exclusive public performance rights, those who wish to perform songs publicly need permission need to so. Performing-rights licenses apply to different media such as radio, TV, music websites, Internet radio, and other digital music services, as well as venues such as nightclubs, hotels, amusement parks, and arenas.[2] There are a vast number

---

2. PROs do not license to movie theaters in the United States. This is the result of antitrust claims brought decades ago having to do with certain publishers being owned by the same companies that also owned movie theaters. Movie producers therefore must and do secure public-performance rights directly from composers for new music or music publishers for preexisting songs.

of such users in the U.S., so it would be virtually impossible for individual songwriters or publishers to license all of them. In fact, performances of copyrighted music even a hundred years ago were so numerous, geographically diverse, and transitory that it was virtually impossible for each songwriter or his music publisher to monitor them all. In 1914, a group of prominent songwriters including Irving Berlin, Jerome Kern, and John Philip Sousa, and music publishers, came together to create ASCAP (American Society of Composers, Authors, and Publishers), the first American performing-rights organization (also known as a PRO), in order to license users, collect public-performance royalties, and pay those royalties to the publishers and songwriters. In 1939, the broadcast community helped establish a competitor to ASCAP called BMI (Broadcast Music, Inc.). A third, much smaller PRO, SESAC (which used to stand for "Society of European Stage Authors and Composers") subsequently emerged. SESAC originally represented contemporary classical music but now represents and licenses all kinds of music.

The primary purpose of ASCAP, BMI, and SESAC is to ensure that music creators are fairly compensated for the public performance of their works. These organizations license public-performance rights on behalf of their writers and publisher members by each PRO granting "blanket licenses" to users. A blanket license includes the right to publicly perform all the songs represented by the PRO. The PROs collect license fees from each such licensee and, after deducting expenses, distribute the income to their writers and publisher members. Although they compete with each other, together these three PROs license the performing rights in virtually all the previously recorded music in the United States and, through their reciprocal relations with foreign PROs, virtually all the previously recorded music in the world. PROs worldwide include:

Australia: APRA	Austria: AKM
Belgium: SABAM	Brazil: SBACEM
Brazil: SICAM	Brazil: UBC
Canada: SOCAN	China: MCSC
England: PRS	France: SACEM
Germany: GEMA	Greece: AEPI
India: IPRS	Ireland: IMRO
Israel: ΛCUM	Italy: SIAE
Japan: JASRAC	Mexico: SACM
Poland: ZAIKS	Russia: RAO
South Africa: SAMRO	Spain: SGAE

Active links to these PROs are supplied in the Resources section of the DVD included in this book.

PROs represent a very important source of income for writers and publishers. Surprisingly, the cloud hanging over the music industry—the decline of record sales—has a flip side, due to the fact that publishers have actually enjoyed an *increase* in public-performance revenue over the past ten years. ASCAP, for example, has collected more than $2.7 billion over the last three years. Take a look at these figures:

Approx. REVENUES (in million) in Year...		
	ASCAP	BMI
2009	$995	$905
2008	$933	$901
2007	$863	$839
2006	$785	$780
2005	$749	$728
2004	$699	$673
2003	$668	$630

As more and more opportunities arise for music licensing, thanks in large measure to new technologies such as music apps, video games, and ringtones, publishers have been able to benefit from the general increase in Internet performance and usage and have not suffered as much as the recording industry from file sharing and streaming. In fact, the music-publishing business is doing well compared to the recording industry. I asked the president and CEO of the National Music Publishers' Association, David Israelite, the reason for this, and here is his response:

> The music-publishing industry is fortunate that we have a bundle of rights that produce income in different ways. While mechanical revenue is down significantly, performance income has mostly held steady, and publishers have become more aggressive in seeking alternative revenues from sources such as synchronization, lyrics and tablature, and merchandising.

The fees charged by the PROs to acquire blanket licenses are usually based on a small percentage of income. There is a mutual benefit to blanket licensing for the PROs and their licensees. The PROs collect money from users of music on a continuing basis for their members. The licensees acquire comfort that they can play any song in the PRO's repertory without fear of copyright infringement. It would be virtually impossible, for example, for a radio station to negotiate a license for every song it plays with each songwriter or publisher.

PROs pay their songwriter and publisher members by assigning value to each performance of their songs, which is determined by various factors such as the amount of license fees collected in a medium (television, cable, radio, etc.), the type of performance (visual vocal, background music, theme song, jingle, etc.), and the economic significance of the licensee (for example, how much a particular TV or radio station pays the PRO). Allocations for each song are made through various methods such as sampling, review of playlists and logs, and other methods that are intended to capture the actual use of music as accurately as possible.

Each PRO pays 50 percent of income to its publisher members and 50 percent directly to the writers. This is important, because the publishers cannot deduct any administration fees from the writer's share. They also cannot deduct any advances they may have paid the writers. This practice started with ASCAP, which, as we discussed, was created by some of the most successful songwriters of all time.

We will explore the licenses that the PROs use for digital media, including webcasting and interactive streaming, in subsequent chapters. For more about the PROs' membership requirements, their formulas for paying royalties, and the services they provide to young songwriters, such as showcases and networking opportunities, check out ASCAP.com, BMI.com, and SESAC.com.

Dramatic Works

PROs do not grant public-performance licenses for dramatic works. The term *dramatic works* refers to productions that use music to directly advance the plot, such as an opera, musical comedy, or ballet. Public-performance rights for music in dramatic works are called "grand rights." The producer of a dramatic work must negotiate such rights directly with the publisher or composer.

Artists and Labels: Rules and Business Practices

Overview

The Copyright Act protects sound recordings produced on and after February 15, 1972. Sound recordings first fixed before February 15, 1972, may nonetheless enjoy protection under the common-law or antipiracy statutes of the various states.[3] The owners of sound-recording copyrights enjoy all the same rights as those who own musical compositions, except, as we will discuss, public-performance rights. Generally, if an artist is signed to a label, the record company will own the master pursuant to contract.

Master-Use Licenses

A master-use license grants permission to use a preexisting recording of music for audiovisual projects such as a movie or in a new record such as an audio compilation. For instance, a movie producer who wishes to use a recording of music in his or her film will need to negotiate a master-use license with the copyright owner of the master—usually a record company. Similar to synch licenses, there is no compulsory rate for master-use licenses. Note that record companies usually do not own the song embodied in their masters. Thus, in order to use Frank Sinatra's recording of Kander and Ebb's "New York, New York" in a film or a TV show, the producer would need a synch license from the music publisher of the song as well as a master-use license from the record company that owns the Sinatra recording.

---

3. State antipiracy laws generally mirror the federal laws. Most states have unauthorized-duplication statutes that make it illegal to copy, reproduce, and distribute sound recordings without authorization. Those statutes apply to songs recorded before February 15, 1972—the date that sound recordings were added.

Public-Performance Rights

The Copyright Act does not recognize a public-performance right in sound recordings (except, as we will discuss in Chapter 3, for digital audio transmission). Therefore, a license is not needed to publicly perform a recording of music (in contrast to any copyrighted music embodied in the recording). For example, Yankee Stadium needs a public-performance license to play the song embodied in the Sinatra recording of "New York, New York" after Yankees ball games but does not need a license from the record company that owns the recording. Also, radio stations need a public-performance license to broadcast copyrighted songs. Radio stations (except for digital stations) do not need a public-performance license to play recorded music.

See Chapter 10 on how the record companies are trying to change the law to make public performance of their masters on radio subject to their permission and receipt of payment.

Record Companies

Record companies make and sell records. But first they must acquire the rights in the performances on a recording. Unlike a song, which is created by one person or one band or is a simple collaboration between a lyricist and a composer, a master is a collaborative enterprise usually involving multiple parties including the artist, the producer, and the background singers and musicians. Therefore, the performances embodied on a master are a result of various creative contributions. Yet the record company will usually be the only copyright owner of the master. This ownership is generally accomplished as follows: The record company acquires rights in the artist's performance under the recording contract with the artist (see discussion below). For backup musicians who are members of the AFofM (American Federation of Musicians) and the backup vocalists who are members of AFTRA (American Federation of Television and Radio Artists), a transfer of rights is included in the standard union contract to which the record companies are signatories. Record producers also make many creative contributions to the recording. Producers help select the songs, the arranger, and the side musicians, and they supervise the recording session as well as the mixing and mastering process. The record company will generally insist that the artist enter into an agreement with the producer under which the producer transfers all his or her rights to the record company.

Recording Agreements

A detailed analysis of recording agreements is beyond the scope of this book. However, we can outline basic terms of the standard deal. These terms have been offered by the major labels and most independent labels for decades, and they have served as the foundation on which the recording industry has done business.

Exclusivity

A standard record contract requires the artist to record music exclusively for the record company. This means that only the record company has the right to distribute records and music videos containing the artist's performances created during the term of the agreement. The artist may perform live concerts without permission. Generally, the exclusivity clause, no matter how broadly drafted, will not be enforced in such a manner as to prevent the artist from performing on a television program, although technically a TV show usually entails a recording. For instance, Sony Music produced a TV series featuring performances of new and some established recording artists. The show was called *Sessions at West 54th* and aired initially on PBS. Many artists who performed on the show were not signed to Sony. Those artists did not secure the consent of their record companies to perform on *Sessions*. But when Sony wanted to include their performances in a "best of" CD, it needed to secure the permission of the record companies for each artist who was not signed to Sony.

Duration and Options

Perhaps the most important provision in the record contract is its duration. Customarily, the record companies require the artist to deliver one or two albums followed by a series of "options" under which the record company can require the artist to deliver additional albums. A typical record deal may have five option periods or more and may require two albums during each option period. The record company can terminate the contract at any time. The artist cannot. The result of this structure is that the record company can drop the artist even before the first album is released, or it can require an artist to record multiple albums over a number of years that may encompass an artist's entire career. In the 1990s, George Michael wanted to terminate his relationship with Columbia Records. But his recording contract required him to record more albums at Columbia's option. Michael brought a lawsuit in England to get out of his contract. He alleged, among other things, that Columbia's option for additional albums should be unenforceable because it made him a virtual slave of the record company. He also argued that since every major record company has these options for additional records, he had no real choice and no real bargaining power. He lost the case. The English court found that he entered the contract voluntarily and that he could not prove collusion between the major labels. From the record companies' point of view, the rationale for options is that the label makes a very substantial financial investment in an artist's career, and it wants to be around to share in the artist's success.

Advances and Royalties

The record company may provide a "budget" from which the artist pays for the production of an album and retains any money not used during the course of production. Alternatively, the record company may pay for the costs of production directly and pay an "advance" to the artist on top of production expenses. As we discuss in the next section, in either scenario, all of these payments are recoupable from the artist's royalties.

The normal recording royalty for new artists and artists with niche audiences, like jazz musicians, ranges from 10 to 15 percent of the suggested retail price of a record. Ten percent of a $15 CD is $1.50, but there are all sorts of deductions, such as packaging (25 to 35 percent of retail) and producer fees (which range from 3 to 5 percent and are deducted directly from the artist's royalty), that significantly reduce that $1.50. These deductions vary from label to label, but normally the royalty is in the range of 75 cents to $1 after all the deductions are subtracted.

Recoupment

All the money that a label spends to produce an album, whether it pays the artist to make the album or pays for costs itself, is treated as "recoupable advances." In addition, at least 50 percent of independent-promotion and video costs are generally treated as advances, as well as any money that the label pays directly to the artist. Under the standard record contract, the artist is supposed to repay all these advances to the label. This repayment happens through "recoupment." Suppose that recording costs and the artist's share of promotion and video expenses add up to a million dollars. In record-company parlance, the artist recoups at his royalty rate. If the artist's royalty is $1, the album must sell one million units before the artist has repaid the record company. Some artists' advocates claim this is unfair, because if the record company has sold a million units at a wholesale price of, for instance, $7 a unit, the record company has pocketed $7 million. In other words, the record company has already made enough money to pay itself back for all its costs and make a profit. But the record companies argue that very few albums ever sell a million units, and they usually barely break even or lose money on most releases. In other words, they need the surpluses from the hits to subsidize all the losers.

In any event, this is the way the game has been played. The result is that very successful artists who sell millions of units recoup and make substantial royalties. The record companies also reward such artists with huge advances. However, relatively few artists ever reach this level of success.

Controlled Composition Clauses

"Controlled compositions" are songs written or cowritten by the artist or the producer of the track in which the song is embodied. Typically, the recording company will pay 75 percent of the minimum statutory rate (see above for the current "stat" rate) for these compositions. Also, they usually impose a "cap" of ten songs per album. So if the artist writes twelve songs, he will be paid for only ten at 75 percent of stat rate. In addition, even if the artist wrote only two songs, if the company has to pay another writer or writers for ten songs, the artist gets zilch. Many in the songwriting community have complained about this practice for years, claiming there is no justification for it except that all the major labels do it and so artists have little choice other than to accept it. It is true that if an artist becomes a huge success, he or she may be able to negotiate the controlled-composition clause out of the contract, as well as increase the recording royalty. Generally all artists, even stars, grant the label a free promotional synch license for use of controlled compositions in music videos.

Limitations on Rights to the Master

While the record company usually owns the master, this does not mean that it has unlimited rights to use the master. The label's rights are limited by the contract with the artist. For example, the artist will usually convey to the label the right to license masters for use in movies and television programs. However, the artist will usually retain consent over the use of masters to endorse a product or service.

The "360" Deal

In the past, record companies focused on making money from selling records. It was a very profitable business. Income rose from hundreds of millions in the early 1960s to billions in the 1990s.

This spurt in income was fueled by a new format—the CD—allowing the labels to sell all the old records that they had sold on vinyl and cassette in a shiny new format. But the artists got to keep money earned from live performances, endorsements, and music publishing. In fact, all of these sources of income were vital, because most artists never recouped recording costs and therefore never earned a dime in recording royalties. The record companies would argue that they made the artist successful and that the additional income from these other revenue sources was a byproduct of their efforts.

Now the labels are desperate for cash due to declining CD sales. Digital sales are rising, but far too slowly to offset the rapid decline of the CD. So the labels are trying to get a piece of the income from these other sources.

They revised their standard recording agreement to get 10 to 20 percent or more in the following areas:

▶ Touring and live performances.
▶ Merchandise—and not just on T-shirt sales. The labels are seeking income from corporate sponsorships, endorsements, and any goods or services carrying the artists' names or likenesses.
▶ Publishing—under a 360-degree deal, the labels are trying to take a cut of the artists' income from songs that they write.

These agreements, covering multiple revenue sources beyond sales of recordings, are called *360-degree deals*. For a major artist like Coldplay, if the label succeeds in getting a piece of live performance, it may have to put up a huge advance, or serious money for tour support and promotion revenue. The same will happen if it wants a percentage of a major artist's merchandise, promotion, or publishing. The bad news for new artists is that these deals can take the form of "passive participation." The labels make no additional advance payments and do no additional work; they just take a piece. So for new artists, a 360-degree deal can be terrible bargain and may provide additional incentive for artists to do it on their own!

According to leading entertainment lawyer Elliot Groffman, "Too many people are falling for the cry that they can't sell CDs so they need more rights. My concern is that we are going to allow [labels] to eat part of the artist's lunch while [labels] are starting to figure out the new distribution models, then in five to ten years they're going to control distribution again and control a good portion of the artist's income."

Copyright Registration: Why Do It, and How?

Why Register?

Copyright registration is a legal formality intended to make a public record of the basic facts of a particular copyright. Registration is not a prerequisite for copyright protection—a copyright comes into existence when the work is created. However, there are reasons why registration is important and provides great advantages to copyright owners. Those reasons are laid out at the U.S. Copyright office's website as follows:

1. Registration establishes a public record of the copyright claim.
2. Before an infringement suit may be filed in court, registration is necessary for works of U.S. origin.
3. If made before or within five years of publication, registration will establish prima facie evidence in court of the validity of the copyright and of the facts stated in the certificate.
4. If registration is made within three months after publication of the work or prior to an infringement of the work, statutory damages and attorney's fees will be available to the copyright owner in court actions. Otherwise, only an award of actual damages and profits is available to the copyright owner.
5. Registration allows the owner of the copyright to record the registration with the U.S. Customs Service for protection against the importation of infringing copies.

The fourth factor above is absolutely crucial. Without registration, a copyright owner cannot obtain statutory damages or attorney's fees. Statutory damages can be awarded up to $150,000 in cases of "willful" infringement—that is, where someone intentionally violated your copyright. For instance, you would be entitled to an award of up to that amount if someone intentionally took the hook of your song to create a new tune, or if they made copies of your record without your permission and sold them in the street, to retail stores, or on the Internet. If you do not comply with the registration requirements, you will have to prove "actual" damages, and proving this can often be very difficult or even impossible. In addition, the award of attorney's fees can be an extremely important incentive to any lawyer, let alone a highly experienced copyright attorney who is skilled in litigation. If you don't register your work, you can have a great case and never find a good lawyer because even if he or she wins the case for you, there may not be enough money to compensate him for his time. You should definitely register each song and master you produce. The U.S. Copyright Office has made that procedure extremely easy and very inexpensive. The steps and the prices are laid out below.

In case you have not heard this or read it in a book, note that the only way to secure the benefits of copyright registration is to register with the U.S. Copyright Office. These benefits cannot be obtained by sending a copy of your song or master to yourself (even by certified or registered mail) or sending your song or master to any other organization, union, or group.

How to Register

To register a work, including a song or a master, you need to submit a completed application form, a nonrefundable filing fee of $35, and a nonreturnable copy of the work. More details are provided below—but you can get all the details from the website of the U.S. Copyright Office (www.copyright.gov). Here are answers to some of the most important questions:

Where can I get application forms? Since the last edition of this book was published, the Copyright Office has begun to allow online registration rather than requiring the filing of hard copies of the application. You can find and complete the form online at http://www.copyright.gov/eco (*eco* is an acronym for Electronic Copyright Office). The fee is $35. It is also necessary to provide a "deposit" of the work, but this can be sent online as well by forwarding MP3s.

May I register more than one work on the same application? You may register "unpublished" works as a collection on one application with one title for the entire collection if the copyright claimant in all the elements and in the collection as a whole is the same. "Published" works may be registered as a collection only if they were actually first published as a collection. In regard to music, the Copyright Act defines *publication* as follows:

> [T]he distribution of copies or phonorecords of a work to the public by sale or other transfer of ownership, or by rental, lease, or lending. The offering to distribute copies or phonorecords to a group of persons for purposes of further distribution, public performance, or public display constitutes publication. A public performance or display of a work does not of itself constitute publication.

Therefore, if you are an artist who writes your own material and have released an album for sale, you have "published" it and can register all the music in the album in one application. Recently I worked with a client who wrote and recorded several tracks on his album and used other writers' songs for other recordings. We filed one application for the masters and songs that he wrote, and another for his copyright in the sound recordings that included songs written by third parties. If you are songwriter who has written but not commercially exploited your songs, you can register them all in one application.

Can you register the copyright in your website? Yes, the original authorship appearing on a website may be protected by copyright. This includes original writings, artwork, photographs, music, and sound. Procedures for registering the contents of a website may be found in Circular 66, Copyright Registration for Online Works.

The U.S. Copyright Office's website (www.copyright.gov) is an invaluable source of information not only on registration, but also on how copyright law protects songs and masters.

Duration of Copyright

The term *public domain* refers to the status of a work having no copyright protection and therefore belonging to the "public." When a work is in or has "fallen" into the public domain, it is available for unrestricted use by anyone. Permission and/or payment are not required for use. Once a work falls into the public domain (has become "PD"), it can never be recaptured by the owner (except for certain foreign-originated works eligible for restoration of copyright under section 104A of the Copyright Act).

Copyright protection does not last forever. Many musical compositions, such as most of the great classic repertoire, are now PD. Generally, a work goes into the public domain after a specific period of time. This section outlines what that period is.

Works Originally Created on or after January 1, 1978

A work that has been created (fixed in tangible form for the first time) on or after January 1, 1978, is automatically protected from the moment of its creation and is ordinarily given a term enduring for the author's life plus an additional 70 years after the author's death. In the case of a "joint work prepared by two or more authors," the term lasts for 70 years after the last surviving author's death. For works "made for hire," also sometimes referred to as a "corporate copyright," the duration of copyright will be 95 years from publication or 120 years from creation, whichever is shorter. A *work made for hire* generally refers to a work made by an employee of a corporation, such as a staff writer at a company that creates commercial jingles. A work for hire may also refer to a person who is commissioned to do a job under certain circumstances. For whether masters are works for hire under standard recording agreements, see the section below, Works for Hire in Recording Contracts.

The term of copyright used to be life plus 50, and for a corporate copyright the term was 75 years from publication or 100 years from creation, whichever was shorter. The duration of copyright was extended under the Sonny Bono Term Extension Act, signed into law on October 27, 1998. The act is named after its sponsor, the pop star and former husband of Cher who became a Republican congressman before his untimely demise in a skiing accident. The act is also sometimes referred to as the Mickey Mouse Protection Act, as it was heavily supported by Disney and other corporations that make a great deal of money by licensing their copyrights.

Many have criticized the extension. It is interesting to consider that originally, copyright protection endured only fourteen years. Professor Lawrence Lessig, the principal attorney representing a party challenging the constitutionality of the law, has argued that the law was designed to protect big corporations who use the copyright law to control culture and extract profits at the expense of those who would use previous works to contribute to society. On the other hand, your songs and masters are protected for a longer period than ever before. You should protect them by taking the steps to register them set forth above.

Works Originally Created before January 1, 1978, but Not Published or Registered by That Date

These works have been automatically brought under the statute and are now given federal copyright protection. The duration of copyright in these works will generally be computed in the same way as for works created on or after January 1, 1978; the life-plus-70 or 95/120-year terms will apply to them, as well. The law provides that in no case will the term of copyright for works in this category expire before December 31, 2002, and for works published on or before December 31, 2002, the term of copyright will not expire before December 31, 2047. For the definition of *publication*, see the section above on registration, and for further information see the U.S. Copyright Office website, Circular 1, Copyright Basics, section "Publication."

Works Originally Created and Published or Registered before January 1, 1978

For works published or registered before 1978, copyright was secured either on the date a work was published with a copyright notice or on the date of registration if the work was registered in unpublished form. In either case, the copyright endures for a first term of 28 years from the date it was secured. During the last (28th) year of the first term, the copyright is eligible for renewal. The Copyright Act of 1976 extended the renewal term from 28 to 47 years for copyrights that were subsisting on January 1, 1978, making these works eligible for a total term of protection of

75 years. Public Law 105-298, enacted on October 27, 1998, further extended the renewal term of copyrights still subsisting on that date by an additional 20 years, providing for a renewal term of 67 years and a total term of protection of 95 years.

Works for Hire in Recording Contracts

Standard recording agreements, including those offered by the major labels—that is, EMI, Sony, Warner, and Universal—as well most important indie labels, stipulate that any recordings of music made by the artist during the term of the agreement are "works for hire," or if for any reason they are not deemed to be works for hire, the artist assigns the copyrights in the master recordings made under the agreement to the record label. Despite this standard clause, do artists retain any rights in their masters?

The Copyright Act of 1976, which went into effect in 1978, makes a crucial distinction between a work for hire and a work created by an artist or author that is not a work for hire. The act provides for only two legal categories of work for hire:

A "work made for hire" is: (1) a work prepared by an employee within the scope of his or her employment; or (2) a work specially ordered or commissioned for use as a contribution to a collective work, as a part of a motion picture or other audiovisual work, as a translation, as a supplementary work, as a compilation, as an instructional text, as a test, as answer material for a test, or as an atlas, if the parties expressly agree in a written instrument signed by them that the work shall be considered a work made for hire.

Note that a master or phonorecord is not included among the works listed in (2). Therefore, unless an artist is deemed to be "an employee," the work-for-hire language in the standard recording agreement may not be enforceable.

The importance of this distinction is that if a work is not deemed to be a work for hire, even if the artist assigned the copyright in the master to the record company, the grant can be "recaptured" by the artist at any time during a period of five years beginning at the end of thirty-five years from the date of execution of the grant. Notices of intent to terminate can be filed ten years before that. Therefore, if the artist entered into a standard recording agreement in 1978, he or she could file a notice to the record companies in 2003, and such notices have already been sent. It is yet to be determined whether the work-for-hire language in the standard record-company agreements is valid.[4] Therefore, it is conceivable that the record companies could eventually lose the right to distribute tens of thousands of records or more. A more comprehensive analysis of this issue goes beyond the scope of this book, but an artist who has entered into a record contract in 1978 or thereafter should consult with competent counsel.

---

4. "The question thus remains unaddressed whether sound recordings created in 1978 and thereafter can qualify as works made for hire," David Nimmer, *Copyright Illuminated: Refocusing the Diffuse U.S Statute* (Aspen 2008). Perhaps one reason for this is that even if artists were able to recapture the copyright in their share of the sound recording, the record label would still be able to claim authorship in the contributions of the producers, engineers, side musicians, background singers, and anyone else who contributed creatively to the record.

Fair Use

Fair use is a complete defense to copyright infringement. Under Section 107 of the Copyright Act, the defense applies where a work is used "for purposes such as criticism, comment, news reporting, teaching . . . scholarship or research." In evaluating whether the fair-use defense is available, courts must evaluate (1) the purpose and character of the use, including whether such use is of a commercial nature or is for nonprofit educational purposes; (2) the nature of the work; (3) the amount and substantiality of the portion used in relation to the copyrighted work as a whole; and (4) the effect of the use upon the potential market for or value of the copyrighted work.

In the context of the music business, fair use arises frequently in the context of parody. In order to constitute fair use, a parody of a song must be targeted at the original work and not merely borrow its style. In the 2 Live Crew case, the Supreme Court of the United States determined that that band's parody of "Pretty Woman" was a fair use because it poked fun at the original even though it used some of the lyrics and melody of the original song. (*Campbell vs. Acuff-Rose Music, Inc.*, 510 U.S. 569 [1994])

Outside of the parody, however, the following cases show that deciding what is or is not fair use depends on the particular facts of each case.

Performing a Thirty-Second Excerpt to Sell Ringtones is NOT Fair Use

U.S. vs. American Society of Composers, Authors, and Publishers (S.D.N.Y., 2009)

Ringtones became a fashion statement in the 1990s, as consumers wanted to have the latest hits play when their phone rang. Additionally, where callers used to hear the sound of a phone ringing *as they waited for* someone to pick up, consumers bought ringback tones to play for people who called them. See Chapter 7 for the business history and current licensing structure applicable to ringtones and ringbacks.

In this court case, AT&T set up online and mobile stores to sell ringtones and ringbacks. For the purpose of attracting customers, they allowed people to listen to thirty-second previews of songs but failed to seek the permission from the copyright owners. ASCAP challenged this practice in a rate proceeding before the federal court in New York delegated to handle such controversies. ASCAP argued that AT&T's usage was completely commercial in nature, done to increase sales, and therefore should have been licensed. ASCAP also pointed out that in its online storefront, AT&T promoted other products alongside music and that playing excerpts of music helped sell these products as well as ringtones. Finally, they argued that dozens of other organizations already license these same exact previews and that AT&T simply did not want to compensate songwriters in ways that everyone else already does. AT&T pointed out that they were -using only thirty-second excerpts, not full songs, and their use of these excerpts would not affect the potential market for sale of full songs.

The court ruled in favor of ASCAP, holding that:

> AT&T erred in assuming that the performance of previews of music compositions on its
> Internet website would be ruled a fair use of the copyrighted material and, therefore, did

not include such previews in its license fee proposal. Although AT&T does not charge for previews, they clearly increase the revenue from sales of Ringtones and Answer Tones, which are made after an average of between three and four previews for each sale. Thus, a fee should be paid for these performances of music to generate revenue.

The court went on to emphasize that AT&T was using the music to facilitate sales of AT&T's products as well as ringtones, that it was customary in the music business to pay for use of excerpts, and that AT&T's usage exploited the melody or chorus, which is often the most interesting and entertaining portion a song.

Using Fifteen-Second Excerpts in a Documentary IS Fair Use Since the Use Was "Transformative"

Lennon vs. Premise Media Corp., 556 F.Supp.2d 310 (S.D.N.Y., 2008)

Expelled was a 2008 documentary directed and narrated by the political pundit and satirist Ben Stein. The movie addressed the "Intelligent Design" movement, which some educators espouse as an alternative to Darwin's theory of evolution, and the ongoing difficulty that various scientists have when attempting to practice their faith alongside their field of study. At one point in the movie, several speakers express negative views of religion and advocate for religion's diminished role in society. The producers of the documentary criticized this view as "merely lifting a page out of John Lennon's songbook" and then followed up with fifteen seconds of the song "Imagine," written by John Lennon. While the song was played, subtitles displayed the lyrics "Nothing to kill or die for / And no religion too." Behind the subtitles are images of black-and white footage, ranging from children frolicking to a military parade, and then a close-up of former Soviet ruler Joseph Stalin. No license was obtained for the commercial use of this excerpt, but licenses were secured for all the other music used in the movie.

Yoko Ono Lennon and her sons, Julian and Sean Lennon, sought to enforce John Lennon's copyright by requesting issuance of a preliminary injunction by the federal court in the Southern District of New York. The court, however, ruled that the defendants were likely to prevail on their affirmative defense of fair use. The court took into account that the original song was three minutes long but the excerpt was only fifteen seconds long. The plaintiffs rightly pointed out that that the excerpt was the hook of the original song and therefore had greater value and impact. The court, however, found that the use was a form of criticism of the song itself and that the movie directly commented upon the music. Rather than using the music as entertainment, the movie was "transformative," in that it was using the music to make the point that, stretched to the furthest degree, the concepts celebrated in "Imagine" were compatible with totalitarianism. The court also emphasized that this transformative use would not usurp the market for licensing the original song.

The foregoing cases demonstrate that fair use is fact-specific. There are no bold lines separating what is fair use and what is not. Each case may depend on the temperament and philosophy of the court before which the case is tried.

Minimum Use, Fair Use, and Sampling

In addition to fair use, the doctrine of "de minimis" use has provided wiggle room to many creators, especially in the area of digital sampling of music. Courts have dismissed copyright-infringement cases on the grounds that the alleged infringer's use of the copyrighted work was so insignificant as to be *de minimis*. However, in 2004 in Bridgeport Music, Inc. vs. Dimension Films, the U.S. Court of Appeals for the Sixth Circuit, which includes Nashville, explicitly declined to recognize a *de minimis* standard for sampling musical recordings. The court ruled that any sampling of prerecorded sounds is an infringement of the sound-recording copyright in the original master, no matter how little was used or whether the material used is even recognizable. The court stated in its decision, "[I]f you cannot pirate the whole sound recording, can you 'lift' or 'sample' something less than the whole? Our answer to that question is in the negative." The court declared: "Get a license or do not sample. We do not see this as stifling creativity in any significant way." *Bridgeport Music, Inc. vs. Dimension Films (6th Cir. 2004)*. The Sixth Circuit's decision in the *Bridgeport* case effectively eliminated the *de minimis* doctrine for recorded music in the Sixth Circuit. The court justified its decision by relying on a provision of the Copyright Act that states that owners of sound recordings can sue for copyright infringement only if the new work actually took elements of the recording itself rather than recreating the sound embodied in the original recording. The court reasoned that this implies that taking any part of the recording was copyright infringement. Many copyright scholars disagree with this analysis. They point out that the language relied on by the court is actually a limitation on the right of sound-recording owners to claim copyright infringement. It was not intended to confer greater rights on owners of sound recordings than owners of other copyrighted works!

Whether the decision was wrong or right, a firestorm of criticism erupted from both the music and the scholarly community. In the wake of all the criticism, the Sixth Circuit agreed to reconsider its decision. Although its revised opinion started by regurgitating its initial analysis and even confirmed its "new bright-line" rule that all sampling of music recordings can never be *de minimis,* the revised opinion ultimately took an extra step that has the effect of completely modifying the earlier decision. The court added at the very end of its reconsidered opinion: "Since the district judge found no infringement, there was no necessity to consider the affirmative defense of 'fair use.' On remand, the trial judge is free to consider the defense and we express no opinion on its applicability." The case was settled after it was remanded, but this language clearly shows that the court found that the initial decision did not preclude the availability of other defenses, such as fair use, even in the context of sampling. Therefore, in the Sixth Circuit, although defendants may not rely on the de minimis doctrine to say that they copied such a small amount that they are not liable for copyright infringement, they may still argue that their use of the sample remains a fair use—that is, that the use is transformative, that it is used for noncommercial purpose, that it copied only a small amount, that the original had a thin copyright, or that the copying did not harm the market for the original work or its derivatives.

Creative Commons: An Alternative to Copyright

Creative Commons, founded by Harvard Professor Lawrence Lessig and two other technology and intellectual-property experts, offers musicians, songwriters, and other creators an alternative to copyright law. The idea underlying Creative Commons is that some people may not want to exercise all of the intellectual-property rights the law affords them. According to the Creative Commons website:

> We believe there is an unmet demand for an easy yet reliable way to tell the world "Some rights reserved" or even "No rights reserved." Many people have long since concluded that all-out copyright doesn't help them gain the exposure and widespread distribution they want. Many entrepreneurs and artists have come to prefer relying on innovative business models rather than full-fledged copyright to secure a return on their creative investment. Still others get fulfillment from contributing to and participating in an intellectual commons. For whatever reasons, it is clear that many citizens of the Internet want to share their work—and the power to reuse, modify, and distribute their work—with others on generous terms. Creative Commons intends to help people express this preference for sharing by offering the world a set of licenses on our website, at no charge.

Creative Commons provides creators with a choice of licenses that they can append to their works. Under a Creative Commons (CC) license, a composer, for example, can choose to allow others to use her compositions in new songs, such as a remix, in exchange for credit and/or compensation if the remix is released commercially. Under another type of CC license, a songwriter could waive the right to compensation, including public-performance fees, entirely.

Under traditional copyright law, if a creator makes his work, such as song, available to the public, it comes with many strings attached. Specifically, as we discussed earlier in this chapter, the copyright law reserves to the creator the exclusive rights to distribute, copy, publicly perform, or create derivative works. That means that even if I buy a song from iTunes, I have no right to redistribute it, publicly perform it, or make derivative works from it. A derivative work is one that is based on another work but is not an exact, verbatim copy. Mash-ups and remixes are examples of derivative works; another example is a movie based on a novel. Although the fair-use doctrine may protect some forms of derivative use, as we discussed earlier in this chapter, each court must decide what use is "fair," and an artist can never be certain her use will be judged to be a fair use. However, a creator can use a Creative Commons license to make it absolutely clear that someone else may reuse their work with impunity. A creator can use Creative Commons as an alternative to the restrictive nature of copyright.

To take advantage of Creative Commons, creators go to the Creative Commons website (wiki. creativecommons.org), choose a license that works best for them, and then follows instructions to include certain HTML code in the work. This code will automatically generate a license button and a statement that the work is licensed under a Creative Commons license. The html code will also include the metadata that enables the work to be found via Creative Commons–enabled search engines.

Below are descriptions of various types of Creative Commons licenses, starting with the most restrictive and ending with the most accommodating type of license you can choose.

Attribution Noncommercial No Derivatives (by-nc-nd)

This license is often called the "free advertising" license, because it allows others to download your works and share them with others as long as they mention you and link back to you, but they can't change them in any way or use them commercially

Attribution Noncommercial Share Alike (by-nc-sa)

This license lets others remix, tweak, and build upon your work noncommercially, as long as they credit you and license their new creations under the identical terms. Any derivative work has to be made available under this same license.

Attribution Noncommercial (by-nc)

This license lets others remix, tweak, and build upon your work noncommercially, and although their new works must also acknowledge you and be noncommercial, they don't have to license their derivative works on the same terms.

Attribution No Derivatives (by-nd)

This license allows for redistribution, both commercial and noncommercial, as long as it is passed along unchanged and in whole, with credit to you.

Attribution Share Alike (by-sa)

This license lets others remix, tweak, and build upon your work even for commercial purposes, as long as they credit you and you license the new creations under identical terms. This license is often compared to open-source-software licenses. All new works based on yours will carry the same license, so any derivatives will also allow commercial use.

All Creative Commons licenses provide the "core right" to redistribute a work for noncommercial purposes without modification. But only the Attribution Share Alike license allows people to use the work for commercial purposes without permission from the owner. All other CC licenses require the new user to seek permission from the original creator to use a work commercially. Under the current copyright scheme, if person wants to license a song for use in a film, he would have to negotiate for a synch license. A CC license gives creators the power to allow other people to build upon the work but also allows the creator to maintain some control. According to Professor Lessig, "the project does not compete with copyright; it complements it." Its aim is not to defeat the rights of authors, but to make it easier for authors and creators to exercise their rights more flexibly and cheaply. "The difference," he told me in an interview, "will enable creativity to spread more easily."

Creative Commons therefore allows people to make a choice to give up specific and precise rights that otherwise they wouldn't be able to sacrifice based on the copyright law's "All Rights Reserved" model. Creative Commons uses the phrase "Some Rights Reserved," and the idea is that you're giving up specific things in a specific context and that's all. Any other use is covered by the whole well-tested body of copyright law. Today, approximately sixty million CC-licensed works exist, including many songs and musical recordings.

In 2005, Creative Commons and *Wired* magazine launched the Fine Art of Sampling Contest, in which contestants sampled Creative Commons–licensed tracks from artists such as Chuck D, the Beastie Boys, and David Byrne to create their own composition. The top winning entries were subsequently compiled onto a CD entitled *The Wired CD: Ripped. Sampled. Mashed. Shared.* Here is an excerpt of my interview with the executive editor of *Wired,* Thomas Goetz, about the compilation.

SG: What was the genesis of the CD, and how did you pull it off?

TG: The CD came about because we knew about Creative Commons, which is a great group that's out there trying to reform or take a new approach to copyright with the backdrop of an extremely restrictive model. The intellectual-property industries—the entertainment industries principally—have taken a maximalist approach toward intellectual property. They want to lock down all their rights. In the music business, it's coming against the otherwise wonderful opportunities that technology offers. Digital technology allows something like file sharing, which is a great way to learn about new music and a great way to sample music. Digital technology also allows people to be much more creative with their music; —look at GarageBand with Apple computers—with a few clicks, users can write and compose whole new songs and have it be available for fleshed-out compositions. So there's this polemical difference between what the music industry is doing on one hand, and the opportunities digital technology offers on the other. Creative Commons is trying to present the third way: find a middle ground where the rights holders are able to grant certain specific permissions and let people use the music in certain specific ways. And, as a correlative, hopefully they get more exposure, more promotion, and more people interacting with and using the music. The Creative Commons idea was out there in theory, so we thought we'd try and take the muscle of *Wired* magazine, which has some pretty good cred, and see if we could talk people into actually using the licenses, see if we could talk major artists into putting these licenses to the test.

SG: Are there any new tracks, or are these all cuts from existing albums?

TG: We tried to put together a CD that not only has this cool, big, high-concept idea behind it—the Creative Commons licenses—we also wanted to put together a CD that people could just listen to and get good songs, so we tried to get exclusive songs. The Beastie Boys' song is an exclusive track—it's an outtake from their new album; David Byrne's song is an exclusive track; they're mostly kind of rare B sides. A couple of them are tracks off of new or upcoming albums.

SG: It's ironic that tracks that may never have gotten a lot of exposure are now available to be used to create even more new music.

TG: Absolutely. The CD was a way to start the experiment and hopefully open up the floodgates to what Creative Commons could accomplish.

SG: Did you work with any of the artists directly?

TG: We were talking to managers, we were talking with bands—we largely avoided trying to go through labels, because the labels hear you messing around with masters and copyright and they run screaming the other way. So we tried to go to people who might be aware of this issue, aware of how the copyright model in this industry is kind of broken and people who might have an open ear toward that idea. It took us ten months to a year.

SG: All of the tracks on the CD are subject to a Creative Commons license, but some of the works are subject to different licenses—David Byrne's track, "My Fair Lady," is subject to a license that states: "Sampling Plus: Songs under this license allow noncommercial sharing and commercial sampling, but advertising uses are restricted." But the license for the Beasties' "Now Get Busy" states: "Noncommercial Sampling Plus: Songs under this license allow noncommercial sharing and noncommercial sampling." What rights would these two different licenses give you?

TG: Let me give you a little background: Creative Commons has about a dozen licenses or a dozen kinds of licenses on their website. They are all fully valid licenses that have been drawn up by their lawyers, and they apply to circumstances for different reasons. So if you want to create something and you want to give it away and have somebody do whatever the hell they want to do with it, then you can use a certain kind of license. If you want somebody to be able to use something but you want them to give you credit, than that's a slightly different kind of license. There's this whole armada of licenses, and it's a little confusing, but it's actually a great virtue of the Creative Commons models, because it allows people to make a choice to give up specific and precise rights that otherwise they wouldn't be able to sacrifice based on the All Rights Reserved model. Creative Commons has this good phrase "Some Rights Reserved," and the idea is that you're giving up specific things in a specific context and that's all. Any other use is covered by the whole well-tested body of copyright law.

In the case of our CD, Creative Commons came up with something called the Sampling license. This would allow people to sample songs, take a little cut from a song and use it in another song, and you wouldn't have to call a lawyer first. You're giving before-the-fact permission for that.

Then they have something called the Sampling Plus license, which not only allows the use of samples, but also allows commercial sampling. When talking with Creative Commons, it became clear that there might actually be a use for another kind of license—a Noncommercial Sampling license—so what we use on our CD is both a Sampling Plus, which allows file sharing and then commercial sampling, and then there's the Noncommercial Sampling Plus license, which is what the Beastie Boys, My Morning Jacket, and Chuck D chose, and that license allows file sharing and noncommercial sampling. With one of the Sampling Plus licenses, somebody could come along—say Eminem finds a little loop on the Rapture song that he really loves, and he puts it into a song and the song goes number one. The Rapture isn't going to get a penny out of it. That's kind of the whole point of the license. They've opened the doors to some wider creativity, and they aren't looking for commercial gain.

SG: But wouldn't Eminem have to give them credit?

TG: Yes, absolutely.

SG: So that's the quid pro quo. The artist gets credit, and theoretically more people get interested in his work, knowing that they used his work in their song.

TG: Exactly. The idea was that basically the whole heritage of music was a sharing, creative process. It was something where one musician heard something based on what a predecessor had done; somebody else came along, built on that, used a line, tweaked a riff. There was a great history in the 1950s of these rock-and-roll "answer" songs, and all that's gone away now because people are so conscious of the rights.

SG: The Beastie Boys opted for the more restrictive license. You can sample, but for noncommercial use only. Is that because of their record company?

TG: The whole point of the licenses is that different people have different choices. Different licenses let people tailor their choices according to what they're comfortable with. I think that when the Beastie Boys chose the commercial license, it probably has something to do with the fact that they're more aware or have more experience than other bands. They sample for a living, so they know what you gain and what you lose. But the fact that the Beastie Boys were willing and eager to put a song out there—allowing file sharing to go on and allowing people to chop up the song and put it on their website and share it with other people, and they get full permission for that—I think they've done an amazing thing.

SG: I think you're right, but as a lawyer who worked for a record company, I do want to make a point: If the artist is with a record company, there may be a limit on what the effect or usefulness of Creative Commons may be, because the artist gives up both commercial and promotional rights in the distribution of his music. In effect, under the standard recording agreement, an artist can't grant a Creative Commons license without the permission of his record company, and some record companies are going to be less liberal than others.

TG: Right—no one had gone to artists of this caliber and said, use this license, give up your rights. We asked a lot more people than we got, and lots of people were terrified by that idea, and rightfully so. The record industry has sued over seven thousand people for file sharing, and here we were asking these artists to say file sharing is okay for the song, so it's a seriously gutsy move on these guys' parts.

SG: And a seriously gutsy move on your part. I wouldn't have wanted to be the one trying to get the record companies to give permission to use the Creative Commons license! But congratulations on getting a fine piece of work out there.

In fact, some established players in the music business are dead set against Creative Commons. ASCAP recently sent a fund-raising letter to its members calling on them to fight organizations like Creative Commons and other supporters of the "free culture movement," claiming that such organizations work to undermine copyright. ASCAP's letter stated that organizations such as Creative Commons "are mobilizing . . . to undermine 'Copyright'" and that "these groups simply do not want to pay for the use of our music . . . [T]heir mission is to spread the word that our music should be free."

Creative Commons responded to this letter in the news section of its website on June 30, 2010:

CC licenses *are* legal tools that creators can use to offer certain usage rights to the public, while reserving other rights. Without copyright, these tools don't work. Artists and record labels that want to make their music available to the public for certain uses, like noncommercial sharing or remixing, should consider using CC licenses. Artists and labels that want to reserve all of their copyright rights should absolutely not use CC licenses.

It seems to me that ASCAP's real concern is that if enough writers waive their right to receive royalties, this could impact their bottom line. ASCAP, together with sister performing rights organizations BMI and SESAC, currently represents almost all commercially popular songs. If, for example, 10 percent of songs became subject to gratis licenses under Creative Commons, the value of a blanket license from the PROs, including ASCAP, would decrease, which could drive their license fees down.

To find out more about Creative Commons, go to www.creativecommons.org. You can also listen to an interview with Professor Lessig in the podcast section of my website. In the interview, we explore Creative Commons in more detail, as well as other issues raised by his latest book, *Free Culture: How Big Media Uses Technology and the Law to Lock Down Culture and Control Creativity.*

Additional Resources

There are many books about music and copyright law. These are among the best:

Moses Avalon, *Confessions of a Record Producer: How to Survive the Scams and Shams of the Music Business* (4th ed., Hal Leonard, 2009).
Jeffrey Brabec and Todd Brabec, *Music, Money, and Success: The Insider's Guide to Making Money in the Music Business* (6th ed., Schirmer, 2008).

Robert Clarida, *Copyright Law Deskbook* (BNA Books, 2009).

Donald Farber, ed., *Entertainment Industry Contracts: Negotiating and Drafting Guide,* (vol. 4, Music), (Matthew Bender, 1992). Sample contracts and commentary.

Melville B. and David Nimmer, *Nimmer on Copyright* (Matthew Bender, 2004). Treatise on copyright law.

Donald S. Passman, *All You Need to Know About the Music Business* (7th ed., Simon and Schuster, 2009).

Peter M. Thall, *What They'll Never Tell You About the Music Business: The Myths, the Secrets, The Lies (and a Few Truths)* (2nd ed., Billboard Books, 2007).

Chapter 2

Practical Advice in Response to Clients' Most-Asked Questions

This chapter addresses the questions that I hear most often when potential clients call me. Those questions are:

1. Somebody stole my song: What can I do? How much can I get? When can I get it, and how much will it cost?
2. How can I protect my name, or my band or label's name? Should I register the name, and how much will it cost?
3. How can a music lawyer help me; will they shop my record, and how much will it cost?

In regard to (1) and (2), I enlisted the aid of leading experts who specialize in copyright litigation and trademark law. For the third question, I turned to veteran music attorneys Don Passman and Peter Thall.

Somebody Stole My Song! What Can I Do? How Much Can I Get? When Can I Get It, and How Much Will It Cost?

In this interview, copyright attorney Robert Clarida gives a brilliant cost–benefit analysis of starting a legal action for copyright infringement specifically relating to music. Bob is a partner at the leading IP (intellectual-property) firm Cowan Liebowitz & Latman. He also serves as adjunct professor of copyright law at Columbia Law School. Aside from his JD, Bob earned a PhD in music composition. He is the author of the *Copyright Law Deskbook* (BNA, 2009) and also edited this book.

SG: Hi, Bob. Let's suppose that a potential client calls you, introduces himself, and says, "I heard a song on the radio and it is almost the same as my song!" Take us through the conversation you would have with the client. What would your preliminary questions be?

BC: First, I would want to hear the songs, but I see that's your next question, so I'll get to it in a minute. Assuming the songs are similar, it would be essential to establish that the client's song was actually somehow made accessible to the defendant. No matter how similar two songs are, there's no copyright infringement if the second song was created independently, without the artist ever having heard the first one. Copyright infringement requires copying, and you can't copy something you never heard. A lot of infringement cases fail on this basis, because frequently the client has not released his or her song commercially in a big way—maybe they've played it at a few gigs, or it was on the local radio station once, or maybe it's on their MySpace or Facebook page, maybe you can even buy it on iTunes. In those kinds of cases it can very hard to establish that there was a "reasonable opportunity" for the defendant to hear the song, which is what the law requires. Sure, it's theoretically possible, but "mere possibility" isn't enough, and speculation isn't enough.

But if there was a "reasonable opportunity" for the defendant to hear the song, the case can go forward—even if the defendant claims they didn't actually hear the song (as of course they will). So let's say the client was an opening act for the defendant one night, and played the song at the gig, they have a video of it that their mother took, whatever. The defendant would clearly have a reasonable opportunity to have heard the song, even if they might say they were out in the tour bus relaxing while the opening act was on. That's just a credibility question, of whether you believe defendant's story. Clearly they had a reasonable opportunity, and it will be up to the jury to decide whom to believe.

Frequently, the client will have sent demos of the song to various record labels, handed a demo to a producer at a party, things like that. In those cases, you really have to establish a connection, or a "channel of communication," between the person who got the demo and the creative team that made the record. Just sending something to the mailroom of a big label is not enough to establish access as to every subsequent record that label releases, or even any record by that label. The courts call this "bare corporate receipt," and it never succeeds in establishing access.

If there is "widespread dissemination" of a song, however, meaning extensive airplay, access is established. The George Harrison case over "He's So Fine" and the Michael Bolton case over the Isley Brothers' "Love Is a Wonderful Thing" are both examples of that—there's no way a defendant can plausibly say they never heard the earlier record, even though as I recall the Isleys' tune was not a huge hit.

SG: Of course, you would have to have to hear and compare the two songs, correct? How similar do they have to be for copyright infringement? It is often said there are a finite number of chords in pop music and there are always going to be some similarities to preexisting songs.

BC: First, there's a kind of sliding scale, related to access. If you have a very clear case of access, less similarity may be needed to show infringement, but if access is really far-fetched, the similarity has to be very compelling. There's even a concept of "striking similarity" some courts have used to say that if two songs are exactly alike in some unusual, quirky way, that can be enough to show access all by itself. For example, if our client had written a song with the word "supercalifragilisticexpialidocious" in it, before *Mary Poppins,* the mere presence of that word in *Mary Poppins* would be virtually impossible to explain, except to say it was copied. There's not really a good argument that it was independently created.

But even with a strong or even "striking" similarity, there may be no infringement. To take the *Mary Poppins* example, if the only similarity was that one word, with no rhythmic or melodic or harmonic similarities, the second song would probably still not infringe. One "striking" word may be proof of copying, but that doesn't mean it's proof of infringement. What you need is "substantial similarity" with respect to the protectable elements of the client's song, and one word, even a made-up word, is probably not enough—I think everyone could go out tomorrow and use the word *supercalifragilisticexpialidocious* in a song and they'd be okay. What you can't do, though, is also take any significant portion of the melody and harmony and rhythm of the *Mary Poppins* song, because then you're going to have recognizable similarity as to protectable elements. There's a recent case called *Bridgeport vs. UMG,* involving a hip-hop group called Public Announcement that had made a very inconspicuous use of the lyric and melody of "bow-wow-wow-yippee-yo-yippee-yay" from George Clinton's "Atomic Dog." They were held to be infringers: they took the melody, rhythm, and lyric of George Clinton's hook and used in their own song. That was too much, even as part of the background during the fade-out. Similarly with Michael Bolton, who was held to infringe the Isley Brothers' "Love Is a Wonderful Thing" in his song of the same name, although there's really not much similarity besides the lyric and title. There's a great website people should check out, started by Charles Cronin, that's got music clips from the actual songs at issue in virtually every music-infringement case ever decided; it's a joint project by Columbia and UCLA at cip.law.ucla.edu. The best way to get a sense of what infringes and what doesn't is to spend some time on that site and get familiar with what the courts have already done. It's hugely instructive, even though you might come away thinking the cases are all over the map, which they arguably are.

One big point I need to make, though, is that a lot of pop songs (and metal songs, and smooth-jazz songs, and bluegrass songs, etc.) sound very much alike, simply because people are writing within certain shared patterns and conventions. Some melodic figures and chord progressions which may strike the client as unique and original (because they've never heard them before) are actually pretty common once you start looking for them, and another song with those same features will probably not be infringing, however much the client may feel it's a rip-off. That's why it's usually not enough to have a song that's kinda sorta the same, it's really got to be exactly the same, and for more than just a few notes, to be an infringement. Once you knock out all the commonplace stuff, which the court will do, there's often not much left of the claim. I got a PhD in music composition before I was a lawyer, and I can analyze melody and harmony better than most expert witnesses, at least judging from the expert reports I've seen, but no matter what kind of chart or graph an expert might make to show similarities, it's ultimately the ear of a layperson on the jury that has to make the call. If your client can play the two songs back-to-back for ten total strangers, without telling them what result he's looking for, and nine of them call it a rip-off, you've got a case. If you need to show some color-coded chart made by an expert, think again before bringing the claim.

SG: Once you hear the two songs, and assuming you find there is sufficient similarity between the songs for copyright infringement, then whom would be the target be? Suppose the offending song was recorded and sung by "Johnny Rapper." Would you only go against Johnny, or his record company and music publisher, as well?

BC: Typically, you'd sue as many people as you can plausibly link to the sale of the infringing song: the artist, the label, the publisher, the producer; and there's often several publishers, and maybe several producers, so you'd put them all in the caption. Probably not iTunes or Walmart—although retailers are often sued in other kinds of copyright cases, like with fabric designs, for example, you don't see it so much in music claims. Clearly they are distributing the infringing work, though, and making money at it, so there's no reason the law shouldn't reach them. Maybe we'll start seeing more of that, since record sales are being concentrated in such few places now.

SG: I suppose the very next conversation with the client is "Is it worth it?" For instance, would you recommend sending a "demand" before filing a lawsuit, to save money, and if so, what would that letter say?

BC: Yes, I would send a demand letter in almost every case, unless there was some reason to think that the defendant would react by starting a declaratory judgment action in some distant place. Usually, a defendant in a case like this will not do that, because they will hope and expect that it can all go away either by ignoring it or throwing a little money at it, certainly less than they'd have to spend on litigating. So they probably won't start a lawsuit. The demand letter will basically say what your claim is: the client is the owner of copyright in a song called XYZ, registered in the Copyright Office no. PA1234567. If it's not registered, now is the time to register it; you may even want to register on an expedited "special handling" basis before you send out your demand letter, to make the letter more impactful. You will then go on to identify the infringing song, say that it is copied from and substantially similar to protectable elements of the client's song XYZ, and that it therefore violates the Copyright Act, 17 U.S.C. 101 et seq. Then comes the demand: the defendant must stop all further use and exploitation of the song, account for all money received to date from exploitation of the song, and pay a sum not less than the amount they've made to date or they will act at their peril.

SG: In your experience, what is the likelihood that a strong letter will result in a tangible benefit for the client? Or is it most often the case that such letters are ignored and nothing will happen unless a lawsuit is filed?

BC: It depends on a lot of things. If you have a really strong case, and the defendant is being represented by a responsible grown-up, and you have a credible copyright lawyer writing the letter, there can be a quick settlement. I've certainly seen that happen; it never makes sense for a defendant to pour a bunch of money into a lawsuit if they know they'll have to litigate and they know they'll lose. If the client doesn't seem to have the wherewithal to sue, however, or if the case is thin, or if the defendant is just ignoring the problem or reacting to it with bluster rather than rational thought, it will take more than a letter to get them thinking clearly about the spot they're in. There are middle steps between a demand letter and starting a full-blown lawsuit, though. If the song is on the web somewhere, you can send a DMCA notice to the host of the site on which it appears, and often the host will take it down. If the defendant is hosting its own site, this will obviously not be effective, and even with a third-party host, the defendant could send a counter-notice and get the song put back up, but they may not want to bother to do so. You can draft a complaint, and send to the defendant with a letter saying we plan to file this in X days if we can't resolve our dispute. You can draft a complaint, file it with the court, but not formally serve it on defendants, and say, "We have commenced this action, we will serve it on you in X days if, etc." This has the advantage of essentially precluding a declaratory judgment action, if you have reason to worry about that (for example, if the defendant is in California and you're in New York, you don't want them to beat you to the courthouse and file in California). Or you can go all the way, formally serve the complaint on defendants with a summons, which starts their clock for having to hire a lawyer and respond within twenty days or they're in default.

SG: Suppose you send the letter but hear nothing back and a lawsuit must be filed—what would you tell the client as to how much money he is likely to recover and how long will it take? Let's focus on timing of recovery first; isn't it true the client may have to wait a long time to see any money? The "He's So Fine" case against George Harrison[1] took twelve years for a final decision on liability and damages! Is this standard?

BC: It can take a very long time to get a final result from a court: a year or more until you get to a jury; then maybe another year or more until an appeal is argued and decided, if someone appeals; and then maybe another proceeding on remand if the appeal doesn't resolve all the issues. But bear in mind that most cases settle at some point in the process, often fairly early through mediation or simple negotiation. Once the parties start paying tens of thousands every month in legal bills—and they will, if the case is being vigorously litigated—they quickly begin to see the value in settling even if they think they'd ultimately prevail.

SG: Couldn't you try for a preliminary injunction (PI)? That could take much less time, prevent the defendant from selling the song, and force a quick settlement.

BC: You could, but that would front-load the expenses in a big way. You'd have to spend those tens of thousands immediately to get a PI ready, and even if you win the PI you'd probably have to post a bond, which the court holds as security in case it turns out that you really don't win and the defendant's business has been halted for no good reason. Sometimes it's warranted, and the leverage can be great if you win, because a defendant may have to stop selling a record (or showing a movie with an infringing song in the soundtrack) just as it's taking off, but it's a very expensive proposition. I guess, like anything else, if you're willing to take a big risk you might get a big reward.

SG: Now let's talk about damages. Just because the client has registered the song doesn't mean they will get the maximum statutory damages of $150,000, correct? What will the client have to prove to get that?

BC: Well, the statutory-damage number you mention, $150,000, is the top of the range for willful

---

1. Following George Harrison's release of "My Sweet Lord," the musical similarities between it and the Chiffons' hit "He's So Fine" led to a lengthy legal battle. In the U.S. federal court decision, *Bright Tunes Music vs. Harrisongs Music* (SDNY 1976), Harrison was found to have "subconsciously" copied the earlier song. He was ordered to surrender the majority of royalties from "My Sweet Lord."

infringement. So the first thing you'd have to prove would be willfulness, basically meaning that the defendant knew they were ripping off your client and they did it anyway. If the infringement was something less than willful, like where the defendant credibly says, "I really didn't know what I was doing was a rip-off, it was just a tune that came into my head" (George Harrison said that, if you read his court transcript), the maximum for statutory damages is $30,000. For any statutory-damage award, willful or not, you'd also have to show some kind of connection between the number you're asking for and the actual harm suffered—statutory damages are not supposed to be a windfall. But if the defendant's song has been successful, the client would go for actual damages.

SG: Well, what about actual damages? If the song made a million bucks, and the client wins the case, how much does he get?

BC: Actual damages are basically the profits made by the defendant from the infringing song. That can be a huge number, and you don't have to show willfulness or anything, just that there was an infringement and the defendant made profits of X. "Profits" is basically gross revenue less the associated costs, including general overhead (unless the infringement is willful—there are some cases saying the defendant can't deduct general overhead for a willful infringement, so it would pay to prove willfulness even though you don't have to). The court doesn't necessarily award the whole profits number, though; it can only award the profits attributable to the infringement. Where a song is very substantially copied, the court would probably attribute the whole profits to the stolen material, but if the infringement is very short and fleeting, like the little George Clinton reference in the fade-out of the Public Announcement track, the court can and should apportion the profits and only award the amount it can reasonably attribute to the infringement.

SG: If the client registered the song, and he wins the case, will the court always award attorneys' fees?

BC: No, even if the client registered before the infringement. The best they can know for sure is that they are *eligible* for an award of attorneys' fees, not that they will automatically get them. (If they didn't register before the infringement, or within ninety days of publishing their work, they aren't even eligible for attorneys' fees.) Winning parties in copyright cases often get a fee award, but the main issue is whether the defendant's position is "objectively unreasonable." If the defense to an infringement claim is plausible enough to get to a jury trial, meaning that it survives a summary judgment motion, it is probably not objectively unreasonable. Also, the client needs to bear in mind that the defendant can get fees if it wins, and the plaintiff's position is shown to be objectively unreasonable.

SG: Can you give us an idea of what it costs to start a lawsuit for copyright infringement?

BC: As I discussed earlier, there are several intermediate steps between a demand letter and serving a complaint, one of which is to "start a lawsuit" by filing the complaint but not formally serving it. That can often get settlement talks happening, and it gives the parties up to four months to work something out before they have to start litigating. You don't have to be rich to do that, but it might cost several thousand dollars to draft a complaint even if the case is very straightforward. A cease-and-desist letter is much cheaper but also puts essentially no pressure on defendants, and they can easily blow it off indefinitely if they so choose (again, if they have no responsible grown-ups around). Obviously, the best answer to almost every dispute is a settlement, which is why almost all cases settle. And a settlement is much easier for a defendant to do if they have "deep pockets." So if you're asking for a $50,000 settlement from Goldman Sachs—maybe if they used the client's song on their website or something—that $50,000 is easier for them to part with than it would be for some formerly high-living musician who's now in bankruptcy. I think the depth of the defendant's pockets is more relevant to how much you settle for, rather than whether you take any action at all. Even if the infringer is broke, you still want them to stop using the client's music. Also, there are other ways to resolve a dispute besides money. Maybe the defendant is an established artist who would give the client credit as a co-writer or producer on the infringing track, or some future track, or agree to record several of the client's tunes on their next album, or something else that would be of value to the client but would not involve the defendant writing a big check. Often people don't think about these sorts of proposals until the lawsuit is under way and there's a mediation or settlement conference, but there's no reason to wait that long. Unless you want to spend more money on your lawyer, which I certainly don't want to discourage.

How Can I Protect My Name, the Name of My Band, or the Name of My Company? Should I Register with the Trademark Office, and How Much Will It Cost?

This interview answers the questions above and goes well beyond to present the best trademark-law primer for musicians, bands, and labels that I have seen. I want to express my thanks to James Trigg and Ashford Tucker of Kilpatrick Townsend & Stockton LLP, a full-service law firm with a specialization in copyright and trademark law. They spent a great deal of time and attention to address each of my questions, which will be clearly evident once you read this section. James is a partner whose practice focuses on copyright and trademark issues arising in the context of the Internet. Additionally, he has advised a variety of entertainers and creators on domestic and international trademark and branding issues, and he is an adjunct professor of trademark law at the University of Georgia School of Law. Ashford is an associate who provides domestic and international trademark-portfolio counseling to clients in a variety of industries, including music. Ashford also used to write for the online music publication *Pitchfork*.

SG: Can you run down the basics: What is a trademark, and why is it important to artists and bands?

JT and AT: A trademark serves to identify the source of goods or services. When we see marks like COCA-COLA, MICROSOFT, BUDWEISER and BMW, we instantly associate them with the products sold in conjunction with them, and we rely on these names to assist us in distinguishing one product or service from another. Thus, generally, trademark law seeks to prevent consumer confusion by allowing trademark owners to control the use of their marks so that consumers can rely on a trademark as an indication of a product or service's unique characteristics.

The law of trademarks applies to the fields of music, film, literature, and art just as readily as it does to soda, software, beer, and cars. Of course, most of us do not like to think of the arts as a "commodity," something that merely is bought and sold. Similarly, artists themselves at times may be reluctant to view their names or their creations as commercial trademarks that identify them to the public in exactly the same way that BUDWEISER identifies Anheuser-Busch. Nonetheless, by taking steps to protect their names, entertainers and artists can assume greater control of their identities and the way that those identities are perceived by the public.

Protectable Forms of Marks

Trademarks can assume innumerable forms, the only qualification being that they serve a source-identifying function for their owners. Naturally, there are traditional word marks: R.E.M., WEEZER, and NINE INCH NAILS all are trademarks that have been registered by their respective owners with the United States Patent and Trademark Office (PTO). Word marks can also take the form of personal names. For example, Madonna, Paul McCartney, and Faith Hill all have obtained trademark protection for their performing names.

Additionally, some artists and record labels (e.g., Grateful Dead, Aerosmith, and Sub Pop) have developed and registered as trademarks distinctive logos and designs that serve to identify them to the public.

Notably, Kiss owns trademark registrations for its stylized KISS logo and the distinctive face paint worn by its members.

Quasi-Protectable Marks

Titles of literary and artistic works, while not completely unprotectable, receive limited benefits under trademark law. A band generally cannot register trademark rights in the title of a single album or song to prevent other artists from using it. A title of a single work, however, may be protectable, and indeed federally registrable, for use in connection with ancillary merchandise, such as toys or clothing. Also, a title may be protectable through litigation if the artist can show that it has achieved "secondary meaning"—in other words, show that consumers have come to exclusively associate that title with the artist or entity that originated the title.[2]

---

2. *Paramount Pictures Corp. vs. Dorney Park Coaster Co.,* 698 F. Supp. 1274 (E.D. Pa. 1988) (owners of rights in the film *Top Gun* were able to shut down the operators of a TOP GUN amusement park ride where the ride invoked elements of the film).

The general prohibition on registering titles does not apply where there is a series of works involved. For example, singer Meat Loaf owns a federal trademark registration for the mark BAT OUT OF HELL, which he has used as the title of a three-album series.

SG: How does someone establish rights in a name?

JT and AT: Trademark rights in the United States can arise from use and from the trademark registration process. Trademark registration is discussed in Section 2.c. below. Under United States trademark law, a party can establish "common law" trademark rights simply by virtue of using the mark in commerce. Generally, "use in commerce" for the purpose of establishing rights means displaying the trademark to prospective purchasers in a manner that associates the mark with the mark owner's goods, services, or business.

Absent a federal registration, the trademark owner's rights in a mark are limited geographically to the scope of the owner's reputation. Therefore, absent a federal registration, it is entirely possible for two different entities to share rights in an identical mark for identical services if:

(1) The second party to adopt the mark offers its products or services in a geographic area so remote from that of the prior user that it is unlikely the public will be confused or deceived; and,
(2) The second party's adoption is in good faith (without knowledge of the prior user's use) and outside of the prior user's area of market penetration and "zone of protection."

In these circumstances, each user is entitled to prevent the other from entering into its "zone of protection" and both parties have the right to expand into "unoccupied territory" so long as their areas of operation remain remote. Thus, for example, a band in Atlanta, Georgia, with only a regional reputation in the southeastern United States can peacefully coexist with a band in Seattle, Washington, using the identical name. As long as each group stays within its zone of recognition, no confusion is likely. However, problems can begin to emerge if the Atlanta band signs a major-label recording contract that provides opportunities for nationwide touring and record distribution. In this event, the Atlanta group will need to resolve the potential trademark dispute with its Seattle counterpart, or else face the possibility of committing trademark infringement when it sells records and tours in the Pacific Northwest.

For any band beginning to enjoy a taste of success in the music business, it is worthwhile to check the PTO website's registration database (available at www.uspto.gov) and to do some targeted Google searches to ensure that their name is available for wider use.

SG: What is the benefit of a federal trademark registration, and how much does it cost? Is it necessary to hire a lawyer to do it?

The Benefits of a Federal Registration

JT and AT: Today, most artists and labels achieve recognition beyond mere regional exposure simply by posting music to the Internet. Online uses (offering streaming or downloads via MySpace or Bandcamp), online sales (selling MP3s via iTunes or Amazon MP3), and far-reaching concert events/tours are all common ways for musicians and labels to promote themselves. Accordingly, artists and labels may seek to avoid potential territorial squabbles like the above-described Atlanta/Seattle example by acquiring a federal trademark registration. Among other things, filing an application to register a mark constitutes nationwide constructive notice of the applicant's claimed rights in the mark. Although a federal trademark registration does not defeat the rights of a remote geographical trademark user who began using the mark prior to the application filing date, the registration provides its owner with superior rights as against any parties who begin using the mark after the filing date of the application.

The case of *Stuart vs. Collins*[3] demonstrates the benefits of a federal trademark registration in the music context. The *Stuart* case involved a little-known rock musician named Thomas Stuart who performed in a group called THE RUBBERBAND. Although the group's primary area of operation was in the southeastern United States, Stuart procured a federal trademark registration for the band's name. Subsequent to the registration date of Stuart's mark, well-known funk bassist Bootsy Collins began to tour and release records under the name BOOTSY'S RUBBER BAND. Stuart filed suit and ultimately was awarded $250,000 after prevailing on his infringement claim. There is no question that Stuart's case was enhanced by his federal registration. Absent this registration, Stuart's rights would have been limited to his immediate zone of reputation, and the value of his claim would have been diminished accordingly.

The *Stuart* case may be contrasted with the case of *Sunenblick vs. Harrell*.[4] In *Sunenblick,* a small jazz record label using the mark UPTOWN RECORDS without a federal registration brought suit against a larger R&B/rap label employing the same mark. The court found no likelihood of confusion between these uses, relying in part upon the small size of the plaintiff's label and upon the fact that the parties catered to different musical genres. It is worth querying whether the result of this case would have been different if the plaintiff had the benefit of a federal registration. Indeed, had the plaintiff's mark been registered, it is possible that the plaintiff's claim to the mark would have been brought to the defendant's attention at an earlier time, and the defendant may have been deterred from adopting the identical mark in the first place.

The Application Process

JT and AT: A federal trademark application may be based upon the applicant's preexisting use of the mark in interstate commerce, or upon a bona fide intent to use the mark in interstate commerce at a future time. Effectively, the intent-to-use basis allows an artist to reserve an unused name for future use by filing a trademark application based on the artist's genuine intent to use the name in the future.

While not legally required, it is generally worthwhile to consult a trademark attorney to navigate the somewhat complicated federal trademark application process. A proper federal trademark application must be signed by the applicant and must include (1) a description of the goods and/

---

3. 489 F. Supp. 827 (S.D.N.Y. 1980).
4. 895 F. Supp. 616 (S.D.N.Y. 1995).

or services the applicant seeks to protect, separated according to their proper class(es); (2) a filing fee of $325 per class of goods or services (assuming electronic filing); (3) a depiction of the mark; and, in the case of use-based applications, (4) specimens that evidence the mark's usage. Generally, musical artists applying for registration should seek to protect their sound recordings (Class 9) and entertainment services including concert performances (Class 41), at minimum. Additionally, they may consider protecting ancillary merchandise such as printed goods (Class 16) and clothing (Class 25). More sophisticated music retailers, be they artists, labels, or others, may seek to protect other services such as retail store services (Class 35) or online streaming services (Class 38). Accordingly, PTO filing fees for a trademark application may vary from several hundred dollars to thousands of dollars, depending on the variety of uses for which the applicant seeks to register the mark. Many trademark attorneys offer flat-fee per-class services that include PTO filing fees. Hiring an attorney to handle a two-class, use-based trademark application that encounters no serious complications in the review process generally will cost a band between $1,500 and $2,500, including PTO fees. Intent-to-use applications typically cost more because there are additional PTO fees involved. Also, conducting proper trademark searches can add to the cost of the process but can be well worth the expense.

Once on file, applications are reviewed by examining attorneys at the PTO, who compare the mark against prior registrations and applications to ensure that it is not confusingly similar to any previous marks. Examining attorneys also review the applications to make sure they do not consist of "merely descriptive" or "generic" terms, which are generally unregistrable. If the examining attorney deems the mark to be fit for registration, the application will be "published for opposition" in the PTO's Official Gazette. Interested parties then have thirty days from the publication date to oppose the application. Provided that the application survives the publication process, the mark will then become registered, if it is a use-based application, or it will be "allowed," if the application is based on intent to use. In the case of an intent-to-use application, the registration will not issue until the applicant has provided the PTO with proof that the mark is being used in commerce.

SG: Is it worth it? At what point should an artist or label think of registering a name?

JT and AT: Once an artist or label begins using a trademark in interstate commerce, theoretically there is no point too soon to apply for a federal registration. Practically speaking, however, paying rent and covering basic necessities (e.g., eating, maintaining a tour van) are major concerns for struggling musicians or small-label owners, so a trademark registration understandably may rank low on the priority list. But, on the other hand, if an artist or label achieves some measure of success and can afford to apply for a federal registration, the cost of doing so is money well spent.

Practically assessing the ongoing general decline in music sales, any performing artist hoping to make a living in the music business likely will sell ancillary merchandise such as clothing and posters. At first these sales may yield only gas money, but eventually they can create a substantial income stream for an artist. As described above, a federal trademark registration puts the nation on notice of the rights the owner asserts in the trademark, thereby avoiding potential territorial squabbles over a mark going forward. The sooner a band or label does this, the better. In the end, a successful artist or label's trademark becomes an extremely valuable piece of property, and owning a registration serves to streamline enforcement procedures and provide a serious deterrent to counterfeiters. Artists who achieve widespread notoriety often have the opportunity to enter into lucrative merchandise-licensing contracts, and a party on the other side of such a deal will expect an artist to protect its trademark from counterfeiters. The most effective first step to protecting a mark is applying for a federal registration.

If a trademark owner fails to take protective measures, competing uses of similar marks can weaken the mark by diluting the distinctiveness of the owner's designations, thereby reducing the public's association between a particular mark and its owner. Large corporate trademark owners annually spend tens (sometimes hundreds) of thousands of dollars to register their marks, to police them in the marketplace, and, where necessary, to bring lawsuits to enforce their rights when other parties tread too closely. While most artists and labels typically do not spend this level of money to police their marks in the marketplace, they should note that with the use and ownership of a trademark comes an obligation to protect the trademark. Even though a fledgling artist or label likely cannot afford the significant costs of litigation often associated with an aggressive trademark-enforcement strategy, registering a trademark is still a good idea because it grants a nationwide "zone of protection" and puts all other potential users of the mark on notice of the artist or label's use of the trademark. It is advisable to consult an attorney about a proper enforcement strategy, and in many cases a registration combined with a simple demand letter (crafted by or with the advice of an attorney) can be sufficient to deter infringing activity.

SG: How do courts analyze cases of trademark infringement?

JT and AT: Using trademarks, bands, artists, and record labels have the ability to distinguish their unique goods and services from their competitors in the marketplace. The test for determining whether a junior user's trademark infringes a senior user's rights is whether the junior party's mark is likely to cause confusion. This test applies regardless of whether the plaintiff's mark is registered. Courts examine a variety of factors in order to assess whether two marks are confusingly similar, including: (1) the strength or weakness of the plaintiff's mark[5]; (2) the similarity of the two marks in terms of sound, appearance, and meaning; (3) the similarity of the parties' products or services; (4) the similarity of purchasers and the channels of trade for the products or services; (5) the similarity of advertising media; (6) the degree of care that purchasers are likely to exercise;

---

5. The strongest trademarks are those that are arbitrary or fanciful in relationship (bear no relation) to the products or services with which they are used. On the other hand, marks that describe the products or services with which they are sold are weaker and may be register only with a showing of "secondary meaning," or that consumers associate the mark with the goods or services. Generic marks are unprotectable. For example, the APPLE mark is a strong trademark when used to sell computers, because the mark bears no relation to the goods. By contrast, an APPLE mark cannot be protected as a trademark to sell actual apples, because in this context the mark is the generic term for the goods.

(7) the defendant's bad faith (or lack thereof); and (8) evidence of actual confusion among purchasers. (These factors vary slightly based on jurisdiction, but the differences are not significant.) A party who loses a trademark infringement suit can be forced to stop using the trademark at issue and to pay money to the other side, sometimes including the other side's attorneys' fees. The amount of money awarded in trademark damages may be significantly increased where the infringer acted willfully and/or used a counterfeit mark. Monetary damages are typically measured in terms of actual damages suffered by the plaintiff and/or in terms of the profits enjoyed by the defendant as a result of the infringing use.

Potential for a dispute exists especially where there is a possibility of confusion stemming from two bands using an identical or highly similar trademark/band name to offer identical or highly similar goods and services (e.g., recorded music and concert performances). For example, if we (James and Ashford) began selling our own original recorded rock music under the name GRATEFUL DEAD, there is a significant chance that any consumer purchasing our music would do so with the belief that we were the "real" Grateful Dead and would doubtless be disappointed to hear whatever we recorded instead of the original band. This likelihood of confusion would be increased if we also used the Grateful Dead's famous "steal your face" logo (shown above). And if we marketed our rock band's concerts under the name AEROSMITH, concertgoers probably would feel cheated when James and Ashford took the stage. For further illustration, note that if we used the name AIRSWIFT, standing alone, it might not infringe the AEROSMITH mark; but, if we used the AIRSWIFT name in conjunction with a "wing" motif and Aerosmith's unique typeface (shown above), there could be an infringement problem. Trademark law should and generally would provide the Grateful Dead and Aerosmith with the ability to stop us from using their names or logos, or from using confusingly similar names and logos.

Accordingly, prior to investing time or money in developing a trademark, it is worthwhile to do a thorough online search for others in the industry using that trademark, to make sure to avoid the current or future possibility of a trademark dispute. And a trademark attorney can provide a more detailed domestic or international trademark search service, as well as a legal opinion on any potential trademark issues, for a party concerned about investing in a particular trademark.

SG: How can you protect your name in foreign countries, and why?

JT and AT: Unlike copyright law, trademark law is territorial. The Berne Convention copyright treaty allows a U.S.-based artist to enforce her copyright in a song in over 160 countries, including almost every market of general significance. By contrast, even if a party establishes trademark rights in the United States through widespread use and/or federal registration, that party's rights in the trademark end at the U.S. border. Other nations regulate trademarks according to their own laws. Some countries—most notably, the United States, the United Kingdom, Canada, and Australia—allow a party to establish common-law rights based on use of a trademark. Many international trademark regimes are first-to-file regimes, so an artist seeking to protect her use of a trademark in these countries should apply for a trademark registration. We recommend meeting with an attorney to discuss international trademark protection options whenever international trademark issues arise.

Domain Names

SG: Let's start with basics: How does one register a domain name?

JT and AT: Domain-name registrars like Go Daddy (www.godaddy.com) and Network Solutions (www.networksolutions.com) offer domain-name-registration services, generally for between ten and fifteen dollars per domain name. The straightforward registration process involves filling out online forms and paying for the domain-name registration.

SG: What protection does registering give?

JT and AT: Registration of a domain name alone does not provide any kind of legal protection. Registering the domain name simply reserves it for use by the owner, effectively planting a flag in a piece of cyberspace ground. Practically speaking, registering and then using a domain name may establish common-law rights in a trademark incorporated within the domain name. But it bears noting that registering and using a domain name incorporating another's trademark can in some situations subject one to legal liability—just as planting a flag and building a tent in someone else's front yard could create trouble offline.

SG: What if someone else has already registered the domain name an artist or label seeks?

JT and AT: The answer to this question depends in large part on whether the domain name includes a trademark in which the domain-name owner has legitimate rights. In such a case, there is generally little an artist or label can do to acquire the domain name, aside from making an offer to purchase the name. This option may be expensive, and it may be cheaper to come up with a creative variation on the desired domain name. Because of the many domain name extensions now available, registering a ".net" or ".biz" or ".tv" domain name may provide the best solution. Or adding the term "band" or "music" or "rocks" to the name may solve the problem.

If the domain name incorporates a trademark in which the artist or label already has established trademark rights, the artist or label may be able to take legal action to have the domain name transferred to it, especially in cases where the domain-name owner is merely squatting on the domain name and the artist or label has strong rights in the mark. One potential course of action is filing a suit in federal court under the Anticybersquatting Consumer Protection Act (ACPA). Notably, a party suing under ACPA may seek monetary damages. But litigation is expensive and generally not advisable for a party simply seeking transfer of a domain name.

A faster, cheaper option for recovery of a domain name is an arbitration mechanism created by the Internet Corporation for Assigned Names and Numbers called the Uniform Domain-Name Dispute Resolution Policy (UDRP). An action brought under the UDRP allows a complaining party to secure the transfer of a domain-name registration where she can establish: (1) that the domain name in question is identical or confusingly similar to a trademark or service mark in which the complainant has rights; (2) that the registrant has no rights or legitimate interests in the domain name; and (3) that the domain name has been registered and used in bad faith. It bears noting that the party bringing a UDRP action cannot seek monetary damages. But, while the amount of legal fees associated with a UDRP action varies based on a number of factors, filing a UDRP generally costs a mere fraction of what litigation in federal court typically costs. The crucial element in a UDRP proceeding is to establish that the registrant is a bad-faith "cybersquatter." This often involves convincing an arbitrator that the registrant has procured the name with the intent to sell it to the rightful owner, or with the intent to improperly profit from it, such as through online advertising or affiliate marketing programs.

SG: If they are available, should an artist or label acquire all the top-level domain names (TLDs) for its name—that is, <name.com>, <name.biz>, <name.net>, etc.?

JT and AT: Generally, yes. If they are available, an artist or label can probably purchase all of the major ones mentioned above for less than a hundred dollars and easily should be able to redirect them all to its website. Note that it may be worthwhile to acquire country-specific TLDs in some scenarios. For instance, if an artist or label does a great deal of business in Japan, it is worthwhile to purchase the <name.jp> domain name. The relatively small costs of these domain-name registrations would seem extremely cheap in hindsight if, after an artist or label achieved great notoriety, a cybersquatter began using one or more of these domain names and forced the artist or label to take legal action.

SG: Obviously, people can register a domain name without a lawyer's help. When is it necessary to consult with a lawyer about domain names?

JT and AT: It is highly advisable to consult an attorney about a domain-name dispute. If someone has registered or is using an infringing domain name, or if an artist receives notice that its use of a domain name infringes another's trademark, an attorney should be consulted. Notably, an experienced attorney may be able to file one of the above-described UDRP proceedings on an artist's behalf for as little as a few thousand dollars.

Band Names

SG: Suppose you are in a band and someone leaves and continues using the band's name. What do you do?

JT and AT: The answer to this question depends first on whether the band has a contract that governs this situation. If a band agreement states that the exiting member has the right to use the name, then the remaining members likely have no claim against the exiting member. If the agreement states that the exiting member has no right to use the name, then the remaining members likely may bring a breach-of-contract claim and potentially a trademark-infringement claim against the departing member. Generally, remaining band members in such a scenario who feel they may have claims to bring against the leaving member should consult an attorney to determine the extent of their rights in the band name under the band agreement.

If there is no band agreement in place, these situations become far thornier. If the band's name is valuable, it is likely that the parties will hire attorneys to litigate over use of the band's name.

SG: Are there any notable cases about this issue?

JT and AT: The cases in this area demonstrate the default rule that trademark law will not prevent a former band member from making a truthful representation of former affiliation with her former band, so long as the former band member (1) does so in a manner that is not confusing and (2) has not agreed to refrain from such representations. In *Kassbaum vs. Steppenwolf Productions, Inc.*,[6] the Ninth Circuit held that the former bassist from Steppenwolf was not barred by contract law or trademark law from using the phrases "Formerly of Steppenwolf," "Original Member of Steppenwolf," and "Original Founding Member of Steppenwolf" in promotional materials for a new band, provided that these phrases were less prominent than references to the new band.

In *HEC Enterprises, Ltd. vs. Deep Purple, Inc.*,[7] the management company for the rock group Deep Purple brought suit to enjoin a former member of the band from using the names DEEP PURPLE and NEW DEEP PURPLE in connection with live musical performances. Notwithstanding the fact that the "original" Deep Purple had ceased performing several years prior to the former member's resurrection of the name, the court found that the mark DEEP PURPLE was still in use given that the group's recordings remained in distribution. Having established that the original group's management owned valid rights in the name, the court enjoined the defendants from making further use of the names DEEP PURPLE and NEW DEEP PURPLE and awarded damages and attorneys' fees to the plaintiffs.

In *Brother Records, Inc. vs. Jardine*,[8] a corporation (BRI) formed by members of the Beach Boys and which owned the rights to the THE BEACH BOYS trademark sued Beach Boy Al Jardine to stop him from using the following names: Al Jardine of the Beach Boys and Family & Friends; the Beach Boys "Family and Friends"; Beach Boys Family & Friends; the Beach Boys, Family & Friends; Beach Boys and Family; as well as, simply, the Beach Boys. This case provides an example of a situation where a band used an agreement to create a corporation, the corporation owned and licensed the rights in the band's name, and the corporation was able to stop an unlicensed band member from using the band's name.

Most notably, the *Brother Records* court addressed the issue of nominative fair use, which Jardine raised as a defense. This doctrine allows a defendant to use a plaintiff's trademark to refer back to the plaintiff's goods and services in situations where (1) the product or service at issue is not readily recognizable without use of the trademark; (2) only so much of the trademark is used as is reasonably necessary to identify the product or service; and (3) the user does nothing that

---

6. 236 F.3d 487 (9th Cir. 2000).
7. 213 U.S.P.Q. 991 (C.D. Cal. 1980).
8. 318 F.3d 900 (9th Cir. 2003), rev'd on other grounds, *KP Permanent Make-Up, Inc. vs. Lasting Impression I, Inc.*, 543 U.S. 111 (U.S. 2004).

would, in conjunction with the mark, suggest sponsorship or endorsement by the trademark holder.[9] The court held that Jardine's use of his former band's name infringed BRI's trademark because Jardine's use indicated that the Beach Boys sponsored or endorsed his concerts. For example, some of Jardine's promotional materials displayed "The Beach Boys" more prominently than "Family and Friends," and Jardine's management testified that they recommended using the THE BEACH BOYS name to create or enhance the value of the concert tour. Finally, the fact that some promoters and concertgoers were actually confused—they could not differentiate between a Jardine concert and Beach Boy Mike Love's nearby, licensed "The Beach Boys" concert—worked strongly against Jardine's case.

SG: Would you recommend a band contract, and if so, what do you recommend the contract say about the band's name?

JT and AT: For any band that has attained commercial success, or that is on the brink of such success, a band contract is advisable, and such a document should provide an explanation of who owns the band's trademarks as well as make provisions for ownership in the event one or more members should leave the band. Often these agreements allow former band members to promote themselves as "formerly of [band's name]," although typically there are limitations placed on how this can be done. For example, there may be a time restriction to how long this representation can be made, and there also may be limits placed upon the type size and font in which the band name appears.

SG: Without going into too much detail, because we could write a book on just this question alone, what other provisions should be in a band agreement?

JT and AT: Most crucially, a band agreement should provide how any conceivable band property or streams of income will be split among the band's members. Property includes tangible items like a van, a tour bus, or instruments and recording gear. And property includes intangible items like copyrights in the band's songs or in any visual designs used by the band, and trademarks in any band names or logos. Streams of income include record and publishing royalties, touring income, and merchandising income, among many potential others. Band agreements may also, among other things, establish the band as a particular type of business entity and delineate between actual members of the band and mere touring musicians. Much of the substance of a band agreement will depend on the negotiating leverage the different members bring to the table—for example, Johnny who writes all the songs for a successful band likely can dictate more terms than Jimmy who just joined and can barely play his bass.

---

9. *Id.* at 908. By contrast, the doctrine of statutory or "classic" fair use allows a defendant to use a plaintiff's trademark to describe the defendant's goods where the defendant uses the plaintiff's trademark in a descriptive manner and thus the use is not fairly characterized as trademark use.

SG: Would you recommend hiring a lawyer for this? If so, do the other people in the band need their own lawyer, or can one lawyer be used for all the band members? And, if using just one lawyer, how does the lawyer avoid conflicts of interest?

JT and AT: Bands should consult an attorney to create any kind of band agreement. And, if they can afford them, band members certainly can hire their own individual attorneys. While hiring multiple attorneys maximizes each member's ability to protect herself in the agreement, it will be costly and it may not be conducive to reaching an agreement in a timely fashion. Generally speaking, a band can consult a single attorney about a band agreement as long as the attorney makes the band aware of the potential conflicts of interest in that situation. A conscientious attorney may require the band to sign a waiver stating, among other things, that the lawyer has explained the conflicts of interest at stake and the band agrees to proceed with the lawyer acting effectively as the band's clerk, memorializing the band's wishes and not intervening on behalf of any member's individual interests. In thornier band-agreement situations, such as when a band has had several members come and go, a band's everyday attorney may prefer to refer the band agreement to another attorney rather than be forced to help the band with an agreement that potentially could favor one member over another

How Can a Music Lawyer Help Me?
Will They Shop My Music, and How Much Will It Cost?

I sat down with Don Passman, author of *All You Need to Know About the Music Business,* and we discussed a number of issues. The full interview is included in Part IV of the book, but during the interview I asked the following questions about lawyers: When do you need one? How do you find a good one? How much will it cost, and most importantly, what if you don't have a lot of money?

Here is his response:

DP: Lawyers in the music business can come in quite early if they like your music. A lot of them will help shop it. So you can come to a lawyer when you've got some recorded demos and actually have them help you get a deal. The way you find one is there's a lot of techniques, which are set out in my book. But essentially, do some research—there are a number of websites that include lists of music lawyers. And there are other ways to access lawyers, including bar association referrals. After that, it's a matter of checking them out. If you find somebody you like, ask for references from other people who have worked with them. In terms of the money, some of the younger lawyers will charge a relatively small amount up front and then take a percentage, and they'll roll the dice with you.

In terms of finding the right lawyer, my opinion is that the recommendations of other people involved in the music business who have worked with a particular lawyer are probably the best way of finding a good one, because they have had the experience of working with the lawyer they are recommending. You can also search the web for music lawyers and then check out the lawyers' websites to see their experience and other clients that they represent.

Most well-connected and knowledgeable music lawyers are based in New York City, Los Angeles, Nashville, or Atlanta because those cities are where the most successful labels, music publishers and producers do business. Although you may not live in these cities, it is still possible to have effective relationship with your music lawyer. Working with an attorney is not the same as, for example, a doctor, who needs to see you to evaluate and treat your medical issues. In terms of music law, your music and documents, which you can transmit online, by fax, or by snail mail, are the "body" that the lawyer is evaluating and assisting. In fact, many entertainment lawyers only see their clients well after they have started working with them, if they personally meet them at all.

Fees

I also asked Passman about clients who may need a lawyer but are short on funds:

SG: What about money? Say you are approached by a manager or small label and you want to hire a lawyer to review the contract but you have no money.

> **DP:** Well, that's tricky. I mean, if you find a lawyer that believes in your music or sometimes on the basis of the fact that a label is interested, you can get a lawyer to go roll the dice with you. Again, some of them will work with you on a percentage and take a chance.

I would add to Don's answer that sometimes if a manager, producer, or label think you are going to be successful and really want to work with you, they will pay a reasonable amount so you can hire a lawyer. I have had clients who are small labels and producers, who have footed the bill for a new artist to hire a lawyer. In the "old" days, when major labels signed scores of artists with huge advances, the lawyers would often review and negotiate the contracts for a percentage of the advance. This was a no-brainer, because the lawyers knew they were going to get paid. Now, however, many deals involve no money up front. Many indie labels and production companies expect the artist to provide a fully produced album or EP. Again, a good test to see if a label is serious about working with you, and willing to put time and resources behind selling your records and advancing your career, is whether they will allocate funds so you can hire a lawyer to review the contract they are offering you.

If you can't get the company or person who wants you to sign you to put up funds for legal fees, my suggestion is to do some research on the lawyer you want to use before you call him or her. Then contact the lawyer by e-mail to explain your situation. And only then follow up by a phone call. The lawyer will sense that you are a serious person and be more willing to work for you for a smaller than usual fee. Even if he or she can't work with you, the lawyer will be much more likely to take time on the phone to give you some useful advice.

Generally, entertainment lawyers will work on an hourly basis. Occasionally they will charge an all-in fee to handle a particular assignment like a trademark registration or to review an agreement. If you retain one on an hourly basis, don't be shy about asking for a detailed breakdown of the attorney's work. I like to use a retainer agreement that provides an hourly rate and states that I will keep my clients informed of the hours billed.

Shopping

Don Passman correctly pointed out that lawyers can help shop records. Some music lawyers have very close relationships with powerful people in the music business, but the reader should be advised that the number of these lawyers is limited and not every lawyer has these connections. When I was working as a lawyer for Sony Music, we would deal with only about a couple of dozen law firms or solo practitioners on a regular basis. Those lawyers usually did have long-standing relationships with powerful people in the business, and the same lawyers still work with producers, production companies, and managers on a regular basis. Often a manager or producer will ask a lawyer to use his relationships to advance an artist's career. But if you are not represented by a successful producer or manager, chances are small that you will get one of these lawyers interested in shopping your music, unless you pay a retainer in advance. If you do get a lawyer interested in shopping your music, make sure that he has industry connections before paying anything, and never pay a lawyer to shop your music if he hasn't heard it! If the lawyer is credible, he needs to believe in your music before sending it to people in the business with whom he has strong relationships.

I asked veteran music lawyer Peter Thall about shopping music. In addition to authoring *What They Never Told You About the Music Business,* Peter has represented artists such as Miles Davis and Paul Simon.

> **PT:** I no longer "shop" artists per se. I never liked that designation anyway. Some lawyers send out dozens of CDs to their A&R contacts at record labels to see if they "stick." They take a fee for "shopping." I never did that. I have always preferred to "present an artist" to a label. But that takes a team of people—often including the publisher, manager, agent, if any—and a presentation that is compelling. And it requires an understanding of the music, the community in which the artist is based, and the musical tastes and nature of the particular record label. It is not very often that a record label will take a lawyer's word that an act is worth listening to, but given the onslaught of incoming material, A&R people are happy to respond to lawyers' solicitations because the source is a trusted one. In addition, believe it or not, the A&R staff knows that the lawyers' contact information/address etc. is stable and they won't be left holding a phone with no wire attached when they eventually try to contact the party offering the artist. My fees are more in line with New York lawyers'. Unlike California lawyers, we don't usually take percentages (how much more can an artist handle, after all?), or at least long-term percentages; but establishing a flat fee for "shopping" and another one when the deal is completed, when the act has no money, is very tricky for both parties. A lawyer should be paid for his/her time and for a particularly excellent result if the client agrees. Seeking a balance between that and zero in case the pursuit of a record deal fails is the result we always seek but do not always attain.

Peter's comments reflect a great deal of experience and wisdom. I would only add that it makes sense to target one or two goals, such as a particular record company or management firm, and let the lawyer shop your music to them for a specific fee. If you are satisfied that the lawyer is working diligently on your behalf and believes in your music, you can expand your search and increase the retainer to cover the additional time.

Chapter 3

Overview of Digital Music Law

T his chapter is intended to provide a snapshot of digital music law. Chapters 4 and 5 will explore the new rules in detail as they apply to webcasting, downloading, tethered (or limited) downloads, and interactive streaming. We start with summaries of the relevant statutes that, in addition to the Copyright Act, provide the basic rules for transmission of music on the Internet. We then define those delivery methods and outline how the rules apply to each.

Statutes Applicable to Digital Music: AHRA, DPRSRA, and DMCA

Audio Home Recording Act

The Audio Home Recording Act of 1992 (AHRA) was the first piece of major legislation affecting digital music.

The act imposes a levy on "digital audio recording device(s)" (such as a digital tape recorder) and "digital audio recording medium(s)" (for example, blank digital audiotapes or CDs) to compensate copyright owners and artists for sales lost due to copying. The payments are made to the U.S. Copyright Office, which then distributes the royalties to copyright owners and creators, including labels, artists, music publishers, and songwriters. The income generated by the levy has been negligible, because the AHRA does not apply to new generations of technology, including personal computers and MP3 players. But the act does provide a model, which we will discuss in Chapter 9, for a possible solution to the woes that currently ail the music business.

In addition to paying the levy, digital audio recording devices that are covered by the AHRA must include a system that prohibits "serial" copying. The most common system in use is the Serial Copy Management System (SCMS), which permits first-generation digital-to-digital copies of prerecorded music but prohibits serial copies. In exchange for complying with the act, the copyright owners waive the right to claim copyright infringement against both the manufacturers of covered devices and consumers who use those devices to make copies of copyrighted music for their own personal use.

Private Copying

Many people rip their CDs—that is, copy and save the songs as computer files—and copy those files to their MP3 players for portable listening. But is this legal? The AHRA states in relevant part: "No action may be brought . . . alleging infringement of copyright based on . . . the noncommercial use by a consumer of such a device or medium [i.e., a device or medium subject to the act] for making musical recordings." The statute therefore exempts personal copying for noncommercial purposes on devices and blank media covered by the act. But a computer is not subject to AHRA. Neither are MP3 players. The Ninth Circuit stated in *RIAA vs. Diamond Multimedia (the "Rio" case) (9th Cir. 1999)* that using a computer to make a copy of recorded music for private, noncommercial use was "entirely consistent with the purposes of the act." But this statement was "dicta," that is, it was not central to the ruling in the case, and is generally treated by other courts as extraneous material to which they need not be bound. There is no direct law on this point. Yet the practice of ripping a CD to a computer and copying the file to an MP3 player for personal use has not been challenged. According to some experts, it is an issue that the record labels and music publishers don't want to fight over, because they are afraid they would lose and/or incur the wrath of both consumers and the electronics business.

The RIAA has never pursued the issue of private copying. An article in the *Washington Post*, published at around the same time of the second edition of this book, claimed that the RIAA was actually pursuing a case against a man who admitted that he ripped his CD collection and stored the music on his personal computer. But the RIAA insisted that they were suing him only for making those files available over a P2P service. The *Post* article may have been based on statements made by an RIAA lawyer that were later retracted by the RIAA.

The Digital Performance Right in Sound Recordings Act

The Digital Performance Right in Sound Recordings Act of 1995 (DPRSRA) created a new right for owners of sound recordings. Under the DPRSRA, owners of copyrights in sound recordings were given exclusive "public performance" rights for the purposes of "digital audio transmissions." This means that an online music service cannot play any prerecorded music protected by copyright without a license. As we pointed out in the Public-Performance Rights section in Chapter 1, the labels do not have a right to prohibit or license the public performance of sound recordings on traditional (analog) radio. They tried repeatedly to acquire such a right but failed, at least in part because the broadcast community has consistently rallied against it. But the labels were able to convince Congress to give them a public-performance right for digital transmission. They argued convincingly that digital transmissions can be reproduced without loss of quality, which could lead to massive copying and ultimately a massive decline in sales of recorded music.

The Digital Millennium Copyright Act

The Digital Millennium Copyright Act (DMCA) of 1998 provided for a statutory license that grants certain digital-music providers called "webcasters" the automatic right to use sound recordings in their noninteractive streamed programming, sometimes referred to as "Internet radio." This means that notwithstanding the new digital public-performance right in sound recordings under the DPRSRA, certain digital music services are entitled to use prerecorded music without the labels' specific permission, provided they comply with certain eligibility requirements and pay fees mandated by the act.

Webcasters are entitled to a statutory license under the DMCA only if they comply with certain fairly stringent "eligibility" requirements. For instance, in any three-hour period, a webcaster may not play more than three songs from a particular album (with no more than two consecutively) or four songs by a particular artist or from a boxed set (with no more than three consecutively). We will set out other important eligibility criteria in the next chapter. Webcasters who stream content that does not meet the criteria of the statutory license have to negotiate a separate license with the copyright owners of the sound recordings that they want to use.

A nonprofit entity, SoundExchange, was established to oversee the administration, collection, and payment of the royalties to sound-recording copyright owners and to the artists, who share the income from this statute on a fifty–fifty basis.

Note that there was no need to create a new public-performance right for songs, as the law was already clear that their public performance through any means of transmission, be it analog or digital, was protected. The same performing rights organizations (ASCAP, BMI, and SESAC) that offer public performance licenses to radio and TV stations also offer blanket public-performance licenses to Internet-based music services. We will outline how this works in the context of webcasting, downloading, and interactive streaming below and in more detail in the succeeding chapters.

Webcasting, Tethered Downloading, Interactive Streaming, and Downloading

Webcasting

Webcasting, as discussed above, generally refers to the noninteractive streaming of audio on the Internet (Internet radio). We have explained how eligible webcasters are entitled to a statutory license for use of masters. A synch license for songs, which is a license for the fixation of a song with a visual image, as in a film or TV show, is not necessary for audio webcasting. However, a public-performance license, which is available from the PROs, is necessary for performing the songs.

Downloading

Downloading music is accomplished through services such as iTunes, where you can download and own a copy of a music recording permanently. With regard to masters, there is no compulsory license for downloads. You will need the permission of the owners of the copyrights in the sound recordings. The copyrights in recordings of unsigned artists are generally owned by the artists themselves. But the copyrights of artists signed to labels are usually controlled by the labels, and obtaining permission from them can be difficult and expensive. With regard to songs, a statutory license does apply. Under Section 115 of the Copyright Act, downloads of records embodying songs are referred to as *digital phonorecord deliveries,* or DPDs. These downloads are subject to the same rates applying to traditional copying of musical compositions on CDs or cassettes (currently $.091 for songs five minutes or less, or $.0175 per minute or fraction thereof per copy for songs over five minutes). As we discuss in more detail in Chapter 5, downloads do not constitute "public performances," so no public-performance license (from ASCAP, BMI, or SESAC) is required.

Tethered Download, aka Limited Download Services, and Interactive Streaming

Tethered or "limited" download services allow people to download songs for a limited period of time—that is, for as long as they pay their subscription fees. If they stop paying the subscription fee (generally on a monthly basis), the music disappears from their hard drives and any other device on which they have copied the music. Rhapsody is the best-known example of a limited-download service.

Interactive streaming refers to real-time delivery of music, where that the listener has the ability to choose to hear any particular song. Limited-download subscription services such as Rhapsody incorporate this way of consuming music, but YouTube is an example of a pure interactive-streaming service: you can listen to anything you want when you want.

Application of the Rules to Webcasting, Tethered Downloads, Interactive Streaming, and Downloading

Here is an outline of how the rules discussed above apply to:

▶ Webcasting or Internet radio
▶ Downloading
▶ Tethered downloads and interactive streaming

Application of the Rules: The Songs

1. *Webcasting or Internet radio.* Unless you own the songs, or they are in the public domain, you need a public-performance license available from the PROs: ASCAP, BMI, or SESAC. See Chapter 4 for details of how much the webcasters must pay for public-performance rights. Webcasters do not need a mechanical license for the use of the songs, since no copies are made.
2. *Downloading.* You need a mechanical license to allow people to make copies of the songs. However, you are entitled to a compulsory license under which you must pay the statutory rate: 9.1 cents per song or 1.75 cents per minute or fraction thereof over five minutes. This license is available from Harry Fox. Downloads are not considered public performances, because a performance does not take place when a song is downloaded. ASCAP tried, but failed, to get two federal courts to conclude otherwise. These cases are discussed in Chapter 5.
3. *Tethered Downloads and Interactive Streaming.* With regard to mechanicals, although teth-ered-downloading services allow people to make copies, they exist only temporarily (as

long as the user keeps on paying subscriber fees). For years, the services that offer limited downloads and the publishers could not reach an agreement on how much the services should pay the publishers. However, in 2008 they came to an agreement that was later adopted in the form of regulations by the Copyright Royalty Tribunal. The agreement and the regulations provided for the first-time mechanical royalty rates for interactive streaming and limited downloads, including for subscription and ad-supported services. Limited download and interactive-streaming services will generally pay a mechanical royalty of 10.5 percent of revenue, less any amounts owed for performance royalties. In certain instances, royalty-free promotional streaming is allowed. See Chapter 5 for more details.

Interactive streaming is also a public performance requiring permission from the PROs. Applicable rates are discussed in Chapter 5.

Application of the Rules to Sound Recordings

1. *Webcasting or Internet radio.* Webcasters are entitled to a compulsory license for use of masters if they comply with certain rules set forth in the DMCA. The license is administered by the not-for-profit organization SoundExchange. The rates vary according to whether your service is commercial or noncommercial, and other criteria. The rules that make webcasters eligible for a compulsory license, the role of SoundExchange and the applicable rates, are discussed in detail in Chapter 4.
2. *Downloading.* You need permission from the owners of the recordings—usually the record companies.
3. *Tethered Downloading and Interactive Streaming.* You need permission from the owners of the music recordings—usually the record companies. See Chapter 5 for a discussion of how services providing tethered downloads and/or interactive steaming must pay the labels and how the labels pay (or don't pay) the artists.

Chapter 4
Focus on Webcasting

Under the Digital Millennium Copyright Act, eligible webcasters may use any recorded music they wish in exchange for paying rates established in accordance with the law. This chapter tells you who is eligible and what the rates are. We also analyze the rates that webcasters must pay for the songs embodied in the recordings. As we discuss in detail below, webcasters have to pay the organization SoundExchange for use of recorded music, and they pay the performing-rights organizations ASCAP, BMI, and SESAC for use of the songs.

What Is Webcasting?

Webcasting, sometimes referred to as "Internet radio," generally refers to the noninteractive streaming of audio on the Internet. It presents listeners with a continuous stream of audio that cannot be downloaded, paused, or replayed, much like traditional broadcast media. Although webcasting started on the web, many webcasts are now available on mobile multimedia devices, including the iPhone, iPad, Blackberry, the Palm OS, and phones using Google's Android mobile-operating system. Although the content can originate from various sources, including live and sporting events, this chapter focuses on webcasters that transmit prerecorded music. There are basically two types of webcasters of prerecorded music: stand-alone services such as Pandora and AOL Radio, and terrestrial radio stations that simultaneously stream the same transmission in digital form on the Internet.

Major commercial stand-alone services such as AOL Radio often feature dozens of different channels of highly themed genres of music programming. But small webcasters, such as those who utilize Live365.com, may program only one or two channels consisting of their favorite music. Many webcasters, such as Pandora, AOL, and Last.fm, are ad-supported services. but some, such as Napster and Rhapsody, which make money from selling subscriptions, offer Internet radio as well as on-demand streaming. Other webcasters will use music to try to sell listeners other goods, such as band merchandise or concert tickets. Some webcasters, such as Radio Paradise, ask their listeners to make voluntary donations, although Radio Paradise also makes money by allowing people to shop in various online stores such as Amazon MP3 and iTunes and receives an affiliate's share of revenue from each sale. Broadcast radio stations that choose to stream online, that is, webcast their signal, will usually use the same methods of raising revenue that they do in their analog world. National Public Radio (NPR), which offers its broadcast on the web, supports this operation the same way it supports its radio component—by corporate, government, and listener contributions. Commercial radio stations that also webcast may seek additional money from advertisers for the further exposure that the Internet provides.

Certain webcasters, most notably Pandora, Last.fm, and Slacker, offer listeners the ability to customize their own station(s) by inputting their favorite songs or artists. Although the stream is considered customized, it is noninteractive. The stations become more and more personalized as users react positively or negatively to each suggested song. Pandora utilizes the Music Genome Project—a system created by the Pandora team that describes the musical attributes associated with every song in its library—in order to make more precise guesses at what a listener may or may not like. In this way, Pandora suggests music based on similar subtle attributes rather than broad categorical likeness, as in being from the same genre, for instance. Pandora also utilizes a metadata system—All Music Guide—in an attempt to augment the user's experience of listening to a particular piece of music. All Music Guide offers biographical information about the artist, what album a song is from, other albums by the same artist, other songs which resemble this song, and so on.

Last.fm calls itself the world's largest social music network and welcomes new artists. (See Chapter 11, Other Music Sites to Utilize, for details on this aspect of Last.fm.) Similar to Pandora, you can log in and enter your favorite artist and Last.fm will create a radio station based on similar-sounding artists (in this way it is quite like Pandora, except it does not make associations by individual songs). It is successful at making recommendations because it uses "scrobbling" to create personalized radio stations. "Scrobbling" a song means that when you listen to it, the name of the song is sent to Last.fm and added to your music profile. Once you have signed up and downloaded Last.fm, you can scrobble songs you listen to on your computer or iPod automatically. This means that every track you have in your music library will be entered into the Last.fm database and will be available for others online to see. It also allows users to place widgets playing their favorite music on various social-networking sites, such as Facebook, Myspace, and Skype.

Pandora is the clear front-runner among stand-alone online radio services, according to online listeners surveyed by Vision Critical in May 2010. Pandora was cited as the favorite by 27 percent, and 42 percent had listened in the past year. No other service garnered more than a single-digit response.

Personalization, the ability to skip songs, and fewer commercials were the top reasons cited by Pandora listeners for using the service.

However, simulcasters, which are terrestrial broadcasters that also stream their programming on the Internet, dominated online radio listening according to a January 2010 Bridge Ratings analysis. The report found that 84 percent of the total online Internet radio listening group regularly listened to AM/FM simulcast streams in a typical week; 62 percent regularly listened to stand-alone Internet radio streams such as Pandora. The report showed that these two groups often listened to both types of streams but that terrestrial streamers predominately spent most of their time with terrestrial simulcast streams and vice versa. CBS Radio, which is the second-biggest radio network (owned by Viacom), simulcasts 130 over-the-air stations. Clear Channel also added more web-based channels to its online radio platform. They also launched subscription-based services, which are commercial-free, for some of their top syndicated talk show hosts. In addition, terrestrial broadcasters have also developed apps for people to listen to on

Use of Web-Only Radio/Music Services, Mar 2010
% of US internet users

Pandora
42%
27%

Rhapsody
6%
2%

Last.fm
5%
3%

Yahoo! Music
5%
2%

AOL
4%
3%

iTunes
4%
1%

Slacker
3%
2%

YouTube
3%
1%

Live365
3%
1%

Project Playlist
2%
1%

■ Listened to in past year   ■ Favorite service

Note: ages 18+; listened to web-only radio/streaming in past month
Source: Vision Critical, "Radio Futures 2010" in association with Radio And Internet Newsletter (RAIN), May 18, 2010

117148   www.eMarketer.com

smart phones (see Chapter 10 for a more detailed discussion on apps.) For instance, in 2010, two of the largest radio broadcasters, Citadel and Entercom, launched smart-phone apps, customized for their individual stations and offering streaming access to over-the-air broadcasts, as well as on-demand audio and video streaming, podcasts, and blogs.

Why Is Webcasting Important?

Since the last edition of this book was published approximately three years ago, webcasting has become increasingly popular. According to Bridge Ratings, Internet radio listening has doubled over the past three years.[1]

---

1. http://www.radiostreamingnews.com/2010/04/internet-radio-traditional-radios.html.

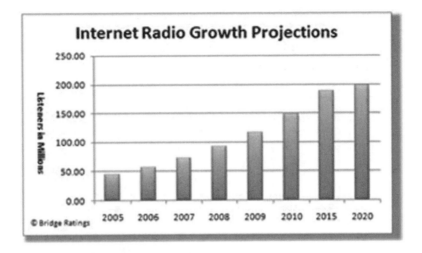

According to Bridge's estimates, Internet radio will have 185 million listeners by 2020, although 250 million will still be listening to terrestrial radio. This second graph also indicates the increasing popularity of Internet radio:

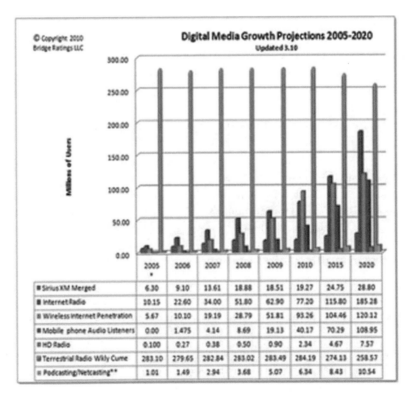

	2005 *	2006	2007	2008	2009	2010	2015	2020
■ Sirius XM Merged	6.30	9.10	13.61	18.88	18.51	19.27	24.75	28.80
■ Internet Radio	10.15	22.60	34.00	51.80	62.90	77.20	115.80	185.28
■ Wireless Internet Penetration	5.67	10.10	19.19	28.79	51.81	93.26	104.46	120.12
■ Mobile phone Audio Listeners	0.00	1.475	4.14	8.69	19.13	40.17	70.29	108.95
■ HD Radio	0.100	0.27	0.38	0.50	0.90	2.34	4.67	7.57
■ Terrestrial Radio Wkly Cume	283.10	279.65	282.84	283.02	283.49	284.19	274.13	258.57
■ Podcasting/Netcasting**	1.01	1.49	2.94	3.68	5.07	6.34	8.43	10.54

ZenithOptimedia has reported that in 2009, advertisers spent approximately $260 million on Internet radio, up 28 percent from 2008. Bridge Ratings analysis puts that number up 12.5 percent to $324 million and $394 million by 2011. Bridge further estimates that advertising on Internet radio will grow dramatically in the next ten years to over $1.6 billion.

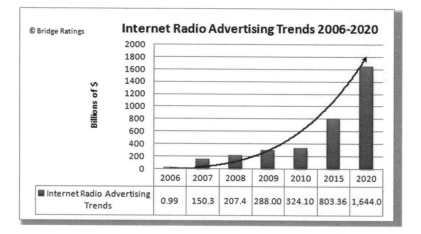

© Bridge Ratings

Internet Radio Advertising Trends 2006-2020

Billions of $	2006	2007	2008	2009	2010	2015	2020
■ Internet Radio Advertising Trends	0.99	150.3	207.4	288.00	324.10	803.36	1,644.0

Estimates in the above chart are based on a composite calculation of all ad revenue generated through Internet radio. These include streaming ad revenue, with the remainder divided among audio ads, music-video ad revenues, buttons, banners, and sponsorships.

One of the most exciting things that webcasting offers in terms of music is the enormous variety of programming it can provide. Broadcast radio is profoundly constricted, compared with the Internet, by the limited broadcast spectrum. The number of channels available on standard AM/FM radio is limited in most locations to a couple of dozen choices. Those choices are further limited by the domination of commercial radio by a handful of corporate conglomerates such as Infinity Radio and Clear Channel. A great deal of mainstream commercial radio sounds like one long commercial "interrupted" by shouting shock jocks and conservative talk-show hosts. Webcasting makes it possible for a potentially unlimited number of independent voices to be heard. Internet radio, as opposed to traditional broadcast radio, offers listeners an unlimited number of musical choices, as well as the chance to program their favorite types of music.

Shifting Trends in Youth Radio Listening

The Edison Research report "Radio's Future II: The 2010 American Youth Study," sponsored by Radio-Info.com, highlights the shifting sands of media usage among U.S. teens and young adults, and the results are striking. If young people are the voice of the future, then terrestrial radio is in trouble.

Waking up to the radio was a routine for twelve- to twenty-four-year-olds a decade ago, but the number who do so has sharply dwindled since. As many young people have given up their music and newspaper habits, the Internet has replaced much of that activity. This dramatic change is made clear in the next graph:

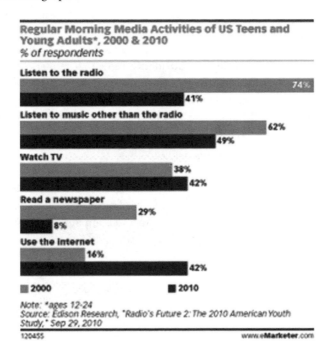

Regular Morning Media Activities of US Teens and Young Adults*, 2000 & 2010
% of respondents

Listen to the radio
74%
41%

Listen to music other than the radio
62%
49%

Watch TV
38%
42%

Read a newspaper
29%
8%

Use the Internet
16%
42%

■ 2000   ■ 2010

Note: *ages 12-24
Source: Edison Research, "Radio's Future 2: The 2010 American Youth Study," Sep 29, 2010

120455   www.eMarketer.com

The same trend is observable in total time spent with various media. In 2000, teens and young adults were spending close to two hours and forty-five minutes listening to the radio each day. By 2010, that amount had fallen to an hour and a half. Time spent online had risen from an hour a day to almost three hours.

Time Spent with Select Media in the Past 24 Hours According to US Teens and Young Adults*, 2000 & 2010
hrs:mins

	2000	2010
On the internet	0:59	2:52
Watching TV	2:37	2:47
Listening to the radio	2:43	1:24
Playing video games	0:42	1:10
Talking on the telephone	1:44	1:04
Reading magazines	0:24	0:11
Reading newspapers	0:17	0:08

Note: *ages 12-24
Source: Edison Research, "Radio's Future 2: The 2010 American Youth Study," Sep 29, 2010

120452   www.eMarketer.com

Compulsory License for Recorded Music: What Is It, and How Do I Get One?

The recording labels have always wanted to get the radio stations to pay them to play their records. The Recording Industry Association of America (RIAA) is the trade group that represents the U.S. recording industry. According to the RIAA website:

> The lack of a broad sound-recording performance right that applies to U.S. terrestrial broadcasts is an historical accident. In almost every other country broadcasters pay for their use of the sound recordings upon which their business is based. For decades, the U.S. recording industry fought unsuccessfully to change this anomaly while broadcasters built very profitable businesses on the creative works of artists and record companies. The broadcasters were simply too strong on Capitol Hill.

As the RIAA points out, the broadcast industry has succeeded in preventing the labels from amending the copyright law to create an exclusive right of public performance for sound recordings. Normal radio stations therefore still do not pay record companies to play music. However, in the last several years the recording industry has had some success in pushing legislation called the Performance Rights Act, which would impose royalties on terrestrial radio stations. See Chapter 10 for details on the legislation and its chances for passage.

Nevertheless, in 1995, the labels succeeded in getting Congress to establish a sound-recording performance right for digital transmissions by enacting the Digital Performance Right in Sound Recordings Act. The RIAA's take on it:

> [W]ith the birth of digital transmission technology, Congress understood the importance of establishing a sound recording performance right for digital transmissions, and did so in 1995 with the Digital Performance Right in Sound Recordings Act (DPRSRA). In doing so, Congress "grandfathered" the old world of terrestrial broadcasting, but required everyone (including broadcasters) operating in the new world of digital transmissions to pay their fair share for using copyrighted sound recordings in their business.

The labels successfully argued that, unlike with analog signals, listeners could copy digital transmissions of music and make a recording of the same quality as a CD. Such copying could therefore compete with CD sales, so the owners of sound recordings should be compensated. By giving the labels an exclusive right of public performance for sound recordings, they could charge webcasters a license fee to play their records.

The DMCA

In 1998, Congress enacted the Digital Millennium Copyright Act (DMCA), under which eligible services may secure a statutory license for the use of sound recordings instead of having to negotiate with individual artists and labels. This statutory license, incorporated into Sec. 114 of the U.S. Copyright Act, covers public performances by four classes of digital music services:

- ▶ Eligible nonsubscription services (i.e., noninteractive webcasters and simulcasters that charge no fees)
- ▶ Preexisting subscription services (i.e., residential subscription services providing music over digital cable or satellite television)
- ▶ New subscription services (i.e., noninteractive webcasters and simulcasters that charge a fee)
- ▶ Preexisting satellite digital audio radio services (i.e., Sirius XM satellite radio service)

The last category of satellite radio, which specifically includes Sirius XM, is not technically "webcasts," because the service is delivered principally through satellites directly to devices that play the transmissions, including special receivers installed in millions of automobiles. However, it makes sense that satellite radio is covered by the DMCA's compulsory license provisions, because satellite radio is noninteractive and delivered by digital transmission. Sirius started up in 1990 and XM in 1992. In 2008, Sirius acquired XM. The service provides subscribers with dozens of commercial-free music channels, as well as other programming.

The Conditions a Webcaster Has to Meet in Order to Qualify for the Statutory License

The DMCA established conditions that a webcaster must satisfy in order to be eligible for a statutory license. The most important one is that eligible transmissions must be "noninteractive," that is, not on-demand or personalized programming. A listener cannot be allowed to select particular songs or create playlists. A 2009 federal appeals court decision illustrates the meaning of noninteractive. In 2001, a group of major record companies sued LAUNCHcast, one of the earliest music webcasters. Eight years later, the Second Circuit handed down a decision in *Arista Records, LLC, et al. vs. Launch Media, Inc.* The issue was whether a webcasting service that provides users with individualized Internet radio stations—the content of which can be affected by users' ratings of songs, artists, and albums—is an interactive service within the meaning of the DMCA. The court noted that a service would be interactive "if a user can either (1) request—and have played—a particular sound recording, or (2) receive a transmission of a program "specially created for the user." In holding that the LAUNCHcast service did not allow users sufficient control over the playlist to qualify as "interactive," the court determined that LAUNCHcast was not required to pay individually negotiated license fees to rights holders. The decision assures that services such as Last.fm and Pandora, which also allow users to create their own channels using complicated algorithms generated by the sites, will avoid legal attack for not being interactive.

A number of other conditions are set forth in the DMCA, including the following, which is referred to as the "sound recording performance complement." A webcaster may not play, in any three-hour period:

More than three songs from a particular album, including no more than two consecutively, or four songs by a particular artist or from a boxed set, including no more than three consecutively. The point of this condition is to prevent listeners from being tempted to record a digital transmission of, for example, a Sinatra album, or an hour of Elton John music.

Other important eligibility criteria are as follows:

▶ *Obligation to identify song, artist, and album.* When performing a sound recording, a webcaster must identify the track, album, and featured artist.
▶ *Prior announcements not permitted.* Advance song or artist playlists may not be published.
▶ Archived programming. Archived programs—those that are posted on a website for listeners to hear repeatedly on demand—may not be less than five hours in duration and may reside on a website for no more than a total of two weeks.
▶ *Looped programming.* Looped or continuous programs—those that are performed continuously, automatically starting over when finished—may not be less than three hours in duration.

Certain other conditions apply. For the full list, see the RIAA's section on webcasting at www.riaa.com. The most important obligation that a webcaster has under DMCA's statutory license is to pay the required fees. The section below discusses the agency that collects those fees and what it does with the money. We then turn our attention to what the rates are and how they were established.

The Role of SoundExchange

Originally a division of the RIAA, SoundExchange is now an independent nonprofit performance-rights entity jointly controlled by artists and sound-recording copyright owners through an eighteen-member board of directors with nine artist representatives and nine copyright-owner representatives. The U.S. Copyright Office has designated SoundExchange to collect and pay out fees derived from the statutory license for digital transmission of masters provided under the DMCA.

SoundExchange is authorized to deduct reasonable administrative fees and thereafter pay the recording copyright owners, generally the record companies, 50 percent, and the artists the other 50 percent. The "featured artist" receives 45 percent of the total artist share. This money is paid directly to these artists, not the record companies. Nonfeatured artists receive 5 percent; 2.5 percent is paid to American Federation of Television and Radio Artists (AFTRA) on behalf of nonfeatured vocalists, and 2.5 percent is paid to the American Federation of Musicians (AFofM) on behalf of background musicians. Inquiries about royalties that may be owed to nonfeatured musicians or nonfeatured vocalists can be directed to the AFofM and AFTRA Intellectual Property Rights Distribution Fund, which is a joint project of both unions, at www.raroyalties.org.

It is significant that the law requires SoundExchange to pay the artists directly. If the payments were made to the record companies on the artists' behalf, the labels could deduct such payments from the amount that the artists owe them for "un-recouped" production and marketing costs. Since most artists are un-recouped—that is, have not sold enough records to repay the record companies for production and marketing expenses—the artists might never receive any of the money paid by SoundExchange if the law did not require payment directly to them.

All royalties collected by SoundExchange are accompanied by extensive electronic play logs submitted by the licensee (the party who licenses the music), the service offering the digital transmission to consumers. These logs are "matched" to a database of unique sound-recording information, and are in turn referenced to an owner of the sound recording and featured artist. This allows SoundExchange to accurately match unique performances with record companies and artists, and pay exactly what has been earned. According to its website, SoundExchange has matched "millions" of digital performances from play logs submitted by the subscription services. SoundExchange made its first payments in 2001. After a slow beginning, SoundExchange has begun to rapidly increase its annual payment to artists and labels. SoundExchange paid out $17.5 million for the first nine months of 2004. By 2010, they paid out $537 million.

Current Rates Payable by Webcasters to SoundExchange for Recorded Music

The DMCA does not actually stipulate the fees that webcasters have to pay for recorded music. Instead, Congress provided that the rates should represent what they would have been if negotiated in the marketplace between a willing buyer and a willing seller. The DMCA additionally stipulates that if the webcasters and the copyright owners (usually record companies) cannot agree on the royalty rates for the license, the rates are to be established by the office of the Librarian of Congress. And that is exactly what happened. The librarian initially established rates in 2001. Then, in 2007, the Copyright Royalty Board (CRB), a three-judge panel assembled to adjust rates for various compulsory licenses for music, including online streaming, raised the rates, which for large commercial webcasters were based on a per-play rate of a fraction of a penny. The CRB, urged by the record industry, increased the rates, but the increase set by the CRB was so steep that, if enforced, many webcasters would no longer be able to continue in business. One prominent streaming service, Pandora, threatened to pull the plug. A protracted struggle between thewebcasters and the record companies ensued. Talks between the webcasters, represented principally by the Digital Media Association (DiMA) and SoundExchange, eventually broke down and Congress took action, passing the Webcaster Settlement Act. That piece of legislation suspended the operation of the rates announced by the CRB and mandated that the parties return to the negotiating table. Finally, in 2010, SoundExchange and the webcasters announced they had come to agreement on new rates.

Commercial Webcasters

The new rates basically distinguish between commercial webcasters on the one hand, and non-commercial and educational webcasters on the other. The commercial webcasters fall into three categories: (1) large webcasters that earn over $1.25 million, (2) small webcasters earning less than $1.25 million but more than $5,000, and (3) "microcasters" making less than $5,000.

Commercial webcasters are further distinguished into two categories: "pureplay" and non-pureplay. Pureplay webcasters are those that earn money exclusively from webcasting. Pandora is the most prominent example of a pureplay webcaster. They make money from advertising in conjunction with performing music. Non-pureplay webcasters use music to lure people into a site in order to sell them other products, such as CDs and DVDs. Yahoo!'s LAUNCHcast was an example of a non-pureplay site, before they sold it to CBS Radio.[2] Both kinds of commercial webcasters, pureplay and non-pureplay, must pay a per-performance fee, that is, a fraction of a penny for every song played. Non-pureplay rates are significantly higher than pureplay rates. On the other hand, pureplay webcasters must pay the *greater* of the per-performance fee or *25 percent of their gross income*.[3] The rationale for this structure is that non-pureplay webcasters will not have to pay a percentage of their gross income, including sales of merchandise. Therefore, they should pay a larger penny rate per stream. Pureplay webcasters get a break on the per performance fees but must pay 25 percent of their advertising revenues if that number exceeds their per-performance total.

The per-performance fee for non-pureplay webcasters in 2010 is .0017. For example, if 100,000 users listen to 100 songs a day, the calculation will be as follows:

100,000 x 100 x .0017 = $17,000

Assuming that this consumption level continues every day for a year, a large non-pureplay webcaster will have to pay approximately $6,205,000.

The per-performance fee for pureplay webcasters in 2010 is .00097. Using the same figures, if 100,000 users listen to 100 songs a day, the calculation will be as follows:

100,000 x 100 x .00097 = $9,700

Assuming that this consumption level continues every day for a year, a large pureplay webcaster will have to pay approximately $3,540,500. Although this number is significantly less than the non-pureplay per-performance amount, the pureplay webcaster must pay 25 percent of their income if it's greater than the per-play amount. For non-pureplay webcasters that sell merchandise in addition to securing advertising money from music, the latter amount will generally be higher than the per-performance fee. Small webcasters, regardless of whether they are pureplay or not, must pay a percentage of their income. Finally, microcasters get a break under the new rates. Those making less than $5,000 have to pay only $600 total and have no reporting requirements. The following grid summarizes the rates for commercial webcasters:

---

2. With the rise of royalty rates, Yahoo! signed a deal with CBS Radio that effectively eliminated LAUNCHcast as it had previously existed, replacing it with 150 preprogrammed stations as well as CBS's local music, news/talk, and sports stations. AOL also found the royalty rate for non-pureplay too high to continue. They also handed off control of their stations to CBS in exchange for a royalty participation.

3. There is also a pureplay rate for small webcasters that make less than $1.25 million. Those rates are listed in the grid below. A SoundExchange staffer told me that non-pureplay webcasters are free to elect the pureplay rates, although this would usually result in having to pay more money. In addition to the rates negotiated by Soundexchange, there are "default" rates set by the CRB. If a webcaster does not elect a specific option, they will pay the default rates, which are generally higher, he said, than the negotiated commercial rates. Due to the complexity of the rate schedules negotiated by SoundExchange, as well as the default rates set forth by the CRB, plus the various reporting requirements in accordance with each category, a webcaster should seek the advice of a knowledgeable attorney before entering into a license.

Groups	Qualification	Rates
Commercial Webcasters	Commercial webcasters with annual revenues of $1.25 million or more.	2009 $0.0016 2010 $0.0017 2011 $0.0018 2012 $0.0020 2013 $0.0021 2014 $0.0022 2015 $0.0024 An annual minimum fee of $500 per station or channel is required, which is applied against the service's total annual liability, and is capped at $50,000. SEE BELOW FOR MORE DETAILS.
Large Pureplay Webcasters	Commercial webcaster with annual revenues of $1.25 million or more.	The *greater* of the penny rate below: 2010 $0.00097 2011 $0.00102 2012 $0.00110 2013 $0.00120 2014 $0.00130 2015 $0.00140 or 25% of gross income
Small Webcasters	Commercial webcasters with annual revenues totaling less than $1.25 million.	Small webcasters pay the *greater* of: 7% of annual expenses or 10% of annual gross revenues up to $250,000 12% of annual Gross Revenues over $250,000
Small Pureplay Webcasters	Commercial webcasters with annual revenues totaling less than $1.25 million.	Small pureplay webcasters pay the *greater* of: 7% of annual expenses or 14% of annual gross revenues up to $250,000 14% of annual Gross.
Microcasters	Services with less than 18,027 aggregate tuning hours per year, annual revenues of less than $5000. SEE BELOW FOR DETAILS	Microcasters are only required to pay an annual minimum fee of $500, and an additional $100 proxy fee in lieu of reporting requirements.

In regard to the minimum fee of $500 per "station or channel" for large commercial webcasters, such webcasters often have multiple channels for different kinds of music. For instance, AOL has over 350 channels. The basic categories, such as alternative, blues, Christian, dance, and so forth, are supplemented by more specific formats. If you click on Blues in the AOL radio site, you can listen to "Acoustic Blues," "All Blues," "Blues Women," "Electric Blues," "Top Blues," and "Radio Mojo." "Rock" includes over forty stations, such as channels for "Accoustic Rock," "Jam Bands," "Adult Rock," "Lite Rock," and "British Invasion." Note that the $500 per-station fee is deductible from the royalty and is applied against per-performance royalty liability. It's also limited to $50,000 per year regardless of the number of channels.

In regard to microcasters, they must have less than $5,000 in income and also less than 18,027 aggregate tuning hours. Aggregate tuning hours are the aggregate number of hours that listeners are tuned in. For example, an aggregate tuning hour could be four listeners who each listen for fifteen minutes; two who listen for thirty minutes, or one person listening for an hour. In the past, some services had problems reporting individual streaming of tracks and could aggregate only the total listening each hour.

Educational and Noncommercial Rates

Educational webcasters are defined as services that are primarily (or substantially) operated by students enrolled in an educational institution. Noncommercial webcasters are noninteractive, non-subscription digital audio transmission services registered as tax-exempt under Section 501 of the Internal Revenue Code, and/or owned by a state or federal government entity, and/or affiliated with an accredited institution of learning. Both educational and noncommercial webcasters pay exactly the same rates: a $500 annual minimum fee per channel or station for usage up to 159,140 aggregated tuning hours per channel or station monthly. Any usage above that cap will accrue a per-performance rate for each track played. Overages will be paid at the per-performance rate as follows:

2010	$0.0016
2011	$0.0017
2012	$0.0020
2013	$0.0022
2014	$0.0023
2015	$0.0025

Noncommercial Radio Stations Operated by the Corporation for Public Broadcasting (CPB)

National Public Radio stations pay a flat fee negotiated by CPB with SoundExchange. For the years from 2005 to 2010, that fee was $1.85 million and covered all NPR stations. For the years from 2011 to 2015, the fee is $2.4 million, payable in five installments of $450,000 each.

Satellite Radio: Sirius XM

Satellite radio is defined as noninteractive digital audio services that transmit audio recordings by satellite and that completed their first transmission before July 1998. The only service meeting these terms is SIRIUS/XM Radio.

Their rates are significantly lower than for large commercial webcasters:
2010: 7.0 percent
2011: 7.5 percent
2012: 8.0 percent

A new rate will be set by the CRB sometime in 2012, if voluntary negotiations fail for the period from 2013 to 2017.

Business Establishments

Finally, a webcaster that confines itself to servicing commercial establishments, that is, a background music service, pays 10 percent of annual gross revenues, and a $10,000 minimum fee per station or channel is required.

Public-Performance Rights

Any performance of songs by broadcast or by digital transmission, including a webcast, requires a public performance. As noted in Chapter 1, Section 106(4) of the Copyright Act gives the copyright owner of a song the exclusive right to "perform the copyrighted work publicly." The act states that "to perform a work 'publicly' means to perform a work at a physical place open to the public," *and:*

> [T]o **transmit** or otherwise communicate a performance or display of the work . . . **to the public, by means of any device or process**, whether the members of the public capable of receiving the performance or display receive it in the same place or in separate places and at the same time or at different times.
> *Section 101 of the Copyright Act. Emphasis added.*

Playing music on standard broadcast radio, for instance, is a public performance because radio "transmits" songs to the public. Similarly, playing songs on the Internet or on satellite radio is also a transmission to the public. Therefore, any webcaster who wishes to transmit copyrighted songs must secure a public-performance license. A webcaster can obtain public-performance licenses to play virtually any song ever recorded by securing a blanket license from one of the three PROs (ASCAP, BMI, or SESAC).

Current Rates Payable by Webcasters to ASCAP, BMI, and SESAC for Songs

ASCAP offers two different types of license for Internet services. One is called "Non-Interactive Internet Services." The other is called "Interactive Services." The first of these applies to webcasting because it is designed for Internet sites and services whose Internet transmissions do not enable users to select individual songs. (We'll discuss the other ASCAP Internet licenses in the next chapter.) ASCAP's repertory, the largest in the world, contains more than 7.5 million copyrighted musical works of every style and genre, in addition to works in the repertories of over sixty affiliated foreign performing-rights organizations.

The ASCAP Non-Interactive Services license provides three different rate schedules. The licensee may choose any one of the three schedules. The first is the greater of 1.85 percent of a website's revenues, or .0006 percent multiplied by the number of "Service Sessions."[4] The second and third schedules are alternatives designed to give some flexibility depending on how much music is used. For instance, under the second schedule, the percentage of revenues is 2.76 percent, but the amount against which this percentage is multiplied is adjusted to reflect income derived directly from the use of music on the site. The minimum annual fee is $288.

The third schedule provides a higher rate (5.1 percent), but gross revenues are prorated by the number of ASCAP songs used. This is especially useful where a site uses a lot of music from new and indie artists and the website secures permission for public performance directly from the artist/composers. In that case, the site may not use a lot of songs for which it needs ASCAP's permission.

Note that each schedule provides an alternative formula based on "Service Sessions." Before choosing between the schedules, it is important to actually do the math for different scenarios to determine which works best for a particular site.

BMI's "Website Music Performance Agreement" applies to webcasting as well as interactive streaming of music (see next chapter). This agreement is based on a percentage of revenues and offers two choices at the licensee's option: 1.75 percent of gross revenues, or 2.5 percent of revenues derived from music sections of the site. The gross-revenue calculation can be used if webcasting music is a primary feature on your website. The second option allows you to reduce the revenues subject to fee by factoring the traffic to pages with music in relation to your total website traffic. You can choose the most economical calculation for your particular website upon submitting your first quarterly revenue report, and you can change the calculation under which you file up to four times in a calendar year, depending on which is best suited to your business. If your business model changes and you decide to add more music to your site, you can switch calculations and save money. Under the terms of the license agreement, you are required to submit separate quarterly financial reports as well as quarterly music-use reports.

---

4. A Service Session is defined in the ASCAP license as "an individual visit and/or access to your Non-Interactive Service by a User. If any such visit or access exceeds one hour in duration, each period of one hour, or portion in excess of one hour, is treated as a single 'Service Session.' For example, if a User visits or accesses your Service twice in one day, once for fifteen minutes and a second time for forty minutes, that User has generated two 'Service Sessions.' If a User visits or accessed your Service for an uninterrupted period of two and a half hours, that User has generated three Service Sessions."

BMI's minimum-payment schedules for 2010 was $320. BMI makes licensing for the Internet easy by allowing licensees to secure a license online through their website (see the Digital Licensing Center at www.BMI.com). You can even automatically calculate the amount you will have to pay. Today BMI serves nearly 6,500 different websites and digital music offerings, offering blanket licenses permitting use of all 4.5 million songs in the BMI repertoire. If your website's primary function is to promote your company's offline business, or if it generates little or no directly attributable revenue, BMI offers a "Corporate Image" license, which includes a rate based on traffic. BMI also offer a special website license for bona-fide nonprofit 501(C)(3) organizations.

SESAC's Internet license agreement requires webcasters to pay the greater of: .0049 multiplied by revenues generated by the site, or .001680 multiplied by "aggregate tuning hours," defined as the total number of hours of music delivered to listeners. The minimum semiannual fee for 2010 is $194.

Chapter 5

Focus on Tethered Downloading, Interactive Streaming, and Downloading

In this chapter we discuss tethered-downloading, interactive-streaming, and downloading services, what they pay the labels and the publishers, what the labels pay the artists, and what the publishers pay the writers.

Tethered-Downloading and Interactive-Streaming Services

Napster and Rhapsody are both examples of "tethered-downloading" services. As we discussed in Chapter 3, a tethered download is a music file that resides on your hard drive, but only as long as you subscribe to the service. Once you stop paying, the file disappears. However, Napster and Rhapsody are also interactive-streaming services, in the sense that you can select any song and listen to it, without downloading it.

Napster and Rhapsody are the most successful subscription services in the United States. However, neither of them is doing very well. The total number of Rhapsody subscribers as of 2010 is 650,000, and that number is down from 675,000 in 2009. The total number of Napster subscribers as of 2008—700,000—was only somewhat better than Rhapsody's. Also, in 2008, Napster was acquired by Best Buy for only $121 million. One of the major reasons for the ill health of these services is that they are not included in the basic fees charged by broadband providers or by mobile operators. One has to pay an additional fee to secure these services. A basic subscription for Rhapsody currently costs $9.99, which allows unlimited access to their music, but only for one computer or mobile device. For an additional $5, one can store and listen to music on up to three computers and/or mobile devices. Napster charges $5 a month for its basic subscription and an additional $5 for its mobile services. Napster also offers an annual subscription for $50 for the basic service, or $96 to include the mobile service. With the Napster mobile subscription, one can sync the music to an iPod or iPhone.

YouTube is an example of a pure interactive-streaming service, because downloads are not offered. Unlike Napster and Rhapsody, YouTube is free and is supported by advertising income.

Download Stores

At this time, iTunes is the leading download store. As recorded in the preface of this book, it enjoys 66 percent of the digital music market, followed by Amazon MP3 at 13 percent and Walmart at

11 percent. iTunes was notorious for battling with the labels in regard to the $.99 download. The labels wanted "variable pricing," arguing that newer releases should be priced higher than catalog material. Initially, iTunes offered all of its songs for $.99. Since April 2009, there are three different prices for songs on iTunes: $.69, $.99 or $1.29, with the highest price for the most current and/or popular songs.

Amazon MP3's download service allows the user to download music to iTunes or Windows Media Player. The music can be played on an iPod or other mobile devices, such as iPhones or Blackberrys. The user can download one song for a price ranging from $.89 to $.99, or download an entire album for $5.99 to $9.99. An album can be purchased for as little as $3.99, when the album is in its first week of release. At other times, Amazon offers a "daily deal" special of albums for $5, part of its campaign to gain market share from iTunes.[1]

Emusic, another download store, works somewhat differently than the prior three. iTunes, Amazon MP3, and Walmart do not charge fees other than per song or per album. Emusic, on the other hand, charges a basic subscription fee of $11.99 for twenty-four songs a month, $15.89 for thirty-five songs, or $20.79 for fifty songs. Unused downloads do not carry over to the following month; rather, the account is recharged with the amount of songs that one purchases the following month. Users can make playlists when the songs are downloaded onto iTunes or Windows Media Player.

DRM

At its inception, iTunes encoded its music files with Digital Rights Management (DRM). DRM is a code that restricts people from full access to the music. For instance, DRM prohibited people from making multiple copies of the music file. In addition, iPods included a code that prevented people from downloading to the iPod any songs that were not coded with the DRM in the iTunes store; although the iPod did accept naked MP3s. Since 2008, the labels withdrew DRM, protection making nonprotected MP3s available on all the download stores. This had the unexpected result of weakening Emusic, because that service offered unprotected MP3s from its start. Thus an important and unique quality that Emusic possessed was lost. In addition, Emusic started as a download store for independent music only. It had no deals with major labels until the labels dropped DRM. Now that Emusic carries songs from the major labels, it has lost some of its credibility with the indie community.

How Much Do the Digital Music Services Pay the Labels?

As we discussed in Chapter 3, there is no compulsory license or industrywide agreement regulating how much these services pay the labels, and indeed the labels can and often do deny permission. The labels are well known for demanding large upfront advances from new digital music services that do not qualify as webcasters.

---

1. *Billboard,* December 18, 2010, p. 28.

Download Services

In regard to downloading services such as iTunes, it is well known that iTunes generally pays 70 cents on each 99-cent download. Therefore, they generally pay 70 percent of revenues to the labels. My experience as an attorney representing start-ups is that labels will not seriously entertain proposals from new download services without being offered a great deal of money up front.

Interactive-Subscription and Advertising-Supported Services

Although labels' deals are confidential, certain public-record materials, such as testimony of a senior Warner Music attorney before the Copyright Royalty Board (CRB) in 2009, show that the labels generally charge tethered-download subscription-based services, such as Napster, on the basis of the *greater of* the following (1) a per-play rate, similar to the rates charged by SoundExchange for webcasters (see Chapter 4); (2) a share of subscription revenue based on the proportionate number of plays of tracks controlled by that label; or (3) nonrefundable advances. According to the testimony of the Warner Music attorney, "[e]ven when . . . advance payments are recoupable against future royalty payments, they essentially serve as minimum revenue guarantees, which can be significantly higher than the minimum payment requirements under the statutory rate." There has been much controversy alleging that these advance payments are so high that they have forced the subscription services to charge fees higher than most people want to pay and have suppressed their growth.

Other key provisions of labels' contract with subscription services are as follows:

▶ Strict security measures
▶ Limits on the types of devices that can be used with a given service
▶ Specification of the audio quality of streams
▶ Providing for extensive and uniform reporting requirements
▶ Technical and financial audit rights

Often the labels will also negotiate "holdback" rights, so that they can create exclusive deals for certain content, enabling them to derive greater value, including lucrative sponsorship revenues. But this also means that consumers may be driven to unauthorized sites or sharing to listen to the music they most want to hear.

Finally, according to the testimony of the Warner attorney, the label's negotiated agreements are typically of short duration, especially for new services. "Thus," he stated, "with any given service, WMG is able to commit to a particular deal structure in the short term, knowing that it will be able to re-assess the structure's long-term financial viability when technology and consumer preferences inevitably change."

In regard to advertising-based services, which derive income entirely from advertising, the Warner lawyer gave fewer details, although he pointed out that most of that label's deals in the United States are with ad-supported video models and that Warner tends "to view the ad-supported audio business model with caution, because it has yet to generate stable revenue streams."

How Much Do the Labels Pay the Artists?

At the core of any recording agreement is the understanding that the artist receives compensation for the label's commercial use of his or her recordings. But what do labels pay artists in regard to income from download stores such as iTunes and subscription services such as Rhapsody and Napster? A recent case involving Eminem throws light on how the labels deal with this issue.

Eminem's Lawsuit Against Universal Music

The question of how much the artist will receive from download sales was recently raised by Eminem's lawsuit against his own record company, Universal Music (*F.B.T. Productions, LLC vs. Aftermath Records*). Eminem recently sued Aftermath, a label owned by Universal Music, when he found out that they were treating income from downloads from iTunes, Amazon MP3, and other such stores as a "sale" rather than a "license." This is a crucial distinction: Under the standard artist's agreement, including Eminem's, the artist is entitled to 50 percent of the income when a label "licenses" his recordings. A traditional example of a license is when the label permits a producer to use a track in a movie or TV show. Sometimes a label may permit a third party to use one of its artists tracks in a compilation such as a Christmas album. This is also a classic example of a license.

But sales of records are treated very differently for purposes of paying the artist. The typical artist royalty is only 10–20 percent of retail, not 50 percent. Eminem's royalty was 12 percent, escalating to 20 percent depending on records sales. In treating downloads of Eminem's music as "sales," the label paid him only his normal royalty, rather than 50 percent of what the company received. Typically, iTunes will pay the record companies 70 cents for every 99-cent download. The record company is responsible for paying the songwriters the mechanical royalty, generally 9.1 cents. That leaves approximately 60 cents. Instead of crediting Eminem half of that amount, that is, 30 cents per download, Aftermath instead credited him only 12–20 percent of 99 cents, minus any deductions authorized by his contract. Although I don't have access to his contract, such deductions may have included a "new tech" deduction of up to 25 percent for electronic sales; a 10 percent deduction for "net sales," which used to be justified when records were made of shellac and could break; and even a packaging deduction of 25 percent, although there are no packaging costs for downloads. Even if there were no deductions, and Eminem was paid on the basis of 20 percent of retail, he would still make a lot less money than if the label treated income from downloads as income from a license. In fact, David Frey, the manager of Cheap Trick, told me that the band was receiving less than 4 cents on downloads from Sony.

A federal court in California ruled against Eminem, but the Federal Court of Appeals for the Ninth Circuit, which includes California, reversed, holding in favor of Eminem, stating that the licensing provisions of Eminem's contract applied rather than the sales provisions, because the deals between Universal and iTunes and other online stores were licenses. In other words, Universal was not selling any records to iTunes; rather, they were licensing the tracks to them. The appeals court first noted that Eminem's contract did not specifically define "sales" or "licenses." The court also provided two grounds for the decision. First, they quoted the Webster's dictionary definition of a *license* as "permission to act" and stated that Universal "entered into an agreement that permitted iTunes, cellular phone carriers, and other third parties to use its sound recordings to produce and sell permanent downloads." It concluded that those agreements therefore qualified as licenses. The second ground was that the case law interpreting the Copyright Act favored Eminem. Under that case law, the court found that it is clear that where a copyright owner retains title in copyright material, limits the uses to which the material may be put, and is compensated periodically based on the transferee's exploitation of copyrighted material, the transaction is a license. The court found that it was clear that Universal's agreements with the third-party download vendors were "licenses" to use the Eminem master recordings for specific authorized purposed—to create and distribute permanent downloads in exchange for periodic payments based on the volume of downloads, without any transfer in title of Universal's copyrights in the recordings. The court concluded:

"Thus, federal copyright law supports and reinforces our conclusion that [Universal's] agreements permitting third parties to use its sound recordings to produce and sell permanent downloads . . . are licenses."In late October, the Ninth Circuit court refused to reconsider its ruling. The Eminem case is a huge victory for artists in their efforts to get their fair share of money from online use of their recordings. The reason is that major portions of the labels' catalogs are still subject to contracts that are the same as Eminem's deal. It is true that since the beginning of downloading in the early 2000s, the labels have revised the basic artist agreement such that the artist is to receive from downloads the same royalty that he would receive from ordinary record sales. So even if the label licenses recordings to iTunes instead of selling them, if the artists entered into their deals with the labels after the early 2000s, they will generally receive a normal royalty of 10–20 percent rather than the 50 percent license fee. However, these revised contracts cover only recent signings.

Artist's Royalties from Subscription Services

The decision in the Eminem case also applies to subscription services. Many labels also changed their contracts so that they can pay less money to artists from subscription services such as Rhapsody and the new Napster. By definition, subscriptions do not involve sales, since the consumer is paying a monthly fee to gain access to all the music in the service's catalog. But instead of receiving 50 percent of the label's income from what Rhapsody and Napster pay the labels, the standard contracts now state that the artist will receive the *equivalent* of his royalty for normal sales with respect to any income from electronic consummation of his music. Therefore, instead of receiving the normal license rate of 50 percent from income derived from the subscription service, the artist will receive only the equivalent of his royalty for normal sales, usually 10 to 20 percent. However, under the Eminem case, the artists would receive 50 percent if they had contracts that were written before the labels revised their deals.

Of course the artist's share will be further diminished when the label prorates the income that they receive from the subscription service in proportion to the number of times the artist's music is streamed. Each contract must be individually scrutinized, but generally if the labels receive $1 million from a subscription service, and there were 100,000 streams or tethered downloads of that label's music, the labels will pay each of their artists in proportion to the number of streams or downloads of that artist's music. So if 5,000 of the 100,000 streams or downloads were of a particular artist's music, that artist would receive 5 percent of the $1 million earned from the services, multiplied by his normal royalty rate. If the royalty rate is 10 percent, he will receive 5 percent of $1 million multiplied by 10 percent, that is, $5,000.

How Much Do the Digital Music Services Pay the Publishers?

Downloading

A mechanical license is required to make a copy of a song embodied in a sound recording. The income that results from these licenses is referred to as *mechanical* royalties. Those royalties (currently the greater of 9.1 cents, or 1.65 cents per minute of playing time or fraction thereof) are paid to music publishers, who generally share 50 percent with the songwriter. As we explained in Chapter 1, the Copyright Act provides a compulsory license with regard to mechanical duplication of songs. This means the copyright owner cannot deny consent, provided that the song has been previously recorded and released to the public. This compulsory license also applies to downloading of songs. Section 115 of the Copyright Act refers to downloading as "digital phonorecord deliveries" (DPDs). The relevant language is as follows:

> When phonorecords of a nondramatic musical work have been distributed to the public in the United States under the authority of the copyright owner, any other person, including those who make phonorecords *or digital phonorecord deliveries,* may, by complying with the provisions of this section, obtain a compulsory license to make and distribute phonorecords of the work. A person may obtain a compulsory license only if his or her primary purpose in making phonorecords is to distribute them to the public for private use, *including by means of a digital phonorecord delivery.* [Emphasis added.]

As we discussed in Chapter 1, the act provides that parties making and distributing copies subject to the compulsory mechanical license can provide notice and pay the copyright owners directly. But those provisions require monthly accounting and filing with the copyright owner and a detailed annual statement certified by a public accountant. However, those who offer downloads of songs can, just as those who make and distribute copies of CDs, use the Harry Fox Agency to obtain mechanical licenses instead of complying with these onerous provisions. As we discussed, the Fox Agency acts as licensing agent for the vast majority of music publishers, who in turn represent the interests of more than 160,000 songwriters. Although the rate is the same whether the licensee deals directly with the copyright owners or with the Fox Agency, the license issued by Fox requires only quarterly accounting instead of monthly statements and alleviates the necessity of finding and paying each copyright owner. The Fox Agency does that work for you. Many music publishers depend on the Fox Agency to handle DPD licenses just as they do old-fashioned mechanical licenses.

Downloading Is Not a Public Performance

As discussed in Chapter 1, ASCAP, BMI, and SESAC represent public-performance rights in the vast majority of all songs still under copyright in the United States, and through their agreements with foreign performing-rights organizations, they represent virtually all the songs still protected by copyright that have been recorded throughout the world. As discussed in Chapter 1, public-performance licenses are NOT required for downloading music if no sound is heard during the downloading process. Downloading for later playback is the same as buying a record. When you buy a record and listen to it at home, there is no public performance of music. When you play the music at home, it is considered to be a private performance.

On the other hand, downloading does involve a transmission "to the public," which is one of the definitions of public performance in the act. Based on this fact, ASCAP started a lawsuit against various downloading services. However, in 2010, the Federal Circuit Court for the Second Circuit including New York affirmed a lower federal court's ruling that downloading was not a public performance. In *United States vs. ASCAP*, the Southern District of New York, which oversees the ASCAP consent decree, held that when a musical work is downloaded online, the work is only reproduced and not publicly performed. AOL, Yahoo!, and RealNetworks applied to ASCAP for the right to publicly perform ASCAP-controlled musical works online through downloading and streaming. The parties were unable to arrive at a mutually acceptable royalty rate, and ASCAP applied to the court, pursuant to the consent decree, for a determination of reasonable royalty terms for the various forms of delivery. The web applicants conceded that the streaming of a musical work constitutes a public performance but argued that downloading does not. Thus, they argued, downloading should not require a public performance license at all. On motions for partial summary judgment, the court agreed. Recognizing that the question was a matter of first impression (an issue not previously decided by a court), it reasoned that under Section 101 a "performance" occurs when a work is "recite[d], render[ed], [or] play[ed], . . . either directly or by means of any device or process." Thus, "in order for a song to be performed, it must be transmitted in a manner designed for contemporaneous perception." While "the term 'perform' should be broadly construed," the court stated, "we can conceive of no construction that extends it to the copying of a digital file from one computer to another in the absence of any perceptible rendition." The court cited additional support for its reading, including several prior online music decisions, the 2001 DMCA Section 104 Report of the Copyright Office, and the 1995 white paper on digital copyright by the Commerce Department, all of which discuss downloading as a violation of the distribution or reproduction right, not as a public performance. Accordingly, the court granted the web parties' motion for partial summary judgment that downloading of a musical file is not a public performance.

Tethered Download and Subscription Services

As we discussed in Chapter 3, in 2008, organizations representing the digital music services and the music publishers came to an agreement and the Copyright Royalty Tribunal adopted regulations that provided, for the first time, a mechanical royalty rate pertaining to limited downloading and interactive streaming, including for subscription and ad-supported services. Limited-download and interactive-streaming services will generally pay a mechanical royalty of 10.5 percent of "service revenue," less any amounts owed for performance royalties. In certain instances, royalty-free promotional streaming is allowed.

The regulations define *service revenue* broadly to mean all revenues received from end users, plus advertising on pages in the site that offer music, minus agency fees up to 15 percent. The royalty of 10.5 percent is applied to each "play" of each musical recording in proportion to other musical recordings. Thus if the service earns $1 million, and one song is played .025 percent among all the other songs in the service, that song will earn .025 percent of the $1 million after deducting any payments to the PROs. In addition, there are "royalty flows" for specific types of services. For instance for nonportable subscription services that allow end users limited downloads on their computers but not mobile devices, there is a 50-cent-per-subscriber minimum, but for a subscription service that allows end users to download music to a portable device the minimum is 80 cents. The rules pertaining to use of music to promote the service are complex but generally provide that the royalty is not due for limited trial periods and other promotional activities.

A news release by the RIAA summarized the agreement as follows:

▶ The agreement proposes mechanical royalty rates that cover both limited downloads and interactive streaming, including when offered by subscription and ad-supported services.
▶ The percentage rate structure in the agreement provides much-needed flexibility for new business models.
▶ The agreement permits the use without payment of certain kinds of promotional streams, in the interest of encouraging paid uses of musical compositions.
▶ The agreement confirms that the mechanical licenses issued under its provisions will include all reproduction and distribution rights necessary to provide the licensed limited downloads or interactive streams.
▶ Outside the scope of the draft regulations, the parties confirmed that noninteractive audio-only streaming services do not require reproduction or distribution licenses from copyright owners.

I asked David Israelite, chairman of the National Music Publishers Association, which was key in pushing this deal to completion, how the deal was working. This is how he responded:

The agreement has worked well. While interactive-streaming services have not been producing as much revenue as some have hoped, the rate and licensing arrangement has created an environment where these services can flourish. I cannot estimate total revenues paid. Rhapsody and Napster are parties to the agreement, but more importantly, the settlement is now the law after the CRB codified the settlement. It is no longer relevant who signed the original agreement (YouTube did not) since it is now the law of the land.

Public Performance

As stated above, downloading services do not require public-performance licenses, but interactive streaming of songs does, because a performance is involved when a user streams a song. The rates charged by the PROs are the same as the rates pertaining to webcasting set forth in Chapter 4, except that ASCAP distinguishes between webcasting and interactive streaming. ASCAP provides a separate license for interactive streaming, under which the fee is $344 annually. The fee for web-casting is less, at $288 annually. ASCAP's formula for interactive streaming is slightly higher than its formula for noninteractive streaming. For noninteractive streaming, the formula is the greater of 1.85 percent of a webcaster's revenue or .0006 percent multiplied by the number of service sessions (individual visits to the site lasting up to one hour; see Chapter 4 for more details). For interactive streaming, the formula is the greater of 3 percent of the site's revenues, or .0009 percent multiplied by the number of service sessions. In addition, ASCAP includes alternative schedules deigned to give flexibility depending on how much music is used. This is similar to ASCAP's approach to noninteractive streaming. For instance, under ASCAP's second schedule for interactive streaming, the website can limit its payment to pages that transmit music and the income derived therefrom, provided the website must pay a slightly higher royalty or per-session use. Details on the licensing can be secured at ASCAP's website under its Agreement for Interactive Services.

How Much Do the Publishers Pay the Writers?

Downloading and Subscription Services

As noted in the introduction to this book, the publishers generally share income on a fifty-fifty basis with the writers, except for sheet music, which is paid on a royalty basis. However, if the writer has a "co-pub" agreement, then her share of revenues from downloading and interactive streaming will be 75 percent. In addition, powerful writers may have "admin deals," under which the publisher will take a smaller fee from 10-15 percent and the writers will receive the balance. For more information about these various deals, please see the introduction. These percentages all apply to income the publishers receive from downloading and from fees payable by subscription services.

Public Performance

In regard to public performance of songs, interactive-streaming services as well as webcasting, these monies are payable by the services to ASCAP, BMI, and SESAC when they pay the writers and the publishers. In the typical publishing deal, 50 percent of said monies will be paid directly to the writer, and 50 percent to the music publisher. In a co-pub deal, the writer will have her own publishing company, and that publisher will get 50 percent of the publisher's share and the writer will receive 100 percent of the writer's share. Altogether, the writer gets 75 percent.

Chapter 6

Music-Licensing Fundamentals

T his chapter is designed to provide an overview of music licensing. Songwriters, composers, labels, and artists can make significant income from licensing music for audio compilations, television, motion pictures, and other media. This chapter will set forth the fundamentals of music licensing for:

- ▶ Audio compilations
- ▶ Home video
- ▶ Television
- ▶ Motion pictures
- ▶ Advertising
- ▶ Musical theater

Audio Compilations

Compilation albums usually contain songs that have been previously released, such as "best of" collections (i.e., *The Very Best of Elvis Presley*). Other compilations can be genre-based and can be a lucrative way of selling old music in new packages. Time-Life, for instance, sells hundreds of different compilations with themes designed to attract baby boomers and their parents, such as *Legends, The Ultimate Rock Collection,* and *The Ultimate Love Songs Collection.* Other compilations are collections of songs that were used in a movie or TV show. Recently, for instance, I licensed a dozen songs for a CD compilation; each song had originally been included in a documentary called *Airplay* that focused on the history of American DJs. The licensing of compilations is fairly straightforward.

Songs

If a compilation consists of songs that have previously been released, they are subject to the compulsory mechanical license. As we discussed in Chapter 1, the Harry Fox Agency (HFA) is set up to issue mechanical licenses that incorporate the statutory mechanical rate of 9.1 cents for songs five minutes or less, or 1.75 cents per minute or fraction thereof over five minutes. All you need to do is fill out forms provided by Fox, which are now available online, indicating the names of the songs, the writers, and the publishers. Here are the requirements:

- ▶ Song title
- ▶ Songwriter's name(s)
- ▶ Publisher name
- ▶ Playing time for each selection (especially if the song is over five minutes in length)
- ▶ Release date
- ▶ Artist name
- ▶ Title of album

The form can be filled out and sent to HFA online. They will generate a contract that can be signed electronically. You never even have to print out the licenses. HFA, as we pointed out in Chapter 1, also has a database, www.songfile.com, that you can use to find the writers and publishers, as do ASCAP, BMI, and SESAC for their respective songs. Upon securing a license, the distributor can pay after the record is released. In the rare occasion that HFA does not represent a song, you will have to go to the publisher. If the publisher does not respond, you can acquire a mechanical license through the Copyright Office. However, the procedures required under the compulsory-license provisions in the Copyright Act are burdensome, such as those calling for monthly rather than quarterly accounting and notice conforming to strict regulation. Of course, if the song is in the public domain (PD), as most of the classical repertoire is, you will not need permission. However, new arrangements of PD songs may be protected by copyright, and in that case you will need a license. Check for an arrangement credit on the packaging of CD, cassette, or vinyl record from which you derived the music.

Masters

You must negotiate with the owners of the masters for compilations. There is no compulsory rate. The standard rate is 10 to 12 cents per track. The labels may request a percentage of the retail price of the compilation, such as 10 percent plus a floor of 10 cents or more. In addition, they will seek advances. For instance, an advance of 10,000 units is commonly required. Sometimes a more difficult problem than establishing a fair rate is getting a license at all. Record companies are extremely reluctant to license tracks that are still selling well. They fear the compilation may compete with their own albums or "best of" records. Since there is no compulsory license for use of masters, they can just deny permission, and frequently do. Finally, each record company will usually ask for most favored nations (MFN) protection. As we will discuss in more detail below, this means that if label X insists on more money than label Y agreed to accept, and label Y conditioned its consent on MFN treatment, you will have to pay Y the additional amount.

Home Video

I am often called upon to clear the following types of audiovisual programs for home video:

- ▶ Music-based documentaries
- ▶ Audiovisual recordings of music concerts
- ▶ Old TV shows (such as old episodes of music-based shows such as *Soul Train,* or episodic comedies such as *Webster,* which used excerpts of music in some episodes)

▶ Instructional videos (for instance, a DVD on how to play guitar)

▶ Wedding videos (use of music in DVDs of weddings or other special events)

As we shall discuss later in this chapter, when music is cleared for a motion feature, usually the licenses are for "broad rights," that is, all media including home video as well as theatrical release and all forms of TV.

The words "home video" generally refer to DVDs, although downloading is now generally accepted as another form of home video and most copyright owners will include downloading as another form of home-video distribution. They will not charge additional fees, although a few music publishers still try to extract an additional payment for downloading. On-demand streaming is not considered to be a form of home video, and a separate fee must be negotiated.

Generally the music publishers, who administer the licensing of home-video rights on behalf of their writers, will require a "penny rate" for each song in a program. That rate is generally 10–12 cents. Sometimes a publisher will accept a lower penny rate if, as in the case of a music documentary, only a brief excerpt of a song is used. Music publishers will also usually require an advance based on units, generally 2,500 to 10,000. So, for example, if there are twelve songs in a music concert program and each is licensed for 10 cents with an advance of 5,000 units, the amount to be paid for each sold will be $1.20. However, the advance of $500 for each song means that that no royalty will be paid on the first 5,000 units.

Generally the producer of the program will be responsible for the initial advance and will negotiate with the distributor that the distributor shall pay for any units over that. However, who pays for the music will be subject to negotiation, in each case, between the producer and the distributor, and occasionally the distributor will agree to pay the advances as well as the royalty payable if sales exceed the advance.

Some music publishers will insist on a "roll-over" payment if the number of units sold exceed the advance. For example if the royalty is 10 cents and the advance is $1,000 for the first 10,000 units, if 1 unit in addition to the 10,000 is sold, another $1,000 shall become due. Other publishers will allow for periodic accounting so that royalties will be payable for the exact number of units sold.

The duration of most penny-rate home-video licenses is usually seven years. The territory is generally the United States and Canada. In other territories, usually there is an industrywide agreement in place between music publishers and distributors. For instance, in England the rate is 6.25 percent of PPD (publisher's price to dealers, i.e., the wholesale price), and in Japan the rate is 5 percent wholesale. These payments are usually made to collection societies, which turn around and pay the music publishers. For instance, in England the fee is payable to MCPS, and in Japan to JASRAC. So if a video is sold in England for £4, the distributor will have to pay 6.25 percent of £5 for all the music in the program. With programs with a great deal of music, such as a music-based documentary or concert, this system is much more favorable than a penny rate. For instance, if a concert video has fifteen songs and each one costs 10 cents for a total of $1.50 per unit, then the royalty due will be $1.50 per unit. If the wholesale price for that program is $10, 6.25 percent would be 62.5 cents, but American publishers generally refuse to accept this kind of formula.

Occasionally a producer will try to secure a "buyout" instead of a royalty. A buyout means that no royalty will be payable after the buyout fee is paid. Most publishers will insist that the buyout fee is greater than the normal advance as quid pro quo for waiving a royalty. Therefore, a producer who wants to pay a buyout fee is making a "bet" that sales will justify a greater upfront payment. Suppose, for instance, a publisher will accept a $1,500 for home-video buyout. If the same publisher would have accepted a 10 cent penny rate, then the producer will come out ahead if he sells more than 15,000 units. The following chart demonstrates this point.

Penny rate at 10 cents

7,500 units	$750
15,000 units	$1500
30,000 units	$3000

Buy out for $1500

7,500 units	$1500
15,000 units	$1500
30,000 units	$1500

The duration of a buyout license will usually be five to ten years. After that, if the distributor wants to sell units, she must go back and negotiate new licenses.

Most Favored Nations

One of the most important concepts in clearing home-video rights is "most favored nations" (MFN). In international trade, MFN means that the country that is the recipient of this treatment must receive equal trade advantages as the "most favored nation" by the country granting such treatment. In regard to music clearances, MFN refers to the clause in most publishers' contracts that states that if any other publisher is treated more favorably, then that publisher will be treated equally as well, notwithstanding the terms in the agreement. For instance, if ten different publishers who control songs in a program, and nine agree to 10 cents, but one insists on 12 cents, then the MFN rate is 12 cents. The following is a typical MFN clause:

It is hereby agreed and understood that if Licensee shall pay to any third party a greater royalty and/or advance payment than those paid to Licensor hereunder with respect to any musical composition performed in the Product, Licensee shall pay to Licensor such greater royalty and/or advance payment, retroactive to the date of the agreement.

MFN can produce harsh results. Some music documentaries can include dozens of small excerpts of music, and if one publisher insists on a higher rate, the impact on clearance costs could be catastrophic. For instance, if a doc includes brief excerpts of fifty songs and the publishers all agree to accept 6 cents for each excerpt, then the per-unit fee will be $3. But if one publisher wants 12 cents, then the per unit fee will be $6, and this may make it impossible for a distributor to make a profit, since they also have to pay for manufacturing, packaging, and shipping. There are various methods of avoiding the harsh results that MFN can sometimes produce. The easiest way of doing it, of course, is to clear the songs before the program is made. If a song comes in too high, it can be excluded.

Recorded Music

So far I have been discussing what music publishers charge for use of songs in a program. Sometimes it is necessary to clear a record label, as well. This happens when the original master is used. For instance, a documentary about an artist may include music from an album. In that case, it would be necessary to secure a license from the owner of the album, usually a record company, as well as a license from a music publisher for the underlying song. The license for the song is referred to as a "synch" license. The license for the master is referred to as a "master use" license. Usually the record company will accept the same terms as the music publisher has accepted. Live concerts do not require clearing masters, because they are not being used in the show as the artist is performing live. However, if the artist was merely lip-synching or "performing to track," then it would be necessary to clear the master. In documentaries, a producer will often use footage containing a live performance. For instance, a documentary about Elvis Presley may include an excerpt of him performing a song on the old *Ed Sullivan Show*. In that case, you would not need to secure a license from the record company, because the license for the footage will include the right to use the sound in the footage.

Instructional Videos

Some of my clients produce and sell DVDs of professional musicians teaching viewers how to play guitar or other instruments. Licenses for recorded music are generally not required, because the performers featured in the video are not using the original recordings. With regard to the songs, my experience is that the publishers are generally cooperative and will grant reasonable terms. A standard license would be 10 to 12 cents per song per unit sold, with an advance of 5,000 units for a duration of five to seven years. However, newer songs may be more difficult to clear, because some writers may not want their songs to be associated with an instructional video. Also, even older songs, if they were huge hits, may be equally difficult. Nothing is lost by requesting a license, though. If the producer of an instructional video wishes to build a website instead of selling DVDs, publishers may accept a flat fee for a limited term such as one to three years, or they may seek a percentage of revenues if the website charges a subscription fee.

Wedding Videos

I receive a number of calls from professional videographers or family members who want to use music in a video of a special occasion such as wedding or birthday. They tell me that they only want to make a few dozen copies and ask whether they need permission. The answer is that they do—if they use copyrighted music and even if they give the videos away for free. And many owners of popular songs will not want their music associated with someone's event. On the other hand, I have had success in licensing some popular songs for fees around $500 for a limited run of copies. This is particularly doable for "non-approval" songs. These are songs that a music publisher can license without the permission of writers or their estates. The more recent and commercially successful the song, the more likely it will be subject to approval. If the original recording is desired, then it will also be necessary to obtain the approval of the owner of the master, usually a record company. Those who want to use music in a wedding video should consider a music library from which they can license or buy music in all kinds of genres for a small fee.

Television Programs

There is a basic distinction in licensing music for documentaries and concert programs for television and licensing music for network and cable shows. Let's discuss documentaries and concert programs first.

Documentaries and Concerts

In clearing music for documentaries and music concert programs, there are a number of variables to be considered, including the fee, duration, and territory.

The synch fee: The fee payable for the use of a song in a concert or documentary can be from a few hundred dollars to well over a thousand depending on the rights requested. For instance, if a producer asks for "all forms of TV," the price will be higher than if a specific form of television is requested, such as "basic cable." Therefore, I advise my clients to ask for the specific rights they absolutely need. For instance, if the show will air only on a specific television service, such as A&E, I will ask for the right to air the show on A&E only in order to get the lowest price.

Foreign TV rights: Usually foreign TV rights will be negotiated as an option. This is because many of my clients have no deal for foreign TV until after the show airs in the United States. If we request foreign TV rights as an option, then we don't have to pay for those rights until we license the show for foreign broadcast. The fee for foreign rights usually is approximately equal to the fee for U.S. rights. For instance, I recently cleared twelve songs in a documentary on a pop singer for $750 for U.S. cable and $750 for foreign TV.

Duration: The producer's deal with a particular television service, such as a basic-cable service or network, may require the producer to acquire a minimum number of years. Networks generally require at least a year, but basic-cable services usually require a minimum of three years.

Usage: Use of an excerpt of a song may cost less than use of a full performance. Also, if a song is heard but no one is seen performing it ("background use"), the song may be cheaper to license than if someone is depicted singing or playing an instrument ("visual vocal" use).

Promotional use: Producers generally want the right to use a song that is included in the documentary or concert to advertise the program in a commercial or online promo. Many publishers will limit promotional use to "in context" promotion. This means you are allowed to use the music to promote the program only by using excerpts of the program including the music—you can't strip the music and use it in a different way than it is actually used in the show.

Most favored nations: All the considerations that we discussed in the home-video section of this chapter above apply to concerts and documentaries on TV. Basically, the publishers insist that if you pay one other publisher more money than they have agreed to accept, you must pay them the additional amount. However, sometimes, MFN can be used as a way of securing all the music in a program on reasonable terms. Suppose a publisher controls a number of songs in the program and grants a favorable rate; that rate can then be used to secure the same rate from the other publishers. On the other hand, if one publisher demands more than all the others, you may have to pay more for all the other songs or delete the high-priced song.

Recorded music: All the rules above apply to music recordings. Generally, the owners of the master recording will insist on MFN treatment with the owners of the songs. As we previously discussed, concerts generally do not require master clearances, because the music was performed live unless the artist lip-synched the song. If a producer of a documentary used music from a record, then a master clearance will be required, and just as with home video, the record label will usually accept the same fees and terms that were negotiated with the music publishers.

Special Rules for Public Broadcast Stations

The Copyright Act provides for special rules for use of copyrighted materials, including music, on public broadcasting stations. Generally, producers are not obligated to clear songs or masters for programs produced for PBS or other public broadcasting stations as defined in the act. The relevant sections of the act are 114 and 118.

In regard to songs, Section 118 provides for a statutory license subject to federally prescribed rates. PBS, on the producers' behalf—with funding from the Corporation for Public Broadcasting—will pay the federally prescribed fees to the copyright owners. But Section 118 does not provide for a statutory license with respect to the use of the songs in the home-video distribution of the program or for foreign TV. So producers have to acquire synch licenses for these uses.

In regard to masters, Section 114(b) reads in relevant part:

> The exclusive rights of the owner of copyright in a sound recording ... do not apply to sound recordings included in educational television and radio programs ... distributed or transmitted by or through public broadcasting entities ... Provided that copies or phonorecords of said programs are not commercially distributed by or through public broadcasting entities to the general public.

Therefore, no payment is required for use of masters in programs on public television. But note that the last sentence quoted above means that if the program is released as a DVD, the producer *will* have to secure master-use licenses if music from records was used in the program.

Cable and Network Shows

Licensing music for popular TV shows has become a lucrative source of income for the music business. The price for a song on a popular network, say HBO or Showtime, usually ranges from $2,500 to $10,000 or more, depending primarily on the identity of the song. It's a pretty good bet that a Lady Gaga song or Rolling Stones hit will be lot more expensive than a song by a relatively unknown band. Another important consideration is how badly the producer wants the song. For example, I recently licensed a relatively obscure song to HBO for $12,500. The program was a docudrama budgeted at about $5 million that focused on historical incidents and included a scene about the musical comedy in which the song was originally performed. HBO wanted the song to make the docudrama more authentic.

In addition to being a source of income, TV shows can also help promote a song or an artist. For instance, the band Death Cab for Cutie became much more popular and sold a lot more records after their music was featured on *The O.C.* In his book *Ripped*, Greg Kot noted that "shows such as *Six Feet Under, The O.C.,* and *Grey's Anatomy* turned into a cottage industry to breaking new bands." More recently, the band One Republic achieved mainstream success thanks largely to having several of their songs featured on *Gossip Girl.* Specifically, the song "Apologize," featured on one episode of *Gossip Girl,* later went on to sell three million digital downloads and more than one million ringtones. Other One Republic songs that got a boost from being on *Gossip Girl* include: "All the Right Moves," "Stop and Stare," and "Secrets."

Another way that popular shows can promote new music is through the web. Such music-intensive series as *Gossip Girl* and *The Hills* include track listings on their websites so fans can identify each song in each episode. The sites also include links to iTunes where fans can buy the tracks featured in the shows. A leading music supervisor in the industry and for shows such as *Gossip Girl* and *Grey's Anatomy,* Alexandra Patsavas, has said:

> What "The OC" did for indie rock, we'd like "Gossip Girl" to do for pop. I'm relying on old favorites while exploring current pop music . . . and since the show revolves primarily around high school students in New York, we'll definitely be using some New York based bands. But these kids listen to the radio too, so there will be that music, too.

Needless to say, promotion of music on TV shows has become a phenomenon, and artists heavily rely on these shows to advance their careers.

It should be noted, though, that licensing music for TV is not a panacea for new bands. The truth is that most new music in shows such as *Gossip Girl* and *The Hills* is from artists already signed with labels and music publishers, who have close ties with the music supervisors who select the music for these shows. On the other hand, there are companies such as LoveCat Music (www.lovecatmusic.com) that will represent unsigned bands and submit their music on their behalf. Also, lawyers with relationships with music supervisors can sometimes be helpful in shopping music for TV and movies.

With regard to the terms for licensing for popular shows, there is lot less flexibility than licensing music for documentaries and concerts. There are two reasons for this. The first is that over the years, the networks and cable services have perceived a market for their shows not only in reruns, but also for home video and foreign territories. And now there is the dream of making big money from the shows on the web through services such as Hulu or Netflix. Therefore, the networks and cable services want all rights and media—they do not want to be limited to just television; they want buyouts. The licenses are generally usually unilateral and demand all media and all territories for a minimum of ten years. The second reason that licenses for music in popular TV shows are much less subject to negotiation than for documentaries and concert programs is that generally, the latter are created by independent producers with less money and therefore less leverage than networks and cable services,

Motion Pictures

The price of clearing music for movies will be primarily determined by the budget and the potential audience for the film. For instance, publishers and labels know that student or "art" films with budgets in the thousands of dollars and a potential audience of thousands of people or fewer cannot afford to pay a great deal of money for music. Of course, they may decide not to grant a license at all, but if they do, the price will be commensurate with the budget and potential audience. The cost of including one song in a major motion picture, on the other hand, can and often does exceed six figures. The price gets higher depending on the identity of the song, with hit songs demanding the highest fees and the use that is made of the music, with use of music over the credits, whether the opening or end credits, fetching highest amounts. Even with a student or independent art movie, the publishers and labels may include a clause that requires additional payments should the movie actually generate a substantial amount of income. For instance, the fee for a popular song in a movie with a budget of a million dollars could be set at $10,000 but require, if box office exceeds $250,000, another payment of $10,000.

Rights: Even before popular TV programs were asking for buyout, producers of major motion pictures and major studios were demanding buyouts for all media. With regard to licensing music for movies, this practice is referred to as acquiring "broad rights." As discussed above, *broad rights* generally refers to all rights, including theatrical distribution, all forms of TV throughout the world, home video, and the Internet. From the perspective of indie producers who are less well financed than their Hollywood cousins, acquiring broad rights even for an obscure song or master can be prohibitive. For independent movie makers, using options can significantly save money.

Options: Suppose you are an independent producer who is still looking for a theatrical distributor for your film. You may or may not find it. Perhaps the only form of distribution you will be able to find is home video. Obviously, you will not need broad rights. You need only the rights in the music that are necessary for the method of distribution you actually use. You can structure the license to give you options for each of these media—for instance, home video including downloading, Internet streaming, foreign TV, U.S. and cable TV. You have to "exercise" the option, that is, pay for the rights, only once you have secured your deal. So you can save a lot of money by negotiating options instead of paying for rights you may not need. I know a producer who made deals for broad rights for all the music in his movie. Sadly, he never got a deal for distribution. He paid close to $50,000 for music for a movie that is still sitting in his loft.

Festival licenses: Most music publishers and labels will give producers the right to show their movies at festivals for $250 or less for each song or track. When you secure a festival license, you can save time by negotiating options for other rights.

MFN: A record company will usually insist on MFN treatment with the owners of the song embodied in the master. The music publisher of a song will also usually insist on MFN treatment with the owner of the master of that song. But producers can usually avoid MFN treatment between different songs and masters. Both labels and publishers recognize that the use of a song or master over the credits, for example, is much more important and therefore should be more expensive than other uses of music in the movie. It is just as well recognized that the use of monster pop hit such as a classic Rolling Stones song is a lot more valuable than a song by an unknown artist.

Advertising

A Brief History of Music in Advertising

Prior to the 1980s, music in television advertisements was generally limited to jingles and incidental music. I grew up with catchy product-related jingles like "See the U.S.A. in your Chevrolet" and Coke's "I'd Like to Teach the World to Sing." Ads like these revolved around the music, which was written by writers who were on the payroll for advertising companies. Companies looking to boost product sales would commission these writers to produce a jingle on a "work-for-hire" basis.

This system eventually faded away during the 1980s and was replaced by a commercial landscape in which advertisements were supplemented by popular prerecorded music. The use of previously recorded pop songs in television advertisements began in earnest in 1985 when Burger King used the original recording of Aretha Franklin's song "Freeway of Love" in an on-air ad for the restaurant. Then, in 1987, Nike used the original recording of the Beatles' song "Revolution" in an advertisement for a new line of sneakers. The floodgates for using pop music in television ads had been opened.

In 1995, audiences around the country were used to hearing some of their favorite songs in television ads. But it still made news when Microsoft paid the Rolling Stones a rumored $9 million for the use of "Start Me Up" in their Windows 95 campaign. The Microsoft campaign was one of many examples of a commercial not only borrowing interest from music, but also borrowing our interests, milking our memories and desires, and selling them back to us.

Of course, "Start Me Up" was licensed by Microsoft because it was a popular tune. What's happening now is that unknown songs by emerging artists are becoming hits overnight as a result of their association with these national ad campaigns. Think, for instance, of the iPod Touch commercial featuring Cansei de Ser Sexy's "Music Is My Hot, Hot Sex." Eighteen-year-old Nick Haley posted a homemade iPod advertisement to YouTube using the song. Apple executives caught wind of the video, were instantly enamored by the music, and contacted Haley to rework the ad for television. The teenager says his inspiration came from the lyrics "My music is where I'd like you to touch." The band's guitarist, Ana Rezende, told *Spinner* in October 2007, "How he found our song, I have no idea, but we're really happy that he did."

Using Ads to Promote Music

Getting your music licensed for commercials can be extremely financially rewarding (as in the case of the Rolling Stones' deal with Microsoft), but artists are generally eager to ink this kind of deal for more than just the money. In the summer of 2007, Volkswagen licensed the right to use all the songs in a brand-new album by alternative rock band Wilco for use in its new television ad campaign.

Here is what Wilco posted on its website in reference to the deal:

> As many of you are aware, Volkswagen has recently begun running a series of TV commercials featuring Wilco music. Why? This is a subject we've discussed internally many times over the years regarding movies, TV shows and even the odd advertisement. With the commercial radio airplay route getting more difficult for many bands (including Wilco) we see this as another way to get the music out there. As with most of the above (with the debatable exception of radio) the band gets paid for this. And, we feel okay about VWs. Several of us even drive them.

So, licensing your music in advertising gets you paid, but it also, perhaps more significantly, gets you nationwide exposure that could help increase your record sales significantly. It also promotes your brandability and, as we know, merchandise sales can amount to a significant portion of an artist's overall income.

It's important to note the apologetic tone in Wilco's statement. As an alternative rock band, Wilco worried that its involvement in corporate advertising would be regarded as "sellout" behavior. But Wilco has maneuvered its career with savvy and done what any emerging artist should do: take advantage of the outlets available for distribution. Other major artists have done the same. Some examples include Sting licensing to Jaguar, Iggy Pop to Royal Caribbean, Bob Dylan to Victoria's Secret, Led Zeppelin to Cadillac, and Aerosmith to Buick and Dodge.

Apple commercials are a good example of how advertising can promote an artist. Since 2003, commercials for Apple's products have propelled the careers of many bands and music artists. For example, the band Jet went on to sell 3.5 million copies of their album after one of their songs was used in the iPod commercial between 2003 and 2004. Feist had similar success after her single "1234" was used in an iPod commercial in 2007. Digital sales of "1234" doubled after the song was used by Apple, and hits on YouTube increased by 1,000 percent from the previous month.

Also in 2007, CSS's song "Music Is My Hot, Hot Sex" was featured on an iPod touch commercial and went on to sell many singles. It should be noted that there was no such response when the CSS single was played on a Zune commercial a year earlier. CSS's agent, Tony Kiewel, was quoted as saying, "This is one of those rare instances where we can point to a single event and say, this is for sure what's driving all of our record sales."

In 2008, singer Yael Naim, an unknown artist from Israel, was able to get her album launched in the United States thanks to Apple's use of her song "New Soul" for their MacBook Air commercial. "New Soul" later reached number seven on the Billboard Hot 100 Chart. Apple also launched the career of the band the Ting Tings when an iPod commercial included their now popular song "Shut Up and Let Me Go." After the song was used in the commercial, "Shut Up and Let Me Go" hit number one on *Billboard*'s Hot Dance Club Songs chart.

These are all examples of how advertisers can make a huge difference in an artist's career. However, it is important for artists to have their music used by the "right" advertiser, not used on just any commercial. Apple has been the "right" advertiser for a lot of these artists because the innovation and creativity of their commercials that sets a platform for these new artists to be heard, as well as Apple's association with iTunes.

License Fees

Fees for contemporary mega-hits. As one may expect, the highest quotes, or fees charged, may be for recent smash hits. There may be little room for negotiation here, because once a song is licensed, its value to another sponsor is radically reduced. Therefore, the copyright owner, who is usually either the publisher and/or the writer, may hold out for the highest royalty price, assuming that the writer is even willing to license the song for a commercial use. The only meaningful leverage is to solicit lower quotes for comparable songs. In any event, the going rate for such hit songs may be a million dollars or more.

Fees for catalog songs. An advertiser may be willing to settle for a song that may be recognizable but not currently on the charts. Of course one can expect to pay less for a catalog song than for a contemporary smash hit, but a routine call to a publisher asking for the "standard fee" for use of such a song in a national television campaign may well precipitate a response such as: "We will not license any song in our catalog for less than $150,000 to $250,000 for a one-year period" (a typical duration for a license of music for a television campaign, discussed below). A pop standard such as "Strangers in the Night," or "Wicked Game" (which was used in a television campaign by Jaguar) may garner prices well beyond the standard range. The bottom line is that the more popular the song, the more it will be in demand for commercial use, and the higher the demand, the higher the royalty price. On the other hand, there are many songs in the catalogs of major and smaller publishers alike that, although recognizable when originally released, have neither received significant television or radio airplay nor have been used in movies or commercials for some time. The fee for such songs, which are of proven quality and which may work perfectly for a client's product, may well be negotiated lower than the standard range. The bottom line is that an offer, even if less than the publisher's standard, is better than no money at all. A publisher may also be hopeful that the advertising campaign will rekindle interest in its song. For instance, the Gap's use of KC and the Sunshine Band's "Get Down Tonight" revived catalog sales for the band's records. In addition, the tips that appear in the last part of this section may be helpful in getting the lowest possible rates for songs in this category.

I was recently called upon to license a couple of R&B hits from the 1970s for a major insurance company. The client wanted to use the songs in national TV commercials and was seeking to use the songs to connect with baby boomers to sell them life insurance. For a three-month window, the price was $100,000 for each song. That was just for the songs. The company rerecorded the masters and so did not have to clear the record companies. The same client wanted to use another monster hit from the late 1960s for a TV spot plus a greeting card to include a chip that would play the song when the recipient opened the card. The total price was $700,000, including the song and the original master: $350,000 to the publisher and $350,000 for the song.

There are also certain sections of a publisher's catalog composed of jazz, new-age, and R&B songs that are catchy but have never had any real commercial success. The publisher may be eager to make a deal for these underutilized songs. Although the songs never received a great deal of public play and would not be recognizable to the consumer, they may fit the spirit and texture of an advertising campaign quite well. These songs may be secured for substantially less than the standard range. However, one can still expect to pay more taking this approach than by going to a music library or "jingle" house and licensing or commissioning a work specifically for a commercial.

Fees for songs by baby bands. Publishers also represent songs by unknown artists. They may want to use a national advertising campaign to gain exposure for such baby bands (just as they may wish to gain exposure for older songs that have not been popular for years). If this is the case, one has a reasonable chance to negotiate a deal well below the standard range.

Other Terms in Licenses for Use of Music in Ads

In addition to the identity of the song itself, there are several factors that will be key ingredients in the quote provided by the publisher. As in any negotiation, the initial quote will probably start on the high end. If any of these factors favor the advertiser, however, they may be used to reduce the initial quote.

Manner of use: If one only needs a song to play in the background while, for instance, a spokesman is making a pitch, one can argue for a reduced rate. In addition, sometimes the lyrics to a song are not needed. Since, in effect, one is only using half of the song, one may be able to negotiate a reduced rate.

Branding: Publishers may start off with a quote that includes the concept that an advertiser will use no music other than the licensed song to promote the product or services. This is sometimes referred to as "branding." If an advertiser will actually use different music for different commercials, this should be emphasized as a possible way of reducing the fee.

Radio and other media: A publisher will often demand an extra 5 percent to 15 percent for use of a song in radio spots. This charge is usually negotiated as an option to run concurrently with the television advertisement. However, for obscure, catalog, or baby-band songs, it may be possible to include radio without an additional charge. This may provide the song with some much-needed publicity and public-performance income. (See the conversation of public-performance income in the first Practical Tip below.) This may be used as leverage to get as many media as possible (such as theatrical use preceding movies) without an extra charge. Securing Internet rights, however, particularly when one is not willing to pay additional fees, may be more difficult (see the conversation on clearing music for new media in the next chapter).

Territory: The quotes for mega-hits, catalog songs, and baby bands set forth above assume that the territory for an advertising campaign is limited to the United States, its possessions, and its territories. Of course, one can dramatically reduce the initial fee where an advertisement is targeting a specific geographic market. For example, a very low fee may be negotiated for use in just one geographical market. Sometimes, an advertiser may wish to start a commercial in specific cities and, if the commercial proves to be successful with viewers, expand the commercial to the entire country. In that case, one may structure an option for the entire United States for a one-year period after the initial limited run.

Publishers will generally try to negotiate an additional 10 percent to 20 percent charge for the use of commercials in Canada. If a song is less than a major hit or a pop standard, it may be possible to negotiate Canadian rights into the basic fee, or at least reduce the standard increase.

Options for extending the term: The quotes referred to above are also based on the assumption of a one-year license. This gives an advertiser time to roll out its campaign and generate momentum. Of course, those fees may be negotiated down for a shorter period. Options generally cost 5 percent to 15 percent for each additional period. For instance, if the fee is $10,000 for a thirteen-week period, a publisher may ask for $11,000 to exercise an option for the next thirteen weeks. Or the additional charge may be avoided by paying, for example, $20,000 up front.

Recorded Music

If the owners of a product or service, or their advertising agency, wish to use a particular recording of a song, rather than rerecord the song, they must secure permission from the owner of the master recording as well as the owner of the song. Generally, the master will be controlled by a record company. Typically, the record company will insist on a fee equal to that of the publisher—this is a variation of the "most favored nations" concept. For an agency wishing to use a popular recording by a big-name artist, this could double an already substantial payment to the music publisher. But the master-use license fee can be avoided by rerecording the song. For instance, one of my clients rerecorded "Groovin'" by the Young Rascals for a TV spot and saved $175,000, the fee payable for the song.

Sound-Alikes

If an advertiser rerecords the song, however, they take a risk if they use a "sound-alike"—a recording intended to imitate the sound of a popular record or the style of a popular recording artist. In the case of "Groovin'," my client rerecorded the song on a synthesizer, and the result could not be mistaken for the original recording by the Young Rascals. But in the 1980s, singer Bette Midler sued over a sound-alike version of her recording of "Do You Wanna Dance," which was used in a Ford commercial. And she won. The Federal Court of Appeals decided:

We need not and do not go so far as to hold that every imitation of a voice to advertise merchandise is actionable. We hold only that when a distinctive voice of a professional singer is widely known and is deliberately imitated in order to sell a product, the sellers have appropriated what is not theirs and have committed a tort in California. Midler has made a showing, sufficient to defeat summary judgment, that the defendants here for their own profit in selling their product did appropriate part of her identity.

Bette Midler vs. Ford Motor Company (9th Cir. 1988). The court found it relevant that the advertising company, Young & Rubicam, actually asked Midler if they could use her voice. She denied permission. They then asked one of Midler's backup singers if she could make herself sound "as much as possible" like the Bette Midler recording of "Do You Wanna Dance." Midler won the case even though Young & Rubicam secured a license from the copyright owner of the song and owned all the rights to the new recording.

On a similar note, legendary singer-songwriter Tom Waits, who has steadfastly declined to license his music for commercial use, filed several lawsuits against advertisers who used his material without permission. Waits first lawsuit was against Frito-Lay for imitating his voice to sell chips. The Ninth Circuit Court of Appeals affirmed an award of $2.375 million in his favor (*Waits vs. Frito-Lay* (1992). Similar to the Midler case, the advertiser approached Waits to perform one of his songs in an advertisement. Waits declined the offer, and Frito-Lay hired a Waits impersonator to sing a jingle in a style and manner similar to Waits. Waits won the lawsuit, becoming one of the first artists to successfully sue a company for using an impersonator without permission. The Midler and Waits cases show that an advertiser should proceed with caution in producing a commercial using a "sound-alike" recording.

Practical Tips for Clearing Music in Ads

When clearing songs for commercials, it's important to remind publishers that they, and the writers they represent, are paid *twice* if an advertiser uses their song. The advertiser pays for the synch license (and this could easily be five figures on up for a national campaign). In addition, the publisher's performing rights organization (ASCAP, BMI, or SESAC) pays the publisher, and the writer, each time the ad is broadcast. Public-performance income generated can be substantial. If a publisher declines to license the song, it and the writer it represents therefore have much to lose. It's important to remind the publisher of these facts when negotiating a deal.

Give them a budget: Some publishers will work with you if you let them know how much you or your client is willing to spend. As discussed above, ask a publisher for a standard range for a catalog song and the publisher will start with $150,000 and up. If you suggest $50,000, the publisher may suggest songs that are in your or your client's price range. In fact, the publisher may give you CDs containing those songs to listen to and choose from.

Consult the experts: There are music-clearance professionals who are extremely experienced in negotiating these deals. You may wish to avail yourself of that expertise.

Approach the writer: If you know the writers or composers, it may be better to approach them first. Writers may be more eager to make a deal for a song than publishers who represent many other writers whose work may bring in higher fees. In certain cases, the writer may be able to make a deal without the publisher's consent, but even if the publisher is the exclusive agent for making the deal, the writer may be your advocate for a reasonable rate.

Don't focus on the number of spots, unless you are producing only one: The publisher may ask for more money for the use of a song if it focuses on the fact that the producer plans to make more than one version of a commercial containing the song. You may want to avoid the issue and hope that the license provided by the publisher will not limit your right to use the songs in more than one television spot. If you focus the publisher on the notion that you want to make a dozen different spots using the publisher's song, the publisher may ask for more money. Of course, the more sophisticated publishers will bring up this point during the course of negotiations. If you wish to use the music in only one spot, however, it is to your advantage to emphasize that in an attempt to reduce the fee.

Consider using stock music or a jingle house: If you are not looking for a recognizable song, you may be better off not approaching a music publisher at all. There are many music libraries and jingle houses that may be able to provide music composed on a work-for-hire basis that will work for your commercial. They are also more likely to control the masters, as well.

Musical Theater

With the success of *Jersey Boys* and more recently *American Idiot,* more and more producers are dreaming of bringing a musical based on pop hits to Broadway. Over the past year, I have been called on to clear songs for two musical-theater productions. One was based on the life and music of a famous artist from the 1960s, and the other was a musical based on a comic book about debutantes from Texas. In the first case, I received a couple of rejections of songs where the music publisher did not want to be part of play. This is a reminder that sometimes it's just not possible to get all the music you would like for a certain project.

However, if permission is given, the standard financial arrangement is much more favorable for a producer of musical theater than for a producer of a documentary, feature film, or TV program: There is no upfront cost. The standard business practice for clearing music for theater is to pay the publishers a percentage—usually 5 percent—of box-office gross receipts without any upfront advance. The sweetest part is that 5 percent is the total that has to be paid. Each publisher is paid a prorated portion of that amount depending on the number of songs used in the show. For instance, if there are ten songs, each song is credited with 0.5 percent of gross box office.

In order to secure a license, the following information will generally need to be provided:

▶ Identity of the producer
▶ Synopsis of the musical
▶ Scene description of music use
▶ Start date
▶ Length of production term

- ▶ Performance territory
- ▶ Total number of scheduled performances
- ▶ Theater size (number of seats)
- ▶ Ticket price (USD)
- ▶ Duration of music/timing
- ▶ Version of song used (i.e., live, CD)/artist recording (if applicable)
- ▶ Lyric change (if applicable)
- ▶ Total number of songs used in project

Publishers will generally limit the term to one year. They want to see that the producer is actually mounting the production and pays them the royalty on a regular basis before granting a longer term. Permission may be hard to get if the producer wants to change the lyrics. If they do agree, they usually want to own the copyright in the new lyric. Usually there is no need to clear the record company, as the music will be performed live by the cast.

Practical Tips for Music Licensing

This interview originally ran in the journal *Entertainment Law & Finance*. I am republishing these tips because they are still relevant in clearing music for any project.

ELF: What kinds of projects do you work on?

Steve Gordon (SG): TV, movies, documentaries, compilation albums, DVDs, and Internet-based projects. I recently worked on several interesting jobs in cooperation with Universal Media Inc. [a company specializing in finding footage and music]. These projects included a documentary on Latin jazz for the Smithsonian Institution, a companion record album for Smithsonian Folkways Recordings, a network TV special featuring the music of Elvis Presley, and a PBS special featuring Frank Sinatra's duet performances from his old TV series, to be released as a home video and on foreign TV. Currently, I'm working on an independent movie about a serial murderer who targets punk-rock fans, containing more than two dozen songs and masters. I also represent a publicly traded Internet content provider that is continually securing rights in all kinds of content, including music, videos, and computer games.

ELF: What is the process for securing copyright clearances?

SG: The process is basically the same for any kind of project. Research the songs, strategize with the client, negotiate the terms, and review or, in certain instances, prepare the licenses. In regard to the last item, music publishers and labels will usually provide their own licenses. However, occasionally a small label, publisher, or unsigned artist will request that you draft the license.

With respect to research, the kind of material to be cleared will dictate the nature of research to be performed. For instance, for musical compositions, the ASCAP and BMI databases are excellent sources for identifying the writers and music publishers. Each of these databases may have to be explored because each performing-rights organization provides information only on the songs in its own repertory. SESAC also administers certain songs that will not be included on the ASCAP or BMI sites. In addition, the Harry Fox Agency provides information concerning songs that it represents [see www.Songfile.com]. If your client is using musical recordings, the packaging and liner notes can supply information such as the name of the record company and artist and the release date. If the client is using excerpts of TV, movie, or video footage, someone should view the credits from the original TV program, movie, or music video to determine the TV service, studio, or record label that controls the copyright in the footage. The musical artists, actors, and other persons (or their estates) appearing in the footage may also have to be cleared depending on various circumstances, including whether there is a musical performance in the footage.

Once you have identified those who control rights in the material to be used, you are almost ready to approach the owners and negotiate terms. But first you must strategize with the client. This conversation should include what rights will be required, that is, media, territory, duration; what you think it will cost; and what to propose to the licensors. This process is the real "art" of licensing. With knowledge of the applicable business practices and pricing, you can advise your client on the approximate amount of money he or she will have to pay for clearances; alert him or her to potential problems, such as material that may be too expensive and may have to be replaced; and develop a letter addressed to the owners accurately reflecting the precise rights that your client needs and proposing the lowest reasonable fee or royalty. The proposed payment, which obviously must be approved by the client, should be as low as possible and include a cogent explanation of the reasons that the owner should accept such a rate. At the same time, the proposal should not be so out of whack with standard business practices that the owner feels insulted.

The negotiation process involves a discussion with the copyright owner or its representative about the project, plus continual follow-up. Many of the projects on which I work will not make a great deal of money for any individual copyright owner. For that reason, many of these requests usually are low-priority items to the people from whom I am seeking permission. To do this work, therefore, a combination of courtesy and persistence is recommended.

Ultimately, if the licensor doesn't accept your terms, you will have to negotiate compromises or even advise the client to drop the desired music. For instance, trying to get a hit song for an independent movie may not happen, because the song owner may not like your client's project, or may not wish to license it to anyone at any price, or may propose a fee well beyond your client's ability to pay.

Finally, the owner will send the license, and it is my responsibility to make sure that the terms in the license exactly match the understanding between my client and the owner.

ELF: What issues arise specifically in the case of independent movies?

SG: From a clearance point of view, the most important difference between an independent film and a major studio production is that an independent producer usually has a lot less money to spend on anything, including music. Therefore, an independent filmmaker may have to curb his or her desire for securing "name-brand" talent. For instance, if your client wants to use "Satisfaction" under the opening credits, that is going to cost big bucks indeed, unless he or she happens to be a personal friend of Mick Jagger, and even then, don't assume a huge discount.

Even if Mick Jagger is your client's best friend, the people who administer the Stones' copyrights may never have heard of your client. Music publishers and labels generally will adjust their rates downward based on the size of a movie's budget. But don't expect to pay a nominal fee for a hit song just because your client's budget is modest. Independent film producers should also understand that no matter how popular or recognizable the music in a movie is, people don't watch movies to listen to music. A lawyer or clearance person can work with a savvy producer to create a great soundtrack without busting the budget. For instance, many music publishers, labels, and managers may be eager to place new songs written by "baby bands" that will be more reasonably priced than songs written by established acts. Another alternative is a "stock" music house. Generally, these firms can license both the song and the master, and therefore offer one-stop shopping as well as low prices. Finally, a composer or songwriter/producer can be hired to write music for specific scenes, or a complete score. There are many talented but hungry songwriters who would be happy to work on a client's project for a credit and a reasonable fee.

Another way to work within a client's budget is to set up the quote request as a series of options. Generally, a film festival license can be secured for a small fee, because music publishers and labels recognize that festivals are not commercial enterprises. Additional rights, such as theatrical, free TV, cable, and home video, can be requested as options. Each one may be exercised by paying a specific fee. "Broad rights"—which include theatrical, TV, and home video—can be expensive. In case your client does not succeed in securing commercial theatrical distribution, these options will allow him or her to gain exposure for the movie (on cable TV, for instance) for a reasonable fee without paying for unnecessary rights.

ELF: Please describe the deal points (e.g., term, territory, royalties, or fees).

SG: The term will vary depending on the nature of the project. Of course, you always would like to secure perpetual rights for your client. But that may not always be possible. For instance, in regard to a TV project, music publishers and labels will customarily limit the term to three to five years. A longer period will cost a lot more money. One way to accommodate future uses is, again, to set up options. The original term can be three years, with an option for another three. That way, your client doesn't have to pay the additional fees unless he or she actually exploits the program for a longer term. Movie and TV producers will generally seek worldwide to maximize the audience for, and income from, their projects. Producers of album compilations, on the other hand, may wish to target the United States and Canada market only. So the scope of the territory provision will depend on the business interests of your client. Of course, the most important item in virtually all clearance licenses will be the money. Generally, flat fees will be required for TV and movies, because that is the standard business practice. On the other hand, if you license a song or master for an album or a home video, you can expect to pay a penny rate per unit. How much you pay will depend primarily on the nature of the project. In regard to a compilation album, although there are exceptions, the owner of the track (generally a record company) will require a per-unit penny rate against an advance. If the penny rate is 10 cents, then an advance payment of $1,000 may be required, with a "rollover" payment of another $1,000 for sales exceeding 10,000, and additional rollover payments after that for each block of 10,000 units. The underlying song will be subject to a statutory mechanical license, currently 8 cents per unit [*author's note: the rate is now 9.21 cents*], although it may be possible to secure reductions from such rate in certain circumstances (if a charitable purpose is involved, for example). Clearing music for a motion picture is a whole different ball game, because there is no compulsory license for use of musical compositions in audiovisual works. The money demanded for even a never-quite-famous song can easily reach six figures for a movie to be distributed by a major studio. The owner of the master, usually the record company, probably will want at least an equal amount for the master recording.

ELF: What is meant by the phrase "most favored nations?"

SG: Also referred to as "MFN," this is a business practice that can affect all the terms of a license. It means that you cannot treat the owner or licensor of content less well than any other owner or licensor of content used in a similar manner. The practice is very common in regard to concert TV programs featuring a dozen full-length musical performances. No one who licenses any song for such a program wants to get less money or give more rights than any other licensor. MFN also plays a big role in audio compilation albums. It exists but is less common in regard to clearing music for movies, because in a movie each piece of music is often used in a different way. For instance, one song may be used over the credits, another song may be used for only a few moments in the background of a scene, and another song may be heard as a theme throughout the movie.

ELF: What are some reasons that a copyright clearance cannot be secured?

SG: Money is the most common reason. In regard to a movie, although some baby bands, composers, or songwriters may love the exposure that your client can create, established artists and bands may not need the exposure. They already have it. Therefore, the price can be prohibitively high. To give a recent example from my own practice, we could not get the price of a Bee Gees song down for an independent movie. So we replaced it with a new song composed by my client. Another problem is that the copyright owner, or his or her representative, may not wish to be associated with your client's project for whatever reason. I once had a problem with getting permission to use "Macarena" for a Chipmunks video. Apparently, the composers did not relish the idea of their song being performed by cartoon characters.

ELF: What are the possible penalties if copyright clearances are not secured?

SG: Perhaps the worst-case scenario is an injunction, which is available as a remedy for copyright infringement. Your client's project could be shut down completely. If it's yanked out of distribution, not only are potential profits lost, but there also could be serious expenses incurred in retrieving the product from warehouses or retail outlets (as there would be if a DVD were involved). Of course, copyright owners have other remedies available to them, including statutory damages and attorney fees, if they properly registered their works. Therefore, the price of using a copyright without permission can be quite steep indeed.

ELF: What is the role of a music supervisor?

SG: A good music supervisor can identify music that could enhance your client's project. But, due to budget constraints, experienced music supervisors make their living working with big studio productions. When they can be afforded, they have knowledge and contacts that could prove valuable, especially when it comes to finding new, cutting-edge music. The client can't depend on lawyers or clearance people to be his or her "ears." Depending on the budget, therefore, the client may have to be his or her own music supervisor, although a knowledgeable lawyer with good industry contacts can be very helpful.

ELF: What is involved in licensing music for Internet-based projects? How is it or other new technologies an emerging area for clearances?

SG: New technologies, including the Internet, have created new uses for all kinds of content. New business practices and forms of licensing have also emerged. The issues and rules can be quite complex, depending on what you are trying to do (e.g., webcasting, streaming, or downloading) and the kind of content you are trying to clear (interactive games, music, etc.). Perhaps the fastest-growing areas of music licensing are interactive webcasting and video on demand. Already, satellite systems and digital-cable modem services are offering content on demand. Concert specials accommodate themselves beautifully to these new technologies. Eventually, concert videos may also be available on the web on an on-demand basis. Therefore, in addition to clearing a concert special for TV and home video, clearance people will find themselves clearing for on-demand uses. This will entail educating the licensor as to the new technologies and, in the case of webcasting, assuring copyright owners that your client will protect the owners' copyrights with encryption technologies to prevent piracy.

Billboard Commentary: Music Documentary Filmmakers Deserve a Break on Licensing Fees

I thought it would be appropriate to end this chapter with a commentary that I published in *Billboard* in November 2009. It explains the value of the work of some of my clients in using the documentary format to introduce music to new audiences and is an appeal to the copyright owners to consider that value in negotiating rates for their music.

Celluloid Heroes

Music Documentary Filmmakers Deserve A Break On Licensing Fees

BY STEVE GORDON

I believe in copyright and the right of artists and songwriters to make a decent living. But as a lawyer who represents the makers of music documentaries, I also believe that the owners of music copyrights should exercise greater flexibility when dealing with my clients.

Unlike feature films, which license music to enhance scenes, my clients often celebrate the music itself, and usually shoot their documentaries on limited budgets. Examples of recent projects I've worked with include "Big Pun: The Legacy," a documentary about the first Latin rapper to go platinum; "Let Freedom Sing," a movie celebrating the music that inspired the civil rights movement; "Punk Attitude," a survey about the punk era; "And You Don't Stop: 30 Years of Hip-Hop," a multipart series about the history of hip-hop for VH1; and two documentaries about Elvis Presley for network TV, "Elvis Lives" and "Elvis by the Presleys."

Because music documentaries can be an effective means of introducing new generations of audiences to legacy artists, labels and publishers should recognize that they're good for business. When I worked at Sony Music, Ken Burns' "Jazz" series on PBS spurred sales of our jazz catalog titles. For "Elvis by the Presleys," what was then known as Sony BMG released a companion CD because the label recognized the power of the documentary to move product.

But too often, owners of music copyrights fail to recognize the promotional value of such works, forcing producers of music documentaries to always weigh the value of using as much music as possible against the cost of doing so. Generally, labels and publishers charge

Music documentaries can be an effective means of introducing new generations of audiences to legacy artists; labels and publishers should recognize that they're good for business.

less for use of their music in documentaries than in feature films because they know that documentary budgets are typically much smaller. But greater flexibility is needed.

Complicating matters is the fact that labels and publishers nearly always insist on "most favored nation" treatment, meaning that if the producers pay more money for one song, they must pay that higher amount to the owners of all the other songs in the film. Recently I was clearing the music

rights for a documentary on the history of gospel music. Although most of the songs in the program were so old that they were in the public domain and didn't require payment, about a dozen other songs were still protected by copyright. One of them was more widely known than the others, but fortunately the song's owner agreed to license it at a reasonable rate. This was essential to the project because if the owner had asked for more, we would've had to pay the same amount for all the other non-public-domain songs, which would've exceeded our budget.

Under U.S. copyright law, producers of documentaries for PBS or other public broadcasting stations aren't obligated to pay for publishing rights or the use of master recordings for music they use in their works. Instead, PBS, with funding from the Corp. for Public Broadcasting, pays copyright owners the relevant licensing costs.

But this provision of U.S. law doesn't exempt PBS documentary producers from having to pay for the cost of licensing compositions and master recordings when their documentaries are released on DVD or in foreign territories. This is important because PBS stations often like to give away DVDs of music documentaries during pledge drives in return for contributions and filmmakers usually want options to distribute their work on foreign TV or other media to recoup production costs.

As a clearance professional, I always try to get the most reasonable rates and the most expansive rights for my clients' documentaries, even as I remain conscious and respectful of the value of the music as well. Publishers and labels, however, should recognize that these celebrations and histories of their music are great promotional tools and should enable documentary filmmakers to make the best work possible. · · ·

Steve Gordon is an entertainment lawyer and the author of "The Future of the Music Business," published by Hal Leonard. He also hosts a podcast by the same name at MyRealBroadcast.com.

Chapter 7
Licensing Music for New Media

Digital technologies have created some exciting new possibilities for licensing both songs and prerecorded music. This chapter explores the legal and business issues pertaining to licensing music for:

▶ Websites
▶ Ringtones
▶ Video games

Websites

This section is written as a guide for those who wish to license music for use on their website. Of course, if you are an artist or indie label, you will use your own music. But this section is intended for those who wish to use another artist's music on their site.

There is no compulsory license for use of a song on a website, because a website is visual and the compulsory license provisions of the Copyright Act pertain to audio uses only. In addition, if you wish to use the original recording of a song, you will need the permission of the owner of the copyright in the sound recording, usually a record company. As we discuss below, the price for obtaining permission for "hot" songs and recordings may well be beyond the budget of many website owners. But there are affordable ways of adding music to your site.

Free

Licensing music for a website is easy if you write and record your own music. You own it; you can use it any way you want. You can also ask a musician friend to write and record music for the website in exchange for a promotional credit.

Public Domain

You can also use music in the "public domain" (see Chapter 1) for free. But be careful. Even music by Mozart—whose compositions are in the public domain (PD)—may be embodied in a sound recording that is still protected by copyright. The solution is to rerecord the PD music to avoid using a copyrighted master. A music library will own rerecordings of PD material that can be licensed at a reasonable rate.

Small Fee

It's easy to find a local musician to write and record new music for your website. Local clubs, Craigslist, and local music schools are good places to start your search. You can also go to a music library for music of every genre, from children's music to hip-hop. Some libraries offer royalty-free buyouts for a minimal fee for one track, or you can subscribe for a small fee to have the music rotate and pay a small amount for a license to use various songs.

Expensive or Impossible

If you intend to have a famous song such as "Satisfaction" by the Rolling Stones playing in the background of your website, you may be setting yourself up for heartbreak instead of satisfaction. Many record labels and publishers of hit songs will flatly refuse to license the music for less than a whole lot of cash. But if my client is a major fashion label that wants to use the music to accompany slide-show images of their collection, they may be able to afford the tens of thousands of dollars that may cost. On the other hand, a website that wishes to promote the music rather than exploit it to sell a product may be able to secure a reasonable rate. I worked with a major museum that sought to showcase well-known Latin music such as Tito Puente and Gloria Estefan on its website in conjunction with a travelling exhibit about the music, and we were able to secure affordable rates.

Another caveat is that if you want the original recording of a song rather than a rerecord, you will generally have to deal with two different copyright owners: the music publisher for the song, and the record company for the master. For instance, approval for a classic hit by the Jacksons such as "I'll Be There" will entail going to Motown Records for approval on the master as well as Sony ATV for the publishing. An addition layer of approval is required for some artists. For instance, if you want to use a Johnny Mercer song such as "Goody Goody," you will have to approach Warner/Chappell for a license and then wait for Johnny Mercer's estate to approve the deal. If you want "Bridge over Troubled Water," you will have to approach Universal Music Publishing to negotiate the deal and wait for Paul Simon himself to approve it. The situation can get even thornier if there are cowriters, because each writer may have his own publisher. This is especially true for hip-hop catalogs. Snoop Dogg's "Ghetto Symphony," for example, has nine different writers who are represented by at least three different publishers.

If you feel that you really need a hit song for your website, you can try to figure out who you need to get permission from and ask for quotes yourself. The advantage of using a music-clearance professional is that they have the resources to determine the owner and the relationships with the copyright owners to secure a quote. Once you have the quote, you can decide whether it's worth the money before entering into a license.

Ringtones

Business Background

Ringtones are songs that play aloud when a phone receives an incoming call, usually a thirty-second clip. Ringbacks, on the other hand, are the music that you hear when you call someone until they pick up or you get their voicemail. Although many people have always found them annoying, until recently ringtones were considered to be the possible savior of the music business because they experienced explosive growth in the 2000s. In the U.S. market alone, total sales doubled from approximately $150 million in 2003 to more than $300 million in 2004, and then jumped to $600 million by 2006 and peaked at $880 million in 2007. Worldwide use of ringtones and ringbacks was truly amazing. Global revenues from ringtones grew to an incredible $4.6 billion in 2006. In addition, artists saw ringtones as a way to get more exposure, and music lovers saw them as a way of customizing their phones.

However, the explosive growth started to decline after 2007 when worldwide sales reached a peak of $4.7 billion. By 2009, ringtone and ringback sales declined in the United States by 15 percent to $750 million. Some observers argue that this decline resulted from people just getting tired of ringtones; these critics perceive ringtones as a fad that has had its day. But another equally good reason for the decline is the availability of free ringtones. In 2005, "smashTheTONES" (now "Mobile17"), became the first third-party solution to allow ringtone creation without download-able software. Later, Apple allowed users of its iPhone to create a ringtone from any song purchased from iTunes. Moreover, a variety of websites let users make ringtones from digital music or other sound files; they can upload directly to their mobile phone with no limit on the number of songs uploaded. Partially due to these opportunities, the average price of a ringtone has plummeted from $2 to approximately $1.

Licensing the Masters

Ringtones began as polyphonic MIDI files that were rerecordings of popular songs—not the original recordings themselves. Therefore, the only clearances required were for the songs. Since these new MIDI recordings were made by ringtone services such as Zingy and Modtones, they owned the new masters and would then turn around and license the music to cell-phone service providers such as Verizon and AT&T. Now, however, "mastertones" dominate the market. By 2007, mastertones accounted for 91 percent of all ringtone sales. Mastertones are the original sound recordings, usually in an MP3 format. Their use, of course, requires the permission of the owners of sound recordings, generally the record companies, as well as the owners of the copyrights of the songs. The price of a ringtone ranges from 99 cents to $1.29 on iTunes, from which the record companies usually receive 40 percent.

Of the money that record companies receive from ringtone revenues, they are responsible for any payment due to the artist. The standard recording agreement requires the record company to pay 50 percent of what they receive to the artist. However, that amount is payable only after the artist's account is "recouped." Since most artists are not recouped (that is, they have not earned enough money from record sales to pay back the labels for recording and marketing expenses), the record companies often keep all the money received from ringtones.

Licensing the Songs

The carriers often require the record companies to pay the music publishers for the use of the underlying songs from the labels' share of ringtone revenues. And that requirement has led to an ongoing battle between the labels and the publishers. For years, the publishers insisted on at least

10 percent of revenues from ringtone sales. The average price of a ringtone was $2 or more, so the publishers were seeking 20 cents or more. However, the labels sought to pay the publishers the same penny rate that they pay for downloads of full songs under the compulsory-licensing provisions of the Copyright Act (9.1 cents). The labels argued that the compulsory-licensing provisions of Section 115 applied to ringtones, since a download of a ringtone was not substantially different from a download of a full song. The labels also felt justified in paying a lower rate to the publishers because it was the labels who financed the recordings while the publishers just sat back and collected the money.

After several years of continuous negotiation between the labels on the one side and the music publishers on the other, the labels petitioned the Copyright Office to determine whether ringtones were subject to Section 115. In October 2006, the Copyright Office (*In the Matter of Mechanical and Digital Phonorecord Delivery Rate Adjustment Proceeding, Docket No. RF 2006-1*) concluded that the sale of ringtones did fall within the definition of "digital phonorecord delivery" (DPD) in Section 115. But in her decision, the register of copyrights, Marybeth Peters, did not fix the rate for ringtones at the same rate as downloads. Instead, she concluded, "[I]t is appropriate for the Copyright Royalty Judges to determine royalties to be payable for the making and distribution of ringtones under the compulsory license."

In 2009, the Copyright Royalty Board (CRB), a three-person panel appointed by the Librarian of Congress whose function is to set rates under the Copyright Act, set the rate for ringtones under a compulsory license at 24 cents per ringtone sold—more than twice the statutory rate applicable to downloads of full songs. In the proceeding before the CRB, the RIAA argued for a percentage-of-revenue royalty structure under which the publishers would receive 15 percent of the wholesale revenue derived from the sale of ringtones. Because ringtone prices are plummeting, this would have amounted to less than the download rate of 9.1 cents. Under the RIAA's proposed plan, publishers ultimately would receive around 6 cents per ringtone: 15 percent of the wholesale rate of 40 cents. While the RIAA attempted to appeal the CRB's decision to set the rate at 24 cents, the Federal Court of Appeals for the District of Columbia (*RIAA vs. Librarian of Congress*) upheld the rate in a decision handed down in the spring of 2010.

The CRB determined that a flat rate was more in line with reimbursing copyright owners for the use of their works. In upholding the CRB's determination on this point, the court observed that in other cases it had validated the CRB's preference for a royalty system based on the number of copyrighted works sold—like the penny rate—as being more directly tied to the nature of the right being licensed (as opposed to a percentage-of-revenue rate).

Moreover, the CRB had determined (and the court of appeals agreed) that a percentage revenue model did not make as much sense for the sale of individual copyrighted works as it would in the case of media that is streamed or broadcast. It is relatively easy to measure how many copies of a ringtone are sold, and thus easy to calculate a flat amount; conversely, such calculation is more difficult to accomplish with accuracy in the case of satellite radio, for example. Since those difficulties were not present in this situation, a flat-rate royalty structure made more sense.

I asked David Israelite, president and CEO of the National Music Publishers Association, about his thoughts on the new 24-cent rate, and why there is a federally mandated rate for the use of *songs* in ringtones and not for musical recordings. This was his reply:

It is important to understand that songwriters and music publishers had preferred that ringtones not be covered by Section 115. Prior to the Copyright Royalty Board process, ringtones rates were negotiated in a free market. It was only because the RIAA made a motion in the trial that ringtones be covered (a motion that NMPA opposed) that we have a federally mandated rate. Once the RIAA won the issue as a novel question of law that ringtones are covered by Section 115, the CRB then set a rate based on the market rates that existed at the time. So, I do think that 24 cents is fair, although we would have preferred that such matters be settled at the negotiating table and not in the courtroom. As to why there is a federally mandated rate for the use of *songs* in ringtones and not for musical recordings, it is simply because of the historical anomaly that the musical composition copyright finds itself regulated by Section 115 while the master recording copyright does not. There is no logical reason for it, and I would prefer that both copyrights be in a free market and not regulated by government.

Ringtones Are Not a Public Performance

Until a federal court in New York decided the matter in 2009 (*United States of America vs. ASCAP*), it was not totally clear whether publishers were entitled to a public-performance fee from ringtones as well as a mechanical royalty.

In October of 2009, we received a definite answer: NO. The federal district court, which oversees rates set by ASCAP, granted Verizon's request for summary judgment against ASCAP, shooting down its argument that mobile-phone providers should pay public-performance royalties for the ringtones that they sell.

As noted above, the sale of ringtones already requires the seller to pay mechanical royalties to the publisher (songwriter) and recording artist, just like MP3s or CDs. ASCAP claimed that when the ringtone is downloaded by a customer or plays when a mobile phone rings, this constitutes a public performance. Judge Denise Cote ruled that there is no public performance under U.S. copyright law, so there can be no infringement of that right. The first claim addressed was the transmission of a digital file from a mobile provider to the customer's phone. Judge Cote pointed out, "ASCAP does not contend . . . that a Verizon customer can actually listen to a ringtone while she is downloading it; it acknowledges that the ringtone cannot be played before the transmission is concluded." In other words, a *data* download isn't a performance. She also concluded that because the transmission is sent to a single individual, by definition it's not public.

But what about when the phone rings? The judge wrote. "customers do not play ringtones with any expectation of profit. The playing of a ringtone by any Verizon customers in public is thus exempt under 17 U.S.C. § 110(4) and does not require them to obtain a public performance license."

Video Games

In 2009, NPD Group, a market research company, found U.S. retail sales of video games, including portable and console hardware, software, and accessories, generated revenues of close to $20 billion. Music plays an important part in the success of the video-game industry. For many years, videos games have incorporated music in the background, over the credits, or at certain points in the action of the game. As discussed in the "Licensing Parameters" section below, much of this material is composed in-house or outsourced on a work-for-hire basis. However, in the past several years, many video games have given music a greater role, using both previously released tracks (by superstars as well as underground hits) and music specifically composed, produced, and recorded for particular games.

One very popular series that has been very innovative in terms of music is Grand Theft Auto. Originally launched in 1997, the game started using music in "radio stations" in 2001. As many readers will know, each game in this series allows players to take on the role of a criminal in a big city, typically an individual who rises through the ranks of organized crime throughout the course of the game. The player is given various missions by kingpins in the city underworld, and these must be completed to progress through the storyline. Grand Theft Auto introduced three main locations: Liberty City, based on New York City; Vice City, based on Miami; and finally San Andreas, based on Los Angeles, Las Vegas, and San Francisco. Grand Theft Auto III and subsequent games adopted the use of radio stations that players can listen to while driving around these simulated cities. These radio stations can be listened to when driving various vehicles in the game, or at the start menu. Grand Theft radio stations include licensed music and original music made specifically for the game, as well as DJ chat and spoof advertising. Grand Theft Auto IV included nineteen in-game radio stations (twenty in the PC edition) and over two hundred tracks. The soundtrack could be expanded by purchasing two bundles of downloadable content that each add over fifty songs and a talk-radio program to the existing radio stations. The radio stations play songs in a random order and will still start at a random point whenever the player enters a vehicle. The music is extremely diverse and includes classic hip-hop, rap, R&B, electronic and house music, fusion, funk, rock, and jazz.

Along with the in-game radio stations, other credited music is heard exclusively at certain points in the game. This includes the opening-credits sequence and when walking through the interiors of certain buildings in the game. Most of the music heard on the in-game radio stations is available for download through the Amazon MP3 digital music store. Beginning with the release of the Lost and Damned in February 2009, soundtrack sales have been available in the iTunes Store.

Video games incorporating music as the featured product, rather than in the background or as accompaniment, have existed for over a decade (including Dance Dance Revolution, Pump It Up, Guitar Freaks, and DrumMania), but here I'll focus on Guitar Hero, as in 2005 its massive success made a real impact on the music industry. Guitar Hero was originally published by RedOctane and Harmonix Music Systems and distributed by Activision on Play Station 2. Players use a guitar-shaped game controller to simulate playing lead, bass, or rhythm guitar on numerous rock music songs by matching notes that scroll onscreen to colored fret buttons on the controller, strumming the controller in time to the music in order to score points. Although most Guitar Hero games supported only simulated guitar, with the introduction of Guitar Hero World Tour in 2008, the game includes support for a four-player band including vocals and drums. The series initially used mostly cover versions of songs, but most recent titles feature soundtracks that use original masters and, in some cases, special rerecordings of the songs created just for the game. The Guitar Hero series features a selection of songs ranging from the 1960s to present-day rock music, from classic artists like Aerosmith, Metallica, and Van Halen to indie bands like Interpol and Wolfmother.

Guitar Hero has been a major economic success, selling more than twenty-five million units worldwide and earning more than $2 billion. This success makes Guitar Hero the third-largest game franchise after the Mario and Madden NFL franchises. The third main title of the series, Guitar Hero III: Legends of Rock, is also claimed by Activision to be the first single video game title to exceed $1 billion in sales.

Guitar Hero is not the only music-based game that has enjoyed great success. In 2006, MTV acquired Harmonix, which developed the Rock Band series of music games, which is in the same vein as Guitar Hero. In 2007, Harmonix and MTV Games released Rock Band through Electronic Arts. The PlayStation 3, Nintendo's Wii, and Xbox 360 versions appeared at the end of 2007. Rock Band expanded upon the game play popularized by the original Guitar Hero games by adding a drum kit as well as guitars and allowed players to sing as well as play simulated instruments. Guitar Hero eventually caught up with these innovations, but Rock Band experienced great success. As of October 9, 2008, the game has sold four million units and generated global revenues of $600 million. The sales of Rock Band have helped Viacom, which owns MTV, to become the fifth-largest video-game publisher in the United States.

A notable feature of both Guitar Hero and Rock Band is that players can download additional songs. Many of the Guitar Hero games developed for the recent generation of consoles (Xbox 360, PlayStation 3, and Wii) support downloadable content, allowing players to purchase new songs to play in the respective games. Songs each cost $2 through the various online stores for the console's platform. In regard to Rock Band, song packs containing three songs cost $5.49, and individual songs cost between 99 cents and $2.99. The price for a downloadable album varies, depending on how many songs are on the album. In the midst of the dramatic decline in CD sales and the flattening out of digital sales, sales in connection with games have been a rare bright spot for the record business. As of December 2008, over 30 million downloadable song purchases have been made from the Rock Band music store. Viacom estimates that it is averaging the sale of one million downloadable songs every nine days. In 2008, NPD Group reported that 22 percent of players of Guitar Hero and Rock Band purchased music, including CDs and downloads, that they heard while playing those games. Players of Guitar Hero III, which was released in late 2007, downloaded five million songs between 2007 and 2008. Each song was priced at $2.50, which meant major revenue for labels and artists. Other bands enjoyed a boost in sales. As reported by USA Today, digital downloads of Dragonforce's "Through the Fire and Flames" went from 2,000 per week to a staggering 37,825 during the last week of 2007, thanks to being featured on Guitar Hero III. The game also introduced the band to a whole new fan base.

In the midst of dwindling opportunities to break new music on commercial radio or MTV, the success of Guitar Hero and Rock Band encouraged some bands to create new recordings just for the games. When the iconic Canadian rock band Rush created an alternate version of their song "Working Man" for Rock Band, it was met with so much praise from players that the group released the alternate version song for download through iTunes. As this approach proved popular, Guitar Hero commissioned Aerosmith to rerecord some of their songs exclusively for the game. The video game James Bond 007: Blood Stone, released in November 2010, contains a new Joss Stone song, "I'll Take It All," written and performed by her and Eurhythmics guitarist Dave Stewart, created exclusively for the game. Record companies occasionally launch new music releases though the games. For example, Warner Records released Metallica's 2008 album *Death Magnetic* through Guitar Hero simultaneously with its initial commercial release. In turn, Guitar Hero not only offered the album in its entirety through the video game, but also included an exclusive rendition of the band's song "Suicide & Redemption." Stories like these inspired "Little Steven" Van Zandt of Bruce Springsteen and *Sopranos* fame to gush that "in the history of rock 'n' roll, *Rock Band* may just turn out to be up there with the rise of FM radio, CDs, or MTV."

Notwithstanding this success, in the last couple of years, sales of music-based electronic video games have declined. According to NPD, sales of these games decreased by approximately 40 percent in 2009. Some blame oversaturation, with Rock Band and Guitar Hero releasing too many games. Others say there has been a lack of innovation. Two new high-profile games released in 2009, Guitar Hero 5 and The Beatles: Rock Band, were expected to help sales, but neither met analysts' expectations. When first released, The Beatles: Rock Band sold 595,000 units in its first month—far short of the expected one-million mark. Guitar Hero 5 sold only 500,000 units in its first month, whereas Guitar Hero III had sold an outstanding 1.4 million units. Moreover, in late December 2010, Viacom sold its Rock Band franchise to investment firm Columbus Nova LLC. Viacom didn't disclose the terms of the deal. However, analysts polled by the *Los Angeles Times* estimated a sale price of lower than $100 million. The company bought it in 2006 for $175 million.

Perhaps sales of music-based games will be revived through innovation. Current Wii hit Just Dance is an early indicator that dance games based on motion controls have great potential. When playing Just Dance, users hold a device called a "Wii Remote," which has motion-sensing capability. It allows users to interact with and manipulate items on a screen by making a gesture with one of their body parts and pointing at the screen. The Wii Remote tracks the user's movement while the viewer looks at a dancer on the screen and tries to emulate the movements. Ubisoft's Wii-exclusive Just Dance franchise—including Just Dance, Just Dance 2, and Just Dance Kids—has sold more than an estimated ten million units worldwide as of January 2011. Moreover, the dance category allows for a broader sampling of music. While Guitar Hero and Rock Band focus heavily on the use of specific instruments, dance games can incorporate all musical styles, so long as they're danceable. This gives all sorts of bands the opportunity to get their music into these games. Cynthia Sexton, executive vice president of global brand partnerships at EMI Music—which contributed about half of the thirty-two songs on the Just Dance soundtrack—said dance games are already starting to pay off. "For me as a label person and for our artists, it just means more revenue," she says. "I won't tell you what the check looked like, but it was very, very healthy. And I look forward to the next game, whatever that is."

Last but not least, in November 2010, Microsoft launched Kinect, a $150 add-on for the popular Xbox 360 console. Touted by Microsoft as "a controller-free gaming entertainment experience," the Kinect does not depend on any remote but rather tracks body movements and voice through cameras and microphones so that the player can be completely immersed in various games, whether it be Ping-Pong, car racing, or yoga. Microsoft has one-upped Sony and Nintendo by eliminating game controls. Instead, Kinect peers out into a room, locks on to people, and follows their motions. Players activate it with a wave of a hand, navigate menus with an arm swoosh, and then run, jump, swing, duck, lunge, lean, and dance to direct their onscreen avatars in each game.

Kinect also understands voice commands. People can tell the machine to change games or mute the volume. Harmonix, which sells the Rock Band music game, will offer Dance Central, a game made for Kinect that teaches dance routines to songs like Lady Gaga's "Poker Face" and Young MC's "Bust a Move." According to Tracy Rosenthal-Newsom, a vice president at Harmonix: "We've been trying to find technology that would allow the player to use their whole body. We wanted to remove the technology and really allow people to dance." Commentators see Kinect as the next big thing not only in games but in artificial intelligence, and it may revive interest in music-based games and in the entire gaming industry.

Licensing Parameters

Now that we know music is a vital element in many video games, and that video games now play a greater role in promoting new music and offsetting the decline of traditional revenues, what are the parameters of the deals?

Most video games simply use music as background material. Often, music plays in the background of various game scenes, much like in a movie. Music is also used a means of control. For example, every time you hear a guitar playing a certain theme, the player is prompted to do something else in the game. This kind of music is generally created in-house by musician employees of the game developer or outsourced on a work-for-hire basis. As discussed in Chapter 1, work for hire means that the musicians/composers who create this material generally transfer all their rights in the music and the recordings to the producer. The price of this work, if outsourced, is often paid based on the amount of music composed and delivered. Generally, the price can be $1,500 per minute and up. Respected composers/musicians with a track record for composing for games can make quite a bit more. Note that these work-for-hire agreements generally apply to both the master and the underlying musical composition.

Deals for music in video games such as *Grand Theft Auto* that use prerecorded music from well-known artists can vary from a buyout for all delivery platforms over a period of years, to an advance against a penny rate. A buyout will allow the game publisher to use the music without paying royalties based on unit sales. Generally, the copyright owner in the song (usually a music publisher) and the master (usually a label) will retain the right to use the song and the track for any other purpose, with the game developer gaining the nonexclusive right to use the music in the game only. But sometimes the licenses will prohibit the copyright owners from licensing the same music in other video games, or at least in other video games that fall into the same genre and that directly compete with the licensee's game. These buyouts can range from $2,500 to $10,000 or more depending on the popularity of the song or the artist and the music budget of the game developer. Alternatively, a game developer can offer a penny rate for the use of each song in a game that features prerecorded music. An offer of 10 cents per unit sold is typical; the advance is often based on a figure such as 10,000 units (the advance therefore would be $1,000). The copyright owners also may insist on roll-over payments for royalties. In that case, the game publisher must pay an additional $1,000 after it has sold the first 10,000 units, and an additional $1,000 after the next 20,000, rather than paying on actual units sold in each contract accounting period. Like a buyout, a royalty deal would be nonexclusive, giving the music publisher and label the right to enter into other licenses for the music or to sell CDs or downloads. For both buyouts and royalty deals, the game producer will usually make a deal with the music publisher for the song first, and then the label will accept the same deal for the master. The reason for approaching the publisher first is that if the music publisher doesn't want to do the deal, the game publisher will not be able to use the song regardless of whether the label agrees to license the master. But if the record company refuses to license a track, the gamer can always rerecord the song if the publisher consents.

Licensing for games such as Guitar Hero or Rock Band falls into two categories—licenses for use of the songs and masters in the game, and then ancillary sales though services like Amazon MP3 or iTunes. The latter is generally handled like other downloads, with iTunes and Amazon getting their cut and the balance going to the label or publisher, although the game producer may negotiate a premium for each sale. Where a band such as Aerosmith collaborates with the game developers and contributes its masters, the band may negotiate for acquiring a share of the receipts on sales of the game, as well as fees for use of the music.

Note that the compulsory-license rate of 9.1 cents per song per copy does not apply to the use of musical compositions in a video game, because, as with movies and television, these are audio-visual uses, and the compulsory license applies solely to audio-only uses.

Soundtracks

While there have been instances where game producers have spun off soundtracks based on music contained in their games, Noah Robischon, author of the November 2004 *New York Times* article "Hey, Cool Music: And There's a Video Game, Too?" reported that stand-alone video-game soundtracks have not met with great success. The critically acclaimed orchestral soundtrack for Halo by Microsoft sold only 40,000 copies. Similarly, the seven-CD box set for Grand Theft Auto: Vice City, which featured a slew of 1980s radio hits, sold fewer than 30,000 units.

The compulsory license and the rate established by Copyright Act would apply to the inclusion and distribution of these songs in audio soundtracks. However, the record companies generally demand a rate higher than 9.1 cents for the masters (often 10–12 cents), plus an advance against at least 10,000 units.

Part II
Crisis and Solutions— The Recording Industry in Transition

Chapter 8

A Brief History of the Digital Music Business

In the last ten years, income earned from recorded music has plummeted in the United States and around the world. As reported in the preface of this book, Tom Silverman estimates that the drop is 80 percent, accounting for inflation. Some would dispute this figure, but it is undeniable that gross income for recorded music in the United States and worldwide is down by at least 50 percent. During the decline, many critics argued that the music itself was to blame—that it was simply not as good as the recorded music that preceded the 2000s. Most experts now agree that unauthorized file sharing and CD burning precipitated the recording industry's decline. Eric Garland, the CEO of BigChampagne, the leading firm that measures activity across peer-to-peer networks, reported: "Consider this: song for song, more music [is] acquired on peer-to-peer networks . . . than through retail sales of compact discs worldwide. Or, to put it another way, file sharing is bigger than the record business."

This chapter recaps the brief but brutal history of the record industry's battles with unauthorized music file sharing and its own customers.

Whatever problems the music industry may face at this time, music itself is more popular and more diverse, and listened to by more people, than ever. In addition to radio, TV, and live venues, we now listen to music on the Internet, MP3 players, smart phones, satellite and digital radio, and cable. What the crisis in the recording industry does mean is that the traditional music business is being replaced by something else. One of the big questions is whether the major record labels, which still distribute approximately 80 percent of recorded music that is purchased, will survive. In the mid-1980s, multinational corporations began gobbling up independent labels to create vast multinational money machines. The business was very tempting. Rock-and-roll continued to capture the public's imagination, and many bands were selling in the millions. Superstars, led by Michael Jackson, were selling tens of millions of records. An album could take a million dollars to produce and a couple more million to market and promote, but if a record sold, for example, at $7 dollars wholesale, the payoff for a successful album was spectacularly lucrative. In his recent book *Howling at the Moon,* the former president of CBS Records, Walter Yetnikoff, reports that when he got to CBS Records in the early 1960s, the most popular artists were Mitch Miller and Jerry Vale. Gross sales were only $250 million. When he left in the late 1980s, sales exceeded $2.5 billion. No wonder a business that consisted of hundreds of independent companies became coopted by five multinational corporations—the accountants saw money in the music and rushed in to reap the profits for their stockholders.

Now, however, it seems possible that we will have a world where the record business will go back to small entrepreneurs once again. The Electronic Frontier Foundation defines itself as the nation's leading nonprofit interest group devoted to protecting American freedoms in the digital environment. Although it does not condone the widespread copyright infringement going on over the Internet, it does criticize the recording industry for the way it responded to the crisis of online piracy:

> Years have passed since the original Napster demonstrated that American music fans were ready for digital music choices beyond the CD. But, rather than rushing to address that marketplace demand, the music industry dragged its feet, hid behind its lawyers, and branded music fans "thieves."

While there is some truth in this criticism, it doesn't tell the full story. This chapter aims to give a succinct but balanced view of the history of the record industry's struggle to come to terms with digital music and the Internet.

Labels vs. the Consumer Electronics Industry and the Failure of the Secure Digital Music Initiative (SDMI)

This section deals with the labels' failed attempt to place a "digital lock" in computers to stop unauthorized distribution of music.

The Secure Digital Music Initiative (SDMI) was a forum that brought together more than two hundred companies and organizations representing the major record labels, consumer electronics and computer manufacturers, security technology, information technology, and Internet service providers (ISPs). It started functioning in earnest at the beginning of 1999. According to its website, SDMI's charter was to develop "technology specifications that protect the playing, storing, and distributing of digital music such that a new market for digital music may emerge." The open-technology specifications released by SDMI were supposed to "reflect . . . the legitimate needs of the record labels for security of digital music." The website stated: "Record companies have identified the lack of a . . . standard for security as the single greatest impediment to the growth of legitimate markets for electronic distribution of copyrighted music. Likewise, technology companies developing computer software, hardware and consumer electronics devices that will handle new forms of digital music have realized that an important part of these devices is the presence (or absence) of adequate security for electronic music." Evidently, the electronics companies ultimately preferred the absence of standards, because in 2001, SDMI went out of business.

The SDMI website concluded: "Based on all of the factors considered by the SDMI plenary, it was determined that there is not yet consensus for adoption of any combination of the proposed technologies. Accordingly, as of May 18, 2001, SDMI went on permanent hiatus."

So, what happened? In a nutshell, the content owners could not get the electronics industry to play ball. The labels wanted electronics makers to voluntarily include in their computers and CD burners codes that would prevent transmission and downloading of content that was not authorized by the content providers. Ultimately this would have made those computers and other devices less appealing to consumers. One of the problems is that the content owners themselves were partially owned by the electronics business. Specifically, Sony Music was owned by one of the world's leading manufacturers of gadgets including computers, blank optical discs, and all kinds of digital devices to record and copy music. You can imagine how difficult it must have been for the Sony Music executives to strongly advocate for systems that could make their parent company less profitable.

Labels vs. Technology: The Rootkit Disaster

Due to the failure of the electronics business to cooperate with the labels, the labels got desperate enough to try to manipulate technology themselves. In 2005, what was then Sony BMG Music embedded copy protection software in fifty-two new CD releases. The software included a "root-kit" designed to hide the copy protection so that no one could defuse it, but the rootkit also created holes through which malware, worms, and viruses could enter and attack the host computer. When consumers tried to play the CD on their computers, the rootkit was automatically installed on the Windows desktop, and it created security vulnerabilities that led to thousands of PC owners reporting that their computer lost functionality or stopped working completely. Sony BMG reacted by offering a software utility that was meant to remove the rootkit component from affected Microsoft Windows computers, but this removal utility was soon revealed as only exacerbating the security problems and resulted in even more sick or dying PCs. As a result, thousands of parties filed lawsuits against Sony BMG; class actions were commenced in California and New York, the Texas attorney general started a lawsuit, and the Federal Trade Commission started a formal investigation. The company ended up settling all the lawsuits after spending untold millions, recalling all the affected CDs, and never trying to embed code on CDs again. The disaster showed that without the consumer electronics industry's cooperation, the content companies, specifically the record labels, could not shut down free copying and CD burning.

Labels vs. P2P: Napster and Grokster Cases

This section tells the story of a big win, followed by a bitter loss, followed by desperation. In 1999, the music industry was turned on its head when a college student named Shawn Fanning developed a program for sharing music with other students in his dorm. Napster provided a platform and centralized server that allowed users to locate, access, and share compressed digital music files (MP3s) from other users' machines with unprecedented ease. Within a few short months after its launch, Napster started to gain popularity and users beyond the small group of college students who adopted the program in its infancy. When record-company executives found out that people throughout the country, including some of their own kids, were downloading hundreds or thousands of songs for free, they decided that file sharing was a problem they could throw money at and would litigate away. The labels marshaled their resources, economic and legal, and sued Napster in 2000. *A&M Records, Inc. vs. Napster, Inc., 239 F.3rd 1004 (9th Cir. 2001).*[1]

---

1. See the interview with Ted Cohen in Part IV of this book ("The True Story of Napster and the Record Labels") for the history of the failed negotiations that led up to the suit against Napster. Ted, who was a consultant to Napster before becoming a senior executive at EMI, relates that Shawn Fanning and Napster made an offer that the labels had to refuse.

The Ninth Circuit determined that the plaintiffs, who included the major record companies, were likely to prevail against Napster on a theory of contributory infringement—that is, Napster had knowledge of its users' infringing activity and materially contributed to it. The court's analysis was heavily influenced by the fact that Napster created a system that was not only overwhelmingly used for acts of infringement (trading copyrighted songs and masters without the permission of the copyright owners), but that Napster was able to control, access, or block infringement by end users. The court emphasized that Napster had the ability to locate infringing material listed on its indices and had the right to terminate users' access to its system. The court held that Napster was under a duty to police its service and remanded the case to the district court. On remand, the district court enjoined Napster from engaging in or facilitating others to engage in copying, downloading, uploading, transmitting, or distributing copyrighted sound recordings. Following the district court's decision, Napster hobbled along for short period of time until BMG put it out if its misery by buying what was left of the company. Shortly thereafter, it closed forever.[2]

Notwithstanding their legal victory over Napster, things just got worse for the major labels. The P2P community and technology was—and this had become a pattern—one step ahead of the law. While the record companies were litigating Napster to death, a new and even more powerful variation of P2P technology burst onto the scene, typified by services such as Grokster, Morpheus, and later Kazaa. Like Napster, these services allowed people to trade music files without paying a cent, but unlike Napster, they proved to be more resistant to the labels' legal fire power: these services did not control a central database or index where every song was available for users to download and share. Instead, they merely provided software that allowed users to locate and trade files directly with each other. This was the legally decisive fact in the *MGM vs. Grokster* decision.

In *MGM Studios, Inc. vs. Grokster, Ltd., 269 F.Supp.2d 211 (C.D. Cal 2003)*, a federal district court in California ruled that because Grokster, unlike Napster, did not control a central database containing music files, Grokster did not violate copyright law. Since Grokster could not delete copyrighted music even if it wanted to, the court reasoned, this new file-sharing service was as lawful as a VCR. The court relied on the same standard that was used in the *Sony Betamax* case:[3] if a device has "commercially significant non-infringing uses," the creators of the device (in that case, a VCR) cannot be held liable for copyright infringement. Like a VCR, the court reasoned, Grokster simply provided a tool (software) that customers could use to trade both legal public-domain materials and copyrighted materials. Grokster could not be held responsible where ultimately it had no control over the traded content. The Ninth Circuit affirmed the lower court's ruling on appeal, holding that peer-to-peer software developers were not liable for any copyright infringement committed by users of their products, as long as they had no direct ability to stop the acts. However, on

---

2. Although Roxio bought the name and the famous logo that it uses today for its music service, the new Napster has nothing to do with the original.

3. In Sony Corp. of America vs. Universal City Studios, Inc. 464 U.S. 417 (1984), also known as the, *Sony Betamax* case, the Supreme Court ruled that the manufacturers of home-video-recording devices, such as Betamax or other VCRs, cannot be liable for infringement and that making of individual copies of TV shows for purposes of "time-shifting" (recording it now to watch it later) does not constitute copyright infringement. This was because one potential use of the Betamax was for private, noncommercial use in the home such as watching a videotape. The case created a safe harbor for technology that is capable of "commercially significant non-infringing uses."

the last day of the 2005 term, the Supreme Court issued its decision in *MGM vs. Grokster,* reversing the Ninth Circuit. A unanimous court held that Grokster and the other defendants could be secondarily liable for their users' infringements, even though the software and services were capable of legitimate uses.

U.S. Supreme Court Review of the Ninth Circuit's Decision

In October 2004, the plaintiffs in *MGM vs. Grokster,* representing virtually every major record company and Hollywood studio, as well as the National Music Publishers Association (NMPA), which represents all the major publishers, petitioned the U.S. Supreme Court to overturn the Ninth Circuit's ruling that peer-to-peer file-trading networks cannot be held liable for copyright infringement. In November 2004, forty state attorneys general filed a separate amicus brief urging the Supreme Court to review the Ninth Circuit's decision, arguing that P2P networks were becoming "havens for non-copyright-related criminal activity" such as child pornography.

In early December 2004, the Supreme Court announced that it would review the Ninth Circuit's decision. According to *Billboard* magazine, the Supreme Court's decision "will finally clarify the industry's ability to control peer-to-peer technology through existing law." *Billboard* also noted that "entertainment industry lawyers say" that the court's decision "will influence the industry at every level, including its ability to invest in artists and songwriters." (*Billboard* magazine, December 25, 2004).

On June 27, 2005, the Supreme Court, in a unanimous decision, ruled against Grokster and its fellow defendant StreamCast Networks (maker of Morpheus). The court noted that file-sharing services violate federal copyright law when they promote and encourage people to swap copyrighted songs and movies illegally. "We hold that one who distributes a device with the object of promoting its use to infringe copyright, as shown by the clear expression or other affirmative steps taken to foster infringement, is liable for the resulting acts of infringement by third parties," Justice David H. Souter opined. Unlike the *Betamax* case, which turned on the commercially significant noninfringing uses of a device, the Supreme Court in *Grokster* ruled that P2P firms could be held responsible for infringement if they are marketing their products toward infringement. "There is substantial evidence in MGM's favor on all elements of inducement," Souter wrote. Following that ruling in favor of the plaintiff labels and studios, Grokster almost immediately settled the case and announced that it would no longer offer its peer-to-peer file-sharing service.

Shortly thereafter, it was announced that Kazaa, which had also been sued by the recording industry, had also settled with the record industry and motion-picture studios. As part of that settlement, the company agreed to pay $100 million in damages to the four major music companies—Universal Music, Sony BMG, EMI, and Warner Music—and an undisclosed amount to the studios. Sharman, Kazaa's owner, also agreed to convert Kazaa into a legal music-download service.

Although the decision was a victory for both the MPAA and the RIAA, and seriously threatened the existence of certain P2P companies including Grokster, it also confirmed that P2P appears to be legal so long as not marketed and promoted in such a way as to encourage copyright infringement. It is critical to distinguish that the court did not find that P2P or any other new technology is per se illegal—only if the service markets or promotes the service in such a way as to encourage sharing copyrighted files will the service be held liable. In regard to each defendant in this case, the Supreme Court easily detected a bad actor. The court complained: "The record is replete with evidence that from the moment Grokster and StreamCast began to distribute their free software, each one clearly voiced the objective that recipients use it to download copyrighted works, and each took active steps to encourage infringement." The court pointed to three things that Grokster and StreamCast did that showed the intention of promoting illegal activity. (1) They both advertised their software to former users of Napster and specifically stated that their software could be used to trade copyrighted movies, music, and software programs. The court also pointed to various incriminating internal documents such as this one written by StreamCast's chief technology officer: "[t]he goal is to get in trouble with the law and get sued. It's the best way to get in the new[s]." (2) They completely failed to attempt to develop filtering tools to diminish infringing activities. (3) They directly profited from illegal use by getting bigger ad fees as their subscriber base increased due to illicit copying. But Judge Souter stated that without evidence of intentionally "promoting" unlawful activity, Grokster would not have been liable: "Mere knowledge of infringing potential or of actual infringing uses would not be enough here to subject a distributor to liability . . . The inducement rule, instead, premises liability on purposeful, culpable expression and conduct, and thus does nothing to compromise legitimate commerce or discourage innovation having a lawful purpose." He also stated in a now famous footnote (12): "Of course, in the absence of other evidence of intent, a court would be unable to find contributory liability merely based on a failure to take affirmative steps to prevent infringement, if the device otherwise was capable of substantially non-infringing uses. Such a holding would tread too close to the Sony safe harbor." To me, this is a victory for technology and peer-to-peer. The motion-picture and recording-industry petitioners and several of their entertainment-industry amici argued that the *Betamax* safe harbor applied only if lawful uses predominate over unlawful uses—in other words, only if a majority of actual uses were noninfringing. So, if more than 50 percent of uses of the new technology were engaged in illegal copying, the technology itself would be illegal and banned. Under the court's opinion, there could be 99 percent unlawful copying and yet if the service does not promote unlawful copying, it will not be liable.

In 2010, a federal court followed the logic of the Supreme Court's decision in *Grokster* to shut down LimeWire. See Chapter 10 for a discussion of that case.

Labels vs. Fans: RIAA's Lawsuits

Shortly after the *Grokster* decision, facing ever-mounting decreases in CD sales and income, the record industry did the unthinkable: they started suing their own customers. As Cary Sherman of the RIAA said about the industry's dramatic loss in income in the last several years, "You worry more about survival and a little less about popularity."

Among the defendants in the first round of lawsuits were a twelve-year-old and a grandmother. The RIAA's suit against the grandmother was eventually dropped when her son-in-law, an attorney, was able to demonstrate that the RIAA had made a mistake: her computer was incapable of downloading or uploading the songs that she had been accused of stealing. In Chapter 10, we will report on the latest group of lawsuits by the RIAA against music file sharers, and we will discuss whether they have achieved the RIAA's goal of reducing unauthorized music file sharing.

Although the labels would have loved to have made the Internet service providers (ISPs) shut down P2P services such as Grokster and Kazaa, ISPs (which are controlled by companies much bigger than the labels) have been able to immunize themselves from liability under the Digital Millennium Copyright Act of 1999 (DMCA). As noted in the preface of this book, a provision of the act, known as the "safe harbor" provision, protects ISPs from any responsibility for illegal content. Therefore, even though they provided access to P2P services such as Grokster and Kazaa, they are not responsible for their activities. Some believe this is unfair; they argue that the ISPs could take down such unauthorized services if they chose to do so.

Labels Enter the Digital Music Business: MusicNet and Pressplay

This is the story of the label's unsuccessful initial attempts to enter the digital music business. I recall being present at a business-affairs conference at Sony when the original Napster was still active. One of the lawyers gave a presentation on digital downloading. She presented Napster first with the aid of a projector. We could see the service offered a seemingly unlimited music collection. She requested a title from the audience, and someone suggested a popular rock song. She typed into her keyboard, and the title came right up, available for download. Then she asked for another request from the audience. This time it was an obscure blues tune. Again, it came up instantly and was also available for download. Not only, she said, could anyone download it for free in a few seconds—they could transfer it to any other computer they had and send a copy to their friends.

Next, she showed what Sony Music had to offer. In order to buy a Mariah Carey single online, you would have to wade through several web pages in the Sony Music website. Each page was loaded with ads, promotions, and hype. When you finally got to the page where Mariah's music was offered for download, only a few of her songs were available, and each cost more than $3. Although you could download the song to your hard drive, due to the miracle of digital rights management (DRM), you could not transfer the music to any other computer. My heart sank. I thought, how could anyone be so dumb? By the time anybody actually found the web page for Mariah's downloadable singles, they would probably be so irritated they might figure that perhaps the labels deserved not to get paid at all. Looking back on this episode, I think now the labels didn't really want to compete with Napster. They wanted to kill Napster and discourage online delivery of music by keeping the price high and the content difficult to access. They wanted to retain the old way of doing business that made the labels so profitable in the first place.

When the record companies started hemorrhaging money and litigation failed, they finally launched their own legal alternatives to the pirates. Warner, EMI, and BMG started MusicNet, and Sony and Universal launched Pressplay. Both were introduced in 2002, and both were miserable failures. They failed because (1) neither allowed the user to download any music; (2) neither allowed their customers to transfer the music to any other device; (3) each service offered music only from their label parents (so Pressplay, for example, had no music except from Sony and Universal artists); and (4) even in regard to the music of their label parents, a lot was missing either because major artists had not consented or because restrictions were in place in guest artist contract and sampling licenses (which is still a major problem for contemporary digital services, as we discuss in the next chapter).

Universal and Sony sold Pressplay. MusicNet continues in a different form today, having changed its business model to aid other online music store secure licenses for use of music from labels. The point that I am trying to make here is that the labels were not focused on creating the future when they birthed MusicNet and Pressplay. They were too busy trying to kill the future.

Labels Give Away the Store: The Birth of iTunes

When I was a lawyer at Sony Music in the early 2000s, Steve Jobs approached us. He met with the head of the company, Tommy Mottola, and his trusted comptroller Mel Ilberman. Mel had been with Tommy at Champion Entertainment before Tommy became chairman of Sony Music. Mel was a financial guru and a master of record-business economics. Jobs came in offering a digital music store that would provide greater revenues, on a wholesale basis, than any label had ever received before. Instead of the 50 percent wholesale, which was standard, Jobs offered a whopping 70 percent. After their meeting, Ilberman was reported to have said, "That guy is a donkey."

iTunes launched in 2003 to great fanfare, while the labels licked their chops. The problem was that instead of selling albums, the record business became a singles business. Instead of making $8 wholesale for every CD, they made only $.70 for every $.99 download. Music fans, it turned out, were interested in cherry-picking the songs they liked instead of buying complete albums. iTunes became another nail in the coffin of the old record business. Although Jobs has sold over 10 billion songs, as reported earlier in this book, income from recorded music has plummeted by more than 50 percent. The replacement of album sales by singles, facilitated by iTunes, only worsened the crisis created by free file sharing. But Jobs made a fortune—not from music, but from devices. Sales of iPods skyrocketed in the mid-2000s. By September 2010, Jobs had sold 275 million iPods. With the introduction of the iPhone, which incorporated the iPods' capacity to play music, his fortunes increased even more spectacularly. By June of 2010, iPhone sales had climbed to almost 60 million since their launch in June of 2007. Although Ilberman was right that Jobs could not make money from selling music, Apple made a fortune from selling the devices that played the music. Perhaps Jobs was not "a donkey," after all.

Chapter 9
Proposed Solutions

The original edition of this book contained an outline for proposed solutions to the woes facing the recording business based on a commentary that I published in *Billboard* magazine titled "Technological Advances Have Led to a Market Breakdown: Licensing Could Solve Internet Piracy." Although the pace of change in the recording business makes the year in which the article was published, 2003, seem like a lifetime ago, the basic principles in the proposal still hold true and are still being discussed by experts and industry leaders. In this chapter, I will summarize my earlier proposal and then present the views of two leading experts on its viability and reasonableness. In brief, my proposal would impose a levy on ISPs and electronic devices, the proceeds of which would flow to the labels, the artists, and music publishers and songwriters, to compensate them for income lost due to piracy. In exchange, a statutory license would legalize file sharing.

Free music is not free: As Tom Silverman pointed out in the foreword to this book, income from recorded music has dropped by 80 percent, accounting for inflation, from approximately $15 billion in 1999 to $6 billion in 2010. Few would argue that one of the biggest factors precipitating this massive decline is unauthorized file sharing. It has been estimated that 90 percent of music downloaded on the Internet is unauthorized and unpaid for.[1] Last spring, when I was teaching a course at Tel Aviv University in Israel, I asked my forty graduate business school students: How many download music? All the hands went up. When I asked: How many download music legally? Only one student raised her hand. When I asked who downloaded from P2P or BitTorrent sites for free? All the hands went up. Although this story is only an anecdote, I believe it reflects the attitude of a generation of young people who never got into the habit of paying for music because it was so readily available for free. In reality, however, the music is not free at all.

In order to obtain "free" music, you need a computer and a high-speed Internet connection—both cost money. In addition, if you want to listen to your free music on other devices, you

---

1. Despite increased industry efforts, music piracy continues to grow. In the United Kingdom, for example, 1.2 billion songs were downloaded illegally by 7.7 million people in 2010, according to recording-industry trade group British Phonographic Industry (BPI). That compares to only 370 million tracks, including songs on albums, that were bought legally.

will need a CD burner, a blank disc, an MP3 player—most likely you'll purchase all three. All of these devices cost money. In addition, if you want to access music on your smart phone from the Internet, you will need to pay for mobile Internet access. Free music, therefore, is not free at all. You have to pay various companies to get it, but instead of paying the artists and the labels, you are paying the ISPs for fast Internet connections and the electronics business for all those gadgets that you need to enjoy your free music.

High-speed Internet subscriptions are at an all-time high, and the number continues to grow. Sales of devices to play digital music has been one of the few financial success stories in the music industry this past decade. . For instance, on January 22, 2008, Apple reported the best quarterly revenue and earnings in its history to date. Apple posted record revenue of $9.6 billion, 42 percent coming from iPod sales. In September 2009, Apple announced that total cumulative sales of iPods exceeded 220 million units. Steve Jobs has stated that Apple makes little profit from song sales, although Apple uses the store to promote iPod sales. The same can be said of sales of iPhones and iPads, which can also be used to listen to downloaded music. According to independent analysts, sales of iPhones are expected to reach 100 million by 2011. Based on these figures, the electronics businesses are making a fortune from so-called free music. In effect, what is really happening is a redistribution of consumers' dollars away from those who create and sell music to those who sell electronics and high-speed Internet connections.

One of the primary causes of the industry's present woes can be traced back to the Digital Millennium Copyright Act of 1998 (DMCA). In negotiations surrounding the passage of the act, the record labels agreed that the ISPs would receive certain "safe harbors" designed to shelter them from the infringing activities of their customers. In exchange, the content owners received certain concessions, including the right to subpoena the ISPs for names of alleged infringers. Because of this accommodation, when unauthorized file sharing became a huge problem shortly after passage of the act, the labels could not force the ISPs to shut down "pirates" such as Napster. Instead, the labels had to pursue the unauthorized file-sharing services themselves.

Legalize File Sharing in Exchange for a Levy Payable to the Labels, Music Publishers, Artists, and Songwriters

The solution to the record industry's woes could be a federal law providing for a statutory license that would legalize the sharing of music online while compensating copyright owners for sales lost due to piracy. A federal law implementing a statutory license could legalize the transmission of all recorded music for purposes of sharing music over the Internet and downloading permanent, portable copies. Fees would be paid by those directly profiting from file sharing—that is, the makers of CD burners, including computer manufacturers, and the Internet service providers whose customers already pay in part for access to such services as LimeWire and BitTorrent sites. If CD sales continue to decline due to an ever-increasing number of households acquiring computers and high-speed Internet connections, and authorized downloads actually decrease, the amount payable to the fund could be adjusted upward.

The contribution of each ISP and computer manufacturer would be determined by a body designated by the U.S. Copyright Office. SoundExchange, as discussed in Chapter 3, is already in place to collect monies from webcasters and distribute those moneys to artists and labels. These funds would be allocated on the basis of downloads of the song and the master, which could be tracked by counting technology that companies such as BigChampagne have used to monitor downloads on P2P services for years. The fund administrator would then pay each label, artist, and music publisher based on an equitable formula. Such a formula is already in place to pay rights owners under the Audio Home Recording Act, as we explained in Chapter 3.

A statutory license would level the playing field: The original commentary also pointed out that a statutory license could cut through a major obstacle in the labels' capacity to compete in the digital music world. That obstacle has to do with contract restrictions. As a consultant for one of the major authorized online music services, I had to delete approximately 80 percent of hip-hop music, because many standard sampling agreements did not permit sales as singles of tracks on which samples are used. Third-party artists who are "featured" on records with other artists often included the same restrictions. Moreover, some major artists have the right to deny consent to their music being distributed online, and they use this right to withhold their consent for whatever reason. For instance, AC/DC and Kid Rock still refuse to allow online stores to sell their music, even though all their recorded music is available for free on illicit sites or through BitTorrent sites.[2] Even artists who are legally obligated to allow the labels to distribute their music online sometimes force their labels to refrain from releasing their work online by threatening not to deliver their next album on time, or at all, because they are justifiably afraid that they will not be adequately compensated by the labels for authorized downloads (see, for example, the discussion of Eminem's lawsuit against Universal in Chapter 5). For these reasons, the labels are at a major disadvantage in competing with "free" music sites where everything is available.

A statutory license could cut through these knots and ensure fair compensation to the artists and the songwriters. These contractual problems have had a strong negative impact on the record companies' ability to compete with unauthorized P2P systems. P2P and BitTorrent are limited in the amount of music that they offer only by the number of songs that their subscribers make available to each other.

Finally, there are a huge number of recordings of live concerts, many of which were made without permission. The statute could legalize these, as well, by requiring the ISPs and device manufacturers to compensate the rights holders for their customers' consumption.

The proponents of a free market would argue that the market is the best device in establishing a fair price for all private property, including music copyrights. However, the technological advances created by the Internet have led to what economists call a "market breakdown" in the recording business. A statute that legalizes file sharing in exchange for a levy on those who profit from the technologies that make "free music" possible ultimately would benefit everyone: the public would have access to more music without the threat of lawsuits; the labels, artists, music publishers, and songwriters would be fairly compensated; and the technology companies would still have the labels around to find, produce, and promote music to attract more subscribers to

---

2. After years of holding out, the Beatles (Paul, Ringo, Yoko for John, and the family of George Harrison) permitted iTunes to sell the Beatles' music. With great fanfare, Beatles music became available on Apple's iTunes on November 16, 2010. In the first week, more than two million of their songs and 450,000 of their albums were purchased.

high-speed Internet services, as well as more customers for computers, CD burners, MP3 players, and other digital devices.

Feedback: I interviewed Steve Masur, a leading entertainment lawyer and digital-law expert, and the full interview is in Part IV of this book. But among the questions I asked was about the foregoing proposal. Here is my question and his response:

SG: "Free" music is not free at all. ISPs make fortunes from people who need high-speed Internet to get "free" content, and people spend fortunes on computers, MP3 players, and so on so they can hear "free" music. Is the answer to the woes of the music business to put a levy on the ISPs and makers of the devices that allow people to "steal" music?

SM: I don't think so. ISP licensing is at best a "mop up," that cleans up the Internet free uses of marginal value the same way that ASCAP, BMI, and SESAC performance licenses mop up the money that would otherwise be left on the table in bars and restaurants nationwide and around the world. I don't think there is any single answer to the woes of the music business. First, we have to find great music that people feel compelled to buy just because it is good. Then we have to create new music services that are easy to use and promote them well. After addressing these fundamentals, in the background, we have to retrofit our law to work better with the new distribution paradigms. As part of this process, yes, we can consider new ideas for how to mop up payment for uses that are not otherwise addressed by the market. I edited the 2010 International Association of Entertainment Lawyers' book *Collective Licensing at the ISP Level.* This book focuses not on whether ISP licensing is a good idea, but whether it is possible, and how to do it, from the perspective of experts in twenty-two countries. That's because I strongly believe we should stop talking about what's good or bad and instead talk about what might work, and build it.

Steve (Masur) sees a levy on the ISPs as a last resort. I posed the same question to Will Page, chief economist of PRS for Music, which represents over sixty thousand songwriters and music publishers. He writes in his personal capacity.[3] Will, as an economist, perceives that a levy would actually be in the ISPs' economic self-interest. Here are his thoughts:

WP: Before delving in to the rights and wrongs of licensing networks, let's consider the value proposition to the customer of the broadband contract as it currently stands. Here in the UK, monthly broadband bills are in the range of £20 to £25 per month. For the ISP, that price could arguably cover the fixed costs of access to the copper pipe network (Open Reach), operational costs of engineers (White Vans), and marginal costs of customer acquisition and retention (Marketing). Somewhere in there is a margin to keep the shareholders happy and capital for reinvestment in next generation access. For "some" customers, it is plausible that a different proposition is being presented. For those customers, cash saving can be made by cutting back on their expenditure on media (CDs and movies) and entering into a contract with the ISP provider. Content consumption

---

3. The "Economic Insight" paper "Moving Digital Britain Forward Without Leaving Creative Britain Behind" is available here: www.prsformusic.com/economics.

need not diminish under this scenario; indeed, it could increase, as they no longer have to pay. They could, for example, save £50 per month on media by entering into a £20 per month [agreement] on connectivity—where that media is accessible on demand via the torrents. For sure, this tradeoff does not apply to all customers, but it will apply to some, and for those whom it does, clearly there's money being left on the table and intellectual property leaking through the pipes. If we accept this point, then we can recognize value, and that allows us to consider how that value could be measured and priced.

Let's now deal with measurement. Firstly, there are good and bad carrots, good and bad sticks, and similarly, there is good and bad measurement of piracy. Secondly, there has always been measurement of piracy, BigChampagne has been doing this for a decade-plus, but what makes this development in the United Kingdom different is that the government has to measure the problem—not a corporate firm or individual, but an impartial government. Third, if we have impartial measurement, we can not only see what trajectory we are on—is the problem getting better, worse or the same as before—but we can also have a rational conversation about what "good" looks like as a desired outcome. In the Insight paper, I refer to the work of Detica and their piracy index. Detica is one of many players in this field, and I'm not advocating one over the other, but what fascinated me about their piracy measurement index is that you have two dynamics—the population of people using unlicensed sites and the volume of traffic happening on a network. That was really cool—it allowed me to plot my first indifference curve since joining the music industry. What we need to take away from this is that we have to move away from the black-and-white legal world and consider the gray which economics introduce: the interdependencies between content and connectivity, the need for incentives so that both parties can manage the problem.

So, we now recognize value and understand measurement; let's revisit the "problem." Recall, if a problem can be measured and priced, it's a completely different problem from that of the past. Before we think about what the content industry wants to do tomorrow, let's think about connectivity. ISPs themselves are increasingly becoming investors in content, and this means they will have a foot in both camps. On one side, they could have millions of customers paying for access to the dumb pipe of the Internet, and on the other side a large investment in intellectual property in the form of (say) sports rights. The anomaly here is that those sports rights can be bypassed by the consumer by streaming events live from torrent sites. For those ISPs in particular, the paper "Moving Digital Britain Forward" will be not only insightful but also long overdue.

Now, for the content industry and music in particular. Jim Griffin, a longtime inspiration and mentor to me, is quick to point out that the way Bourget approached this problem in Paris in 1851, when he saw the value this his music was bringing to the restaurant and sought compensation through collective licensing and went on to create SACEM, is not that dissimilar from one possible approach that could be taken here. Compensation, through levy, licensing, or dynamic compensation, would monetarily benefit creators and introduce incentives to the market. If it were dynamic compensation, the less the pollution, the less the compensation payments—hence allowing the players to "manage the problem down" either through licensing carrots that work (such as TeliaSonera bundling in Spotify to their ISP package) or the use of sticks that work. Point being, tracking changes in the measurement of piracy population and volume index would enable all the stakeholders to work with whatever works. Working in a vacuum of no knowledge helped no one, and that is exactly where the debate seems to have stalled in the absence of impartial and verifiable measurement of the problem itself. For the music industry, it's time to move on from the "woe is me" reflections about P2P and consider "where do you want to go tomorrow" as well as begin a long-overdue consideration of what "good looks like" and set goals about getting there.

Other Solutions

Voluntary collective licensing: Another possible solution to the recording industry's current economic crisis is voluntary collective licensing. Under this model, copyright holders would voluntarily join together and offer "blanket" licenses. As discussed in Chapter 1, this is how the songwriters and publishers who created ASCAP, and later BMI and SESAC (the PROs), decided to deal with the problem of securing compensation from broadcast radio and television stations, cable, satellite, background music services, nightclubs, hotels, arenas, and so on. Now the PROs license Internet-based music services, as well (see Chapters 3–5).

There are now many P2P services offering software that makes it possible for millions of people to trade music files with each other. Many of these services have expressed an interest in obtaining a license that would make it legal for their users to listen to and download music. The PROs do offer Internet licenses to any service that applies. The major labels do not. Even before being shut down by the labels, Napster was trying hard to negotiate for such a blanket license from the major labels.

As the Electronic Frontier Foundation[4] (EFF) has suggested, blanket licensing would not require any changes to copyright law and leaves price-setting to the copyright owners. According to the EFF, "Something much like this could be developed for file-sharing [for masters.]" Copyright owners could offer blanket licenses on nondiscriminatory terms, to ISPs, to software vendors, or to consumers directly.

The problem, of course, is that this solution has been available to the labels all along. It works only if virtually all copyright owners cooperate and forgo lawsuits in exchange for a reasonable piece of the pie. So far, the big record companies have shown no interest in pursuing a voluntary "collective licensing" plan.

It is worth noting, and one would hope that the major labels have noticed, that while the labels struggle not to lay off more employees and artists, the PROs are doing better than ever. For instance, BMI reported revenues of $673 million for the 2004 fiscal year—6.8 percent more than the prior year. This translated into royalties of more than $573 million for its songwriters, composers, and music publishers. The revenues and royalty distributions were the largest in the company's history. In addition, new media revenues, including those from Internet-based services, were up 70 percent. This kind of success is especially remarkable in a period when market forces and technology continue to batter the record business. BMI also made it through this period without a single business-related layoff, compared to massive layoffs at the big labels.

The following alternative solutions are from the Electronic Frontier Foundation's website (www.eff.org). My comments follow.

---

4. EFF is a nonprofit organization dedicated to defending freedom of thought and expression for new technologies, such as the Internet and the World Wide Web. See www.eff.org for more information.

Individual compulsory licenses: "If artists, songwriters, and copyright holders were required to permit online copying in return for government-specified fees, companies could compete to painlessly collect these fees, do the accounting, and remit them to the artists. The payment to each artist need not directly reflect what each consumer pays, as long as the total across all artists and all consumers balances. Anyone could start such an intermediary company. Some companies might charge a flat rate per month, some might charge per song or per bandwidth, some might offer a single lifetime payment. Consumers would have the option to sign up with whichever of these services was most convenient or least intrusive for them. Consumers who don't download music, or don't mind the risk of a lawsuit, would not be required to buy a license."

This idea parallels my proposal for a statutory license that would legalize file sharing in exchange for a levy on ISPs and manufacturers of electronic devices, including computers and MP3 players, which facilitate music downloading and copying in order to compensate artists and labels for lost sales. The EFF's proposal, however, envisions independent entrepreneurs collecting the levy on behalf of copyright owners and artists instead of a governmental agency or nonprofit such as SoundExchange.

Ad revenue sharing: "Sites like the Internet Underground Music Archive, eMusic.com, and Artistdirect.com provide an online space for fans to listen to music streams, download files, and interact with artists. In the meantime, these fans are viewing advertisements on the site, and the revenues are split between the site and the copyright holders. Like radio, the money that funds the pie comes from advertisers, not consumers. But, unlike radio, artists are rewarded directly. And, since these sites often host a page for member artists, other payment methods are possible at the same time. Internet Underground Music Archive (IUMA), for example, compensates artists for both ad views and song downloads."

As this paragraph points out, sharing of advertising revenue could appropriately compensate rights holders. Advertising is already a key component of many digital-music services, especially those focusing on independent music.

P2P subscriptions: "P2P software vendors could start charging for their service. Music lovers could pay a flat fee for the software or pay per downloaded song. The funds could be distributed to artists and copyright holders through licensing agreements with studios and labels or through a compulsory license. In 2001, Napster and Bertelsmann AG were considering such a subscription service. Although Napster's legal battles with the recording industry removed it from the playing field, recent attempts at a subscription service (such as Apple's iTunes Music Store) show that consumers are willing to pay for downloaded music."

This model depends on the cooperation of the record companies, which has thus far been lacking. However, an individual artist with an established fan base could consider starting a closed P2P network on a subscription basis. The fans would be able to share that artist's music from recordings and live concerts without fear of reprisal from the artist. The artist would be responsible for paying any third-party stakeholders, such as third-party songwriters, producers, and side musicians.

Digital patronage and online tipping: "Direct contribution from music lovers is a very old form of artist compensation, ranging from a simple passing of the hat to the famed patronage of Florence's Medici family. As content has moved to digital form, so has the form of payment. With an online tip jar such as the Amazon MP3 Honor System, artists can ask for donations directly from their websites, in amounts as small as one dollar. Patronage sites such as MusicLink have also emerged, which allow consumers to seek out the musicians and songwriters they'd like to support. Either way, consumers are given an easy, secure method to give directly to the artists they admire."

Bandwidth levies: "Several people have nominated ISPs as collection points for P2P. Every Internet user gets web access from an ISP, and most have a regular financial relationship with one as well. In exchange for protection from lawsuits, ISPs could sell 'licensed' accounts (at an extra charge) to P2P users. Alternatively, they could charge everyone a smaller fee and give their customers blanket protection. The latter model would, however, charge people whether or not they download music."

At least one major ISP, Verizon, publicly announced that they would consider paying such a levy if the record labels agreed to stop suing their customers. The record companies have not publicly supported such a levy to date. They do not want to relinquish control over pricing. Again, the plan advanced at the top of this chapter would include a levy on ISPs as well as the electronics business in order to adequately compensate the labels and artists.

Media tariffs: "Another place to generate revenue is on the media that people use to store music, also known as a 'media tariff.' Canada and Germany tax all recordable CDs and then distribute the funds to artists. In the U.S., we have royalty-paid recordable CDs and data CDs. It's difficult to pay artists accurately with this system alone, but other data (statistics from P2P nets, for instance) could be used to make the disbursement of funds more fair."

According to the folks at BigChampagne, it is possible to measure the popularity of tracks downloaded through P2P networks with precision. For more information on how this is accomplished, listen to the interview with Eric Garland and Joe Fleischer of BigChampagne in the CD-ROM included with this book.

Conclusion: According to the EFF, "There are many options available to make sure that artists receive fair compensation for their creativity. Today, convoluted and outdated copyright law is being used to claim that 60 million Americans are criminals. It's time to look seriously at the alternatives and start a dialogue with Congress to bring copyright law in tune with the digital age."

Chapter 10

Latest Cases and Legislative Initiatives

T his chapter explores the most recent important judicial cases and legislative initiatives affecting the music business. The information discussed in this chapter is current as of December 2010. Please check my blog, www.futureofthemusicbusiness.biz, for updates.

Viacom vs. YouTube

Viacom International Inc. vs. YouTube (S.D.N.Y. 2010)

In 2007, Viacom filed a lawsuit against YouTube and its corporate parent Google for copyright infringement, seeking more than $1 billion in damages. Viacom lost its copyright infringement when Federal Judge Louis L. Stanton decided that YouTube was not responsible for Viacom videos uploaded on its site by its users. Judge Stanton found that requiring all user-content-generated sites such as YouTube to safeguard their content before it's posted would violate the Digital Millennium Copyright Act. The decision was handed down in June 2010.

The DMCA provides immunity from liability for user-generated sites such as YouTube if they comply with the "notice and takedown" provisions in the act. If the site receives a notice from the copyright owner that someone has uploaded infringing material, the site must remove that content. If the site complies, the copyright owner is barred from suing the site. In this case, Viacom served notice of infringing material, and YouTube immediately complied. The decision noted:

> The present case shows that the DMCA notification regime works efficiently: when Viacom over a period of months accumulated some 100,000 videos and then sent a mass take-down notice on February 2, 2007, by the next business day YouTube had removed virtually all of them.

Despite YouTube's compliance with the DMCA, Viacom sued anyway, arguing that Google profited from piracy on YouTube and did not do enough to limit its occurrence.

It is important to note that, to a large extent, the case addressed past conduct, as Viacom said it was not seeking damages for any actions since Google put in its filtering system, known as Content ID, in early 2008. When the system finds a match from a user-submitted clip, it alerts the copyright owners and gives them the option of removing or selling ads on it.[1] It is significant that Google's past practice of merely complying with the notice and takedown provisions of the DMCA was found noninfringing because many startups could not afford to implement such a system. Michael S. Kwun, a lawyer who worked for Google on the case, told the *New York Times,* "I have no idea how much money YouTube spent on developing its content ID system, but if that was required for any new start-up, you wouldn't see any." The decision makes clear that user-generated sites are not legally required to develop such a system and could expect legal protection as long as they took down content when copyright holders complained.

Viacom has announced that it will appeal Judge Stanton's decision.[2]

Universal vs. Grooveshark

UMG vs. Grooveshark (N.Y. Sup. 2010)

Grooveshark is a great example of how some Internet sites engage in activity that may be illegal with the hope of amassing such a huge audience that the copyright owners will do business with them instead of trying to shut them down.[3] Grooveshark allows its users to upload their own music, commonly copyrighted material, onto their site, making it readily available for other users to hear. Like Spotify in Europe, Escape Media's Grooveshark is a "freemium" music service, meaning that you can hear any song in the catalog on demand and save any of them into playlists without paying a cent. The service generates revenue from visual ads embedded in the free version of the service and $3 monthly payments from premium users who pay to have ads removed.

EMI sued Grooveshark for copyright infringement in June 2009. Grooveshark responded by stating, "We find the use of this negotiating strategy counterproductive, as Grooveshark has been willing to conclude an agreement with EMI Records that is economically sustainable for both EMI Records and a start-up company the size of Grooveshark." The lawsuit was dropped when EMI decided to license its catalogs to Grooveshark. When asked whether Grooveshark's deal involves handing over equity to EMI, Grooveshark's vice president of communications, Isaac Moredock, responded that:

---

1. Content ID works as follows: YouTube receives audio or video reference files from content-owning rights holders and metadata to describe their content, as well as what they would like YouTube to do (monetize with advertising, track, or block) when their content is found. YouTube offers this copyright-protection tool to content partners for free. Of course, the newness of content ID brings about problems, including overcensoring of videos mistakenly recognized as copyrighted content, including remixes, parodies, and educational lectures, though it does allow YouTube users to dispute video removals. As soon as a dispute is filed, the video is available immediately, and the claimant must file a formal DMCA notification if they still want the video taken down. This gives users an advantage in uploading fair content without it being unnecessarily purged.

2. Greg Sandoval, "Google Defeats Viacom in Landmark Copyright Case," CNET News (U.S.), June 23, 2010, http://news.cnet.com/8301-31001_3-20008636-261.html. Retrieved June 23, 2010.

3. On December 10, 2010, Google released its "Zeitgeist 2010" roundup, a rundown of the biggest trends through the lens of the biggest search engine. The hottest music app this year, in terms of queries, was Grooveshark, listed as the ninth-fastest-rising search in the entertainment category.

We can't go public with [details about the deal] yet, just because we're going to try to use this as a template to go and sign all the other major labels, and we're hoping that they agree to similar terms. But until we have other major labels onboard, we can't really get into the specifics of the terms—one, for overall safety, and two, because we're trying to keep it ahead of Spotify.

In January 2010, Universal Music Group (UMG) sued Grooveshark for providing free access to music belonging to UMG. In the suit, UMG claims that Grooveshark targets "the very segment of users that are bringing the labels to their knees with illegal downloading." In other words, those who seek pirated music for free on the Internet flock to Grooveshark.

Part of UMG's attack on Grooveshark was to have Apple take down the Grooveshark iPhone application. In response, Grooveshark's CEO, Sam Tarantino, claimed that UMG was not in compliance with DMCA takedown procedures and had never once issued Grooveshark a takedown notification.

An interesting twist in this case is that UMG decided to bring suit in state court—rather than federal—and sued only for acts of infringement relating to recordings produced prior to 1972. The *federal* Copyright Act protects only sound recordings produced after 1972; for recordings produced prior to that, state common law applies. The reason for UMG's strategy is to avoid the DMCA's notice and takedown provisions: since the DMCA is part of the federal Copyright Act, it would not apply to pre-1972 records. In effect, Universal is trying to strip Grooveshark of the defense that the DMCA's notice and takedown provisions would otherwise afford them. However, the federal Copyright Act may be deemed to preempt the state common law, which means that the federal law will be applied instead of the state law when the two conflict. It is an interesting legal effort by Universal, however. Check futureofthemusicbusiness.biz for updates on this case.

Grooveshark vs. Spotify vs. Google: The Race Is On

Grooveshark hopes to beat Spotify in the race to launch the first successful ad-supported comprehensive on-demand streaming service in the United States. In order to beat Spotify in this race, not only does Grooveshark have to survive Universal's legal attack, it must also sign up Sony and Warner, not to mention indie aggregators like IODA and The Orchard. Grooveshark's Isaak Moredock told Wired.com that the company hopes to sign deals with the remaining majors in the next six months: "We are dead set on signing those agreements with the [remaining] labels," he said.

However, even if Grooveshark can land all the majors, it will face stiff competition. Spotify is another "freemium" ad-based service that has already achieved major success in the European countries where it has launched thus far: Sweden, Norway, Finland, the UK, France, Spain, and the Netherlands. Unlike Grooveshark, Spotify already has deals with the majors, but only for access by users in those European countries.

On the other hand, Spotify has several times predicted that it would start up in the States, only to postpone launch. So far, they have been unable to sign the U.S. majors. Grooveshark's surprise deal with EMI gives it a lead in the United States. When it comes to independent bands and labels, Grooveshark has a more inclusive approach than Spotify, which requires bands to sign to a label or aggregator in order to be included in the service. Instead, Grooveshark permits anyone to upload their own music. But there's no question that Spotify has a big advantage of its own—a massive war chest it can use to sign label and publisher deals, a peer-to-peer architecture that saves on bandwidth costs, and a critically praised downloadable app that feels more like iTunes than Grooveshark's web-based service. It can also save files locally in the premium version and has an iPhone app that's already won over fans in Europe.

But even as Spotify and Grooveshark race to succeed as ad-based services, they will walk over the corpses of other ad-based services that died an early death: imeem and SpiralFrog. SpiralFrog never launched, because it ran out of money before paying the steep upfront fees demanded by the major labels, who have long been suspicious of ad-supported models. Another huge warning to both Spotify and Grooveshark is imeem, which actually launched its ad-based all-you-could-listen service in 2006. Unlike SpiralFrog, imeem succeeded in signing deals with all four major labels. However, just two years after its launch, imeem was forced to sell out at less than a paltry million dollars because they could not afford to pay the huge "minimum" advances that the big labels required. Myspace took it over but does not include all the songs that imeem had, and many users of imeem have not followed the service to Myspace.

Spotify and Grooveshark face the same basic problem as imeem: money. Ad-supported services such as imeem simply have not been able to generate the level of revenue required to afford the labels' minimum advances. Now enter Google: as noted in the preface, Google is reportedly planning a cloud-based, ad-supported service that would include all the tracks that iTunes sells, but it would offer all those tracks for free and make them available to any Internet-connected device. Google may be the only service with enough money to afford the labels' demand for high upfront advances. More important, Google may be the only company with enough users to attract the ad revenues necessary to feed the labels and still make a profit.

Network Neutrality: The Battle over the Future of the Internet

Network neutrality is the principle that all Internet content should be treated equally by network providers; that is, ISPs should deliver everyone's content, —and not block any content, plus they should deliver that content at the same speed. The ISPs and some content providers and Internet services such as Google would prefer a system where the ISPs can charge fees for faster speeds to those websites and services that are willing to pay. The ISPs would make more money, and wealthy content providers and online services would gain an advantage over competitors who could not afford to pay such a premium. Many people involved in the music business consider this to be a very important issue. For example, the independent record labels, represented by the American Association of Independent Music (A2IM), take the position that discarding network neutrality would give the major labels and artists an unfair advantage because they could afford to pay for greater bandwidth and faster delivery of their content than the independent labels and artists could afford.

As this book was going to press, FCC chairman Julius Genachowski proposed, and on December 21 the FCC voted three to two in favor of, new rules that would appear to preserve network neutrality, but these have been criticized by progressives including Sen. Al Franken from

Minnesota, along with public-interest and free-speech groups, for being riddled with loopholes. They slammed the rules as a bad compromise and woefully inadequate. The new rules would clearly prevent "fixed-line" broadband providers like Comcast and Qwest (as opposed to mobile services discussed further below) from blocking access to sites and applications. However, the rules are not so clear when it comes to "paid prioritization," which would allow a company to pay an ISP for faster transmission of data. Paid prioritization would result in some websites and applications reaching customers at slower speeds than the ones that pay for faster service.

The relevant rule is as follows:

Rule 3: No Unreasonable Discrimination
A person engaged in the provision of fixed broadband Internet access service, insofar as such person is so engaged, shall not unreasonably discriminate in transmitting lawful network traffic over a consumer's broadband Internet access service. Reasonable network management shall not constitute unreasonable discrimination.

The press release issued by the FCC states in relevant part:

. . . as a general matter, it is unlikely that pay for priority would satisfy the "no unreasonable discrimination" standard. The practice of a broadband Internet access service provider prioritizing its own content, applications, or services, or those of its affiliates, would raise the same significant concerns and would be subject to the same standards and considerations in evaluating reasonableness as third-party pay-for-priority arrangements.

Although the press release suggests that paid prioritization would violate Rule 3, critics argue that because the rules do not explicitly forbid paid prioritization, this could be a first step toward cleaving out high-speed, premium fast lanes from the "public Internet."

Moreover, the rules would allow wireless companies more latitude in putting limits on access to services and applications. Specifically, wireless Internet providers like AT&T and Verizon would be prohibited from blocking websites, but not from blocking applications or services unless those applications directly compete with providers' "voice or video telephony services." So a mobile provider that also has a telephone service could not discriminate against other telephone services, such as Skype. However, other forms of discrimination would be possible. Here's an example from Senator Franken: "Maybe you like Google Maps. Well, tough," Mr. Franken said on Saturday on the Senate floor. "If the FCC passes this weak rule, Verizon will be able to cut off access to the Google Maps app on your phone and force you to use their own mapping program, Verizon Navigator, even if it is not as good. And even if they charge money, when Google Maps is free."

The two Democratic FCC commissioners, Michael Copps and Mignon Clyburn, who voted for the rules with the chairman, acknowledged that they were not as strong as they would have liked. On the other hand, the two Republican commissioners, Meredith Baker and Robert McDowell, who voted against the rules, suggested that the net neutrality rules are an example of government overreach. In an opinion piece in the *Wall Street Journal* on December 23, 2010, Mr. McDowell asserted that "nothing is broken that needs fixing."

In addition to the progressives complaining about their adequacy, and conservatives complaining that they are unnecessary, the rules are subject to a court challenge, particularly in the wake of a previous court case—*Comcast vs. FCC (D.C. Cir. 2010)*—which put into doubt the FCC's authority to make rules on this matter at all. In April 2010, the Federal Appeals Court in Washington, D.C., ruled that the FCC did not have authority to prevent Comcast, which had threatened to do so, from slowing its cable customers' access to the file-sharing service BitTorrent. As a practical matter, the court ruling had no impact on Comcast subscribers, since the company decided not to slow access to BitTorrent. But the court decision can be used to challenge the validity of the FCC's new guidelines, although Comcast and other major ISPs apparently agreed to the new rules before they were announced.[4]

Check www.futureofthemusicbusiness.biz for updates on this important issue.

Public Performance Rights Act: Will the Labels Finally Get Radio to Pay Up?

As reported in Chapter 1, the record companies do not have public-performance rights in their masters except in regard to digital transmission. Therefore, unlike music publishers, who do enjoy those rights, they receive no money from terrestrial radio. During the past several years there has been a major push to try to change that. The Performing Rights Act, a bill proposed by Senator Patrick Leahy (D-VT), would expand protection for public performances of copyrighted sounds recordings. The terms of that bill and its likelihood for passage are presented at the end of this section.

Current Law

When it comes to music, U.S. copyright law protects two distinct copyright owners: (1) the owners of the musical compositions (the song), which is usually a music publisher, or songwriters who control their own publishing; and (2) the owners of the sound recording embodying the song, which is usually a record company, or an artist who is not signed to a label. The Copyright Act gives the copyright owners of songs the exclusive right to perform the copyrighted work publicly. But the Copyright Act does not give public-performance rights to the copyright owners of masters, except for digital transmission. This means that radio broadcasters have to pay publishers and songwriters for the songs they play, but they do not have to pay labels and artists to play the recordings that contain the very same songs. This arrangement has been in place since the beginning of recorded music. The old Copyright Law of 1909 protected a number of different copyrights, including songs, but sound recordings of music, which were in their infancy, were not covered. In 1972, federal law was amended to protect sound recordings, but public performance was deliberately omitted from the types of protection that normally apply to copyright materials. Why? Politics and money!

The broadcast community, which has one of the strongest lobbies in the history of American politics (the National Association of Broadcasters, or NAB), successfully persuaded Congress not give to owners of sound recording public-performance rights. Many congressmen may have been persuaded by the fact that they needed the radios stations' friendships when they ran for office, as radio gave them a platform for staying in touch with the voters and campaigning for office.

---

4. *New York Times*, December 20, 2010.

Although the labels have never been happy with the law, the broadcasters argued that they were promoting the labels' releases and therefore helping the labels sell more records. In fact, labels would often pay the radio stations to play their records, a practice known as "payola." While Congress made payola illegal as a federal offense in 1960, periodic governmental investigations have revealed that it is still practiced clandestinely to the present day. In 2005, New York State Attorney General Eliot Spitzer launched an investigation into major record labels' involvement in the practice of payola. This investigation culminated in big labels like Sony Music Entertainment and Warner Music Group reaching settlements of $10 million and $5 million, respectively. The investigation revealed that labels sent cash payments or gifts like electronic goods, and even sent a Buffalo DJ on holiday to Miami, in exchange for radio play for their artists. Sony acknowledged these practices and admitted that payola was "wrong" and "improper" before apologizing. The money was donated to local charities in aid of music education and appreciation.

However, as the record industry has suffered huge decreases in income from record sales, it has stepped up its lobbying efforts to change the law in order to extract money from the broadcasters.

Out of Step with Other Countries

As the labels emphasize, in every other developed country worldwide, copyright laws grant performers (artists, musicians, and vocalists) and producers (such copyright owners as record companies)— as well as songwriters and publishers— exclusive rights for the public performance of their recordings and compositions. The rates differ from country to country, but each upholds its responsibility to require broadcasters to pay for sound recordings via analog as well as digital transmissions. Internationally, the rates vary according to revenue and programming. For example, in England, the rate is 2 to 5 percent, depending on a station's revenue.

As a result of incongruous copyright laws here and abroad, other countries withhold royalties otherwise payable to U.S. copyright owners, since international owners of sound recordings don't get performance royalties from U.S. radio play. The record companies hope that by pushing Congress to impose a royalty on broadcasters, they will receive additional income not only from U.S. radio stations, but also from foreign performing-rights organizations.

Terms of the Bill and Likelihood of Passage

Over-the-air broadcast stations would be able to use a statutory license and make one payment annually under a rate set through negotiations or by the Copyright Royalty Board for all the music they play, instead of having to negotiate with every copyright owner for each use of music. At the current time, there has been some speculation that the rate would be 1 percent of gross revenue. However, this is just speculative and is not part of the legislation. There have been discussions between the National Association of Broadcasters (NAB) and Music First Coalition for settling on a rate, but nothing concrete has been determined. If the record companies prevail, they'll be rewarded with a fraction of the estimated $20 billion that radio earned in ad revenue last year.

The proposed legislation accommodates small broadcasters and others to assure balance and fairness to broadcasters and artists. More than 75 percent of all commercial radio stations and more than 80 percent of all religious stations would be covered through the planned accommodation.

Small commercial stations, ones that gross revenues of less than $1,250,000 a year, would pay only $5,000 per year; noncommercial stations such as NPR and college radio would pay only $1,000 per year; stations that make only incidental uses of music, such as "talk radio" stations, would not pay for that music; and religious services that are broadcast on radio would be completely exempt.

Proposed amendments to the existing law would make it clear that a new right for recording artists and sound-recording owners cannot adversely affect the rights of, or royalties payable to, songwriters or musical-work copyright owners. The legislation adopts the same payment structure applicable to payments for webcasting, which is 50 percent to the record companies and 50 percent to the recording artists. The "featured artist" would receive 45 percent of the total artist share. This money would be paid directly to these artists, not the record companies. Nonfeatured artists would receive 5 percent: 2.5 percent is paid directly to the American Federation of Television and Radio Artists (AFTRA) on behalf of nonfeatured vocalists, and 2.5 percent is paid to the American Federation of Musicians (AFofM) on behalf of background musicians. In regard to webcasting, SoundExchange collects the money and pays the receiving parties. The bill contemplates that an organization similar to SoundExchange itself would play that role.

There is also a provision in the act for a fund of 1 percent to be set up for side artists and background vocalists. Each group would receive 50 percent, which would be paid to their unions, AFofM and AFTRA.

The Performing Rights Act has yet to be adopted. In April 2010, the Obama administration announced its support of the bill through a letter from the Commerce Department to Senator Leahy. The bill has been approved by the House and Senate judiciary committees and is awaiting floor action in both bodies.

I asked David Israelite, the president of the National Music Publishers' Association (NMPA), for his opinion about the bill, and this was his reply:

> The NMPA supports the Performance Rights Act. Our support, however, is conditioned on three critical factors. First, the final legislation must contain the songwriter protection language that NMPA helped negotiate with all of the parties. This language would ensure, to the best ability possible in legislation, that songwriters are not harmed by having their royalties reduced due to the new income stream for artists and record labels. Second, the legislation must not be attached to any other issues that would impact songwriters and music publishers in a negative way. Finally, the support of the songwriting and music publishing community is premised on the agreement that the RIAA and record labels honor the One Music[5] philosophy that demands similar support by the RIAA and record labels for the rights of songwriters and music publishers when a third party, such as the broadcasters in this instance, are compensating both copyrights in the use of music.

---

5. The National Music Publishers' Association has proposed a concept called "One Music," urging the entire music community to be "supportive of each other regarding the value of music," according to Israelite.

Continuing Importance of Traditional Radio

If you're a music fan, you may hate traditional commercial radio stations. They rarely play new releases, except those from major artists or major labels, and confine the music they play to a limited set of genres, mainly pop and R&B. Plus, there seem to be more commercial breaks than ever. In fact, younger listeners have declined dramatically, in favor of other ways of finding and listening to new music, such as YouTube and Internet radio. But traditional radio remains a hugely important format to artists who are seeking a broader audience and mainstream popularity and success.

Edison Research recently conducted a survey of twelve- to twenty-four-year-olds in the United States. They are a vitally important demographic for new artists, because they actively attend concerts, buy merchandise, and consider artists' endorsements in purchasing of products. A lot has changed, including the number of hours spent listening to terrestrial radio stations, but radio still ranks remarkably high in new music discovery.

With the success of the web and social networks, total listening hours for traditional radio have declined steeply among younger listeners, from an average of 2 hours and 43 minutes per day in 2000 to 1 hour and 24 minutes in 2010. While this decline is undoubtedly significant, the same survey found that 88 percent of those surveyed still discover new music through traditional radio, a figure that narrowly falls short of personal recommendations (at 90 percent) but easily tops formats like YouTube (72 percent), social-networking sites (56 percent), and even Internet radio stations such as Pandora, Last.fm, and Yahoo! Music (42 percent).

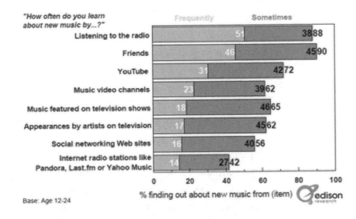

New artists seeking national acclaim cannot reach the masses without breaking on radio, and the major labels still have the best contacts for making that happen, which keeps them relevant even as they suffer through continuing financial misfortune.

Labels vs. LimeWire: The End of P2P?

Arista Records et al. vs. Lime Group (S.D.N.Y. 2010)

In May 2010, LimeWire was found liable of copyright infringement against thirteen major record companies. The lawsuit was filed in 2006. LimeWire created its service in 2000 and at one time was the world's most popular P2P service, with more than fifty million monthly users. U.S. District Court Judge Kimba Wood, citing Grokster's unanimous ruling from 2005 in her decision (see Chapter 8), determined LimeWire was liable for inducing and enabling copyright infringement, noting that LimeWire had failed to implement in a meaningful way any technical barriers that would have made it harder for users of its software to illegally share and download music files. In a motion filed in June 2010, the RIAA asked the court to freeze all assets belonging to the parent company of LimeWire (Lime Group) and its president, Mark Gorton, claiming that the company was "liable for hundreds of millions of dollars (if not even a billion dollars) in statutory damages." In late October, the court granted the record industry's request for a permanent injunction ordering the Lime Group to stop distributing and supporting its file-sharing software, thereby shutting the service down. Lime Group, which is now trying to launch a legitimate music service, agreed to comply with the court order. Shortly before this book was submitted for publication, LimeWire announced that it will be shutting its virtual doors to the public for good on December 31, 2010, ending its ten-year run as a peer-to-peer file-sharing website. Some call this the end of the file-sharing era, but others believe it will not significantly impede illegal downloading. (See "Limited Impact" of RIAA's lawsuits below.)

Update on the RIAA's Lawsuits

Beginning in 2003, the RIAA started suing users of P2P networks. They were hoping to, if not shut down illegal file sharing and downloading, at least significantly reduce it. When the first round of lawsuits was filed in September 2003—targeting 261 defendants around the country—RIAA president Cary Sherman stated: "It is simply to get peer-to-peer users to stop offering music that does not belong to them." The RIAA's goal in targeting music fans instead of businesses was "not to be vindictive or punitive." Rather, they sought to strike fear into the hearts of would-be downloaders. RIAA spokeswoman Cara Duckworth hoped that the lawsuits would create a "general sense of awareness" that sharing copyrighted music without permission is "illegal."

There has been some confusion about the total number of cases that the RIAA filed, as opposed to how many people they actually sued. The answer is that they filed over thirty thousand cases, but they sued only around eighteen thousand people. The explanation for this is that the ISPs voluntarily provided the names of around six thousand people, but the RIAA had to file twelve thousand cases to acquire the names of other alleged infringers. They would do this by filing a subpoena with the ISPs to make them give up the names. These are known as "John Doe" lawsuits, as the names of the infringers are unknown. When the RIAA received the names, they would start an action directly against those people. Therefore, although there were more than thirty thousand cases, the RIAA actually sued only approximately eighteen thousand people

End of the Suits

In late 2008, the RIAA announced they would cease bringing new actions. The reason for this halt seems to be twofold: First, the lawsuits generated horrible publicity, so although the RIAA wanted to "educate" the public that copyright infringement was bad, some of the lawsuits made the organization look like it just wanted to punish people. For instance, in 2003, the RIAA sued a twelve-year-old girl for illegally downloading music from Kazaa. The girl claimed she didn't realize the downloading was illegal, because her mother paid a service fee for Kazaa. Her mother settled with the RIAA for $2,000, the equivalent of $2 per song.

At times the process of suing the alleged infringers looked absurd, since the RIAA did not know who they were suing until the ISPs gave them the defendant's name from their IP address. They sometimes would find out they were suing dead people or people who could not have engaged in file sharing. For example, in 2006, a family in Georgia was sued for copyright infringement on the basis of illegal file sharing, when the family didn't even own a computer. The family claimed they had lived in that location for only a year and that perhaps the previous owner of the house had shared the files. Another example is the RIAA's lawsuit against Gertrude Walton. They accused her of sharing over seven hundred songs. Her daughter sent the RIAA a copy of her death certificate, and they dropped the case against Ms. Walton.

Limited Impact

The second reason for the RIAA deciding not to bring new lawsuits is that the lawsuits had little impact on combating free file sharing. RIAA chairman Mitch Bainwol said that the lawsuits had been successful, claiming that piracy would be even worse without them but that "the marketplace has changed" and new methods of combating piracy would be more effective today. On the other hand, Fred von Lohmann, then a staff attorney with the Electronic Frontier Foundation, said the lawsuits simply did not reduce the number of people trading music online. "If the goal is to reduce file sharing," he said, "it's a failure." Fred is now an attorney with Google.

In use of P2P websites, there are ways to avoid getting caught and to hide your identity.

The first is to use a private versus a public BitTorrent site. A private BitTorrent site is one in which the user must be invited. The only way to be invited is by an active member. A private BitTorrent site restricts use by requiring the user to register with the site.

The second way to hide the user's identity is to ensure the user's computer is not acting as a Supernode. A Supernode is a connection point that allows other users to download material from your computer.

Third, the user can use an intranet. An intranet is a private network that securely shares any part of an organization's information or network operating system within that organization. A prime example of an intranet is a network on a college campus.

Fourth, the user can transfer data through instant messaging systems, like AOL Instant Messenger (AIM).

Fifth, the user can utilize a program that blocks "harmful" IP addresses from connecting to the user's computer.

Almost all the RIAA cases were settled. According to Matt Oppenheim, an attorney who used to work for the RIAA, out of the eighteen thousand total cases, eleven thousand were either immediately settled or not prosecuted for some reason by the labels. The other seven thousand people held out or did not respond, and the RIAA filed named federal lawsuits against them. Out of those seven thousand, most of those people settled, with the exception of the over one hundred defendants who filed counterclaims against the RIAA. The causes of action for these counterclaims were abuse of process and civil conspiracy. Most of the counterclaims were dismissed. The only cases that have gone to trial are against Jammie Thomas and Joel Tenenbaum.

Capitol vs. Thomas-Rasset (Minn. Dist. 2010)

This case was against a Native American woman from Brainerd, Minnesota, named Jammie Thomas (now Jammie Thomas-Rasset), in 2007. The trial took place in Duluth, Minnesota, some 117 miles from the defendant's home, and was most decidedly not a trial by a jury of "her peers," since several members had never used the Internet in their lives. The jury awarded the record companies a total of $222,000, or $9,250 per song file, in "statutory" damages—that is, damages based on a statute rather than on any actual losses to the record companies, or profits made by the "infringer" based on infringement of twenty-four song files, having a combined retail value of $23.76. Conservatively estimating the record companies' lost profits from each song at 40 cents per song file, that would make the verdict 23,125 times the actual damage allegedly sustained. Apparently the key items of evidence, in the jurors' minds, were: (a) the fact that the applicable Kazaa username was the same as the defendant's usual e-mail address, and (b) the fact that the defendant's hard drive had crashed, necessitating replacement, both of which circumstances could have been attributable to her computer having been "zombyized." After the jury returned its verdict, the judge determined that he gave an improper instruction to the jury, and that "merely making songs available in the Kazaa shared folder was insufficient to prove distribution," meaning that making the song files available did not constitute copyright infringement.

The second trial occurred in 2009, with a returned verdict for the labels. Thomas-Rasset claimed she did not download music from Kazaa but that her kids or her ex-boyfriend might have. This time the jury awarded the labels $1.9 million, amounting to $80,000 per song. The judge found the award to be excessive and offered the labels an ultimatum: either reduce the award to $2,250 per song, a total of $54,000, or attend a third trial. The labels chose to go to a third trial, because they were concerned about how giving into a lower damage award would affect future cases.

The third trial occurred in early November 2010 and was decided on November 3. The only issue was the damage award. Joe Sibley, Thomas-Rasset's attorney, claimed that the amount of harm done by illegally downloading the twenty-four songs off Kazaa was $.99 to $1.29 per song, the amount it would cost a user to purchase each song on iTunes. However, there was a secondary issue with regard to damages, which is how much harm was done by Thomas-Rasset's sharing of those twenty-four songs with Kazaa users. No one can calculate the exact amount of harm, because no one knows how many other Kazaa users might have downloaded her songs. As discussed above, when damages are difficult to calculate, the court will impose statutory damages. Statutory damages, an award of money based on the Copyright Act, range from $750 to $150,000 per song, and the jury gets to decide the amount based on that range.

The judge refused to instruct the jurors that the amount of the award was required to bear a reasonable relationship to the actual damages sustained by plaintiffs, and the jury returned a verdict of $62,500 per song, for a total of $1.5 million. In his commentary on the case, attorney Ray Beckerman, who has litigated a number of the RIAA cases on behalf of defendants, blogged as follows:

> No surprises here, given the contents of the jury instructions and verdict form. The only surprises are that (a) the judge felt it necessary to have a predictably futile third trial, (b)

the judge refused to instruct the jury that the statutory damages must bear a reasonable relationship to the actual damages, which is a fundamental tenet of the law regarding copyright infringement, and (c) the judge has so far declined to reach the constitutional issue which is staring him in the face. It also seems odd to me that the judge had not instructed the jury that plaintiffs had proved a copying—i.e. a download—but not a "distribution" as defined in the Copyright Act.

RIAA vs. Tenenbaum (D. Mass 2010)

In August 2007, the RIAA sued Joel Tenenbaum for copyright infringement for downloading and sharing thirty-one music files from Kazaa. The case went to trial in July of 2009, and Tenenbaum was represented by Harvard professor Charles Nesson. During the trial, Tenenbaum admitted to downloading the songs. The court found for the RIAA and awarded $675,000 in statutory damages. However, the damage award was reduced by a U.S. District Court judge in Boston, Nancy Gertner, who stated that the amount was "unconstitutionally excessive" and decreased it to $67,500. The case is now on appeal.

Does Providing Access Equal Distribution?

Copyright owners have, among other exclusive rights, the exclusive rights to copy and to distribute. The RIAA could never prove illegal copying, because the files downloaded by P2P users could have been obtained legally—for instance, by downloading the songs off iTunes. They could only propose that the defendants made their files accessible. This begs the question: did these cases have an impact on clarifying the law on whether merely providing access is distribution?

Electra vs. Perez (D. Or. 2006)

Despite the fact that the above two cases went to trial, perhaps the most important file-sharing case to date is *Electra vs. Perez*. This case is one in which the judge ruled on motion that access is equal to distribution. In this case, the defendant, Perez, allegedly downloaded and made music files available for distribution over the Internet using the file-sharing program Kazaa. The judge stated that to prove copyright infringement, the plaintiff must prove two things: (1) ownership of the alleged infringed material, in this case the music; and (2) that the alleged infringer violated one of the rights granted to a copyright holder. A violation of one of the rights would be either making an unauthorized copy or unauthorized distribution of the music. As to the first issue, Elektra was able to prove copyright ownership of the music. As to the second issue, the judge held that by providing evidence that Perez made copyrighted material available for distribution through Kazaa, Elektra "met the necessary elements of a copyright infringement claim," that is, that providing access constitutes an unauthorized distribution.

The case ended up being dismissed because Elektra discovered that it was Perez's family members, rather than Perez himself, who were responsible for the infringement. However, this case is important because it was the first to announce this position, and the issue was a novel one because the copyright law predates the technology at issue.

RIAA's Latest Tactics

After the RIAA abandoned its strategy of filing individual lawsuits in 2008, it turned instead to a series of preliminary agreements with major ISPs in an attempt to track down and punish copyright violators by cutting their Internet service. Using this model, the RIAA has attempted to enact a "graduated response" system whereby a series of written warnings would be mailed to individuals suspected to be illegally downloading. The first two warnings would consist of antipiracy messages. The third warning would result in the individual's ISP cutting back or suspending their Internet service. However, this strategy has been a toothless effort: as previously discussed, under the Digital Millennium Copyright Act, ISPs are not required to send warning letters to users about their illegal behavior, much less cut or suspend their Internet service. However, the RIAA has gotten certain ISPs to take action, and a reported three million[6] warning letters have been mailed from major U.S. ISPs, including AT&T, Comcast, and Verizon. Yet these same ISPs deny that they would ever interrupt service to customers simply because they were accused of copyright violations by the film or music industries. The RIAA went so far as to enlist the help of Andrew Cuomo, New York State's attorney general, to nudge the ISPs into fighting piracy in the same way he pushed them to combat child pornography. This move rubbed some ISP executives the wrong way, because unlike in the war against child pornography, the Digital Millennium Copyright Act is completely on the side of the ISPs.

Unlike in the United States, the RIAA has had some success with emerging anti-copyright policies in Europe, in particular the HADOPI law in France, and the European Union's Intellectual Property Rights Enforcement Directive. France's HADOPI law is essentially what the RIAA was hoping to adopt in the United States—a graduated response, or "three strikes" program, whereby ISPs must cut or suspend copyright violators' Internet service for up to a year. The Intellectual Property Rights Enforcement Directive is a law that enables copyright holders to obtain a court order that requires ISPs to hand over IP addresses of people accused of infringing on intellectual property. This law has led to coordinated efforts among police forces across six countries, including the UK, Belgium. and Sweden, and has even led to arrests in Sweden.

France's Three-Strikes Law

The HADOPI law in France was introduced in 2009 as a means to control and regulate Internet access and encourage compliance with copyright laws. HADOPI (which stands for "Haute Autorité pour la Diffusion des Ouvres et la Protection des Droits sur Internet") is the government agency created by the eponymous law. Despite strong backing from French president Nicolas Sarkozy, the bill was rejected by the French National Assembly on April 9, 2009. The French government asked for reconsideration of the bill by the French National Assembly, and it was adopted on May 12, 2009, by the assembly and on May 13, 2009, by the French senate. The debate around the law has involved accusations of dubious tactics made against the proponents of the law. A "petition of 10,000 artists" in support of the bill was challenged, and numerous signatures were proven to not

---

6. *Billboard,* December 18, 2010, p. 43

come from people engaging in any artistic activities described by the petition, to belong to nonexistent people, or to belong to artists who denied having signed the petition.

On June 10, 2009, the Constitutional Council of France struck down the central yet controversial portion of HADOPI that would have allowed sanctions against Internet users merely *accused,* as opposed to being convicted, of copyright violations, ruling that because "the Internet is a component of the freedom of expression" and "in French law the presumption of innocence prevails," only a judge could impose sanctions under the law. On October 22, 2009, the Constitutional Council of France approved a revised version of HADOPI, requiring judicial review before revoking a person's Internet access but otherwise resembling the original requirements. The HADOPI law remains highly controversial given that, under its jurisdiction, ISPs are not legally required to send written warnings, but they are required to provide the personal contact information for anonymous IP addresses found to be file sharing and face fines of 1,500 euros a day for failing to provide this information.

The enforcement of this law works as follows:

▶ An e-mail is sent to the connection owner and defined by the IP address involved in the claim. The ISP is then supposed to invite the owner to install a filter on his or her own connection. If a repeated offense is suspected by the copyright holders, their representatives, the ISP, or the HADOPI, in the six months following the first step, the second step of the procedure is started.
▶ A certified letter is sent to the connection owner with similar information sent in the first e-mail. On failure to comply or accusation of repeated offenses by the copyright holders, their representatives, the ISP, or the HADOPI, in the year following the reception of the certified letter, the third step of the procedure is started.
▶ The ISP is required to suspend the Internet service for the Internet connection, object of the claim, for two months to one year. The connection owner is blacklisted, and third-party ISPs are prevented from providing him or her an Internet connection. This service suspension doesn't interrupt billing. Eventual charges involved in the service termination are at the connection owner's expense.

Recourse to a judicial court is not possible for the first two steps of the procedure, and the last step is not stoppable by judicial recourse. The charge of the proof is on the connection owner.

Intellectual Property Rights Enforcement Directive

Enacted in 2004, the European Union's Intellectual Property Rights Enforcement Directive enables copyright holders to obtain court orders to require ISPs to hand over IP addresses of people accused of infringing on intellectual property. Though it was due to be fully implemented by 2006, only the UK, France, Belgium, and Sweden have begun to enforce the directive. However, it has led to arrests of individuals found guilty of illegal downloading.

ACTA—the Future of Copyright Protection?

A new trade agreement being privately negotiated by officials from the United States, the European Union, and other countries could go into effect as early as 2011. The United States and Japan proposed the Anti-Counterfeiting Trade Agreement (ACTA) in 2006 as a plurilateral treaty to help in the fight against piracy and was initially discussed in 2006 and 2007 by the United States, Japan, Canada, the European Union, and Switzerland. Negotiations started in June 2008, with the participation of a broader group of participants including Australia, Mexico, Morocco, New Zealand, Republic of Korea, and Singapore and should be concluded by the end *of 2010*. Like HADOPI, the primary goal of ACTA is to establish a standard protocol whereby ISPs warn and then suspend the service of connection owners found guilty of illegal downloading. It is also possible that ACTA could actually set up criminal penalties for illegal file sharing. A document leaked by the French advocacy group La Quadrature du Net revealed ACTA's Chapter 2 Criminal Provisions, which outlined that "each [copyright violator] shall provide for effective proportionate and dissuasive penalties," including "imprisonment and monetary fines." The UK government has officially declared its opposition to ACTA's criminalization provisions, and many find these provisions to be hugely controversial given that all talks have been held in secret thus far.

Part III
How to Succeed in the New Music Business

Chapter 11

How Artists Can Use New Technologies to Succeed

I n this chapter, we will focus on using social networks, blogs, and other digital tools to promote and market your work. At the outset it is important to note that digital tools have made it easier and cheaper to create new music than ever before. I recently discussed this topic with Rick Karr, who is a former NPR journalist and current professor at the Columbia University Graduate School of Journalism. Rick is also a former musician and record producer. This is what he had to say about the new technologies for creating music:

> Twenty years or so ago, I was investing every penny I had in a small eight-track studio in Chicago, and bands would pay me to come in there and craft their demos. Now the equivalent bands are doing their own thing on their own equipment. And there are hundreds of artists like that within half a mile of where I'm sitting in Brooklyn. The music business used to be about controlling access to the means of production and distribution. Now the former is trivial. And artists are reinventing the sound of music. It used to be that only a band as successful as Queen could layer backing vocals the way that they and Roy Thomas Baker did it. Now anyone can do it. That fascinates me, and it's fomenting a revolution in the sound of music that's every bit as powerful as the revolution in business being driven by the net and widespread computing power.

Thanks to relatively inexpensive home recording solutions, with digital audio workstations like Logic, ProTools, and Ableton Live and a host of affordable audio interfaces, writing and producing music at home has become almost the standard for aspiring artists today. In the old days, artists would pay extremely expensive rates for studio engineers and producers to create their demos—now almost anyone with a pair of good ears can do it themselves. Although most artists do go on to work with studios that have better analog equipment (traditional analog equipment still trumps digital audio tools in terms of sound quality), producing one's demos or first recordings at home can be the quickest and easiest way to get one's music into the ears of others.

Social Networks: How to Get the Most from Them

Within the past few years, social networking has become one of the most important means ever developed to keep in touch with friends, family, and colleagues. But social networks have also become one of the most powerful tools that artists and musicians have ever had to advance their careers. At this time it's essential for artists and labels in every kind of music—from electronic to pop and from jazz to rap—to utilize social networking and the web to both create a presence within various online communities and to promote their music. In this chapter we discuss social networks, blogs, and how to create an effective website for your music.

What Is Social Networking? The Essentials of Creating an Online Presence

With a good product and persistence, it is not difficult for new artists to gain traction through social networks and write-ups in music blogs on the web catering to different musical genres and tastes. It's quite simple to promote one's music and image on various social networking sites like Facebook, Twitter, Myspace, Bandcamp, SoundCloud, and Last.fm. Whether you are a folk, pop, rock, indie, electronic, metal, hip-hop, or R&B artist, it is relatively easy in the age of Web 2.0 to create a vibrant online presence that fans from all over the world can engage with. Social networking has in many ways replaced traditional models of reaching out to potential new fans, and this section (as well as the next chapter of this book, written by online marketing expert Jason Spiewak) is dedicated to describing the various methods and strategies for the optimization of online marketing tools.

Social Networking at a Glance

Network	Number of Active Users (as of August 2010)	Start Date	How Musicians Can Use
Facebook	500 Million	February 2004	Create official Page to stay in touch with Fans, create a Facebook Profile to network with actual friends and colleagues
Twitter	190 Million	July 2006	Engage in conversations with fans, other bands and bloggers
Myspace	66 Million	August 2003	Create a Myspace page to showcase music, upcoming shows, bio, pictures, videos

How to Create a Strong Online Presence Through Facebook and Twitter

Facebook and Twitter are becoming increasingly essential social-networking tools for artists. They rank respectively as the number-one and number-two social-networking sites on the Internet,[1] sandwiching Myspace in terms of monthly unique visitors. Both Facebook and Twitter have streamlined user account pages that make accessing information direct and simple. Let's take a moment to explore Facebook and Twitter and how to best optimize them for your own social-marketing strategies.

Facebook Basics

Launched in 2004 by Harvard student Mark Zuckerberg, Facebook has since become the pre-eminent social network on the Internet. According to Alexa Internet rankings, Facebook is the second-most-visited site on the Internet, after Google (number one) and before YouTube (number three).[2] As of July 2010, Facebook reported an active user count of 500 million and enjoys greatest popularity in the United States, the United Kingdom, and, surprisingly, Indonesia. Anyone age thirteen or older with a valid e-mail address can sign up for the free service.

With a Facebook account, users can create pages that include a wealth of information about their lives. They can include information about their schools, jobs, birthdays, romantic-relationship status, political views, favorite TV shows, movies, books, and music; they can upload photos and videos to their Facebook pages; create events and event invitations; post status updates to their "wall," which can include HTML links, photos, videos, and notices of upcoming events. Through myriad options, users easily create online identities for themselves and then create networks of friends, colleagues, and family members, all of whom have their own page and identity on Facebook. As of December 2010, Facebook added an e-mail component that some say is intended to compete with Google's Gmail.

The beauty of Facebook lies in its interface, specifically designed for extremely tight and intimate networked communication. It is incredibly easy to look up others and add them as friends, and establish a large body of friends. Friends can "like" and comment on each other's status updates and share information through posting on each other's wall. Other features on Facebook include the "poke" and "gifts" options, whereby users receive notification of "pokes" from other friends and pay $1 to send little image icons to each other.

Finally, Facebook provides a "news feed," which is a chronological timeline of all posts from those users. You can view your new posts in isolation from posts provided by your friends by clicking on "Profile." The news feed also displays event invitations, notice of uploaded photos, changes to work/school/location/relationship status, and more. Like Twitter, the news feed creates an immersive and never-ending stream of information that is highly addictive.

---

1. "Top 15 Most Popular Social Networking Websites," http://www.ebizmba.com/articles/social-networking-websites, August 4, 2010.

2. "Top Sites: The Top 500 Sites on the Web," http://www.alexa.com/topsites/global, August 4, 2010.

Facebook for Artists: Do's and Don'ts

Artists can use Facebook in two ways—by utilizing their basic Facebook profile, and by creating an official Facebook "Fan Page."

Do's:

▶ Keep existing friends informed of what's going on with your music, without being excessively self-promoting.

▶ "Friend" contacts that you meet through attending events and playing gigs.

▶ "Friend" contacts that you meet online through other social networks—these could be bloggers, label owners, and/or other musicians in your scene.

▶ Cross-pollinate! Promote the work of others in your scene—invite your friends to events held by other artists and labels, and create status updates with links to press and websites of other artists and labels.

Don'ts:

▶ Don't excessively self-promote—your friends will think that you are interested only in yourself!

▶ Don't be too serious about your own project—you want to keep the tone on your own profile informal.

▶ Don't friend people that you haven't met in person or online before—this is an obnoxious practice and will make you come off as aggressive or overly eager.

The Facebook Page—aka Fan Pages

Perhaps the most powerful tool that Facebook offers to artists and bands is "the page," also sometimes referred to as the Facebook "Fan Page." The page is intended for organizations or people who would like to communicate with a group of people and is also used by public figures and companies to communicate with their fans and customers. It is obvious that artists and record labels are candidates for using this important tool, and they do. The difference between a normal Facebook account and a Facebook page is that you must have a basic Facebook profile for yourself before you can create a Facebook page. Also, you cannot friend other users on Facebook through your page—you can add contacts only through your basic Facebook account. The beauty of the Facebook page is that anyone—any artist, band, or label—can create and maintain a Facebook page from the personal account.

How to Set Up Your Page and How to Use It

To set up a page, you must already have a basic Facebook profile. Then simply visit any page on Facebook, and in the bottom left hand corner you'll see a link that says "Create a Page." Then you will be directed to set up your own page!

The Benefits of Having a Facebook Page

To put it into perspective, one-third of Facebook users—and that's over 100 million people—are a fan of at least one music artist or band page, and the average user becomes a fan of four pages each month. This means that it's absolutely essential to have a page for your solo project, band, or label. Facebook pages can include pictures, a bio, links to press, and other related stories about your project. Through a Facebook page you can create official events through your page identity. You can also keep your fans up-to-date with status updates on your like page—each time you create an update, it will be displayed in your fans' respective news feeds. The status updates can feature new tracks you've made, upcoming shows, recent press, new photos, links to new music videos on YouTube/Vimeo, and more. Furthermore, you can upload and display MP3s using the Facebook Music Player application.

The page is the best way to utilize Facebook for promotional purposes. You can invite your existing friends on Facebook to become a fan of your page, and they can in turn suggest your page to other friends of theirs. Your fans can then stay easily up-to-date with what's going on with your project, simply because your updates will show in their news feeds along with the endless other updates from their friends and other pages.

How to Use the Facebook Page: Do's and Don'ts

Do's:

▶ Use a first-person voice to show fans you are active on the page, and encourage them to post feedback and comments.

▶ Share everyday stories to bring fans closer to you—share behind-the-scenes updates and content, such as candid photos of you at rehearsal, on the road, or just relaxing.

▶ Ask fans a question now and then in your status updates to generate conversation, and show that you're listening by responding with comments to fan replies.

▶ Run a paid Facebook ad campaign, which will target fans of similar bands to generate more interest.

Don'ts:

▶ Don't post more than a couple of status updates each day—you do not want to inundate your fans with unnecessary content and perhaps turn them off from wanting to stay in touch with you.

▶ Don't send excessive mass messages to your entire page membership—send mass messages only when you have an announcement like an album release or a very important gig.

▶ Don't aggressively invite your friends to become fans of your page—invite them once, but don't persistently remind them again and again. Remember that Facebook is a community of friends, not consumers!

Twitter

Since its creation in 2006, Twitter has become the second-most-active social network on the Internet, with over 100 million users worldwide. Twitter is a microblogging service that enables its users to send and read other user messages, called "tweets." Tweets are text-based posts of up to 140 characters displayed on the author's profile page. Users can subscribe to (or "follow" in Twitter-speak) other users' feeds, whereby the user will receive their tweets in reverse chronological stream on their main Twitter homepage. It is described as the SMS of the Internet—SMS stands for Short Message Service, the standard service for worldwide mobile-phone text messages—because users can send tweets from mobile phones and smart-phone Twitter applications. Users can easily cross-pollinate tweets by directing them to the attention of certain users (through the use of the @ symbol, followed by the user's name—for example, "Can't wait for the @brahmsband show tonight!"). You can also create a hashtag, which is a pound or hash symbol before a word that will be the subject of a search by others on twitter. The word used as a hashtag will be later searchable on Twitter (for example, "Can't wait for the @brahmsband show tonight! #brahmsband"). Users could search tweets about Brahms and see what was written about the band. Users can also retweet the tweets of other users (for example, "RT @brahmsband Come see us play tonight @ mercurylounge!").

The tipping point for Twitter's popularity was its promotion during the 2007 South by Southwest film and music festival, during which usage of the service increased from twenty thousand to sixty thousand tweets per day.

Here are a few stats on Twitter's tremendous popularity:

▶ number of tweets, daily: 70 million
▶ number of tweets, monthly: 2 billion
▶ of registered users: 145 million
▶ number of account sign-ups, daily: 300,000[3]

As a social network, Twitter is based on two principles—subscription ("following") and cross-pollination. Following creates the foundation for communication on Twitter, and cross-pollination enriches the content and searchability of your tweets. As an aspiring artist, band, or record label, it's essential to know the subtleties of Twitter and how to best optimize it for promotion of your online identity and brand. Outlined here are successful methods for the optimization of following and cross-pollination:

1. Subscription Strategies

As always, your goal should be to have high online visibility with those who would be interested in your music and brand. Therefore, your goal with Twitter should be to secure a high number of followers, interested in staying in touch with you and up-to-date on what's going on with your project. What are the best ways to secure a high number of followers?

---

3. Source: Matt Graves, communications director @ Twitter, August 2010.

a. *Less is more*—There's a temptation to start mass-following others on Twitter, in the hopes that others will follow you back. Resist this temptation. Twitter does not penalize users for mass following, but it simply does not look good to start mass following on Twitter. There's no guarantee that others will follow you back, and there's no way that others will be able to read your tweets unless they follow you back or visit your profile page. The best thing to do is to selectively and slowly create a list of those you follow, and develop relationships with those few that follow you back. Allow others to follow you first, as well. A smaller, tighter network is vastly stronger than a wide, empty one.

b. *What to say*—Once you have secured followers, be sure to stay in touch with them and engage with them in a meaningful way. Resist the urge to post about mundane minutiae (for example, "Wow Frosted Flakes taste ggrrrrrreatt!"), but also resist the urge to endlessly self-promote. Strike a balance between promoting your own project, supporting the projects of others in your network or scene, and posting about relevant and interesting content. For example, if you are a hip-hop artist, post links to articles or interviews about MCs that have inspired you, in addition to any upcoming shows you have or recent press you've received. If you're a folk musician, post a link to a story about music and activism, in addition to posting about fellow folk artists and your upcoming releases. The more interesting the content you post, the more likely it is that followers will respond to or retweet your tweets, which will help you gain more followers.

2. Cross-Pollination Strategies

Equally as important as tastefully following and being followed is the successful use of cross-pollinating tactics. The correct use of replies, retweets, and hashtags can go a long way in enriching the relevance and searchability of your tweets. Let's explain:

a. *Replies*—Replying to others' tweets is a great way to start dialogue with another user, especially if they haven't started following you yet. If you use the @ symbol with their username directly proceeding (i.e., @brahmsband), your Tweet will be sent to their @ brahmsband list and later show up in search results for that user's account. In addition to starting a dialogue and potentially gaining a new follower, you also show that you are interested in using Twitter to actually communicate with others, as opposed to endless self-promotion. Moreover, other users who reply to you will increase the visibility of your name on Twitter and entice other followers of theirs to start following you.

b. *Retweets*—If you find another user's tweet interesting, you can retweet the post to your own feed, so that your followers can read that user's tweet. It may seem like a redundant practice to quote other users in this way, but it's actually an incredibly useful means to increase your own visibility—if you retweet another user's post, they'll see the post later as being retweeted by you, and your name will also show up in search results in connection with this other user, through your retweet. Furthermore, those who retweet your posts will increase the visibility of your username on Twitter and entice other users to start following you.

c. *Hashtags, or, #increasingyourvisibility*—Hashtags are also a key way to stay in touch on Twitter. Hashtags start with the # symbol, followed by a word or phrase with no spaces, and increase the searchability of your tweet, if you use hashtags that other users might also use. For example, #nowplaying is a very common hashtag that users include with tweets about bands or artists that they are interested in, because many, many users also use that hashtag, making it easy to find out about new bands and artists through Twitter.

Is Myspace Dead?

Launched in August 2003, Myspace was *the* destination for music-related social networking. With both regular user and music accounts, fans and musicians alike could create pages to interact with each other, and musicians could easily friend other musicians, thus creating virtual communities based on mutual genres or location. In June 2006, it was ranked the most popular social-networking site in the United States, but in recent years other sites have risen far past Myspace. In April 2008, Facebook came out on top as the world's premier social network. As other sites like Twitter and YouTube soar in popularity, Myspace seems to be stopping dead in its tracks. The pages became inundated with advertisements, especially after Rupert Murdoch acquired Myspace for $580 million in 2005, and the interface was clunky in comparison to Facebook and YouTube, not to mention the music player crushing MP3s to 96 kbps, a dreadfully low bit rate that often severely distorts the original sound. With the panoply of options for sharing one's music online, is Myspace really necessary anymore?

I posed this very question on my blog while completing the third edition of this book, and the responses were mixed, deeming Myspace either completely dead, a beached whale but still alive, or useful in its own right. One reader linked us to an article[4] he wrote on why Myspace is still valid, and the points of his argument were indeed relevant:

▶ Myspace still attracts millions of unique visitors per month.
▶ Myspace indexes well on Google and other search engines—your Myspace artist page will usually appear at the top of search results, making it easy for others to find your music.
▶ The more play hits you get in your Myspace music player, the more visibility you will have on Myspace itself. Your page will show up higher in Myspace search results, making it easier for potential fans to find out about you and your music.
▶ Myspace is a quick and familiar way for people to check out your music, image, and upcoming tour dates.

All good points. The article cited the following tips to best optimize your Myspace experience:

▶ Don't include more content than is necessary—the more videos, slideshows, and widgets you include on your page, the longer the load time will be, and the more likely new fans

---

4. *Tight Mix,* June 2, 2010 http://tightmixblog.com/social-media/is-Myspace-still-important-for-a-musicians-online-presence/.

will be deterred from hearing your music because your site is simply too cluttered with information.

▶ Don't bother with leaving comments on others' pages—it looks tacky because about half of Myspace comments are now just spam. Consider even removing the comments and "Top Friends" sections from your page, and allow your site to feature just your music, brand, and upcoming shows.

Myspace's New Redesign

Myspace officially rolled out its long-overdue redesign as this book was being delivered to my publisher in December 2010. It made the "s" in MySpace lowercase (now Myspace) and incorporated some new features. Myspace has begun to offer new profile templates for music pages. The new Myspace design is more consistent with Web 2.0 aesthetics, with cleaner presentation of content, simple navigation, and links to other social networks, games, video, and music news. The design overhaul might make Myspace relevant again. Apart from the Web 2.0 style makeover, the new Myspace design offers the following attractive options:

▶ Artists/bands can now upload up to twenty-five songs (as opposed to ten previously).
▶ Dozens of different page themes are now available.
▶ The ability to create a customized marquee header has been added.

Already, acts like Lady Antebellum, Outkast, the Decemberists, Imogen Heap, and the Black Eyed Peas (who have also become pitchmen for the site) have embraced the new Myspace Music design changes. When I visited these artists' profile pages, one of the first things to stand out was the Twitter widget at the top of the page, displaying the band's most recent tweet in quote format. Perhaps I'm not completely used to Twitter yet, but I found this slightly jarring—the attempt at making the Myspace page more open or more human with a Twitter update actually made the page feel more sterile. I would argue that many bands will maintain their pages with the original Myspace layout, simply because it's been the standard for years now, and the new layout is not as customizable as the original. Yet the simplicity of the new design is undeniable, and consumers of music who have grown up in the Web 2.0 era will no doubt be drawn to the new design.

Myspace announced it will focus on promoting curators, it says, "a subset of its audience whose reputation and knowledge around particular entertainment topics and emerging cultural trends make them uniquely influential—by supporting them with the resources, tools and a platform to expand their reach within the Myspace community." That all sounds very impressive, but can Myspace really be saved from obsolescence? Since Rupert Murdoch paid $580 million dollars for it in 2005, its popularity has been on a consistent downward trajectory, and this much-trumpeted overhaul could be too little, too late.

I asked the editor of Digitalmusicnews.com, Paul Resnikoff, for his opinion of Myspace's new design, and this is what he wrote:

Once upon an Internet time, back in 2005, the chaotic look n' feel of the original MySpace was a selling point. Every page was a kludge, a messy teenager's bedroom online. Well, that's no more, and like a club gone stale, MySpace is no longer hot—just like that. And even though MySpace's neater redesign and interface were sorely needed by 2010, the bigger exodus was well underway.

So what does that mean for artists? Sure, the new Myspace is losing traffic by the minute, but don't believe all the hype. Bands are still wise to create, maintain, and interact with their Myspace Music profiles, for a variety of reasons. There's still lots of traffic flow, both from within Myspace and from outside referral points like Google. In fact, Myspace could easily be the first landing pad off of Google, and the first impression that a fan, music supervisor, or other potential business partner sees.

The reality is that audiences are fragmented—sure, they tend to glom around Facebook, Twitter, Google, and YouTube, but there's so much more action beneath those behemoths. In fact, it wasn't too long ago that if a band lacked a Myspace profile, they might as well not have existed. That legacy still counts for something, at least at the time of this writing.

On top of that, Myspace is now making serious efforts to redial its focus back toward music and entertainment. They've lost the social-networking war to Facebook—that game is over—but Facebook isn't interested in music in the way that Myspace is. In fact, Facebook users can now connect into Myspace to follow some of their favorite artists, and MySpace is continuing to make efforts to own this niche. Let's see how this plays out.

Social-Networking Aggregators

Staying in touch on Myspace, Facebook, Twitter, and other social networks can be difficult to juggle after a while. How can you keep up with individually posting at each site? Save yourself some time and sign up with a social-networking aggregate service that can update your posts across the board and collect updates from individual networks. TweetDeck is a useful tool to synchronize the three networks—with TweetDeck you can update your Myspace, Facebook, and Twitter statuses simultaneously, and you can stay in touch that much easier (and faster). Furthermore, services like Disqus allow you to leave comments on blogs and other websites as being from a public social-networking account—this means that comments you leave on blogs or other websites will show up as status updates in the social-networking account you connected Disqus to. This is a key tool for developing lines of communication with bloggers and other online journalists (see the section on blogs below).

How to Go Viral on YouTube and How to Use Ustream

During my years at Sony I was known as the "Video Guy," since I was director of business affairs for all things video at Columbia and Epic, including every music video we did there for ten years, by artists such as Michael Jackson, Bruce Springsteen, Pearl Jam, Billy Joel, Lauryn Hill, Bob Dylan, and Mariah Carey.

The average cost of a video was six figures and up, except for Michael Jackson's, which cost more like a million and up. Now it's possible to make your own video, launch it on YouTube, and get more views than many of the most successful videos we ever broadcasted on MTV. And if you haven't noticed, music videos are hardly played on MTV anymore! YouTube is in fact the new MTV for music, except you don't have be represented by a big label to get a video put up. Since launching in 2005,[5] YouTube has become the number-two search engine in the world (following Google) and has become the Internet's third-most-visited site after Google and Facebook. [6]According to its website, people are watching two billion videos a day on YouTube and uploading hundreds of thousands of videos daily. Recently, Lady Gaga and Justin Bieber both crossed the one-billion-views mark.

YouTube should be considered a primary tool in any aspiring artist's arsenal of social networking strategies, simply due to the fact that tens of millions of people visit YouTube every day, plus anything that's uploaded has a chance of going "viral." What does viral mean? Viral could mean a prank video that gets millions of views. But it could also mean underground producers such as Mysto and Pizzi, who have developed a cultlike audience to watch them make remixes of well-known hits. For instance, a video depicting them working on the remix of "I Got a Feeling" by the Black Eyed Peas garnered over 1.8 million views. But in addition to the viral phenomenon, YouTube can be a means of being "discovered" by the one person who can make you a success. That's precisely what happened with Justin Bieber.

The Justin Bieber Story

When Justin Bieber was twelve years old, he came in second place in a local singing competition for his version of Ne-Yo's "So Sick." His mother, Pattie Mallette, posted the video on YouTube for friends and family to watch, and she continued to upload videos of her son's performances. While searching for videos of a different singer, the former marketing executive of So So Def, Scooter Braun, viewed one of Bieber's videos by accident. He knew talent when he heard it and tracked down Bieber in his hometown of Stratford, Ontario. After some convincing, Mallette agreed to let Braun take Bieber to Atlanta to record demo tapes. A week later, Bieber was singing on a track for Usher, who arranged an audition at Island Def Jam Music Group. Bieber was signed to Island Records in October 2008 and has since moved to Atlanta with his mother to base his career there. Bieber is now a superstar. Without YouTube, you might well never have heard of him!

CSS and iPod Success

CSS (Cansei de Ser Sexy) is a Brazilian pop band that gained notoriety after one of their songs, "Music Is My Hot, Hot Sex," was featured in an iPod commercial. How did it happen? Simple—a fan of theirs, eighteen-year-old Nick Haley, created a homemade fan video for the iPod Touch using their song. Executives at Apple caught wind of this fan video and later got in touch with CSS to license the same song in a *real* iPod commercial. Though CSS had already experienced a level of success prior to this event (they were signed to Sub Pop and had the same song featured in a Zune commercial a year prior), the iPod spot helped sell loads of singles, and their popularity skyrocketed.

---

5. In November 2006, YouTube, LLC was bought by Google for $1.65 billion and now operates as a subsidiary of Google.

6. http://www.alexa.com/topsites, August 10, 2010.

OK Go Becomes a Household Name from Making a $20 Video

Though already signed to Capitol Records, pop rock band OK Go was not selling a lot of records and was facing virtual obscurity—until a homemade video parodying the dance moves of 'N Sync, which cost in total $20 to make, spread like wildfire in the YouTube community. The band's popularity soared, and they subsequently released another homemade video featuring choreographed dancing on treadmills ("This Too Shall Pass"). Again, the video was a viral hit, getting over fourteen million hits in the first two years after its debut, and OK Go has since become famous in the viral video world for releasing a string of massively successful videos (including a series sponsored by State Farm). After becoming a household name, the band was able to leave their label, start their own management company called Paracadute, and still make money.

OK Go's lead singer, Damian Kulash, published a thought-provoking piece on the future of the music industry and how it will be key to have corporate sponsors underwrite content generation:

> My rock band has leapt across treadmills, camouflaged ourselves in wallpaper, performed with the Notre Dame marching band, danced with a dozen trained dogs, made an animation with 2,300 pieces of toast, crammed a day-long continuous shot into 4½ minutes and built the first ever Rube Goldberg machine—least that we know of—to operate in time to music. We are known for our music videos, which we make with the same passion and perseverance we do our songs. Our videos have combined views in excess of 120 million on YouTube alone, with countless millions more from television and repostings all over the Internet.
>
> For most people, the obvious question is: Has this helped sell records? The quick answer is yes. We've sold more than 600,000 records over the last decade. But the more relevant answer is that doesn't really matter. A half a million records is nothing to shake a stick at, but it's the online statistics that set the tone of our business and, ultimately, the size of our income.
>
> We once relied on investment and support from a major label. Now we make a comparable living raising money directly from fans and through licensing and sponsorship. Our bank accounts don't rival Lady Gaga's, but we've got more creative freedom than we did as small fish in her pond.[7]

OK Go is a good example of how a band can continue to make a good living without the help of a label by using social media and sponsorships in today's music business.

How to Broadcast Yourself on Ustream

An exciting new way to engage online audiences is to stream live video of yourself on Ustream. It is a free online service where you can create your own live video broadcast show, with a social-networking follower aspect similar to Twitter. Ustream was founded in March 2007 and has since gained more than two million registered users, who generate 1.5 million-plus hours of live streamed content per month.

---

7. *Business Week,* December 20, 2010.

All you need to use Ustream is a computer, a webcam, and a solid Internet connection—once you sign up for an account on Ustream, you can create a new broadcast show for yourself, and instantly begin streaming the video from your webcam to your own uStream video player for anyone online to view. You can also embed the live video player into your own website, allowing for fans to visit your own website and watch streaming footage of you or your band.

Curious to learn more about Ustream, I created an account for myself. I realized it would be useful for my own podcast—I could do live video broadcasting of the interviews I conduct, as well as various lectures and seminars. On the site, I discovered that the broadcasts were organized by category—so I selected the "music" category, and the first video to show up in the search results was a live broadcast of Bow Wow behind his desk and chatting on a speakerphone with fans about his most recent movie role. The Ustream page reported nearly one thousand active viewers. In addition, a live-chat application directly adjacent to the video player displayed comments from several Bow Wow fans expressing their excitement about watching him live, as well as commenting on the conversation he was carrying on with fans on speakerphone. I then understood how amazing this new technology is—it's now possible to go even further with video than YouTube and create your own live video broadcasts—absolutely free. This site may prove immensely useful for artists and bands who wish to broadcast live streams of their performances, or even of situations like interviews, being in the studio, rehearsing, and so on—to create another way to intimately connect with new audiences.

Music Blogs: The New Tastemakers

At the same time as Facebook and Twitter have captured the attention of tens of millions of users, dedicated music blogs such as Pitchfork and Brooklyn Vegan have become critical to the success of independent artists such as Arcade Fire. For those of you who have been hesitant to take the leap into Internet culture, a blog is simply an online journal (*blog* is an abbreviation of the word *weblog*). As of the end of 2009, there were over 130 million blogs on the Internet, and among these are millions of music blogs, all catering to different genres, styles, and taste preferences. Music blogs are an incredibly useful resource for aspiring musicians, because they are one of the easiest ways to gain Internet publicity and promotion. The dissemination of information on blogs is viral—if one blog features your music, it is possible that other bloggers will take notice and do the same. This section will discuss blogs, bloggers, and blog aggregators, and how to develop lasting friendships with bloggers. If used correctly, blogs may not only generate free publicity online for aspiring artists, but also can lead to positive attention from labels, booking agents, and venues.

Case Study—Arcade Fire and Their Viral Success

Arcade Fire, a band from Montreal, is an excellent example of the power of blogging as a tool for music discovery. Prior to September 2004, they released one EP and toured as an opening act for another band. A combination of the promise demonstrated in their recording and the excitement generated in their live show got them signed to the Chapel Hill, North Carolina, label Merge Records. Merge manufactured and released ten thousand copies of the act's album *Funeral* in mid-September. Around that time, several MP3 blogs that cover rock releases started singing the praises of this album and offered one or more MP3s for download. As a result of this coverage, at least in part, record stores couldn't keep up with growing demand for the album. In mid-October, the band performed at the Merge Records showcase at New York's Mercury Lounge. Several MP3 bloggers and other journalists were spotted in the front row, watching the band and taking photos. Win Butler, the band's front man, told the crowd, "I'd like to thank the Internet." After this showcase, MP3 bloggers got back online and reported how amazing the band's performance was. Even the *New York Times* took notice and quickly informed their readers about this red-hot band. A month later, Arcade Fire played a show at the Bowery Ballroom, which offered more than twice the capacity of their last New York show, and this time the show sold out weeks beforehand. Less than two months after *Funeral*'s initial release, Merge had sold forty thousand copies, making it the fastest-selling album in the label's history. Arcade Fire released their third studio album, The Suburbs, in 2010 to further critical and commercial acclaim, receiving Grammy nominations for Best Alternative Album and Album of the Year.

An Overview of Music Blogs

Blogs are self-published online journals maintained by writers covering an endless range of topics. Here are some quick statistics about blogs:[8]

- ▶ Approximately 133 million blogs exist.
- ▶ 77 percent of Internet users read blogs.
- ▶ Two-thirds of bloggers are male.
- ▶ 60 percent of bloggers are eighteen to forty-four years old.
- ▶ 75 percent of bloggers have college degrees.
- ▶ 75 percent of bloggers are employed full time.

Who Are Bloggers—and More Important, *Music* Bloggers?

Bloggers tend to be literate, nerdy, and very enthusiastic about what they feature or discuss. Music bloggers are no exception—they are fierce music fans, often obsessively so. Some music bloggers love to write about new and yet-undiscovered acts; some choose to feature what larger sites have already featured (artists that have the cultural "stamp of approval"); some write only about hard rock; some only about a very obscure type of dance music; some only about hip-hop. Music bloggers' tastes vary widely, but one thread remains the same—they are devoted music fans who frequently write articles on the bands and artists that they enjoy.

Which Blogs Should I Approach?

The most important factor in getting blog write-ups is to do your research—be absolutely meticulous in finding blogs that write about the kind of music you make. Find blogs that feature the style or genre you are working in, as many blogs are genre-specific and will not post MP3s of artists who fall outside their preferred genres (remember—bloggers are mostly intense music nerds who tend

---

8. "70 Usable Stats from the 2009 State of the Blogosphere," www.thefuturebuzz.com/2009/12/10/blogging-stats-facts-data.

to obsess over a few different genres and feature only artists that fall within their taste spectrum). Also, be sure to seek out blogs that feature artists at your level of visibility. There are plenty of music blogs on the Internet devoted to exposing new artists—seek these blogs out. There's not much point in sending e-mails to blogs that feature more established artists—many bloggers lament receiving hundreds of e-mails a day from aspiring musicians and simply have to delete whatever they don't instantly recognize by name. With a little research you can find many blogs well suited to your type of music and your level of success.[9]

How to Attract Bloggers to Your Music

Let's discuss appropriate ways to contact bloggers. Remember that (1) they receive many e-mails a day from artists just like you, and (2) they are *human*—though many music bloggers make a career simply from writing, the vast majority are either working or in school and take time out of their already busy schedules to maintain a blog. You need to consider ways in which you can get an edge on other artists in actually establishing a rapport with potential writers:

1. *Actually read the blogs:* by following the blogs you'd like to be featured on, and leaving comments about their posts (not spam posts like "You're awesome—check out my band") on a regular basis can help you establish a relationship you can later draw upon when contacting for a write-up. Plus, you'll get a better sense of whether the blog would feature your kind of music at your level of accomplishment.
2. *What to write:* when sending e-mails to bloggers, try to at least find out their first names (located usually in the "about" or "contact" sections of their sites) and send a *personal* e-mail to each blogger. Never send a mass e-mail to two hundred bloggers—they will get turned off and feel slighted. Send a personal e-mail with an individual comment directed toward the blog (i.e., "I read that article about this band, I like your writing," etc.), and then keep your e-mail short and sweet. Come up with a clever one-sentence description of your music, include no more than three tracks to listen to, and then describe your upcoming projects (a forthcoming EP, a remix, a show at this venue). Bloggers tend to love music videos, because they are stimulating for their readers both musically and visually; try to make a video for one of the tracks you send, even if it is a budget, DIY kind of video.
3. *Be sure to include links to other instances of your music online:* Your Myspace, Facebook and Twitter pages are a good place to start. Your SoundCloud, Last.fm, and Bandcamp pages are also good sites to direct to. However, be sure to again not overload your e-mail request—include a maximum of three links.
4. *Don't follow up:* As stated before, bloggers are people with lives just like you. If a blogger likes your music and wants to post it, they will let you know. There is no quicker way to turn off a blogger than to follow up with them on whether they received your e-mail or not.

---

9. A Google search for "music blogs" revealed many websites such as www.music-favourites.blogspot.com that list hundreds of blogs in different genres.

Aggregators

The beauty of blogs is that they are often aggregated—meaning, posts from hundreds of different blogs are gathered onto large sites and displayed together as one all-inclusive RSS feed. Examples include Hypem.com, Elbo.ws, and We Are Hunted. Try to seek out blogs that are aggregated on larger sites, because these posts will be visible for a larger audience. Users of aggregate services are often on the lookout for the next big thing and will scour through MP3s on a daily basis.

Start Your Own Blog

Another useful way to gain traction in the blogging community is to start your own blog and feature artists you enjoy. Then it's possible to establish a rapport with other bloggers first on an intellectual or curatorial basis. Once a relationship has been developed in this way, it will be much easier for you to contact them directly about your own project. Bear in mind that several A&R, PR, and label representatives maintain their own music blogs, so oftentimes maintaining your own blog can be the quickest way to get in touch with those in the business.

Your Website: How to Make It Great

Why Your Own Website Is Essential in Crafting an Online Presence

Perhaps the most important part of your digital arsenal is your website. The primary reason for artists, particularly up-and-coming acts, to invest time, energy, and a modest amount of money in a quality website is that the Internet provides a worldwide audience for your music. Your website can be your press kit, making any physical press kit almost irrelevant in today's world. You can use your website as a vehicle to create a strong and credible web presence. Through your website, you can promote, sell, and distribute your own music as either physical albums or downloads, sell merchandise, and promote live performances and tours.

Some argue that an artist's website is irrelevant in the age of social networks, asking, "Why would I need a website when I already have a Myspace page, a Facebook page, and a Twitter account?" While these pages do offer platforms for content once available only on a dedicated website (including a music player, the ability to link to shopping carts, and mailing lists), it is still nevertheless essential to have a website for the following reasons:

- ▶ A well-developed website will make your project look professional and easily searchable on engines like Google and Yahoo.
- ▶ It allows you to have full control over essential aspects of your online presence, e-commerce, and mailing lists, and it lessens reliance on third-party providers' platforms, rules, and business models. Control and stability in the rocky terrain of the Internet is invaluable, though it does involve some care and maintenance.
- ▶ Your website can serve as a highly connected hub, linking to all your other social-networking accounts—this cohesive element will add further credibility to your Internet presence.

Methods to Easily Create Your Own Website

What you need to bring to the table: There are three essential forms of content that you, as the artist, need to furnish to create a website: a bio, high-quality photos, and at least several high-quality samples of your music. These items have traditionally constituted a basic press package that managers and agents use for radio promotion and to get club gigs and record deals. They are also the core of any good website. Other essential items are tour schedules and a mailing list, so that fans can keep up-to-date with upcoming shows and announcements. Additional materials like videos and links to press write-ups are helpful, as well. Finally, it is necessary to consider a visual layout of the site, or how you want to project your music aesthetically. But before we go any further, let's cover all the bases and outline three elements common to all websites:

1. *Domain name:* The unique ID that points to your website, such as www.stevegordonlaw.com. Domain names include a suffix such as .com, .org, .gov, or .tv. You can purchase domain names from sites called "registrars." For more information on securing and protecting your domain name, see Chapter 2.
2. *Web hosting*: No matter what you have on your website, you'll need a "web host" to make your site available over the Internet. The physical computer where your website exists is called the *server.* A server is a computer or device on a network that manages network resources. GoDaddy.com is an example of a good web hosting service, as they offer domain name registration along with their hosting services in a single, inexpensive package.
3. *Web design*: What shows up when people type in your domain name and are transported to your site. The cost can range from nothing—if you do it yourself or your friend does it for you for free, to a few hundred bucks for a bare-bones site created by a professional (such as my site, www.stevegordonlaw.com, which cost me $500) or a couple of thousand dollars or more for a site designed by a respected commercial service. But bear in mind that the competition for your website design and hosting dollars is fierce, with many competitors, so it is really a buyer's market and you can find great deals.

How you go about obtaining and maintaining these elements is up to you, but there is no way around having all three.

Jargon. The Internet, much like the music business, has its own unique jargon that can be intimidating to those who aren't familiar with it. Here are some additional key terms that will likely turn up quite a bit in developing your website.

▶ *Browser:* The software used to view, manage, and access web pages. The two most popular browsers are Firefox and Microsoft Internet Explorer. Web pages often appear differently depending on the brand and version of the browser intended to view them in.
▶ *Cascading style sheets (CSS):* CSS is a programming language used to describe the presentation semantics (the look and format) of a document written in a markup language, usually HTML.

▶ *Digital Rights Management, or DRM:* Coding computer files, including music files, to limit portability and/or facilitate payment options.

▶ *e-commerce:* A term that refers to the growing retail, service, and business-to-business industries on the World Wide Web. E-commerce websites facilitate the buying and selling of goods and services, including music, over the Internet.

▶ *Flash:* An animation technology. Flash animations are quick to download, are of high quality, and are browser independent, meaning they look the same on different browsers.

▶ *HTML:* Stands for Hypertext Markup Language; a cross-platform text-formatting system for creating web pages, including text, images, sounds, frames, animation, and more. A website is a collection of electronic pages generally mapped out in HTML and designed in CSS.

▶ *Hyperlink or link:* An electronic connection between one web page to either other web pages on the same website, or web pages located on another website.

▶ *Java:* Java is a programming language, created by Sun Microsystems, that can be used to create animation as well as more complex applications such as a calculator.

▶ *JPEG:* Stands for Joint Photographic Experts Group. File format for full-color and black-and-white graphic images.

▶ *RealPlayer, Quicktime, Windows Media Player:* Plug-in applications developed by RealNetworks, Apple, and Microsoft, respectively, that allow users to hear and see audio and video files saved in various file formats. These programs also deliver streaming media, that is, audio or video broadcast live over the Internet. Clicking on certain hyperlinks within a website will cause your web browser to activate these programs.

▶ *URL:* The acronym *URL* stands for "Uniform Resource Locator" and is an address of an individual web page element or web document on the Internet.

▶ *Web 2.0: The term Web 2.0* describes the Internet after the advent of interactive information sharing, interoperability, and user-centered design and the proliferation of social networks. A Web 2.0 site gives its users the free choice to interact or collaborate with each other in a social-media dialogue as creators (prosumers) of user-generated content in a virtual community, in contrast to websites where users (consumers) are limited to the passive viewing of content that was created for them. Examples of Web 2.0 sites include streamlined pages with simple layouts and easy access to relevant information, blogs, and social networks.

Two glossaries offering comprehensive definitions of the above terms and many more are located at www.the-marketing-shop.com/social-networking-terms-web-20 and www.getnetwise.org/glossary.php.

What to Include on Your Website and Why

You should conceptualize what you want your site to look like and what you want to accomplish before designing the actual web page. What is the first thing you want people to see when they log on to the site: flash animation, or an ad for a new release, or an e-mail list sign-up? What kind of color scheme do you want for the site? What visual elements will you use to make the site easy to navigate? These questions are very important if you are building your site yourself. If a site has a good "flow" or aesthetic, it can draw a great deal of attention and enhance your image. Bear in mind that you want your site to have a Web 2.0 flow—you want to make sure that information (photos, MP3s, bio, tour dates) is quickly and easily accessible, that the layout is simple and easy to navigate, and that it offers links to other social networks that you use.

The process by which web pages are created is called "coding" or "scripting." A web designer creates everything you see on a website using Internet programming languages, generally HTML and CSS. HTML is rather complex, and it is not recommended that you undertake the task of coding your website from scratch unless you have a solid background in computers. However, if you do wish to design your own site, there are several programs that can make the process less tedious. Microsoft's FrontPage, Adobe's Creative Suite, and Macromedia's Dreamweaver are software programs that allow the user to create a web page not by "coding," but rather by manipulating the graphical interface. In addition, Macromedia's Flash program has become something of a visual necessity for artist web pages, allowing for an array of stimulating visual designs to be implemented in addition to regular HTML scripting. Flash is usually seen on the "intros" of many artists' sites.

These programs do not require an actual knowledge of HTML, and all of them come bundled with useful tutorials. For those who wish to acquire professional web-development skills, schools of continuing education affiliated with major universities such as the New School or NYU in New York City provide courses in web design at reasonable prices taught by competent instructors.

Templates: Another available option that requires little time and money is purchasing a premade template. Here, you would still need to set up web hosting and acquire your domain name, but the design of the website is already completed for you. All you have to do is make some minor changes to the text of the website in order to tailor it to your band, and upload the site to your hosting company. Unlike creating the website from scratch, using a premade template could generate a fully functional, professional-looking website in a very brief period of time. Websites such as www. freetemplates.com and www.flashtemplates.com offer many free or very inexpensive complete and professional websites, and many of them include music-related themes.

Designers and hosting services: Web designers with rudimentary skills are currently "a dime a dozen." If you don't know someone who does it, they can be easily solicited at sites such as www. craigslist.org. Freelance web designers are always looking to build their résumés by working with highly visible, highly creative people such as artists, and some will even do the work pro bono in exchange for a prominent credit on the site.

Several years ago, I found a designer who was a friend of a friend to build my site. He did a brilliant job for a few hundred bucks, and he found a friend to host my site on his server for free. I registered my domain name myself and I was in business. The process took a week and cost less than $750.

If your budget is a bit larger, professional web designers such as Quabe, Inc. (www.quabe.com) can provide a sharp, innovative, and customized design.

Services offering domain name registration, web design, and hosting: The past five years have seen an explosion of entrepreneurial energy at the intersection of the music business and the Internet.

This has resulted in the emergence of dozens of new and exciting services for artists and music professionals.

An excellent resource for artists and bands is Bandcamp. Bandcamp is a webhosting site for musicians that allows you to upload photos, MP3s, and upcoming tour dates; a shopping cart that allows you to sell downloads of your music and merchandise; and finally, a mailing-list service that allows fans to stay in touch. Furthermore, Bandcamp is truly a Web 2.0 site, in that it also includes syncing with other online music retailers and with other social networks.

Apps for Artists

How They Work

App is short for "application software" and is essentially a website designed to be accessed and viewed on Internet-connected mobile phones. The music industry increasingly sees mobile apps as an important distribution channel. Among the most successful music-based apps are Shazam (which identifies songs on the fly); Internet radio services Last.fm, Pandora, and Slacker; and Tap Tap Revenge, a music-based game. In fact, "Music" is the second-ranked app category on the iPad and iPhone (after News), according to Nielsen.

There are more than 300,000 apps available on iPhone, with five billion downloads, and 120,000 for Google's Android, with one billion downloads.[10] Currently, Blackberry users have access to only a small fraction of that number (approximately 10,000) although companies like Mobile Roadie are in the process of designing thousands more for the Blackberry. The future of apps seems bright, as currently 25 percent of U.S. mobile customers use smart phones including the iPhone, Blackberry, and Android, and by 2011 that percentage is expected to double. Worldwide, the number of mobile phone subscriptions is estimated at over five billion. Moreover, Microsoft recently launched its Windows Phone 7 operating system, which has received positive reviews for its slick design, intuitive interface, and integrated content-aggregation strategy that mixes third-party apps with Microsoft services such as Bing, Zune, and Xbox Live. It is reported that more than 300,000 developers have signed up to its developer program. The chart on the following page shows the lay of the land with respect to the different smart phones' market share and share of worldwide app downloads.

Should You Get One, and How Much Will It Cost?

So should artists have their own apps? Companies such as Mobile Roadie, which designed Madonna's app, charge from $499 for setup and $29 per-month maintenance to $1,999 for setup and $99 per-month for additional features such as horizontal views. iLike is charging artists a onetime fee of $99 and will also participate in a revenue-sharing deal for those that want to charge for their applications (the current plan is for a fifty-fifty split). Artists that give their application away for free will have to pay only the initial fee. An app can be used for the same purposes as a website: promoting new music, videos, and shows; selling merchandise and music; posting news

---

10. "10 Reasons Why Windows Phone 7 Has Its Work Cut Out," http://economictimes.indiatimes.com/tech/hardware/10-reasons-why-windows-phone-7-has-its-work-cut-out/articleshow/7136846.cms.

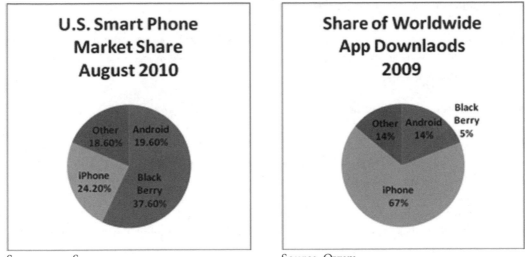

Source: comScore   Source: Ovum

stories; and integrating with social networks. Moreover, the app will look good on the mobile device, whereas a website may look crowded or unreadable and flash-based websites may not be viewable at all. Some examples of artists who have available apps: Jason Carver, Jessica Harp, Jimmy Cliff, John Butler Trio, Kadence, Ingrid Michaelson, and the Cribs. Each showcases music videos, photos, news, photo-jumble games, concert listings, and/or community features that let fans share photos with each other. All of them were made with iLike's iPhone app toolkit. Not only will an app help promote new music, it may also help drive sales. Taylor Swift's Mobile Roadie app helped her to sell 350,000 downloads within the first two weeks of her last album's debut. Apps can also be helpful in creating a buzz around a new album prior to its release.[11] Linkin Park's app, 8-bit Rebellion, granted early access to the first single off their new album.

In some areas of music, such as pop and hip-hop, where acts are trying to gain mass appeal with teenagers, an app may be essential since kids love them. For fans of other kinds of artists, such as artsy electronic music, an app may seem crude and overly commercial. You should judge whether you should build one based on the opinion of your fans. According to Michael Schneider of Mobile Roadie, the biggest benefit of an app over a website is

> a much higher quality user experience, which in turn results in fans coming back more often and spending more money. A native app takes advantage of the phone's native features, which allows for things like smooth transitions, engaging design, and a fun user experience. Native apps can also access things the web can't—for example, adding an event to the calendar on your phone, or using the phone's camera to take a photo or video.

Having read this blurb on his website, I called Michael for additional comments. Here is our discussion:

---

11. *Billboard*, December 18, 2010, p. 26.

SG: What do you mean by a "native" app?

MS: A "native" app is an app that is built for the phone's native language and takes advantage of the phone's user interface and features, as opposed to a "web" app that is HTML-based and can be viewed on any device.

SG: What do you mean by "using the phone's camera to take a photo or video"?

MS: An app user can use the camera to take photos at shows upload them directly into the app. Or users can RSVP to shows from inside the app, and we can automatically add it to their calendar.

Before diving in to the app world, one caveat is in order for artists of any genre. At the time of this writing, some industry experts are advising that HTML 5 could supplant many types of apps—including artist apps—by simply letting developers create a mobile-optimized website that all smart phones can access equally well.

Other Music Sites to Utilize

SoundCloud, Last.fm, and Bandcamp

Although Myspace is arguably still viable, there are several other sites where you can feature your music and promote your records, live gigs, merchandise, and more.

SoundCloud

SoundCloud is an excellent site for posting your tracks, remixes, and DJ sets. With a free account on SoundCloud you can have a profile page that features your music, just like Myspace—but the difference is that you can upload up to 120 minutes of your own music, share your tracks with up to 100 other users, and allow for 100 downloads of each track or mix you post (your tracks do not have to be downloadable if you prefer not to give them away). You can connect with other users by "following" them in the same way you do on Twitter, and other users in turn can follow you. Plus, SoundCloud has created a convenient "dropbox" system for sharing your tracks with other users, allowing you to send your music directly to users you think might want to hear it. SoundCloud also offers a "dropbox" widget that bloggers often use on their own websites—it is a convenient way to submit songs for blogs' consideration and makes their lives much easier without the hundreds of e-mails over the course of a given day, week or month. SoundCloud has a clean and easy-to-use interface with no advertising. The sleek design and quality music uploader (the music sounds much better on SoundCloud than on Myspace) are causing countless bands to make the switch or at least augment their Myspace profiles. SoundCloud's pros and cons:

Pros: Clean interface, quality music uploader, free, unlimited uploads and sharing with a premium account, can make original tracks downloadable, easy to meet new people.

Cons: Free accounts limited to 120 minutes of music and only up to 100 downloads for each track. SoundCloud page is not customizable like Myspace. Instead you have a simple white page (though you can upload art for individual tracks and albums that show up as icons in the music player).

Last.fm

Last.fm is another great resource for posting your music online. Although it is primarily known for being an online radio service, it also has an intelligent tagging system similar to Pandora's (see Chapter 4). An initial search for an artist or genre will result in a continuous radio stream of similar-sounding music. Also, Last.fm has a social-networking component, in that you can make friends and message other users and create or join groups based on your musical tastes and preferences.

To submit your music to Last.fm, you must create a "Music Manager" account—it is the only way for labels and artists to create artist pages, upload songs, and add tags to describe the music. Furthermore, a Music Manager account allows labels and artists to participate in "Powerplay" campaigns, where for $20 Last.fm will guarantee a hundred radio plays of one song to a specific group of users. However, the greatest benefits of the Music Manager account come from tagging your music and comparing it to other artists' work—and the more that others on Last.fm listen to your music, the more often it will be featured on the radio "stations" of similar tags or artists.

Also, Last.fm offers the opportunity to participate in a royalty-sharing scheme—for every time that your song is played on Last.fm's free radio service, you receive a share of the net revenue accrued for each complete play. In order to participate, you must own the copyright for both your songs and the recording and you cannot be a member of SoundExchange (see Chapter 4) or any performing rights organization (see Chapter 1). If you are just starting your music career, then Last.fm's royalty-sharing system may be something to consider. But artists/songwriters who have been on the scene will be better off joining SoundExchange (as an artist) and a performing-rights organization (ASCAP, BMI, or SESAC), because these organizations collect monies for you from many other different sources.

Pros: Great exposure if you can get your music on their radio service; music can be promoted via Powerplay.

Cons: Not much control over the look of your page, and the social-networking component experience is clunky.

Bandcamp

Bandcamp is quickly emerging as the new premier website for showcasing your music. With Bandcamp you can create a fully customizable webpage with an embedded music player (with a bitrate of 128 kbps—much better than Myspace) and shopping cart. Bandcamp allows you to offer your tracks in various formats, for instance MP3, AAC, FLAC, or Ogg, and lets you set the price for your music. In addition, Bandcamp provides all the metadata necessary for your tracks so that they can show up in iTunes complete with artwork, titles, and other information. Plus, the site is search-engine-optimized so that your Bandcamp page shows up first in search-engine results. Finally, Bandcamp reports streaming information to SoundScan, allows you to set up Creative Commons licenses for your music (see Chapter 1), and automatically delivers the e-mail addresses of those who download your music—in effect creating a mailing list for you as more and more visitors download your tracks.

In August 2010, Bandcamp ceased to be a free service—it now takes a share of your revenue from sales of digital downloads, physical albums, and merchandise. The current rate will be 15 percent of each transaction, dropping to 10 percent as soon as your all-time sales exceed $5,000. Bandcamp boasted sales of over $1 million in music from March to August 2010. Perhaps Bandcamp's greatest success story to date is Zoe Keating, a classical cellist whose album *In the Trees* debuted at number seven on the *Billboard* classical chart solely from Bandcamp sales, without a record label or digital distribution on iTunes.

Pros: Free shopping cart, mailing list, SEO, metadata creation, SoundScan reporting, quality music player.

Cons: Bandcamp takes 15 percent of revenue from digital downloads, physical albums, and merchandise.

How to Sell Your Music Online

Today's technologies have enabled artists to carve out their own DIY supply chains and modes of distribution. Today, the tools are ahead of the expertise, and the Internet is constantly reinventing ways for music to be heard and sold—that which was considered incredible in 2003 (Myspace) is now regarded as antiquated or bloated, and new networking sites like Bandcamp and digital distribution sites like TuneCore have assisted artists in even faster and more inexpensive ways. Because of the so-called democratization of the music business, via the rise of home studios and DIY marketing, more records than ever are being released in the United States, and despite falling record sales, there exist ways to make financially successful records on your own. CD Baby and TuneCore are the leaders in helping indie artists sell their records on web stores such as iTunes. Most web stores will not deal directly with individual artists, because that would require a massive increase in work for them in terms of reporting sales to the artist, paying them, making changes that an individual artist may wish to make, and so on. For these reasons, they much prefer to deal with aggregators such as Tune Core or CD Baby, who perform these functions for them.

TuneCore and CD Baby

Derek Sivers founded CD Baby in 1998 as a place to sell his own music and that of bands with whom he was friends. The idea caught on, and more and more bands and artists asked him to distribute their music. Sivers sold CD Baby to Disc Makers in 2008 for $22 million. When CD Baby launched in 1998, the only way they sold music was by mailing physical CDs to those who ordered them from their website. CD Baby continues to do this. Disc Makers also retained Sivers's policy of allowing artists to set their price point for selling physical compact discs. CD Baby retains $4 of every sale, and the remainder gets paid out to the artist.

CD Baby also provides digital distribution on their website and in approximately seventeen third-party online stores.[12] For downloads from their site, CD Baby keeps 25 percent of the purchase price. The artist keeps the rest. For sales on third-party sites, CD Baby keeps 9 percent of income received from any digital store. That is, of course, in addition to the cut taken by the third-party store. So if iTunes takes 30 cents from each $1 sale, the artist will receive approximately 60 cents instead of 70 cents.

CD Baby also requires a setup fee of $35 per album and $9.95 per single for both physical distribution and digital distribution. However, you also need to purchase a UPC bar code for $20 per album and $5 per single to sell your album or singles on third-party digital stores and physical stores. Without purchasing the barcode, your music will be available for purchase through the CD Baby website only, as either a physical CD or digital download. If you have a lot of single songs you want to sell, this can add up. For instance, fifty songs will cost you $250 just for the bar codes. On the other hand, it would still be more expensive to buy your own UCC barcode. They cost $760 for a minimum of 100 barcodes from a company called GS1U.S. The UCC bar code is important— without it, SoundScan cannot monitor your sales, which means that the artist will not qualify for *Billboard* charts (which are based on SoundScan numbers).

While CD Baby is a good way to get your music in digital stores like iTunes, Amazon MP3, and Rhapsody, and they efficiently mail your CDs to people who order physical copies, their third-party physical-distribution service is less attractive. According to the CD Baby website, they have a physical-distribution deal in place with "international retailers, including Super D (one of the world's largest distributors of music and DVDs)." This is a bit misleading; what CD Baby actually does is get your CD listed on international distributors' databases, which retailers can then review in order to choose which albums to stock on their shelves. Unless you actually take the time to develop relationships with record-store owners in various towns (guest-listing them to your shows when you play gigs, visiting the store in person), there's little chance that retailers will stock your CD without knowing and liking your music.

According to their website, these are current stats for CD Baby:

▶ 360,000 different albums sold by artists at CD Baby
▶ Over three million tracks in their digital-distribution catalog
▶ $157 million paid directly to the artists

---

12. CD Baby's website reports that it has strong relationships with the following stores: iTunes, Amazon MP3, eMusic, Rhapsody, Napster, Myspace, Spotify, Liquid Digital, Verizon V-Cast, Shockhound, Nokia, Last.fm, Zune, MediaNet, Tradebit, GreatIndieMusic, and Thumbplay. They also list the "legal" version of Limewire, although as reported in Chapter 10, a federal court has shut down Limewire and the link to the site reports that it's not taking new customers.

How Much CD Baby Pays You

This grid summarizes how CD Baby pays its artists:

Type of Sale	You Get	CD Baby Cut
CDs and Vinyl (includes sales through *physical distribution* partners)	Your chosen purchase price minus $4	CD Baby keeps $4 per unit sold. If your album sells for $13, you get paid $9.
CD Baby.com downloads (single tracks & full-album)	75% of your chosen purchase price	CD Baby keeps 25% of the purchase price with a minimum of 29 cents. For a download that sells for $9.99 you get paid $7.49, and for a single that sells for 99 cents you get paid 70¢.
Digital distribution sales (including iTunes and Amazon MP3.)	91% of net income	CD baby keeps 9% of the net income paid to them by the web stores and you keep the rest.

In addition to distributing your music, CD Baby provides services such as web hosting for $20 per month or $199 per year and renting credit-card swipers to artists for sales at gigs. They charge $30 for the swiper, plus a refundable deposit that is repaid when it is returned. However they also keep 9 percent plus 3.8 percent for credit-card fees (12.8 percent total).

TuneCore

Unlike CD Baby, TuneCore does not sell directly to music consumers—it limits itself to distributing indie artists to third-party digital stores. The advantage that TuneCore offers artists is that they charge only a flat fee for their services. Unlike CD Baby, which charges 9 percent of any monies received from services such as iTunes and Amazon MP3, TuneCore pays 100 percent of monies they receive to the artists. For only $9.99 you can use TuneCore to sell a single to approximately a dozen digital stores.

Price/Type	# Stores including iTunes
$9.99 per Single	19
49.99 per Album	19
$9.99 per ringtone	One store

At the time this manuscript was delivered to my publisher, TuneCore was not using UCC barcodes. SoundScan therefore does not report sales made through TuneCore. While this helps reduce the price that TuneCore charges, it makes it impossible for artists to be ranked in charts based on SoundScan numbers.

Third-party Rights and Exclusivity

It is important to note that an artist must own all the rights in a record or have the authority or permission from the owners. If you didn't write any of the songs, you must find out who the copyright owners are and pay the publisher their mechanical royalties the same way you would for CDs or downloads. See Chapter 1 for how and whom to pay, and how much. Similarly, if you included samples on the record, you are responsible for clearing them before selling through CD Baby or TuneCore. Neither TuneCore nor CD Baby asks that you sell records exclusively through them, but they do insist that you use them exclusively for the stores they represent, so you cannot use both for the same records, as they both sell though iTunes and Amazon MP3.

How to Sell Music from Your Website for Almost Nothing and Keep All the Money

PayPal—Ultimate DIY Sales Model

Apart from selling your music on CD Baby and TuneCore, you can take DIY to the next level by—selling your music through your own website using PayPal. The most evident drawback to this model is that you need to handle mailings of physical releases and pass on links to customers for downloads. However, PayPal takes a much smaller cut than CD Baby—just a little over 1 percent—and unlike TuneCore, there is no per-record fee. But the main benefit is that this method keeps your fans on your site instead of transporting them to iTunes or some other store where you are competing with millions of other titles and your fans can get distracted. Of course, you can sell on your website using your own credit card account, but the monthly fees and transaction costs are usually significantly more than what PayPal would charge. You can also use PayPal to sell merch, concert tickets, or anything else you can think of. There are two different types of merchant accounts on PayPal—Standard and Pro.

With the Standard PayPal service, you can set up payment buttons on your website easily, with no advanced programming skills. The buttons are compatible with most commonly used third-party carts, but you can also do a custom integration into your site. You can use PayPal's tax and shipping calculators to automatically work out sales tax and shipping costs for your orders. Furthermore, you can accept payments in twenty-two currencies from 190 countries and markets worldwide. However, buyers have to leave your site momentarily to go to the PayPal payment page—a downside if you want to have your page look super professional and complete.

How It Works

Step 1: Customer chooses your product on your website.
Step 2: Buyers check out with credit card/PayPal.
Step 3: They review their details.
Step 4: They view their payment confirmation.
Step 5: They return to your site.
Step 6: You get paid.

PayPal Pricing—Website Payments Pro

The difference between Standard and Pro is that with the Pro version, you can process credit-card payments directly on your site—keeping your paying fans close to you and your brand. It works with most major shopping cart applications, and PayPal will handle the following:

► Payment processing
► Reports, statements, billing info, account support, and phone/fax/e-mail orders

There is a $30 monthly fee for this service and transaction fees of 2.2 percent to 2.9 percent depending on sales, with the fee decreasing as your sales increase, plus a transaction fee of 30 cents.

In conclusion, although you have to make your own choices about online distribution, selling directly from your own website is a nice complement to using an aggregator for distribution on iTunes and other digital stores, because it keeps your fans on your website. Using an aggregator, such as TuneCore or CD Baby, is also a good idea, because it allows people who are already on online stores to discover your music.

Chapter 12
Insights from an Online Marketing Guru

Online Marketing Manual by Jason Spiewak, President of Rock Ridge Music

Jason Spiewak's clients include Twisted Sister, Run DMC, RCA Records, and Atlantic Records. In this interview we explore the details of a successful online marketing campaign.

SG: How did you get your start in the music business?

JS: My path into the music business began on the artist side. I played piano and sang for Blue Suede Groove for five years. We released three independent albums and fought the same battles fought by every new band in America. It was trial by fire, though we eventually built a nice following and toured from Canada to Florida, and I'm proud to say that it was how I earned a living for two-plus years after graduating from Penn State.

I took the lessons I learned as an independent artist to an assistant job at Artemis Records. At Artemis I worked long hours and read every piece of paper I could get my hands on while working with artists like Warren Zevon, Steve Earle, Kurupt, Baha Men, and Kittie (whom I later signed at Rock Ridge Music). From Artemis I went to a tiny indie label called Studio E Records. That label moved very slowly, but I learned valuable lessons there about A&R and artist relations. My final big label stop was TVT Records, learning new media, Internet marketing, and search engine optimization while promoting huge urban records from Lil Jon, the Ying Yang Twins, and Pitbull. When I started at TVT, if you googled "pitbull" you would only get information about the dog. Today if you google "pitbull" I'm proud to say that the artist's website still comes up first.

I had the privilege of learning music marketing from some of the best minds in the business—Tom Derr, my partner at Rock Ridge, taught me how to focus on what counts. As he likes to say, "The truth is brief, bullshit is long-winded." Michael Krumper schooled me on the retail marketplace, Daniel Glass helped me understand that music marketing doesn't take place in an office, it takes place on the street and in the clubs, and Christina Zafiris showed me the power of leveraging content online and beyond. All of these lessons and many others continue to serve me at Rock Ridge Music.

In 2004, Tom Derr and I started Rock Ridge Music. At that time, competition was fierce at every turn as the music business faced its largest contraction in over fifty years. Retail shelf space was shrinking, and it was a struggle to ship enough units to keep afloat. We had no choice but to make up for lack of physical sales by selling music online. It was an arena where we could compete based on our knowledge of that market and our relationships. We delivered big-splash visibility for our humble roster at that time. As other labels took notice, we began to offer our online marketing services on a "by-project" basis. At first it was our friends who hired us, and we worked Better Than Ezra and Black Label Society for Artemis and Sevendust for TVT. Then we started chasing the online business, taking meetings at all of the major labels and big indies. We were hired by J Records to work Barry Manilow. The project was so successful that Rock Ridge becoming Barry Manilow's online marketing company for everything from his Vegas show to archival DVDs released by Rhino. We were also hired to create credible rock visibility for Daughtry on his first RCA Records release. Our client base today consists of over thirty labels and releases by over a hundred different artists. Rock Ridge Music became an online marketing company because of our approach and our ability to execute.

Our approach to online marketing is a humble one. It's impossible to know everything about the online world, it changes so rapidly. We try to focus on the music, and we employ certain philosophies to market that music. We want to be on the leading edge of technology without being on the bleeding edge of technology. We are paying enough attention to hopefully identify a wave so that we can catch it and ride it.

Today, Rock Ridge Music offers services in three general areas: we're a record company with distribution through ADA (Warner Music Group), an artist management company, and a marketing services company. In terms of our marketing services, we specialize in new media marketing, which generally includes our online marketing services, viral marketing and promotion, and digital distribution.

SG: So why should someone hire Rock Ridge Music to promote them online? How does Rock Ridge "break" an artist?

JS: It's an old business cliché, "If you don't promote, nothing happens." This may seem obvious, but many new artists fall into the trap of simply uploading their music online and waiting for people to discover how great they are. A song cannot be a hit if no one hears it, and if you don't promote that song, no one will. People often compare underpromoted music to a tree falling in a forest, in that it doesn't make a sound. I would say that it's even more tragic, because the "online forest" is so crowded that a tree wouldn't even have an opportunity to hit the ground. There are simply too many other trees surrounding it. Not only are there a ton of artists out there, but a ton of websites, as well! We create custom bulletins for every project and reach out on an individual basis to the top music and lifestyle sites on the web. We are always learning about new sites, creative ways to promote, applications that help artists move ahead. Rock Ridge Music helps break an artist by creating visibility for their art while navigating the massive online music world.

SG: Do you provide advice on website development, and how should an artist use their website?

JS: Simple is the key, and we are hired to develop websites often. In most cases, an artist website should be an e-commerce hub and a simple funnel for information—one place to offer fans things to purchase, and to provide information and to incorporate all of the dynamic content available for that artist. For example, if you're a touring act with great live shows, your website should provide detailed information regarding your touring, links to buy tickets, and video clips. If you're an act with a radio hit, that song should load as soon as your website does—make that immediate connection for people so they don't have to do any guesswork. If you're a brilliant writer, include a blog feature and share that side of you. And just as important—don't have anything on your website that is not active and reflective of you. Stale content is a massive turnoff for fans. An artist should consider their audience and provide a web environment that is simple and makes sense.

SG: How important is Facebook? Is Myspace dead? How relevant is Twitter? What about YouTube—how do you use it? What other social-networking sites do you use?

JS: The incredible thing about social media is how rapidly it changes. By the time this volume is printed, chances are that my company's specific methodology to deal with social media will be totally different than it is today. So I'm going to focus on my ideas in general terms. Effectively marketing music via social networks involves three parties—the marketer, the advocate, and the consumer. I'll give these folks names in order to hopefully breathe some life into my example— Marty the Marketer, Abby the Advocate, and Colby the Consumer. So let's say that Marty is promoting a new single from Sister Hazel and goes onto the band's Twitter profile and posts a message promoting the song, including a link to preview the track and preorder it on iTunes. The message is seen by Sister Hazel fan Abby, who then reposts it on her profile. Abby's Twitter account is connected to her Facebook page, so her good friend Colby sees the message on Facebook and knows that Abby has really good taste in music, so he decides to click the link to preview the track. The links reach Colby directly, which is why it's very important to offer media-rich marketing messages online. It's this type of delivery that now creates a credible impression with the ability for the consumer to react. In order for marketing messages to be effective in breaking through the clutter online, it's important that the messages be worded cleanly and contain either an offer or an idea.

An offer is a specific value proposition for the consumer. A discount. Complimentary or exclusive music (preferably both). First access to concert tickets. To merchandise. Some specific offer that is communicated simply and clearly. It's okay to include a "hoop" for the consumer to jump through, as long as the hoop is simple. An e-mail in exchange for media. A tweet in exchange for a coupon. But the offer must be there, and the value must be real.

If you don't have an offer to make, it's important to offer the consumer an idea. "Cool" is the modus operandi for most social networkers. The definition of cool is obviously broad—something may be cool to a young mother who is in a network with other young mothers. Something else may be cool to a dude who loves dick and fart jokes. Something else may appeal to senior citizens. The point is that an idea online must have a targeted audience. If you're going for broad appeal, comedy and love are two great universal vehicles. All that said, the idea of trying to be all things to all people is a lost art in social media. "Cool" is essential to having a viral-video success story, and we have learned a lot about this world having been behind several YouTube video success stories, including the popular Psychostick video for "Beer!!!" as well as having served as the record label for Obama Girl's sensational "I've Got a Crush on Obama."

Offers and ideas are the key to successful social media marketing. One mistake that people often make online is recruiting a "street team" or "online army" to promote on their behalf. In my view, asking your fans to call themselves "street teamers" is a tax on your credibility. All you have is your unique voice online—this goes for artists, as well as for Rock Ridge Music as a company. When someone signs up for your mailing list or opts in to your social network, they are automatically part of your inner circle. Treat those people with respect and do not ask them to do for you. Only offer them things they can do for themselves while loving your art.

SG: How important is the quality of the music, or is that genre-specific?

JS: The quality of the music is extraordinarily important. One goal of an effective online marketing campaign is motivating fans to share music with other fans, and if you're promoting great music, it is much more likely that fans will want to share it with others. Genre lines tend to blur online, and that idea becomes less important. I think about the diverse array of music on my computer—30 percent of it may be rock music, 20 percent of it may be pop songs, 20 percent of it may be urban music, and so on—but the songs are all songs I want to hear, regardless of their genre. Greatness is the key. If it's not great, fans will tune it out and find something else that speaks to them.

SG: How important is the look and style of the artist?

JS: Consistency and authenticity are the key elements here. Artists should pick a direction and be consistent with that direction. Find a look that feels comfortable, have some flattering pictures or imaging created to support that look, and use that look across all of your web properties.

SG: Do you suggest working with a separate PR agency or publicist? If so, what do you do that is different than what they do?

JS: It depends what your goals are for a given project. My company specializes in creating visibility on the Internet and driving traffic to a product online, and these efforts are meant to complement a traditional PR campaign. In my opinion, hiring a PR company is a good idea if your project contains a strong non-Internet component such as a large tour, or perhaps a compelling element like a celebrity tie-in. A great PR company can be an excellent complement to a Rock Ridge online campaign—for example, if the PR company is able to secure a large television opportunity, Rock Ridge can then tell that story online and grow interest in the artist before, during, and after the TV appearance.

SG: Do you do "real"-world marketing, too, or just work the "virtual" world?

JS: In my view, it is all "real-world" marketing. The online world is a reflection of what is happening offline. If something is interesting and compelling offline, it will likely have some form of online component. The reverse can also be true. Online marketing, in its best form, is reflective of some effort that is taking place offline, as well.

SG: Which world is more important: "real" or "virtual"?

JS: Both worlds are important, neither more important than the other. The physical world is extremely competitive, and there is a perception that it is easier to compete online. That just isn't true. There are so many new artists making music and uploading that music to the Internet. The goal is to break through all of that clutter, the same way a new band must emerge from obscurity if they perform at local bars and clubs.

SG: What can the artist do to help himself even if he hires you?

JS: I am going to gear my answer toward developing artists who have not broken through from obscurity to the mainstream and say that the artist must continue to do everything they can to help themselves. It takes a solid team to break an artist, and my company can be very helpful in that process. However, the artist must continue to work and be involved. We like to work with artists who work as hard as we do, because those are the artists who often find success.

Chapter 13

Big Money and Mainstream Success: Major Labels and New Business Models

Big Label Deals: Who Gets Them, How, and How Many Are Left?

The tools that we described in Chapter 11 may be sufficient for artists in genres like electronic or acoustic folk who are interested in reaching a select fan base that can support their music by buying records, attending concerts, purchasing merchandise, and so on. Those tools may even be adequate to establish enough of a fan base so an artist can make a living and quit her day gig. But for artists in genres like hip-hop and pop who aspire to reach a worldwide audience and become a household name, more than those tools may be required to rise above the din and connect to hundreds or thousands and eventually millions of new fans. For such artists, a powerful partner is needed to get on commercial radio (which is still vital for breaking most new acts), touring large venues, appearing on national television shows, and securing placements in popular TV shows, well-financed movies, and national ad campaigns. All of these opportunities require connections, clout ,and money. Under the traditional model, the money and influence came from a big record company. When I was a lawyer at Atlantic Records and later Sony Music, we would sign dozens of artists a year at deals starting at $250,000 to over $500,000. That money was provided just to produce an album, and the record company would budget more than that for promotion, marketing, and publicity. And if the artist showed promise after the release of the first album, the marketing budget could easily exceed a million dollars. Those days are largely over. The big deals still exist, but only for a select few. However, the four majors are still important. If you look at the *Billboard* charts, the top ten artists in any of the charts ranging from pop to rap to R&B are usually represented in some way by one of the majors, if not as an owner, then at least as the distributor and label partner. Even though an artist may be signed to a so-called indie label, that company may receive financing and marketing support from, as well as distribution through, a major. For instance, Taylor Swift is signed to a small label called Big Machine Records, launched in 2005 by former DreamWorks Records executive Scott Borchetta. But Big Machine is distributed by and receives marketing support from Universal Music, and Universal was largely responsible for Swift getting on Top 40 radio, playing major venues, and appearing on national television.

For those talented and lucky enough to get them, a deal with a major can still produce the same kind of success that has launched the superstar careers we are all familiar with. The following interviews with the CEO of Atlantic Records and the head of A&R at Disney's Hollywood Records illustrate what the majors still have to offer artists and provide guidance on the best ways of securing deals with them.

Interview with Craig Kallman, Chairman and CEO of Atlantic Records

SG: Can you give us a thumbnail sketch of how you got into the music business?

CK: My dad had a big and eclectic record collection when I was growing up. So I would spend hours devouring new music of all genres. It ranged from Hot Tuna to Taj Mahal to Fairport Convention to Mozart to Black Sabbath. As I began to collect records myself, I would spend my weekends in the downtown mom-and-pop shops like 99 Records and Vinyl Mania. It was there I met Richard Vasquez ,who introduced me to deejaying. I hustled my way into deejaying at the Mansion. That led to getting resident deejay jobs at First City, Danceteria, Area, the Palladium, the Tunnel, Mars et cetera. I also took a bunch of other jobs working for *Billboard*, Factory Records, and New Music Seminar in New York City. While I was at Brown, I worked for the college department of CBS Records. When I graduated from Brown, I went back to deejaying and started an independent label called Big Beat, basically out of my bedroom. I began selling records out of the house I lived in with my dad and borrowing his car and selling them out of the trunk.

SG: In terms of a big label, what was your first big break?

CK: My first major-label deal was for an artist, Tara Kemp, I licensed to Irving Azoff's Giant Records. Soon after, the head of Atlantic Records then, Doug Morris, called me on another act I had, called Jomanda. We got along, and he said he wanted to buy my company and bring me into Atlantic. So I sold Big Beat to Atlantic and started working for him directly. I was lucky to have both Irving and Doug as my two mentors early on in the music business.

SG: How do you spend your time? What's a typical day like?

CK: I get up at six a.m. and start with international calls and then listen to music. I give my son breakfast and take him to school and then come back and listen to more music and go through e-mails. I check in with my partner, Julie Greenwald, when I first get to the office and start the day of meetings and phone calls. I'm very much on the A&R side of the company. Julie Greenwald runs the day-to-day operations. I'm focusing on the signing of new talent, the development of the existing roster, and the making of the records. At night, I am seeing our artists' live shows, seeing new acts perform, and visiting our artists in the studio.

SG: Do you think the role of A&R has changed in the last ten years?

CK: I think it has become incumbent on the A&R staff to be more engaged with their artists than ever. As the business continues to become more complex, the need for an intimate understanding of the artist becomes mandatory, so you can facilitate their vision at every frontier. The round-the-clock engagement with them I think is required.

SG: Who are some of Atlantic's hottest artists right now?

CK: Between Atlantic and our label partners we have Kid Rock, T.I., B.o.B, Christina Perri, and Death Cab for Cutie on Atlantic; Cee Lo and Bruno Mars on Elektra; and Paramore on Fueled by Ramen, to name just a few. Next year we look forward to fantastic new releases from James Blunt, Plan B, Lykke Li, and a new artist from the UK named Rumer.

SG: These days anyone can make a record on their laptops and get their record on iTunes, so why do you still need a label?

CK: There are so many facets to how we can be an important critical partner to the artist. On the recording side, it isn't just the financial component. Obviously a key element to making a record is providing the bands the resources to make the record they want to make. But I think more significant than just the economics are the creative contributions and dialog that exists. It is our job to be a productive sounding board or editor or door opener for new ideas and relationships. Our job is also as an essential curator to allow people to cut through the 15 million bands on Myspace and the blogs to find the ones we believe in. It is the marketing, promotion, publicity arm of this company that has two hundred-plus people dedicated to bringing our artists to market every day. There is a lot of competition for people's attention and traffic to weed through. It is our job to get our bands noticed above the rest around the world. It takes a long time, patience, and investment. That's what artists come to us for.

SG: Let's now compare the indies to the majors. Some people say that with a big label you could get lost rather than at a small one. If you do need a label for all the reasons you mentioned, why would an artist be better off at a big one than at an indie?

CK: Indies are fantastic because they have smaller rosters and can have a more focused musical point of view. But the majors obviously have a lot of resources and manpower that the independents don't have. It all depends on what you need as a band at any given point in your development.

SG: In terms of Top 40 radio, is it necessary to be on a major to get that commercial success?

CK: We have a very big staff to handle the vast number of radio stations in this country. We talk all day to radio to convince them our artists are worthy of being played on their radio station. That takes a big commitment of time and resources.

SG: Do the bigger labels still have the bigger budgets?

CK: I believe that would be true for the majority.

SG: If a bigger label is better, what kind of artists are you looking to sign, and do you recommend that certain artists in certain genres look in a different direction?

CK: A bigger label isn't better, it's just different. It all depends what an artist is looking for in their partner.

SG: What would an artist need that a major could serve better than an indie?

CK: More people and resources is the big distinguishing factor. When the artist needs the big global push to the mainstream, also, I think we have a lot of experience and know-how there.

SG: Les Nubians, an artist fusing world music, soul and R&B, was with EMI in the late 1990s but recently inked a deal with an indie. That label loves the band, and they are going to push very hard for them. If you're an artist, should you be looking to a major or an indie, depending on the genre of music that you are in?

CK: Yes, it depends on the genre and the artist.

SG: Suppose you want to be signed with a major label. How do you go about it?

CK: You want to create your own story as much as you can. You want to build a local fan base and following, by playing live and working online and cultivating that local momentum. We're taking notice of artists, regionally, that are really building their own story for sure.

SG: Do you look at YouTube and Myspace numbers?

CK: We look at everything—every metric out there.

SG: Are the majors signing as many acts as before?

CK: No, we're definitely signing less. Fewer artists with a more comprehensive engagement.

SG: How have the deals changed?

CK: More development deals and obviously 360 deals.

SG: Can you give me an idea of what a 360 deal looks like?

CK: We become a partner in all aspects of the artist's career: touring, merchandising, fan club, everything.

SG: Do you provide resources in all of those areas?

CK: Yes.

SG: Would you say that Atlantic is fairly unique in that respect?

CK: I can only speak for us, but I think that we have been doing it for a number of years now and we made a big investment in all of those areas.

SG: Have the advances declined somewhat?

CK: We try to bring costs in line with the marketplace as much as we can, while continuing to invest as aggressively as it makes sense.

SG: How do you see the future of the business? Will live performance, licensing, and merch become more important than record sales?

CK: I don't have a prediction on how the economic future of all these revenue streams will play out yet. I think it's still about the fundamentals of making amazing records and being able to bring them to market with every component linked in your marketing plan.

SG: What's the future for Atlantic Records?

CK: Our strategy is simply to continue to develop an amazing roster. It is that simple.

SG: Can you give me an example of how you work with an artist on live performances and touring or merchandising? What is your strategy, and how does the label get involved?

CK: We look at their live show and see how we can invest in both their production and their promotion of the live event. It is a constant dialogue on how to maximize the live experience for their fans.

SG: So you're actually working with the venues?

CK: Yes. We work closely with the venues and the promoters.

SG: How does merchandising work?

CK: We have our own merchandising company that works hand in hand with the product managers. Merchandise has become a key component to the marketing plan.

SG: Have you become a partner in publishing, as well?

CK: Sometimes.

SG: It seems that now everything is negotiable?

CK: Yes.

Interview with Jason Jordan, VP of A&R at Disney's Hollywood Music

SG: Give us a thumbnail sketch of how you got in the music business.

JJ: I started my own label when I was thirteen years old, with my twin brother, Joel. We were part of the Philadelphia punk rock and hardcore music scene and really fell in love with some of the bands and music at the time. We had saved some money between odd jobs and managed to figure out how to press up a seven-inch vinyl EP of a recording a band did for us (there was no contract, just a handshake that they would pay for the recording, we would pay for the pressing, and we would split everything fifty-fifty). We sold a thousand of them, tripled our investment, and started a very profitable cottage music business. Joel carried on with the businesses in some format and has until this day, and I took an entirely different path—meeting David Kahne, who hired me as a major label A&R rep in 1994 at the tender age of twenty years old, working for Columbia Records/Sony Music. Four years later, in 1998, I left Sony Music to help one of my mentors, Bob Cavallo, start the new Hollywood Records. I was one of the first A&R hires he made in the beginning. It has been an amazing twelve-plus years at Hollywood Records/Disney Music Group.

SG: Who are Hollywood's hottest artists now? Which ones do you work with?

JJ: We have an amazingly diverse roster of artists. It really spans the spectrum, from pop like Miley Cyrus, the Jonas Brothers, Selena Gomez, Jesse McCartney, and Demi Lovato, to the unbelievable musicianship of Grace Potter and the Nocturnals. We have great rock like Plain White T's, Atreyu, Alpha Rev, and our multiplatinum rock band Breaking Benjamin. I signed both Alpha Rev and Breaking Benjamin, though I work in every genre and enjoy all kinds of music, not just rock.

SG: Traditionally the role of A&R would be to discover new talent and get the artist signed to the label, plus they would supervise their recording projects. Has role of A&R changed in the last ten years?

JJ: Absolutely. It changes more often than every ten years. I'd say one of the most important things an A&R person has to stay on top of is how to maximize the internal machine they are working for. Think like a manager would—as there are creative ways to increase the visibility of an artist at a label and keep it on the radar. Beyond being the internal cheerleader, it's important to remind the label why we signed the artist in the first place and keep the artistic vision in check. That is still incredibly important, as "music" and "business" are words than coexist as long as you're respectful of the art and artists that you ultimately make your money off of. It's being a lot more involved in the day-to-day at the label where the marketing executive may have handled everything before; I think the A&R person absolutely needs to stay involved. A lot of labels are also a lot more research oriented these days than instinctual A&R, so they watch what is happening very closely online, in regional SoundScan reports, radio, you name it. If there is data to be collected, someone is collecting it. Hollywood is not that kind of label. We are lucky to have an amazing relationship with our parent company, which allows for incredible synergy. We also sign what we love, and those decisions have been not been made lightly, as the bar is incredibly high. In this day and age, with what is being spent, the bar has to be high.

SG: Take us through a typical day?

JJ: It honestly changes often. It depends on if I am actively making a record, chasing an artist, or off cycle and just looking and listening. Many times the first two things have collided a lot. For instance, at the moment, I am currently chasing a band that I am dying to sign. So the last couple of weeks of my life involved going to LA more than once and seeing a show that my entire label attended, as well. Since I've returned, I've spent time patiently monitoring the negotiating process between our attorney and the band's. That process is fascinating to me even after sixteen years of doing this job. As you can imagine, I also spend a lot of my days listening to new music, which comes from a variety of varied sources—from attorneys and managers and agents and other music-business professionals to absolutely random sources. I am a music fan first and an A&R person second. I listen to everything and anything, but I'm always listening and looking for what is right for Hollywood Records. I spend a lot of my time taking meetings with managers, artists, writers, producers, and so forth who want to meet about new music they are pitching to me, about songs that are available, or about a new artist. I love that part of my job—waking up each day and thinking I might discover something truly great.

SG: These days anyone can make a record on their laptop and get their record on iTunes. So why do you need a label?

JJ: You don't necessarily need a label. My ethos is absolutely punk, do it yourself. Put it out yourself. Tour yourself. Sell some records and get some fans first. I believe that most bands and artists shouldn't ever contact a label if they haven't put out an EP, at the very least, on their own—both physical and digital. It's so easy to press a CD as well as release it digitally, and the artist gets to keep most of the money. If you actually sell some, then chances are that more than one major label will come knocking on your door first! As majors are signing less and less artists these days, if you're a real musician, then you really can't wait around for someone to discover you. Work with a major label when it makes sense to do so—when you need that extra marketing and promotion power that all of them can provide.

SG: If you need a label, why would an artist be better off at a big one rather than an indie? What does a big label have to offer that small or indie one doesn't?

JJ: I think this is an extension of the last question. I should say that even if an artist doesn't need a label, there are services that even indie labels (as well as at some majors) are better at farming out to third parties—such as independent publicity, online promotion/marketing, and so on. I would only say you would need to go to a major label if you required the absolute in marketing and radio promotion power at this point. Most well-oiled independent labels have the same distribution methods these days as we do—it just boils down to dollars and cents and if they can afford to take something all the way. That would be what I would be weighing if I were an artist with the option to work with a big indie or a major. Plus, of course, who could give you the best deal for the services that are expected.

SG: What kind of artists should look to be signed by a big label, and do you recommend that certain artists in certain genres such as electronic or jazz, go indie rather than big label?

JJ: It's hard to say. I'm surprised by stuff that gets signed all the time, so I would never discourage an artist to shoot for the "big time" if that is what they think a major label deal is. I think certain genres such as electronica and jazz and classical and let's just say "non-mainstream" music might be better serviced by a specialty label in that genre. I don't think anyone would argue against me on that point. Ultimately, if a label thinks something will light a fire or is worth signing because they think it will generate revenue from a synch standpoint, you have to consider that, as well. There are what many would consider "indie" artists living quite comfortably on majors at the moment.

SG: Okay, suppose you are an artist that would be well served by a big label—how do you go about getting signed to one?

JJ: For starters, do it yourself. Put out a record, find a synch, get booked, and become the biggest artist in your own back yard. A major label will find you. It's not a matter of "if" anymore, it's a matter of when. If you're doing it the right way and selling records and tickets and making noise, a label will come calling. You can always try the traditional route of trying to shop it with a lawyer and a manager, but that idea is quite archaic to me. Without the buzz of sales or a story to tell, it's hard for a major label to get excited about much more than the music. Sometimes, though, the music is enough. It's rare, but I love it when that is the case.

SG: Are the majors signing fewer artists? And have recording and marketing budgets gone down, and if so, how dramatically?

JJ: No major label is signing the same amount as they were even the previous year. It's not a business that would or could sustain itself if it kept on consuming at the rate it has been. I think what you will see now and in the future is an overall scaling back of not only labels and their staff sizes, but the amount of acts they sign per year. It will be more realistic and sustainable, which is what Hollywood has already been doing for years. Signing advances went down years ago; it's incredibly rare for anyone to get the kind of big-whale advance they might have seen even less than a decade ago. Records don't cost much to make anymore—with most of the production being done outside of what we could consider a traditional recording studio back in the day. It's hard to put a percentage figure on anything, as all I can really judge is what I see objectively across the industry. As an industry, majors are signing less and for less and asking for more from those deals. Different revenue streams beyond the traditional selling of a master recording.

SG: Since you mentioned "different revenue streams," are all the deals 360 now?

JJ: It all depends on which label you are talking to. At some, yes, absolutely. At ours, we will always ask for what we think is fair and negotiate the rest. There is never a pro-forma, take-it-or-leave-it type of deal for us and certainly not a 360. It's a wild new world out there, and we have to be as flexible to new business opportunities and even revenue streams that haven't been thought of yet.

SG: It used to be that the ticket to big-time success was a big label deal; would you say things have changed?

JJ: I think so. I'd like to point to someone like Ingrid Michaelson, who has had an amazingly strong and successful career from television synchs to writing to being an artist largely without a major label being anywhere near the picture.

SG: Hollywood is owned by Disney. Are there "synergies" involved? In other words, do artists at Hollywood have opportunities to connect with other divisions of the Disney empire, such as movies or television?

JJ: Of course. That is the advantage of working with a company like Hollywood and our relationship with Disney. It is just as powerful for our younger artists as it is for someone like Alpha Rev, whose music we have managed to get featured in a major Disney film as the end-title credit. That is the kind of stuff that never happened when I worked elsewhere and yet is the standard for what we do. A soundtrack or film opportunity or major television appearance or synch or whatever is a great place for a new artist to jump off from. As powerful as radio is, we have to (and love to) work with our parent company to expose our artists in clever and nontraditional ways. It's amazing, actually, as being part of a company like Disney doesn't allow for a lot of "no's" when coming up with new ideas. We are expected to play nicely together, and all of the Disney divisions do, and we love them for liking the music that we work so hard on.

SG: What does the future look like for Hollywood?

JJ: It looks bright. I think we have our most exciting roster at the moment in the twelve years that I have worked at the company. We are moving into an unpredictable and unprecedented time in the record industry and the music business overall. I think Hollywood Records is poised to weather the storms and grow and change as we have been doing over the previous years. I look forward to discovering and working with great music!

Facing Extinction, the Major Labels Adapt: EMI Label Services and an Interview with Its Chief, Michael Harris

The majors are experimenting with alternative business models because they have to. The old way of doing business—investing a lot of money and resources in a horde of new bands and waiting until one has terrific sales to subsidize the losers—is no longer viable, because even the most successful artists are selling a lot fewer records. One example of how a major is experimenting with a new business model is EMI Global Label Services. EMI started this new division several years ago. It offers a "partnership" to an artist under which the artist himself pays the initial cost of creating the album. In return, the label provides a budget that includes three different types of support: "commercial," "marketing," and "back office/supply chain." Commercial consists of sales, brand partnership, and working with the artist to develop merchandise. Marketing focuses upon launching an artist on commercial radio and promoting the artist in the press, as well as and accumulating research about the artist's fan base and the best ways to enhance it. Back office/supply chain involves physical manufacturing, accounting, and digital distribution. These initiatives are offered in a "menu" style that allows the artist to pick and choose the efforts that work best for him.

Financing can entail a modest upfront advance against a distribution fee for the label, instead of the traditional model of a big advance tied to small recording royalty. In this model, the artist retains the lion's share of the monies from record sales and also retains the copyright in the masters. The label retains only a distribution fee, which is a small price to pay for the expertise and leverage that a large record company brings to the table.

EMI Global Label Services is also a tool utilized by third-party labels and established artists because it affords continued independence while providing the valuable expertise and resources of a large record company. In August 2010, the 50 Cent–owned label G-Unit, formally with Interscope Records, signed with EMI Label Services for an exclusive North American distribution deal. Also, Slash is using Label Services to launch his first solo album, due in April 2011 in the United States. This venture allows him to gain the advantage of a big label's expertise in getting the album out to the consumers in an effective way, but allowing for the artist to retain creative control and get back a larger sum of money from sales.

I sat down with Michael Harris, EVP/GM EMI Global Label Services. Here is our discussion:

SG: When did EMI Label Services launch, who launched it, and what inspired its creation?

MH: When Dom Pandiscia took over responsibility for Caroline Distribution in May 2008, he and I developed a strategy of making available the "frontline" marketing team to third parties. Our goal was to react to the cosmic shift in the retail environment and provide artists with an alternative, comprehensive revenue solution designed to maximize their global potential.

SG: What is your role, and can give me a picture of a typical day?

MH: As with most music-industry roles—there is no typical day. If I were to try and summarize what I do from a business standpoint, I would say—deal making, marketing oversight, and sales strategy. However, I like to think of what we do as building bespoke partnerships with third parties in trying to maximize their revenue potential.

SG: What have been your biggest success stories to date and ELS' role in them?

MH: There have been a series of success stories, but a few that standout are:

▶ Bobby Valentino was our first Top 10 debut, as well as our first upstream artist to Capitol Records.

▶ Raekwon's release really put us on the map. In this instance we provided all marketing services to the artist, with the release debuting number four on the Top 200 chart.

▶ Slash, where we provided radio promotion services to the artist. Besides the success at radio, this release showed our versatility through various product offerings (i.e., merchandise bundles, deluxe packages, Abbey Road Live, D2C Platform, etc.).

▶ Matt Nathonson is an example where we took an act on a third-party-distributed label and helped them get the project over the finish line. Matt is signed to Vanguard Records (one of our distributed labels), who had taken a track to Top 10 at the Hot AC format. We were able to partner with them and provide radio-promotion services that helped cross the track over to Top 40. This resulted in 1.3 million incremental digital single sales, as well as 200,000-plus incremental album sales.

SG: Can you give me an example of a case where it did not work out?

MH: I truly don't know if there has been a case where it did not work. We pride ourselves on transparency, which helps negate any false expectations. We are very open with our partners, and if something does not seem to be heading in the right direction, we work hard with them to make it right.

SG: What kind of artists are you looking to partner with?

MH: We mainly partner with established artists where there is already a "brand" identity. However, in certain cases, we will help develop some of our third-party-label acts, for example with the band Taddy Porter, who are signed to Primary Wave, one of our third-party labels. In this case, we have taken a track to rock radio to complement the marketing efforts of the label.

SG: Are your deals 360? That is, do you seek partnership in revenues from other income flows than just record sales, such as touring, publishing, merch, and endorsements?

MH: Our deals are not 360 deals. However, we do offer services in alternative revenue streams such as synch/licensing, merchandising, and brand partnerships on a nonexclusive basis.

SG: You often hear that the record business is on the verge of collapse: true or false?

MH: The record business is not dead, nor is it on the verge of collapse. The record business has to understand how music touches people, and we must be at every one of those touch points to make sure we are helping make that connection and extracting the value that belongs to its creators. I believe EMI is doing an outstanding job of grasping that philosophy and that EMI Label Services is a great example of that.

SG: Is EMI Label Services unique, or do you have competition from the other majors?

MH: Our competitors offer marketing and promotional services, but what makes EMI unique is that we offer the "A-Team" to help work your record. We like to say that the same team that is helping megastars like Katy Perry is helping market your artist.

Part IV
Interviews with Artists and Music Industry Leaders

Chapter 14
Artists Adapting to a Digital World

How to Raise $80,000 in Two Months: Interview with Singer, Songwriter, and Recording Artist Jill Sobule

Successful singer, songwriter, and guitarist Jill Sobule writes about deeply personal and socially conscious issues, including the death penalty, anorexia, homosexuality, the Christian right, and even sexual slavery. Her career first started at two major labels, MCA and Atlantic, and she enjoyed great success in 1995 with the hit single "I Kissed a Girl" (not to be confused with Katy Perry's subsequent single of the same title), which was featured in the film *Clueless*. She signed briefly to Danny Goldberg's Artemis Records but ultimately turned to the DIY model, raising over $75,000 to produce her most recent record.

This interview focuses on how an artist can use the power of the Internet and relationships with fans to succeed.

SG: Your debut album in 1990 was *Things Here Are Different,* and it was released by MCA, a major label. You were only twenty-five years old. How did you get the deal?

JS: You know, it was one of those stories—someone I knew was a music publisher from Nashville, who actually came and saw one of my shows, liked what I did, and wanted to do something with a noncountry feeling. He had me come out there when Nashville had this thing called the Extravaganza, which was like a South by Southwest, and I was discovered.

SG: As Woody Allen said, 90 percent of life is showing up. Did MCA offer you the traditional record contract that the majors used to offer, with the big money advance up front, but a small artist royalty and options for multiple albums?

JS: Yes. Indeed. And what did I know? It was great! It was fantastic. Someone was paying for me to go into a recording studio and put out my record.

SG: Did they pay a big enough advance to surpass recording costs?

JS: They paid, but I didn't get that much, 'cause it went to the manager, and then it went to the lawyer, and then we had Todd Rundgren produce it, who had a high fee. But still, it was way more money than I had waiting tables.

SG: People have seen that the upfront money from majors got eaten up real quick.

JS: Yeah, it does.

SG: According to All Music, which I'm going to quote here, and then I'm going to ask you if it's true, "The album vanished from sight soon after its release and she was dropped by her label MCA. Disheartened and destitute, Sobule moved to Los Angeles and took a job as an assistant to a wedding photographer." True?

JS: Yes! I'm pretty incompetent to do anything else other than write songs, so I had various jobs, and one of them was an assistant to a wedding photographer. I'd go to a wedding every Saturday and Sunday and hold up his light. I just think he liked my company. And we just ate and drank a lot. Actually, MCA did give me another chance. The album was produced by Joe Jackson and some tracks by Wendy and Lisa, but it cost a lot of money, and I'm not sure it was so great, and I was dropped afterward.

SG: Some people say that working with the big record labels is like getting a mortgage on your house, but they get to keep the house.

JS: Yeah, it's ridiculous that I did two records for Atlantic and they own them. It makes no sense.

SG: I have a question about your Atlantic years. I read that your lawyer, Ken Hertz, played your demo tape for an Atlantic executive who was so impressed he quickly signed you to a contract. Is that true? Did your lawyer help you get the deal?

JS: He did. A music lawyer did it, who's still my lawyer today, by the way. In those lean years I stayed in his guest house with him and his family. Now, that's a good music lawyer.

SG: Not only legal advice, but housing and accommodations, as well.

JS: Housing's a good thing.

SG: I was a lawyer with Atlantic in the early 1990s. Did they offer you the standard recording agreement with big advance, a small artist royalty with multiple deductions, and multiple options?

JS: Exactly.

SG: And they got to keep the copyright in the album. How was your experience with Atlantic? Did they at least do a good job of promoting and marketing the records?

JS: Well, no. The A&R guy who I had, I actually really liked. He decided to release "I Kissed a Girl" as a single, and it was kind of a curse and a blessing, because it got a lot of play and sold well. But after that they didn't quite know what to do with me.

SG: Did Atlantic tell you what to do, or did they let you do your own thing?

JS: You know what, I was really lucky, because I always had creative control.

SG: It seems like the big bad record companies weren't that bad.

JS: Well, no. I don't have any complaints, it was just that their time is maybe up. I mean, it was nice to have an advance, and they spend a lot of money on you, but the only problem is, who knows what they use all the money for. And a lot of artists are like myself, I never really recouped or saw any money afterward.

SG: Probably because they recoup at your royalty rate, so if they put in $100,000 and your royalty is $1 per record sold, you have to sell 100,000 records to recoup. But they get the wholesale multiplied by 100,000, but you haven't earned any royalties.

JS: Exactly, and I mean I was still glad that I had the chance at the time when the majors signed artists. I was glad because of it. I made fans I still have to this day. I'm not complaining about that at all, I think it was great.

SG: Did you make any money from mechanicals, because, as you know, a songwriter gets money from the first record sold. Did you see any of that money?

JS: Yeah, I mean there was publishing, but not really anything else. That's the great thing about today, is that I think in those days, except for the advance, it was either real success or poverty for artists. But now people own the means of their production, you know? That's pretty damn great! I'm just using that as an example, too, it's the long tail, really.

SG: Yes, under DIY, and you get to keep all the cash. But before heading out on your own, your next step was signing with the famous indie Artemis Records in 2004. Was your experience working with an indie better, or worse? How would you compare it to working with a major?

JS: It was really the same thing, but with less of an advance and less of a budget, to tell you the truth [*laughs*]!

SG: Jill Sobule, we respect your honesty. There's a risk associated with signing with small record companies, so I guess we underline that point. Now you are doing something really great. You are doing it on your own. I want to talk to you about your last album, *California Years,* and as I've seen the website, you raised money for your last album all on your own. Tell us how much you needed, how much you got, and how you did it.

JS: Needed? I didn't know how much I needed. I just put it up there and said in my wildest dreams I'm not going to make over $75,000, thinking that's a joke. I just wanted to raise money, but I didn't want to say to my fans, just give me money. I put up a site, Jillsnextrecord.com, which had different levels of contribution in exchange for gifts and services in return. So for a certain amount of money, you got in the liner notes. For a certain amount of money, I would sing your name in the last song. There could be house concerts, or I'd write you a theme song (that was my favorite one). And there was the weapons-grade plutonium, which was the $10,000 dollar donation, where in exchange you would come sing a song with me on my record. I didn't think anyone would do it, and someone did it. It was pretty great.

SG: You wrote that also, if you can't sing, you can always play the cowbell. Now, did that person sing, or play the cowbell, or what?

JS: This person sang, and she was actually pretty damn good.

SG: I've gotta listen to this! Which song was this?

JS: It was "Mexican Pharmacy."

SG: We'll have to listen to that one and tell if we can hear the amateur. I noticed that you didn't offer lunch. I think Sarah Palin offers lunch for $50,000.

JS: Oh, I know!

SG: Not to compare you to Sarah Palin.

JS: The woman who bought the Sarah Palin lunch looked like Church Lady from *Saturday Night Live*!

SG: It's one thing, building a website and asking fans to contribute money, and another getting people to actually have them contribute. How did you promote the site?

JS: Well, I had a number of people through a newsletter, who were on my mailing list. I used Myspace and Facebook. I've always been really on top of the social networking. And so I think that really helped. Also, someone from the AP picked it up, and then it went out to all these other news sources, it that was pretty great, I have to say.

SG: How many friends on Facebook or Myspace or Twitter do you have? Can you give us some general numbers?

JS: Well, on Myspace I don't even know, because I don't much use Myspace anymore.

SG: Really? Why?

JS: There's just something about it that I don't like the look of it, I don't know.

SG: I know, when I go to my Myspace page and I see an ad for Toyota or Bad Boy records, I'm wondering, you know, "Is this Toyota's webpage, or is it Puffy's webpage, or is it me?"

JS: Right, right. Well, it's Rupert's space.

SG: It's Rupert's space. I hear you.

JS: Well, on Facebook I've done my personal site and I post to the 5,000-person limit—I'm really active on that, so I've had to start a musician page that I just started a couple weeks ago. But I'm really active on it. Every other day I have a contest, "Who Am I?" where I change my profile picture. Yesterday I was Princessor Empress Theodora; it's sort of silly, but people love it.

SG: I've been to your website, and it has a very simple design. It's basically a map, and in the middle is the new album and you can click on that and find out how to get it. But did you do the site yourself? Was it expensive? Do you have people help you maintain it? Or do you do it all your own?

JS: Webmaster. I've had some incredible artists and graphic designers and web designers help out.

SG: Is it ever a quid pro quo kind of thing, where you do them favors and they do favors for you?

JS: I pay some, but also I'm very big into the barter system these days. Artists helping out each other. It's been really great.

SG: Well, let me talk about your web store for a second. You can buy CDs using PayPal, and I noticed for *California Years* you can use any credit card. Oh, by the way, to give a plug for your website, what is it exactly?

JS: Jillsobule.com.

SG: You can buy T-shirts, as well. Do you actually ship these CDs and T-shirts yourself? Do you have boxes in your living room?

JS: I have a friend who takes a percentage out of the store. And don't forget, you can also get these on Amazon MP3 and iTunes, although we do like you going to my site better.

SG: When I interviewed Moby, I asked him how he got 750,000 followers—so will people just come to you? You don't have to buy mailing lists, or hire a publicist, or anything like that—once you've established your name, people will find you?

JS: Well, I hired a publicist, and I think he did a good job, but I really think that now people don't have to raise as much as I did. There was still a part of me that was going old style with buying a publicist, and you don't necessarily have to do that.

SG: Well, now that we've mentioned it, I don't think we've said that your goal was $75,000 and you actually collected $88,000?

JS: Yea. And I could have gone on, but I didn't, and you know people were saying, "You don't need that much to make a record," but this was for everything, including marketing and publicity—I was trying to do everything that a record company would do. And that's the other thing that I have to mention, is that it's been fun and it's kind of great, but it takes up a lot of time. Unless you've got a bunch of people helping you, and I have a few people, it really is time consuming and it's also kind of like, pioneers. You're still trying to figure it out—it just takes a lot of time, and also it's still kind of a wilderness, which is exciting, but it can be scary, too.

SG: Yeah, but you succeeded. How long did it take you to raise all that money?

JS: Two months.

SG: Wow! It was really worth the effort, don't you think?

JS: Oh, my God, it was! But you know, a lot of that I also looked at as presales.

SG: Oh, I see, presales against the CDs, because your minimum contribution was a free digital download. And then $25 was for an advanced copy of the CD.

JS: Right.

SG: Did you have any inspirations; did you have any models for this? Was anybody doing this before that you know of?

JS: Not that I know of.

SG: Anyway, how's the album doing?

JS: Considering I sold a ton of them presale and afterward, it's been good. I'm going to go on tour soon, and that's the other thing—what's great about this is that it's kind of old school and completely new school. It's new school with all the social networking, but at the same time going out and pounding the streets and selling your merch on the road—that goes back to the way it's always been.

SG: You're going to dozens of cities. Do you have a private airplane?

JS: Yeah, right. I'm gonna borrow a smelly van, that's about it.

SG: Do you sell a lot of CDs at your gigs?

JS: Well, you know, I've been doing it for a long time. I remember when I was opening up for Warren Zevon. We did two tours together, and I just loved him. He was funny, but he could be a curmudgeon (not to me), but he was funny to his fans. I remember he would come out and I would outsell him all the time in merch and I'd say "It's because these people don't know me, and I say to them I'm going to go out and sign after my show so they could come and meet me." And he was like, "Agh! I'm going to try that, too!"—so we'd both go out together, it was nice, you know? So artists have to be just out there and available, really.

SG: I want to end the interview with a few words about licensing. I know that you had a big success on *Fabulous,* which was a very popular show on Nickelodeon for which you wrote the theme song. How did you get the gig?

JS: The writer and creator of the show was my friend, and that was a really great thing. I actually scored the show, and it was my first kind of day job ever, and it was a great day job.

SG: Did it pay well?

JS: You know, can you imagine what Mike Post, the writer of the theme, makes every time when *Law and Order* is on and there's that "konk konk."

SG: As long as you have your copyright. Did you keep yours?

JS: Yes.

SG: So, then, you do get performance royalties on the reruns, as well?

JS: Right.

SG: But not as much as a network program.

JS: No, not as much. It's kind of negligible. But I'm not complaining.

SG: And is it good publicity, promotion for the rest of your career with selling records and all of that, or do people even know that it's you?

JS: I don't think people even knew.

SG: I recently had a singer-songwriter in a movie and he loves it, because even though it's in the trailer for the movie, he can blog about it and other blogs are picking it up, so there's this whole underground buzz going around about this new band in this new movie; it happens to be a George Clooney movie. It's working for him pretty well. Now, you had that big hit, "I Kissed a Girl," and it got picked up in the film *Clueless,* which also featured your song "Supermodel." How did the *Clueless* opportunity come to pass? Did you seek them out, or did they find you?

JS: At the time I was having a hit with "I Kissed a Girl," so, you know, for that month I was the girl of the moment.

SG: How do you get licensing gigs? Do you have an agent or a music publisher?

JS: I go with Bug licensing.

SG: Does Bug helps you find these licensing opportunities?

JS: They mostly come from Bug, but I'm constantly looking for things, and a lot of times it comes from other people—you know, there's so many things out there. By knowing someone, by being a friend of a friend, sometimes seems to work more than having a song plugger.

Chapter 15

Are Indie Labels Better for Artists Than Majors?

Interview with Musician, Composer, and Recording Artist Moby

Moby (né Richard Melville Hall) is a Grammy-nominated producer, songwriter, and recording artist. His 1999 album *Play* holds the record as the top-selling electronica album of all time, having sold over ten million copies worldwide. He has collaborated with some of the brightest and most innovative artists of his generation, including Lou Reed, Kris Kristofferson, David Bowie, Slash, Bono, Michael Stipe, New Order, Public Enemy, and Mission of Burma.

This interview focuses on Moby's views on the record industry and social networking, and his advice on how to make it as an artist in today's music business.

SG: I'd like to talk to you about your most recent album, *Wait for Me,* and about the business of releasing a record in today's market. I noticed you can buy the album in any format—CD, download, even vinyl—from your site.

Moby: I don't know the mechanics or the logistics of how we sell through the site . . . I think we're using some sort of third party.

SG: I noticed that you use a company called Thompson Records, which gives fans the opportunity to buy directly from your site.

Moby: Yes, they're a company in the north of England, and they do a lot of this sort of merchandise fulfillment.

SG: Is EMI still your record company? Do they also help you distribute?

Moby: It's a bit strange. —I basically left EMI, but I'm still with EMI in half the world—originally I had an exclusive worldwide deal with them. The main reason I left was because I felt like EMI and the major labels were sort of spending more time in restricting people's access to music than they were actually spending promoting the music. You know, they were figuring out all these different ways to prevent people from listening to music. To me, that is sort of anathema to what a recording company should actually be doing.

SG: What was your goal in terms of distributing your last album?

Moby: The goal when we were releasing the album, either on our own, or through different partners around the world, was not great sales or great margins, because the truth is no one sells that many records. The goal was not driving the best deal. The goal was trying to make as much unfettered access to music as possible. Like basically just to make the music as widely available as possible and without applying any restrictions to use it.

SG: Well, now that EMI's taken DRM off their records and you can buy unprotected MP3s, would you consider going back?

Moby: DRM was certainly pointless, but it was worse. For example, I had some instances where a radio station would be playing a song off one of my records, but it wasn't at the time that the label wanted them to be playing it, so EMI would actually issue a cease and desist. But with most people I know, the way in which people hear music and buy music has just changed and I don't really see piracy as being a problem. I see piracy as actually being a way that people hear music that they otherwise wouldn't hear.

SG: My take on it is that free music isn't free. The electronics business is making a fortune off of free music, because they are the ones that facilitate it, selling computers with CD burners as well as the ISPs that sell you broadband. Those companies have profited a great deal from the proliferation of so-called piracy. The record labels have suffered. But where do the artists come out in this equation? Are they better off, or worse off?

Moby: I think it's hard to generalize. It really comes down to an artist-by-artist scenario. If you look at the history of institutions, almost every institution, whether it's a church or a political party or a music movement or a record company, tends to start to serve a specific need and it usually starts with a pretty good idea. But then at some point the goal of the institution becomes keeping the institution and business. And record companies came into being because for a long time they were the best way of getting music from the musician to the audience. You know that's the sole way they could justify their existence. And that made a lot of sense. They needed to understand the logistics of "how do you record an orchestra, how do you record a band," and "how do you press up vinyl and get it into the fifty thousand record stores in the United States?" But it seems like most record companies are trying to justify their continued existence by saying, "Hey, we've been around for a long time, therefore we should continue to be around." If you take a philosophy class that's called the "is–ought fallacy"—basically saying that if something is, it ought to be. And I think that record companies either need to reinvent themselves top to bottom, or go away.

SG: Although Little Idiot is the label on which you released your last album, I also noticed Mute on the packaging. So it looks like you have partnered if not with a major, then at least with another label that is known as a prominent "indie." What do they bring to the table?

Moby: I'm partnered, in almost every country except the UK, with a different label. The labels that we partnered with are labels that I think have done quite a good job in establishing their reliability. As we both know, the main job of a record company for the longest time was distribution. They were in production and distribution. They were the ones who knew how to make the records, and they were the ones who knew how to send them out to the rack-joggers and whatnot.

SG: Right. And they also had those big trucks and the warehouses and the factories. All that stuff that isn't quite as necessary as it was before.

Moby: And now when I look at the sales in the UK on my most recent record, literally 90 percent of my sales are from three retail outlets. So for me the role of the record company now is marketing.

SG: Right. And what is Mute doing right?

Moby: What Mute does right is they listen to the records. They get passionate about the records, and they don't have a cookie-cutter approach to marketing. Many people at labels are so over-worked that regardless of the record, they just mark it up the same way. With Mute, every artist gets their own specific marketing plan. And the people who work at Mute really think about it and they really care about the music. Also, what they do right is they keep working on records six months and a year after they've been released. If I look at some of the success I've had, I've never in the course of my career had immediate success with a record. When the album *Play* was released, it went to number one in Europe, but only eleven months after the initial release date. The biggest hit single I ever had in France came eighteen months after a record was released. In hindsight I was looking at the demise of the record companies; it was basically when they started quarterly reporting.

SG: And Mute does better than that?

Moby: I mean, I'm sure they have to be doing quarterly reporting, but they try to take that longer view.

SG: So the majors had to make profits immediately, and if they didn't, they would drop the artist.

Moby: That's the way the majors became once they started quarterly reporting to their owners. A record would come out, and if the record didn't basically prove itself in the first month and a half, the label would move on.

SG: I recall receiving copies of countless drop notices when I was at Sony. If that ethos had been prevalent in the 1970s, Fleetwood Mac would have been dropped. Also Prince and Bruce Springsteen, whose initial albums did not do that well, would have been dropped. So Mute is with you for the long haul?

Moby: I hope . . . you never know. Because who knows what EMI will do with Mute. Who knows if the people working there will continue to work there. Making predictions about who you might be working within a couple years in the music business is probably like making predictions after the Vietnam War about who we would be fighting next.

[*Author's note: Although Mute operates as an indie, it is owned by EMI.*]

SG: I hear you. Well, let's talk about how you're doing. I notice you have 53,000 friends on Myspace, and I can see you are still posting there. So do you think Myspace is still an important place for artists to have a presence? And what's the best way to use it?

Moby: Well, actually I think there's a much bigger site of mine that has more like a million.

SG: I notice you have about 750,000 followers on Twitter. How did you acquire so many followers?

Moby: [*Laughs.*] Um, by being so fantastically interesting. I have no idea. I mean, one of the reasons that I do what I do is because I really like communicating with people. I mean, sure, Myspace and Twitter are great places for marketing, but first and foremost I just like being able to communicate with people. I mean, I'm doing this interview with you because I like talking with you.

SG: I appreciate it.

Moby: You know? And I think sometimes that one of the really nice things about having my own label, is that professional decisions we make are done for all the right reasons. When we think about touring, the first thought is not how much money can we make. The first thought is how can we put on a really good tour, reach the right people, and create something that has integrity that everyone's going to be happy with. And I know that might sound like insincere lip service, but that's actually the way we approach things. It's not that my manager and I are all enlightened [*laughs*], it's just that neither one of us is good at being a mercenary.

SG: It also must be nice to have total creative control.

Moby: Yeah. And being able to do things like the first single from this record—it used an obscure song that can never get played on the radio, and with an obscure video by David Lynch that will never get played on TV, which I can throw on YouTube and is fantastic. And we gave it all away for free, because that seemed like the right thing to do.

SG: Talking about giving things away for free—let's touch on Moby Gratis for a second, because that's a pretty innovative thing. Tell us what it is and how it works and what inspired you to create it.

Moby: Well, I started Mobygratis.com as a way to give free music away to independent filmmakers and film students. The impetus to do so came from a conversation I had with a friend of mine who's an indie filmmaker. He was just complaining and complaining about how difficult it was to license music for movies.

SG: Because it's too expensive to license music for movies?

Moby: Yeah, if you're an indie filmmaker and you have no budget and you want to license a song from a major label. If you have no budget, first of all, a major label is not going to return your call. And if they do return your call, they are going to quote some outlandish, exorbitant fee for whatever title you want to license. And then once you do that, you have to go to the publishing company. And it's just this huge, expensive rigmarole, so I just wanted to help out people who are trying to make independent films.

SG: Now, the key is that it's free for festivals and if they get picked up they have to come back to you, so it's not completely free.

Moby: Well, it's not completely free. If ever the film becomes commercial and the music is licensed commercially, they have to pay a small commercial license. But the commercial license, I've structured it so I can never make money from it. Whatever money is generated goes to the Humane Society. The reason for doing that is if I make sure that I can never ever make a penny from it, then I know I'm doing it for the right reasons.

SG: I'm definitely going to recommend the site to my film-producer clients, because they usually have to spend a small fortune to license music.

Moby: I've actually been criticized for being a little bit too open about giving stuff away. And all I'm saying is that this works for me. I understand that a lot of musicians who really want to get paid as much as they can for their music, I fully respect that and I would never criticize them for having that attitude, because I don't know what anyone else's circumstances are. If someone has alimony payments or needs to buy a dialysis machine, who knows?

SG: Since record sales have declined dramatically, and you're giving music away to the filmmakers, how do you make money?

Moby: Well, I guess I got lucky, because over the years I've saved and invested pretty well. And I have a fairly simple life. You know, I've lived in the same apartment and had the same studio for a long time. I hope this doesn't sound insincere, but my goal as a musician is to try to make music that I love and try to get people to hear it. Basically, what I've found is as a musician today, if they want to be savvy, they'll have diversified revenue streams. They'll figure out how to produce other artists and do remixes and DJ and play live and write film scores and all these different things. And then I've found that the best way to have success is to do what you love. I'm better at doing things that I love and then maybe some money comes in.

SG: You've been so successful at getting your music into movies and television; can you give us a couple of tips?

Moby: My tip is I have no idea—because I mean, this album *Wait for Me* is arguably the most cinematic record I've ever made, and I haven't had a single film license from it. And I've licensed tons and tons of music over the years to films! Clearly, the market is so crowded. And I mean, there's a lot of music being used in the world, but for every piece of music that gets licensed, there's probably about twenty thousand pieces of music that were pitched. I did a panel about radio a couple years ago, and people in radio were asking me how do they compete with Internet radio and how do they compete with NPR. And they were looking for technological ways of doing things. And to me the only way anyone succeeds in the music business is having good content.

SG: So as the blogger Bob Lefsetz likes to say, the first rule for any artist is: "Don't suck!"

Moby: Yeah, I mean if you want to sell more records, make better records. If you want to get your music licensed, make really great music. If you want to have people listen to your radio show, have a really great radio show.

SG: I'm doing my best! [*Laughs.*] I can't believe out of the three-quarter-million people you have on Twitter and Myspace that at least some of them aren't music supervisors.

Moby: I have friends that are music supervisors, and I'd give them advance copies of the record. And with this record, still, not a single license!

SG: Well, I'm sure it's on its way.

Moby: At least for my own peace of mind and my own sanity, there has to just be a degree of acceptance. I try to make the best record I can make, and I try to get people to listen to it. And beyond that? There's nothing I can do.

SG: But you can talk, and you're very articulate! I want to end in an interesting response to an interesting question you were given when you were on WNYC a few weeks ago—the question was, "Are we witnessing the death of the recording business as we know it?" And you said, "At the risk of being undiplomatic, the demise of the record business is one of the best things that has happened to music." What did you mean by that?

Moby: What I meant was that 1999 was a high-water mark for profitability and was at the bottom of the barrel for creativity. You know, I can't think of a worse year . . .

SG: You mean you didn't like Celine Dion?

Moby: [*Laughs.*] I've criticized other musicians in my life, and I've always regretted it, because sometimes they come after me with their posse. So I'm not going to criticize other musicians, and I don't need any more enemies. But I just find that there's almost an inverse relationship between profitability and creativity. And I mean this—I hope I don't sound crazy or new age, but music is sublime. Music is what can change a person's life. It can make them move across country and cut their hair or grow their hair. And it can make, you know, it can make death more palatable, it can be sexy, it can be celebratory, it can be all these different things. So I think our ultimate goal as people in the music business has to be existing in service to music. You know? And if you get rich from it, great! More power to you! But either way, the Beatles and the Rolling Stones, the reason that they're so iconic and so hugely successful is that they made amazing, beautiful records that meant a lot to people. You know? I get that the record companies can, top to bottom, reinvent themselves and be more successful than ever. But I don't think the way to reinvent yourself is putting a new coat of paint on an old, outdated business plan.

SG: Do you think that they'll learn before it's too late?

Moby: I was talking about this with a friend of mine who's been in the music business for a long time, and we were saying that a record company wanting to be your "merch" company is akin to your plumber wanting to fix your car. Their only experience is making records. I just don't see these old, ossified, monolithic companies having the flexibility to adapt to the market today.

SG: Now, that was undiplomatic.

Moby: But at the same time, I hope they can.

SG: Ah. So you're available for consultation?

Moby: I don't know anything. But I'm available for coffee! Beyond that, I don't know what I can offer.

SG: I've enjoyed talking to you a great deal. Do you have any parting shots for our audience before you leave?

Moby: My parting words are: the reason we are all in the music business is because at one point music made us cry, or gave us a profound, sublime experience, and as long as we keep our focus on that, everything will work out.

Chapter 16
A Digital Artist: DJ Spooky, aka That Subliminal Kid

Interview with Paul Miller

Paul D. Miller, aka "DJ Spooky: That Subliminal Kid" is a multimedia artist, composer, and writer. In 2008, Paul edited and published *Sound Unbound,* a compilation of essays focused on the role of sound and digital media in today's society. His multimedia artwork has been featured from the Ludwig Museum in Cologne, Germany, to the Andy Warhol Museum in Pittsburg. Recently he was invited by the island of Vanuatu in South Asia to launch an art colony on the island and create a space that is "a nexus for art, culture and climate awareness." Google featured his work, a collection of digital photos, video, and music inspired by Vanuato, in an exhibit in October 2010 to celebrate their digital art initiative and the opening of their new corporate headquarters in New York City.

SG: What inspired you to put together the *Sound Unbound* anthology, and who were some of the contributors to the book?

PM: I work with MIT Press, and they are focused on technology and a contemporary sort of "aesthetics." So as an artist, writer, and musician, those are three things I focus on: art, writing, and literature. With music, one of the things I've tended to find is that there's always this kind of need for people to keep it very streamlined, very simple. Meanwhile, the world is a very complex, rapidly changing place. When you get thirty-six essays focusing on contemporary music production, contemporary music thinking, contemporary art in relationship to technology, and contemporary technology's relationship to culture. I had people like Daphne Keller, a senior attorney at Google, and artists including Moby, Chuck D from Public Enemy, Brian Eno, and Steve Reich, who wrote the introduction. In all, thirty-six essays by thirty-six radically different people. The idea was like a radical omnivorous situation (i.e., let's open it up and have diverse points of view from very strong people in their specific fields) and also to just create a situation where hip-hop, electronic music, you name it . . . It's unapologetically complex. It's not stupid. Because a lot of stuff is found in books—for example, some of my favorite writers like Jeff Chang, or if you go back in time to other people, like, David Toop's *Rap Attack.* A lot of books just want to keep it really streamlined, really simple. So I wanted to try to say, look, you know the world is complex. Let's try to make something that really reflects that.

SG: This may defeat the purpose, but give us a takeaway from the book. How would you say that digital has affected the art of some of these contributors to your book?

PM: Say, for example, Moby. His piece was about what it was like to have a sample of other people's voices. I thought that was a really interesting thing with his relationship to the Alan Lomax Collection. And the fact that he has been a really an important figure for electronic music for the last fifteen to twenty years. So when you look at Public Enemy's album *It Takes a Nation of Millions*, it was an absolute collage—the whole album was made from small fragments of other people's records. And I love the fact that Chuck D and I are doing a project with Clyde Stubblefield, James Brown's drummer. So the book is kind of a mix tape. I collect the artists' records, and explore as much as possible the collage aesthetics that drive mix tapes and the contemporary art scene that say, "Look, this is a social sculpture." The book has been one of MIT's top sellers in the last couple years and we've had a great run with it.

SG: Tell us about your most recent venture, the Vanuatu Pacifica project. How did it come about, who are some of the people involved, and what do you want to achieve?

PM: The Vanuatu Pacifica Foundation is an artist-run initiative saying, "All right, let's think of an artist residency." Let's think of a forum where people can figure out creative, for lack of a better word, "intervention." How can a culture respond to change? The South Pacific is a really incredible place filled with so many different cultures and different ways of looking at life. So I'm looking at this as kind of a beginning of dialogue where we have artists, lawyers, writers, scientists, composers come out to the island to do mini residencies. We want to see a way to get them in dialogue with the local population and to exchange culture. To see what happens. I want to leave a lot of room for people to think about complexity and nuance and to explore the local population in relationship to their own ecosystem. I want to mix art, music, science, digital media, and explore this notion of sustainability but also allow for exchange of perspective.

SG: I recently attended Google's digital art exhibit in New York featuring your work, and I saw that the people of Vanuato are featured in your work.

PM: Yes, it's a long story, but I started the project kind of as a relationship situation. My girlfriend at the time and I wanted to go away, and we wanted to figure out some places where we could spend some quality time together, and I ended up sort of really enjoying the region and seeing how this was a sort of micro utopia, a micro space, a micro culture. Google's new initiative is intriguing in that they are a company that's focusing on optimizing communication. Figuring out different ways of channeling language. Channeling spoken text, including Google Talk or Google Buzz and so on. Vanuatu has in the most amount of languages for the smallest population in the world. And it's also a place that's been rated by the Happiness Index, which is this group of economists that are trying to study how happiness works. It's been rated as one of the happiest places on earth. So I thought it was an intriguing and complex place to think about during this project.

SG: Well, how do digital tools figure in your work?

PM: Almost everything I do is software based. My iPhone apps, my studio system. I'm making tracks all the time, and so I realize my tools, whether it be from my writing, my art, my film edits, or, you know, looking at how I put together a music track. It's all software. Software doesn't mean anything unless it's connected to something else, so you have to think about networks. And that is the basic core of what digital art means. So I'm really interested in that, although Vanuato is not a center for digital media. It's very remote. There's only one place to check e-mail on the whole island. About fifteen miles away from where we are, so you have to hike.

SG: You couldn't choose a place nearer to an Internet connection?

PM: That's the point. When you think about the contemporary music scene and contemporary music production, it's about the studio as the center of how people make music and so on. But on an island like this, this social form is like a clearing in a beautiful part of the land where people gather and watch each other and play live instruments and so on. So it's a paradox. I'm very intrigued to see how we can make this functional.

SG: How are people on the island responding to your project?

PM: They're very enthusiastic. We've had no problems, and they can't wait to get started. I mean, everybody is just ready to roll.

SG: You guys discovered any local talent?

PM: Yeah. I've checked out some of this music, the music on the island. I haven't had much chance to get really deep into it, because when I was there I was focusing on other things. Music is one component of what I do, so I want to try to keep my role in terms of music. But I'm really focused on the culture in general. Music is just one bit of piece of the puzzle.

SG: Do you have any plans to further collaborate with Google?

PM: Sure. Google's been very supportive of my work, and they have a very interesting mini empire of culture. They're able to figure out very complex applications and apply them to real-time music, real-time literature, real-time art, and those are things that I think are very important right now. I maintain a very open communication with Google.

SG: One of the sections of the book in which this interview will be published is a "how-to" for artists. Do you have any advice for up-and-coming artists on using digital tools to make or distribute their work?

PM: At the end of the day, if you're new to the game, the whole idea is to be an innovator and ignore the rules as they're normally set up and try and come up with unique ways of making content, unique ways of how people perceive your work, and unique ways of how that work reflects the environment it's coming out of. If people view you as fitting in the formula, there's already twenty zillion people doing that already, so you really need to flip the script and try some whole different angles on things. A real innovator cuts through the mix, and I think that's what you do if you have a sense of being organized, and that's half the battle, as well. So one half is innovation; the other half is just being organized about the innovation.

SG: What's coming up next for you, Paul Miller? Are you going back to Vanuatu, or what other projects are you planning?

PM: Basically, I plan on doing a lot of environmental work over the next couple months and years. First and foremost, I just went to the North Pole with a group called Cape Farewell, sort of far north for about four weeks. I took a studio up there, and I was trying to figure out some different ways of creating music compositions, sort of reflection of landscape. But the landscape is melting and shattered and it's completely vanishing. I want to make music about a vanishing space, a vanishing sense of how the environment is transforming that whole region, and I'm trying to make it what I call "Acoustic Portraits." Then next year's the one hundredth anniversary of the discovery of the South Pole. So I'm going to be doing a project around Antarctica. And then I am finishing my next book, called *The Book of Ice*. So those are three projects. I just participated in two others: one is called "The Green Patriot." It's posters and prints looking at environmental issues. And the other is a book called *The Boombox Project*. It's a history of boom boxes.

SG: It sounds like you have a lot on your plate. How can people find out more about the Vanuatu Pacifica project and your other ventures?

PM: Well, the website for the Vanuatu Pacifica foundation is just www.djspooky.com/vanuatu, and that has a lot of information. And my normal website is just www.djspooky.com, and wc have lots and lots of info on that, as well.

SG: I want to thank you, Paul Miller, aka DJ Spooky, for being part of *The Future of the Music Business*.

PM: All right. Rock and roll.

Chapter 17
How to Measure Success in a Digital World

Interview with Eric Garland, Cofounder and CEO of BigChampagne

Eric Garland is the cofounder and CEO of BigChampagne, a media tracking company that was the first to monitor P2P music file sharing. Garland discusses "The Ultimate Chart," a new ranking system that determines the popularity of songs and artists based on online streaming, webcasting, blogs, and social media, as well as SoundScan and traditional radio.

	Artist	Song
1	Katy Perry	Firework
2	Bruno Mars	Grenade
3	Black Eyed Peas	The Time (Dirty Bit)
4	Rihanna	What's My Name
5	Pink	Raise Your Glass
6	Glee Cast	Dog Days Are Over
7	Kesha	We R Who We R
8	Bruno Mars	Just the Way You Are
9	Glee Cast	Hey, Soul Sister
10	Rihanna	Only Girl (in the World)

Sample of BigChampagne Ultimate Chart (December 9, 2010)

Garland also discusses in this interview his take on the most important recent developments in the business and his take on the future, including the future of Spotify in the United States and the replacement of P2P with YouTube as the most popular platform for online music consumption. Considered a visionary in the industry, Garland is a leading speaker on digital music issues.

SG: What were the most important developments in the business in the last two or three years?

EG: The first thing that pops into my mind is that we've gone as an industry from thinking that there would be some silver-bullet solution to all of the challenges of the Internet age, to appreciating in a collective way. It's seeped into the collective unconscious of the business that it's not going to be any one thing. It's going to be a number of businesses that are all going to have to flourish in order to replace all of the value that's been lost in the traditional business.

SG: Can you elaborate?

EG: The CD lost enormous share to Napster and Kazaa and LimeWire and all of that ilk starting a little more than ten years ago, but in the last couple of years we've been thieving from the thieves, meaning free alternatives like the ad-supported version of Spotify, like Myspace music, and most importantly like YouTube. These things have been stealing share from traditional file-sharing platforms, so P2P is losing ground in terms of where people are listening to music, where people stream on demand or download. It wasn't ever really about P2P file sharing as much as it was about this move to unlimited all-you-can-eat on demand. It feels like free music. And P2P may end up having been just one stop along the way.

SG: That sounds like good news for the business, because Spotify and YouTube are ad-supported, and the copyright owners, artists, labels, and songwriters are sharing in revenue from that.

EG: They are! I would like to characterize it as good news, but as you know, elements of the business (particularly the largest music companies) are unconvinced that it's all good news. I think when Spotify comes into the United States it will probably be as a subscription service and not as an ad-supported service. Similarly, a lot of the free ad-supported streaming services have struggled in terms of making their label partners happy with the proceeds. I think, as much as we're glad to see pirate markets give way to legitimate markets, the biggest music companies want those legitimate markets to be much more lucrative than they are.

SG: So you don't see the business rebounding?

EG: People now agree that we're going to need a lot of things to succeed in part to be successful and whole. I thought maybe we were finding the bottom as an industry in some markets, but I think we may see some more bad news coming out of the United States in the next year. Because it doesn't appear that we've stabilized the way we hoped.

SG: What about the idea of a levy on the ISPs' profits to compensate the labels for their loss on record sales?

EG: Isn't it wild that we are seeing things that were heretical when we started talking about them? I remember bringing up this notion of "Well, we might just have to impose payment on existing behaviors—if we can't slow the Internet to a crawl, we might just have to figure out a way to put a toll booth in there." And I remember that notion eight or ten years ago was enough to get me forcibly out of some buildings of some major music companies, and now, you know, all of these things, and particularly cooperative efforts with carriers like mobile carriers and ISPs, are very much on the table. People that rejected them conceptually out of hand just a few short years ago are now starting to raise them.

SG: I raised the issue with Tom Silverman, who wrote the foreword to this book. Tom is actually on the board of the RIAA, and when I asked him why the big labels haven't pushed for a levy on the ISPs, he said the labels would not support it, but he also said if there were a simple announcement that the big labels were going after the ISPs, the labels' value would skyrocket. So let me ask you, why don't you think the big labels ever rallied around this idea?

EG: I think it's pretty straightforward, actually. The music companies in North America and the USA think that they can do better, meaning they would only do that as a sort of a last resort, for the obvious reason that it represents a real loss of control. And at the point where you're just taking a handout basically because your intellectual property is being distributed far and wide without your permission or your consent. They view that as sort of a last/worst, or maybe the second-to-worst outcome. The worst outcome is you don't get paid at all. Second-to-last stop on that train is you get a handout because you can't control the market. And so what they're trying to do is to motivate the largest companies, like Google and major mobile, cable, and satellite carriers, to want to participate in this marketplace, to build businesses together where we can pay a premium for content and exert a lot of control on what people do with that content and how that content travels to and fro. And so I think we're a long way from saying, "Okay, uncle! We'll take the handout." They've got bigger plans.

SG: My theory is that they have been reluctant to push for a levy because they are afraid that half of the funds would be paid directly to the artists. That's how other compulsory-licensing schemes such as those imposed on webcasters work.

EG: Again, it's another form of loss of control, right? When you hand it over to Uncle Sam, he's going to oversee how the monies are allocated. In the private market, *you* get to oversee how the monies get paid out, if at all.

SG: When I mentioned the royalty on the ISPs to Andy Lack, who was chairman of Sony Music at the time, he said it sounded like communism.

EG: And that was the company line for most of the music companies at that time when Andy Lack was in the seat.

SG: At the New Music Seminar, you gave two presentations. One of them was "The Ultimate Chart," which I want to focus on in a minute. But your other presentation was called "By the Numbers," which you presented in conjunction with Tom Silverman. Could you just give a thumbnail version of what you discussed?

EG: For the "By the Numbers" presentation, Tom started with a great analysis of sales trends, going back in some cases back to 1972 to the present. Some of it was unsurprising to anyone who's been paying attention—as you know, we had this terrific bubble in the 1990s, around the extraordinary growth of the CD product, and then we've just seen this thing falling like a stone for most of the past ten years. But Tom went beyond that and did some additional analysis looking at the numbers of artists or the numbers of releases in the form of albums and songs that break through the noise. And he identified a breakthrough point, a threshold, which was around ten thousand units sold, that correlated with these artists breaking out.

SG: Right. And I think he said that of 105,000 albums released in 2009, only a few hundred sold better than ten thousand units.

EG: That's right.

SG: Incredible.

EG: And the number of albums released last year that actually went platinum, that sold one million copies or more? The number that went platinum, care to guess?

SG: I don't even want to hazard a guess, it's too depressing.

EG: If you said a baker's dozen you would be high—it was actually only twelve albums, down from last year, which was down from the year prior. But you think if there were only twelve platinum releases, then where is growth, if at all? And what we found was music consumption, people watching, listening, streaming, downloading is growing at a rate that is striking at that rate of decline. So what we looked at in our presentation was to see where that occurred, and the standout headline is that in many ways, that now occurs on YouTube more than anywhere else. And I think I was even quoted in some of the coverage of our talks saying, if someone asks you, "What's the biggest name in online music?" you would probably inclined to say iTunes. However, I would say YouTube, because by the numbers that dwarfs Apple iTunes in terms of consumption. People are watching an individual video of a popular Justin Bieber or Lady Gaga video hundreds of millions of times on YouTube, and it's that way all the way down the tail. Even relatively obscure things get a lot of views on YouTube.

SG: Again, that is good news for the music business. YouTube generates advertising income. I also listen to Last.fm and Pandora all day instead of the radio. They have few commercial interruptions, and I can see information about the artists at a glance. Last.fm and Pandora are also paying the record companies and the publishers, which is good news.

EG: They are, absolutely. And you're right in keeping with our findings on this statistically. We made a couple of announcements with respect to Pandora—we were able to announce that they had their sixty millionth registered user and that they now represent more than half; more than 50 percent of all Internet radio listening now occurs at Pandora. So they are a monster in the category, and in fact they are now starting to represent whole percentage points of all radio listening, online and off. Pandora now has more than a percent, maybe close to 2 percent of all radio listening. It's just staggering. You know, I've known Tim Westergren since we were both baby startups, and now, when I'm lucky enough that he takes my call, we have a laugh about how one of my favorite pet Internet projects went mainstream in a really big way.

SG: Perhaps when the advertising market comes back, the labels will get their breath back. Because if you look at ASCAP and BMI, which take a piece of advertising revenues, over the last ten years they've actually generated more income in each year than the previous year. So maybe there is hope that the record business can make a comeback based on this model.

EG: There's no question there's hope. I mean directionally, if we look at what's declining precipitously, it's CD sales, but what's growing like a weed is listening and watching on services such as Pandora and YouTube. And that speaks directly to ASCAP and BMI revenues, because when people click the play button, when people listen, when people stream, that's when copyright owners, artists, and songwriters make money.

SG: Let's turn our attention to "The Ultimate Chart." The *New York Times* reported this summer that "This week BigChampagne, a company that tracks online media, announced the Ultimate Chart, a challenger that it says measures music's popularity more fully by counting not only sales and airplay (as *Billboard* does) but also online streams and an array of social-networking services." Bob Lefsetz, the music-industry blogger, was a bit more emphatic. He wrote, "The death of *Billboard* and SoundScan. It's like we're putting glasses on the music industry. Their details are finally coming into focus." With that intro, tell us what is "The Ultimate Chart"? How is it different than the *Billboard* top pop chart, and why is it better?

EG: The Ultimate Chart is the culmination of just what we've been doing as a research outfit for about ten years: we started looking at the original Napster and peer-to-peer before there was any digital music available for sale, for stream, for download in any legitimate form anywhere. When we started measuring traffic on peer-to-peer, we had a really simple but controversial thesis, and that was: This is a precedent for something big. What's happening with the original Napster, we said, is probably the future of the business or points to the future of the business. And it made sense to us that all of that browsing and shopping in record stores would eventually make its way online and that people would listen to and buy and enjoy music increasingly on their computers. And so we took a keen interest in Napster and the things that followed Napster such as Kazaa. We started collecting a lot of quantitative metrics about all of that online activity about music. The only problem was, it was hard to make a chart out of that, that you could put in *Billboard*, because it was really just an infringement chart. At least in the eyes of the business, it was just a painful reminder of all the stuff that was being stolen from them. It took the market a number of years to launch legal outlets for digital music in such a way that we could point to billions of authorized impressions and transactions. A vibrant marketplace, people all over the world enjoying all over the Internet in a way that was noninfringing, right? First, iTunes had to show up, and after it, the floodgates opened and a huge variety of things appeared, including all of the companies we've talked about today, from Pandora to YouTube and everything in between.

SG: The new Napster and Rhapsody and so forth.

EG: And so forth. Exactly. And so what we've done with the Ultimate Chart is a simple furthering of that original thesis. We tried to gather as much information as is available about all of the ways in which people are consuming music—all of the ways in which music is popular, and we measure those things for the first time all in one chart. So it's an expansion on, you know, what have always been the weekly sales and airplay charts. We just made something more inclusive.

SG: Let's get into a little more detail. Your press announcement stated, and I quote, "The Ultimate Chart integrates data from categories including: song and album sales, radio airplay, online audio and video plays and followers. The Ultimate Chart is the first and only chart that looks at all of the ways in which music is popular online and off." That sounds great, but how do you integrate so many diverse ways of listening to music, from authorized downloads to Twitter? Do you assign different weight to each category?

EG: Absolutely. And I'm glad you used that word, "integrate." Because what we've realized in recent years is that that's really the single best word, "integration." It's the single best word to describe what our company does and who we are at heart. We are a data aggregation and integration company, and so, as a technology startup, we developed a lot of good technology and core competencies around reconciling things that appeared at first to be irreconcilable.

SG: Tell us how you allocate value to each use of music to create the Ultimate Chart.

EG: Everything we do with the Ultimate Chart is weighted according to value. Value means, in this case, economic value. So that can be very simple. Ten plays on radio or Internet radio are worth ten times what one play is worth, or it can be much more complicated. For instance, what about a follower on Twitter? What about a friend on Myspace? We created a social-metrics category, which includes things like fans, friends, and followers. And what we do with that category is, rather than make it a component of the Ultimate Chart, we determined that the value of a play or a song may be increased slightly based on all of the other shows of affinity that an artist may have. Although we take it into account, we assign a relative weight. I think the actual formula is 1/100th of the next-smallest measurement, to give those affirmations some effect on the value of your play, and what that means is that if you and I each got 100 plays, but you were much more popular in terms of people liking you and following you and friending you and listening to you, then your 100 plays might be worth 110, and my 100 plays, if nobody cares about me and I have no friends or fans on the Internet, then my 100 plays might be worth 90 and therefore your 110 beats my 90.

SG: For example I'm a Wynton Marsalis fan, and I was at his house and I recorded it when he broke out into spontaneous music after the Saints won the Super Bowl, and I taped that on my Blackberry and uploaded it (with his permission, of course) to my YouTube account. And then he was broadcasting a concert live through Ustream and I relinked that to my Facebook friends and fans. So you're saying all of that is part of your calculations?

EG: For our purposes, all of that is absolutely accounted for, but in the category of social metrics, meaning that is going to be in the very small box of things that can slightly increase or decrease his status based on his actual paid play. But all of his official material, that which is generating revenue for him, is weighted much more heavily.

SG: If you go to www.ultimatechart.com, you can see all the stats for top songs and artists, broken down by sales, broadcast, watching/listening, fans/friends/followers, all scored on a 100-point scale. It seems you are making your calculus a lot more public than *Billboard*.

EG: We want to make it completely transparent, but at the same time this website is not our pro version, which is available through our partners and subscribers. This is a consumer site, so we didn't want to overwhelm, we didn't want to put a lot of math and, you know, put a spreadsheet up on what is essentially meant to be an entertaining website. But yes, transparency is the goal. Listen, if we don't know how we arrive at these things as a business, if we can't audit and scrutinize and critique the horse race, then it's a "rigged" race. Transparency is key.

SG: So are there going to be other charts? Hip-hop, country, et cetera?

EG: Sure. We're very excited about forthcoming genre charts, as you mentioned, format charts that will address all the major categories from urban or hip-hop to pop, to rock, country, and so on. Geographically specific charts and data-source-specific charts. We're going to start publishing information about P2P downloads, publishing information about YouTube views, publishing information about iTunes sales, et cetera. There's a radio station that we're working on now that will make these playable charts. It's a great platform, and we've just been bowled over by the response to it.

Chapter 18

The True Story of Napster and the Labels: How Shawn Fanning Made the Labels an Offer They *Had* to Refuse

Interview with Ted Cohen, Managing Partner of TAG Strategic and Former Senior VP at EMI Music

Ted is a thirty-year music-industry veteran and currently managing partner of Tag Strategic, a digital entertainment-consulting firm. Ted served as senior VP of digital development and distribution at EMI Music and is recognized as one of the leading authorities in the world on the digital music business. In this interview, Ted reveals that labels sought to work out a deal with Napster, but Napster made them an offer they had to refuse. Ted also discusses his views of the most important recent developments in the business and his prescription for success in today's music business.

SG: In a previous interview, I asked Eric Garland about what might bring the industry back from the brink. He replied that a number of different business models will have to flourish if the record business is going to recover. What do you think of Eric's opinion?

TC: When I joined EMI in May of 2000 and continued over my six years there, I tried to express to senior management that it was about choice. In mid-2000 we were talking about doing digital downloads with Liquid Audio, RioBORG, and Amplify.com. This is three years before iTunes. A lot of resistance arose, because of "why do we want to do digital downloads," and "they're going to cherry-pick our library," and "if they're going to pick one track, then a single track should be three, four dollars, because that's the best song on the album and they're not going to buy the album now." So, you know, we started doing full-album downloads. Then we were able to move the needle a bit and get to individual track downloads. The perception that individual track downloads were going to hurt full album downloads was similar to the perception that full album downloads were going to hurt physical CD sales. So then we get past that and iTunes comes along. And iTunes is a combination of track downloads and full album downloads. Just prior to that, Rhapsody comes along. Now, Rhapsody is subscription, so it's ten to fifteen dollars for all-you-can-eat. Basically unlimited access to music, but a recurring monthly charge. Labels, including mine, EMI at the time, were completely against the idea of unlimited access, because now that would hurt track downloads and album downloads. So if we let people have access to all the music they wanted through access, not through ownership, then they might not buy a CD again. I argued very loudly that if we could get consumers to spend ten bucks a month, isn't this a better consumer proposition, first of all, and secondly, isn't it better, as we are trying to expose artists, because in an à la carte track or even an album-download environment, there's a purchase barrier to discovery.

So you have a situation where you've got all these artists you're trying to get exposure for so that they can tour, so that they can become bigger, so that they get to a second and a third album, which is harder and harder these days. . . . So I became very bullish on subscription. And I continue to be bullish on subscription. I'll follow the time line here: We finally license Rhapsody in early 2002. Then the legal Napster comes along. Then in 2003 we do iTunes. Then we move later into the idea of ad-supported services. It was hard to get the labels—again, mine included—to accept the idea that "ad-supported" could work . . . it made them very uncomfortable. I insisted that downloads were only one part of the solution, and that streaming was another part of the solution, because some people may want to own the music, and others may just want access to it. Because of mobile streaming on the iPhone, Android, and Blackberry, the hesitations about streaming are off the table now. So what you have now is ubiquitous access to music wherever you are. Some people subscribe to MOG, or listen to Slacker or Pandora or Spotify or Rhapsody, or any of these streaming services. Then the challenge becomes how do you curate it, or how do you filter it, how do you do editorial. But we now have access in 2010, to upwards of ten, eleven million tracks now, and Grooveshark announced yesterday a $3-per-month web-only access to their service. So we went from MOG offering it at $5, and Rhapsody offering it at $10, and we're now down to $3 per month for access to all the music in the world. How much is the value proposition going to get before consumers buy in? We'll see what happens.

To address Eric's response, yes, the labels have gotten better at looking at multiple solutions, but I joke that with desperation comes more vision, so things that they weren't able to consider three years ago, when business was only down 25 percent, look a little bit more interesting when the business is down 50 percent, so eyes are opening. People are being a little more willing.

SG: Is advertiser-supported streaming on YouTube the most important development in the last two to three years, and if it is, what's the second-most-important development?

TC: That's the most important development. I think it's really an important change of attitude. But another important development has been, and this came out of the iPhone, personalized applications. Different ways of accessing music. I can have Rhapsody on my iPhone, I can have MOG on my iPhone, I can have Slacker. I think Apple has done a great job of popularizing the concept of the application environment, which is now available on most mobile phones. . . . Apple does an amazing job of mainstreaming consumer behavior. They weren't the first people to build a digital music player; that was done by the Rio player in 1998, and the iPod didn't come along until 2001. They weren't the first people to do a touch-screen phone. That was done by Palm way before the iPhone ever came out. But the marketing stream. The ease of use. The simple message to the consumer says, it's about choice.

[*Author's note: See Chapter 10 for fuller discussion of apps.*]

SG: That goes back to your original comment and to Eric Garland's, which is, diversity may be the solution.

TC: It is, and you can't change consumer behavior anymore. Anything we can do is meet them at every itch that they have with a solution that scratches that itch.

SG: You were a speaker at Tom Silverman's New Music Seminar this summer in New York. Could you please give a thumbnail sketch of your presentation, which focused on the history of digital music?

TC: I started in 1964 with the creation of ARPANET (Advanced Research Projects Agency Network), which was the original Internet, to the launch of FTP, which stands for "file transfer protocol." There was a lot of geeky stuff in the beginning—from the personal computer coming out in 1978 and 1979 via IBM, Apple, and Atari, to the launch of the CD in 1983. Basically, I went through the whole time line of how access to digital music has evolved.

SG: I think one of the most important developments was when the Germans created MP3, which Shawn Fanning used to create Napster.

TC: But there's one thing that predates all of that. In 1994, Rob Lord, Jon Luini, and Jeff Patterson created IUMA, the International Underground Music Archive, which was the first place where you could go and download music from any of the artists, and in some cases, some major artists, and put their music up there. But the music was uploaded in the uncompressed WAV format, so it could take you two to three hours to download a song. Along comes MP3 in 1995 or 1996, which was developed by Karlheinz Brandenburg, an audio engineer at the Fraunhofer Institute, and then here's Shawn Fanning sitting at Northeastern University in Boston and he goes, "You know what? We could create a way to index with what's up there and let people in a noncentral basis create a peer-to-peer network where people can experience each other's music." You didn't have to be a technologist to go, "Name a song you like. And then okay, somebody here has it. Would you like it? What else do they have? Oh, who's that artist? I like that one, that one, and that one. But I don't know that one." There was a certain amount of discovery there. You'd look in somebody's folder and see a song or an artist you'd never heard of. This was very exciting. I perceived that there was a way to monetize it.

SG: Did Shawn Fanning and Napster try to make a deal with the labels?

TC: So the folklore goes that Napster tried to make a deal with the music industry, and the music industry stupidly rejected them—but this isn't true. It was only around late 2001 to —early 2002, when Hank Barry was running Napster, that Bertelsmann invested. Bertelsmann invested a ton of money that Napster used to enhance its service and come up with a deal for the labels. And the deal that was put on the table was a flat payment of one billion dollars, which sounds like a lot of money, but at the time the music industry was a fourteen-billion-per-year industry. So if you were going to say, "Here's a billion dollars. We'll guarantee you one billion dollars, but now anybody who wants to go to Napster to get their music, can go to Napster to get their music legally and get anything they want." Overnight you were turning the music industry from a fourteen-billion industry to a one-billion industry without a royalty. There was no percentage, no royalty. It was a flat payment. Here's a billion dollars, get out of our way. So everybody said no. I mean, if I said to you right now, Steve, I will give you two hundred dollars for your car. Okay? Will you give me your car?

SG: Well I don't own one, but if I had one I wouldn't sell it.

TC: But I made you an offer, you turned me down. How shortsighted of you. I mean, this is basically what it was. So again, in the legend of Napster, Napster tried to be nice, but the stupid label people wouldn't listen. It's not true.

SG: But here's what surprises me, Ted. I heard Hilary Rosen recently on an interview with NPR talking about the history of negotiations between Napster and the record labels, and she never got into this. Since she was on the labels' side at that time, it seems surprising she wouldn't talk about this one-billion-dollar-flat-fee offer. Why didn't she tell the story?

TC: I have no idea. Hilary is a really smart woman. I have a lot of respect for her. She's one of the smartest people that I've ever met. But she got frustrated toward the end. I think there was a point where she wanted to see it all go away and have a happy ending—but there wasn't a happy ending there. Unfortunately, the offer that was put on the table came at a time when there was so much animosity between both sides. And so you know it all went away, and it's just unfortunate.

SG: One of the reasons for the New Music Seminar was to provide a road map for success to artists in today's business, and to give snapshots of the current trend. But what was really the best useable advice you heard at the seminar for new artists?

TC: I've been involved with Tommy for the last two years on the seminar. The promise of the Internet was unrestricted access to your fan base. But to paraphrase Tommy, it doesn't guarantee you attention—it gives you the opportunity to be noticed. But there are so many artists out there right now creating music, trying to promote themselves through a Myspace, a Facebook, a Twitter, and so on. Any of the services out there: ReverbNation, TuneCore, Topspin, Hello Music, all these different services. These are tools that you have to use intelligently. And I think that the challenge is to rise above the noise. Because just getting your music onto iTunes, getting your music onto Rhapsody, getting your music played on Pandora, that's the beginning, but that's not the end. All this is doing is providing a basis for you to then build a career. The most important thing is that you have to take responsibility, and you have to take action. And there's no one to blame anymore. You don't have a manager anymore to blame. You don't have an agent, you don't have a label. You don't have any of these people that you can blame. Even if you have a manager, even if you have an agent, the days of saying "It's their fault" are over. You need to take ownership of your career; you need to take responsibility for what happens. And knowing that you have that responsibility, you have to take every reasonable action to let people know how good you are. And you can't sit around waiting to be discovered, or wait for your manager or agent to take care of you. You've gotta be twenty-four/seven on your game and in their face working it. And if you don't want to, then go back to Starbucks and ask me if I want an extra shot of espresso in that coffee.

SG: Well, at this point I need to tell an anecdote in evidence of what we saw and heard at the seminar. One of my assistants is also a musician. And she does electronic dance music. She's got a small niche, but she works it. She did an EP on her laptop and spent $1,000 to get it mastered. And this is what she did for three months—she befriended blogs. She went to the blogs that she knew represented her music well and didn't just send the EP and ask them to review it. She spent time making friends with the bloggers and corresponded directly with them about their opinions on other artists, and after she created the relationships, with about twelve blogs, she then sent them this EP as a courtesy. Didn't even ask them to review it. But some of them did, and they all liked it. And then the posts were aggregated to Hype Machine, which led to more blog attention, and eventually the EP got reviewed in Pitchfork and Brooklyn Vegan, and at that point people started to really take notice. And one thing led to another in terms of networking. Long story short, she got two record deals. One was terrible, even though it was a big German record company. But the other one came from an imprint at Universal, and it was absolutely fair.

TC: Currently I have two artists that I work, both are female, both in their twenties. One of them totally waits around saying, "What have you done for me?" and the other one is calling everyday saying, "What can I do? What can I do?" The one that's doing, the "What can I do?" artist, I'm telling her everything she can do, and she's reporting back to us what she's done. The other artist is really dissatisfied that things aren't going as well for her as she thought they would have six months ago. And I've been very brutally candid with her about the fact that she went out on tour and blogged twice during a monthlong period. That's not staying in touch with your fans. This other artist blogs daily. She e-mails daily, she tweets daily. She works it. And you have to work it. And if you don't work it, and you say, "What are you going to do for me?" that's the old music business. It's about "What do I need to do, tell me what to do, how can I do it?" I help both of them, but you know, sitting there waiting for it to happen, those days are over. Even at a Lady Gaga level, where everything's being done for her, she's relentless. And I talked to somebody about the beginning of her career, and she went after this. You can say now she's with Jimmy Iovine, and she's part of Universal and it's this big machine. But the bottom line is that it was her hunger that sparked all this. Nobody walked up to her and said, "Would you like to be Lady Gaga?" She just basically went for it the same way Madonna went for it. When Madonna was with Warner, she didn't sit around waiting for Warner to do it for her. When I was at Warner in the early 1980s, when Madonna's career first kicked off, she would sit in every marketing meeting in the office. She became like the mascot, and we would let her sit in sales meetings and marketing meetings over in the corner. She wanted to learn. She wanted to know what is sales? What is marketing? What is promotion? What is publicity? And she was like a sponge, she soaked it up and she took what she learned and became, you know, the force that she became. She wanted it so badly that she would do everything reasonable to make it happen. And that's what it takes. It's still about a hunger. It's not about being coddled.

SG: What you just said reminds me of what Don Passman, who represented people like Janet Jackson, told me. He said that the successful artists are the ones who would "walk through walls" to get to where they wanted to go.

TC: Absolutely. So whether it's digital or whether it's analog or whatever, it's about that hunger, and that's the one thing that hasn't changed. An artist that is both smart and hungry is going to succeed.

SG: Talking about hunger, let's turn our attention to the big labels, who have been the biggest losers from the changes that technology has wrought. Income from sales of recorded music is down by more than half in the last ten years. They're shedding employees, and in EMI's case, they may be going out of business, which is sad.

TC: I wouldn't be confident of that yet. Now that Roger Faxon's in charge, he's a really good music man. They've gotten rid of a lot of the issues there. Roger Faxon ran EMI Publishing for the last four to five years. Before that he was part of the EMI group in London. Really smart guys. And they've given him control of both the music label and publishing, and I think you'll see some good things from him. In general, I do agree with you, but the labels are looking at how they need to reinvent themselves, although they were slow to do it. Another thing that people don't talk about, and this is really critical: Name another business in the history of business that was not challenged by a better business model, but challenged rather by the fact that their customers decided to just take from them what they used to pay for. Does anybody go into a Ford dealership and say, "I don't like the price of the Ford. You guys are really out of date, you're really not with it. Cars should only cost five thousand dollars, so I'm going to drive away with one right now 'cause you guys are idiots."

SG: You know, I see it a little differently. I don't think it's all about the consumers not wanting to pay. I think it's about the electronics business and ISPs making a fortune from so-called free music. And they are not only making a fortune, but people who buy new computers or CD burners, who purchase high-speed Internet, they feel entitled because they've already paid.

TC: Well, you hit the word. You know, we went from an age of empowerment, ten years ago, to an age of entitlement. Anyone is entitled to do whatever they want because the technology allows them to do it. And when Verizon was running ads eight years ago that said, "Sign up for Verizon high-speed Internet and download thousands of songs a month," I said to Sarah Deutsch at Verizon, "Are you telling me with a straight face that you think that one of your customers is going to sign up for broadband from Verizon and download thousands of songs a month and then pay one dollar each for? Your message basically said 'sign up for this service and take all the music you want.'" Verizon implied that once you get this high-speed access, you are now entitled to this.

So nobody stopped this, and the ISPs have lived under safe harbor, saying, "We don't know what's happening, we can't tell you what's going on."

SG: The ISPs got that safe harbor under the DMCA because they had more power in Washington than the record business did. So I think in a way that the big labels have been a victim not only of new technology, but of competitor companies with more economic power than they. You know, I blame it on those two forces more than I do on the consumer.

TC: I have a seventeen-year-old son who really doesn't understand what's wrong if people are making stuff available, why he can't download it. He has been a little bit of a film buff the last couple years, and he's really puzzled by why downloading is unacceptable—it's so easy! It's easier to download a movie from Rapidshare than it is to download a movie from a legal site. And he has more control over that movie when he downloads. So that's a problem. You can educate a bit, but you basically have to say I can watch most of the movies I want now, online, streaming them whenever I want on Netflix. The ones I can't stream, they can deliver in the mail to me. And it's a great value proposition. It scared the hell out of the studios, and now the studios are finding Netflix to be the digital equivalent of Best Buy.

SG: So the movie studios are experimenting with new business models with the aim of giving people what they want. Will the record companies do the same? Let's talk about Spotify. That seems to be what people want—it's a free, ad-supported service and you can stream anything you want and it's caught fire in Europe, but the labels won't let it launch in the United States. Why are the record companies allowing it to exist in Europe, and why are they not allowing it here?

TC: Well, first of all they paid very large advances. And the idea was that people would convert over to the paid model. You know, it looked very promising, but the conversion has not been as good as we thought it would be.

SG: Right. They currently have eight million users, and only a few hundred thousand have converted to the premium service.

TC: Yeah, so there's a little bit of a push back now. Well, also because they got such a hero's welcome in Europe about this great service, so when they came over to the United States there was a little bit of an arrogance about it.

SG: It's not just that the European affiliates are more progressive than the Americans.

TC: Well, you know, there was a bit of progressiveness there, and it was probably easier to get done because it wasn't a U.S. service coming over to Europe, so the Europeans probably welcomed them with a little bit more open arms.

SG: Are the labels afraid that the advertising model won't pay off?

TC: Yes, because there was a promise of big advertising revenues at one point, but then we had an economic downturn. Ad revenues dropped in general for the whole business.

SG: Do you have any parting shots?

TC: No, I actually don't have any parting shots. I want everybody to get along better, and I want this all to move forward, because this is almost my thirtieth year working in the business and I really thought this digital problem would have been solved ten years ago.

Chapter 19

How to Make a Hit Song in the Digital Age

Interview with Jay Frank, Senior VP of Country Music Television

Jay Frank is currently the senior VP of music strategy for Country Music Television, better known as CMT. At CMT, he oversees the implementation of music across all platforms, including TV, web, mobile, and VOD. He used to manage music programming at Yahoo! Music, and before that he was the senior music director at the Fox Network. Jay is also the author of a new book called *Future Hit DNA*.

SG: Why did you decide to take the gig at CMT? Are you a huge fan of country music?

JF: I've always been a fan of great songs, and, it didn't really matter what genre it was, and I certainly saw, around the middle of this decade, when all the troubles for the music business really started to steamroll, that per capita, country music seemed to be delivering more great songs. But the real reason why I wanted to move to Nashville and work for Country Music Television was because it's one of the very few jobs where you can work cross-platform. One of the exciting things, right now in the digital age, is the ability to actually combine multiple screens and synchronize them to help artists move forward. To be able to go and take television, radio, the web, mobile and make sure that they're all in synch around artists, and therefore really moving forward an artist's career, was an exciting challenge, and it's been working out really well.

SG: Well, give us a brief idea of how those moving gears work at CMT. Give us an idea of what you mean by those "multiple screens."

JF: Well, CMT.com is the largest country music website, reaching well over three million people a month, and so what we usually do is start an artist by promoting their video on CMT. com, gauging the audience reaction, seeing if it's something that the audience really likes. From there, we'll then go and move it onto the television screen and provide extra promotion there. After we create that familiarity, we go to syndicated radio, where we have a syndicated news feed that goes to 150 country radio stations, and publicize the artist there. We will also use CMT Mobile, which has been growing by leaps and bounds, to publicize the artists. Anywhere that you're going to see the

CMT brand, when we're promoting either a superstar or a new artist, we're promoting them on all these platforms, so that people are really getting a sense of the popularity of a song, and we know that we can move the needle effectively for the artists we work with.

SG: So you use the website to test the waters for a song, before you consider putting it on air?

JF: Absolutely.

SG: Before discussing the book, I'd like to ask the same question I asked my two last guests, Eric Garland and Ted Cohen. And that question was, what was the most important development during the last two or three years? Both of them agreed that the most important development was building a consensus in the business that there's no one silver bullet that will be the remedy to the problems the recording business. They both agreed that it's not going to be any one thing that will bring the business back, but instead the answer is to nurture a variety of different business models. And that the labels are finally realizing that they have to nurture all of these different business models. What do you think?

JF: I'd have to agree, and I'd probably even take it one step further. When you look at the heyday of the music business, in recent terms, the late 1990s into 2000, 2001, one of the reasons why the music business was so healthy then was because the number of outlets for people to actually purchase music was also at its peak. You could go into a plethora of independent stores, and chains like Tower were at their height. You could also go to any mall and you'd have two or three record stores in each. And you had all the big-box retailers coinciding with the expansion of Best Buy, Walmart, and Target. So buying records was easier than ever. In the last few years, the purchasing of physical music has gone down, because most of the big chains have gone out of business, the big-box retailers have shrunk their space considerably, and numerous independent stores are also out of business. What is replacing them, in terms of the number of outlets, is on the Internet. And the difference is rather than everybody doing the same thing, that is, selling downloads, everybody's doing something different. Some people are streaming music in radio—think of Pandora and Last. fm. Other people are doing subscription services—think of Rhapsody. And other people are doing premium models, such as YouTube. All of them are doing different things, and so to replace the numerous outlets that generated the revenue that the music industry is accustomed to, they do now have to shift their thinking to say, I don't just have to move one product, I have to move multiple products. I have to potentially have a hundred-plus different skews for each record that comes out, in order to be able to generate the same revenue. But once an artist and the label wrap their head around that, the revenues may get to a point where it could become close to what you would see in a normal, healthy music business again.

SG: Ted Cohen told me that "desperation creates vision." Perhaps at this point the labels have no choice except to support new platforms.

JF: Well, absolutely. I mean, I haven't seen final numbers for Q2 of 2010, but either in Q2 or Q3 of

2010, the way that sales have been going, it's going to be the tipping point, where more than half of all music purchase transactions will occur online. And you're right, it's that desperation that creates the necessity to realize what the consumer wants. And the reason why I wrote *Future Hit DNA*. It's not just the record labels that have to pay attention to that, it's the artists themselves that have to pay attention. If they're not making music that fits these new digital sales and digital consumption patterns, then the music's just not going to sell.

SG: Well, since you mentioned the book, then let's just jump right to it and make your publicist happy. [*Laughter.*] *Future Hit DNA*'s main thesis seems to be that the elements that made hit songs in the past are changing, and new techniques must be implemented for number-one songs of today. Well, first of all, what inspired you to write this book? Did you write it primarily for songwriters and artists?

JF: Yeah, I wrote it primarily for songwriters, artists, and producers. The business-model conversation that dominated the bulk of the last decade is somewhat of a red herring. If there is music or an artist that really plays well, they will sell at levels that are pretty close to some of the peak years of the music business, Taylor Swift and Lady Gaga being prime examples. Both of which appealed to a younger audience who are supposedly stealing music like no tomorrow, and yet both of them have done in three years' time over two hundred million dollars in music revenue worldwide, just from the recorded-music portion of their businesses. So when you look at that, you go and you say, well geez, file sharing can't really be the only reason artists don't sell as many records, if some of them are generating that much business. When I was at Yahoo!, I would notice patterns of what songs were really driving user interaction online. I was seeing some interesting similarities and, through that, was somewhat able to predict which songs had a higher likelihood of becoming hits, versus some other songs. And, you know, I just started writing it down, and before you knew it, it was an outline for a book, and I just kept going.

SG: The book states that you can synthesize the feedback of millions of music fans to identify, pick, and promote a future hit, well before it touches the mainstream radar. What are the sources of your research?

JF: Obviously, major record companies will have access to tastemakers at all of the major outlets, whether that's going to be your Last.fm, or iTunes, or Amazon MP3, and they're going to be able to get more effective data. But there's also a lot of other sources right now, ranging from, on a high end, BigChampagne, down to, on lower ends, new companies like Next Big Sound, that will actually aggregate all of your social networking and all of your other activities to gauge how quickly a song reacts. If you can compare that to other songs in the genre, or other songs that you, as an artist, released, you might be able to identify which songs are more reactive and more likely to be worthwhile commercially for you to be able to spend your time marketing.

SG: We went through the new chart, the ultimate chart that BigChampagne's Eric Garland developed. Do you subscribe to BigChampagne?

JF: I subscribe. Ultimate Chart is a major step forward. It's not the final step, but it is a major step forward into identifying what is the most popular artist out there right now. Too often, we've now been living in an environment where truth is not what wins out. The online consumer expects actual popularity to govern charts, yet, you know, there are still manipulations going onto other charts. For example, Arcade Fire was the number-one album just before we did this interview, yet it got that way because they charged $3.99 on Amazon MP3. I should say Amazon MP3 charged $3.99, not the band. So that generated a lot more unit sales that inflated the number of sales to make it number one. It would probably have been number two or three, had you actually tried to get it to full price and a lot of those sales not gone through. Same thing with the singles charts.

There's a lot of people out there trying to manipulate the charts; that's what they do. The Ultimate Chart is actually now trying to gauge all of the actual user interactions, whether it's going to be YouTube or whether it's going to be Myspace or Google streams, to really gauge exactly how a consumer is interacting. Again, it's not perfect yet, but it's been a lot better than anything else we've had previously, in my opinion.

SG: Well, I'm sure Eric Garland would be happy to hear that. [*Laughter.*] But, let's get into the nitty-gritty, as it were. In terms of the elements that used to make songs hits, as opposed to today's hits, what were the old elements that made yesterday's hits, and I'm thinking American Songbook— Cole Porter, Gershwin, and Frank Sinatra. And what are the new elements that you must have to have a hit today?

JF: Well, a lot of what I talk about in the book focuses on three major points of the song: the beginning, the middle and the end. Which sounds pretty obvious but is pretty consistent. The beginning is what I tell artists to focus on the most. And that's because the major change, in the last several years, has been music discovery shifting from something that you stumble upon at radio to something that you get on-demand through online streaming. The difference is that when you stumble upon something on the radio, you might stumble upon a song's hook, discover that hook, and say, ooh, this is fairly good, and then eventually like the whole song. Now, when you're discovering online, all discovery is happening at the same point, which is the very beginning of the song, at the zero-second mark. So now you have to say, okay, now the beginning of my song is more crucial than ever. On top of that, you don't have a DJ to help guide you into the song. There is no DJ talking over an introduction to some song. So what you have to do is that you have to actually make the beginning of the song that much more compelling. And the one thing that I've seen, and I saw this all the time, is that the consumer gives a song about ten seconds to impress them. So if you have an introduction to a song that goes sixteen seconds and just kind of meanders along, to get to the part that sets the mood, those songs aren't responding well. You pretty much have about seven seconds before something triggers in the listener's mind to say, eh, this song is not interesting to me, I need to go to the next song. So, more and more, the popular songs are songs that have shorter introductions. As a matter of fact, so far in the first half of this year, the twenty-five top-selling downloads have an average introduction length of just over six seconds.

SG: So the major change here is that there's no DJ describing what's coming up, like, for instance, on Pandora or Last.fm or any other of the services that people use, so you've got to introduce the song well for yourself.

JF: Right, and on top of that, you have a much higher level of volume of discovery at your fingertips. You know, a radio station might add two or three new songs a week, and you're going to discover from that pool. Meanwhile, now any day that you go online, there's thousands of songs that are released every week. It's physically possible, if you were to listen to all the music twenty-four hours a day, seven days a week, for you to hear only 5 percent of what's released in any given week. So that volume of music is always calling out to the person who's trying to discover music. So when they go and hear something and immediately make a split-second decision to say, eh, I'm not that interested in it, there's another song that's calling them. So they will go to a different website, they'll skip ahead to the next song.

SG: Skip ahead, I do that all the time, right.

JF: Yeah, exactly. And the thing is that when you actually press the skip button or go to a different website, in the person's brain they are making a negative association on that artist. So even if that song might actually be good, now, that first listen, that unfairly may have only been listened to for seven seconds, you now have a bigger hurdle to convince that person to like that song and/or that artist. Because they have a negative association, and who's got the time to go back, I've got to go listen to the other 95 percent of the songs that it's impossible for me to hear. So you have to really impress someone quickly, you have to engage them fast, because if you don't, there's just a very high likelihood that they'll never come back.

SG: Your book is supposed to provide a roadmap for producing hit songs by giving fifteen tips. I guess we already discussed one, which is the beginning of the song. We don't have time for all fifteen, but let's go though two or three others that are the most important.

JF: The three most important elements are the beginning, middle, and end. Focusing on the end, I talk a lot in the book about how at the end of the song, an artist should actually put something that makes the ending seem somewhat incomplete, or a false ending. And the reason for that is, with so many songs out there, how do you make a song sticky once someone gets to the end? How can they actually make it memorable? And it's a somewhat obvious trick, but what you can do is, you actually fail to provide a chord resolution, therefore making the end of the song seem incomplete, especially if it happens somewhat abruptly. Then the consumer, the listener, in their minds, is trying to build that song. It's similar to like when you go walking around, and you say, why is that song stuck in my head? Chances are, that song is stuck in your head because you were somewhere, maybe it was a store, maybe it was in your car, and you left that area before the song was completed. And your brain tries to complete that song in your head.

There's a great book called *This Is Your Brain on Music* that really dives into the phenomenon of how that happens. A way that you can trick the listener is to actually create false endings intentionally. So that if a song actually ends without a chord resolution, then the listener's brain will likely keep humming that song or thinking about that song. To the point where if you do it right, it becomes the itch that you can't scratch, which means that it will either (a) create familiarity or (b) you have to listen to the song again in order to be able to feel satiated. But since the song has a false ending, you're just going to create an endless loop. But through that endless loop, you'll actually create song familiarity.

SG: Well, I hope that never happens to me with a Justin Bieber song. [*Laughter.*] I don't want an endless loop of Justin in my head. Can you give us an example of what you're talking about?

JF: One of the best examples, I think recently, is the Ke$ha song "Tik Tok." I think it's a perfectly constructed song for the new digital age. It's got a zero-second intro—it just dives right into the first verse the minute that it starts. There's a lot of other details throughout the song, but then when it gets to the end of the song, it actually plays the first note of the chorus. It's the very ending of the song, and it's a short ending, and a very cold ending, but that first note of the chorus is not actually the chord resolution. The chord resolution actually happens at about the seventh beat into the chorus. So it feels like it's not resolved, even when to some degree it is, and it's starting the chorus, just a little bit, so that your brain will want to start singing that chorus again once you leave that song. Very, very tricky, but very, very effective. One of the reasons why, in less than a year, that song is one of the top-ten-selling downloads of all time now.

SG: You also write about how certain digital media result in higher royalties for an artist. Can you elaborate on this?

JF: This is something that is just now starting to happen, I don't think it's fully there, but I believe it's going to come in the next few years. And that's the notion that every one of these new companies, whether it's going to be iTunes on the sale side, Rhapsody on the subscription services, or even Pandora or Last.fm, they all have to do one thing, which is manage their costs. And the best thing that they can do is keep people on as long as possible while paying out as little as possible. Let's make no bones about it. Much as they're glad that artists are making money from their service, they want to pay out as little as they can. They're a business. So one way they're able to do that is by monitoring which songs are most popular and then figuring out which songs actually cost them the least.

One of the examples I use is that if somebody has a brief punk rock song that may be about two minutes, somebody in one of these services might take notice and say, hey, you know what? It costs us three times as much to stream three two-minute punk-rock songs as it costs us to stream "Stairway to Heaven" or "Hotel California" once. This is because the service must pay each time a song plays, no matter what the duration. So what is their incentive to stream those songs? It's three times as much to stream those punk-rock songs as it is a proven favorite like "Stairway to Heaven" or "Hotel California." If you were a business, you would side with "Hotel California." So my thought is that an artist should take this in consideration when choosing songs to record. Figure out ways to subtly lengthen the song a little bit more, just so that song becomes that much cheaper for a streaming service to play than something else. If a company like, say, AOL, managing sixty or seventy different radio stations, can figure out how to get their average songs from fifteen songs played on the radio per hour to twelve songs, if Pandora can do this, with their millions of radio stations, we're talking millions of dollars in cost savings per year. So it's in their best interests to do that. If an artist can actually make that happen, and subtly, without making the song overstay its welcome, extend the song by a good twenty to thirty seconds, then you have a higher likelihood of making it more cost effective for one of these new digital services to play it and you will get a larger share of the pie because you will be the one most cost effective to that service.

SG: Well, let's take a look at how that works. So I'm Pandora, I'm paying ASCAP and BMI and SESAC a blanket license, a percentage of my revenues. So I don't think that what you're saying would have an impact on paying the performance-rights organizations for the songs, but perhaps the payment to the record companies and artists is affected by what you're saying?

JF: Yeah, the SoundExchange is the one that's most directly affected, because the law reads that you are paying based on per stream. And so to the service it doesn't matter whether the song is two minutes long or ten minutes long, it costs the same.

Also, the artist benefits. If you have a song that's four and a half minutes long versus three and a half minutes long, you make a greater impact on the listener. They may have only an hour to listen to music because they have other things going on in their life. They have a finite period of time to listen to music. If you are able to own more of that time, more of that listening experience, then you are making yourself more competitive by blocking your competition. You're preventing listeners from hearing another person's song.

SG: Okay Jay, I have to play devil's advocate here, and I'm sure you knew this was coming, because there's been a lot of bellyaching that when it comes to pop and R&B especially, there's a deep similarity between the songs, and especially the hits. Now, having given you that complaint, don't you think your book, if everyone followed your advice, may result in even more same-sounding songs?

JF: The answer is yes. Guilty as charged! And I don't necessarily think that's a bad thing. One of the things is that, as much as the record companies get endless amounts of grief, the one thing you have to remember is that, for the most part, they're music fans. They really enjoy music. And when you have pop hits that spin off tons of cash, these companies will usually make investments in the artist and the music. It could be a half million dollars, it could be two million dollars, and they go and find things that they just feel artistically are good and deserve a chance.

One of the biggest problems over the last several years is that they didn't have that cash on hand to develop other artists. You see, there have been plenty of studies that actually say that when a media or entertainment business actually gets into a period of significant homogenization, it actually also becomes the period of biggest creativity, because there's more money flowing to fund that creativity. So what I actually think will happen is that as some of these pop hits become bigger and bigger, and become more monetizable, it will create more cash flow in the business, and these record companies will actually start experimenting more.

SG: I understand what you're saying. In the 1990s while I was at Sony and things were going well and we had a lot of financially successful artists such as Celine Dion, the profits would pay for more interesting artists than Celine. My apologies to Celine. The point is the company was making hundreds of millions in profits, which supported our jazz department and classical departments, which are now more or less gone.

JF: You're right. I mean, at the same time, it may not be everyone's cup of tea, but I remember at that same time, as Sony was signing all those things, they also signed Youssou N'Dour, you know, an African pop artist. That kind of stuff doesn't happen as much nowadays, but I think that stuff will come back, you know, I think we're probably one to two years away from probably having significant enough cash flow that people will start experimenting more.

Auto-Tune

SG: From your lips to God's ears, Jay. One last question about creativity and the way that music sounds today. A lot of people complain about Auto-Tune. As you know, Auto-Tune is software that music producers use to correct pitch, in vocal and instrumental performances, to disguise off-key inaccuracies and mistakes, and that has allowed singers to perform perfectly tuned vocal tracks without the need of singing well. And the backlash is that performances are perceived as kind of phony. You're not hearing human voices, you're hearing machine-generated music, and it's also resulted in many songs sounding more or less alike. What's your opinion on Auto-Tune?

JF: I have two opinions about Auto-Tune. One is that, just like any other technology, you can have people who can take that technology and use it creatively. T-Pain was the first person who really used Auto-Tune well by taking it to its extreme and coming up with a unique sound that worked for him. And I think Will.I.Am is actually doing the same thing right now with his music and utilizing Auto-Tune for some creativity. On the other side of it, one of the biggest problems I have with Auto-Tune is not the homogenization of the song, but the fact that people spend way more time making their sounds perfect versus getting more songs out into the marketplace. I talk a lot in my book about how people need to release more songs more often. Nowadays, when you have two years in between people's albums, and in some cases you might even have a year to a year and a half between singles, people are forgetting about artists. They're moving at the speed of light. And so, all of a sudden, an artist's second album, they might as well be a new artist, because they've lost their fan base in that adjoining time. It's much more effective for an artist to release more singles more often, because then they can actually be able to keep that fan excited, keep them engaged. The artist can experiment more. Because if a fan knows a new song's going to come two or three months later, then they know that if the song is a dud, that's okay, we might get a good one coming up in a couple of weeks. I don't think there's nearly enough of that right now, and one of the biggest problems with Auto-Tune is that rather than just accepting something for being really good and enjoying the spontaneity of the performance, people are spending that much extra time trying to make the song perfect. And I don't think that that necessarily helps it, because, as I think you know all too well, if the underlying song itself isn't good, all the Auto-Tuning in the world isn't going to save it, and all the Auto-Tuning in the world isn't necessarily going to make it that much more sellable. I think it's much more productive for an artist to actually be able to go and actually release more songs more often and actually be able to grow their fan base that way.

SG: What I hear you saying is the problem isn't really the technology itself, it's the way you use it.

JF: That's correct. It's totally in the way you use it. And, you know, from that point, there are plenty of people who use it to homogenize the sound of the song, and I agree with you. I don't think in the long term that helps anybody.

Chapter 20

How to Distribute Music in the Digital Age

Interview with Jason Pascal, Vice President and Senior Counsel at The Orchard

Jason is a business-development executive and attorney who has developed and executed strategies to acquire and distribute digital assets to maximize revenue growth and enhance company brand. He has extensive knowledge of law, sales, business development, and marketing in the digital media arena.

SG: Orchard specializes in digital music. Tell us what that entails—who are your clients, and to whom do you distribute?

JP: The Orchard owns or controls over two million individual tracks. Ten to 15 percent on any given day of the tracks available on iTunes are delivered to iTunes by The Orchard. Our clients are owners of audio and video, that is, record labels, artists, film companies, and so on. Our titles are encoded in over 100 different formats and delivered out to 660 mobile and digital retailers in 75 countries around the world, such as iTunes, Amazon MP3, Napster, eMusic, Rhapsody, Spotify, Zune, Thumbplay, Rdio, Bell Canada, Rogers, and many others. We have operations in 26 markets around the world, and our European headquarters are in London. Our offices in New York City, London, Berlin, Paris, and Barcelona all have local marketing staff to pursue opportunities through digital retailers and to execute sophisticated digital-marketing plans for select releases in order to maximize sales potential.

SG: What is your basic deal with clients? Do you charge a commission?

JP: Our basic deal encompasses worldwide, exclusive distribution via our entire retail network in exchange for a negotiated distribution fee.

SG: Will you ever work with individual artists?

JP: We currently work with individual artists who have a strong management team as well as a proven history of sales.

SG: Distribution without promotion and marketing can be a fruitless endeavor. What other services do you provide in addition to your basic distribution model?

JP: We provide the following additional services:

- ▶ Digital retail marketing for select releases
- ▶ Interactive marketing for select releases, which includes the development and execution of online marketing plans
- ▶ Synch licensing
- ▶ Mechanical administration
- ▶ International sound-recording performance-royalty collection
- ▶ Sophisticated, real-time sales analytics
- ▶ Graphic and web design for an additional fee

SG: You also distribute physical product since buying TVT in 2008. Why did Orchard get into physical distribution? Given the fact you were one of the first digital distributors, that seems like a step back to the past.

JP: TVT was one of the last independents with direct relationships to physical retail. We saw this as an opportunity to bring in new clients for whom physical was crucial but were unable to break off digital from their current distribution relationship. We are selective as to which clients are chosen for physical, and the economics are such that realistic sales projections allow The Orchard and its clients to profit.

SG: Tell us about your role—how long have you been at The Orchard? What do you do, and what gives you the most satisfaction?

JP: I have been at The Orchard for nearly six years, most recently as vice president and senior counsel. I am a senior member of the legal department and work extensively on bringing new clients on the content side into The Orchard for distribution and/or for purchase. I receive the most satisfaction from seeing the deals with the longest "sales cycle" actually close. The monies that take the longest often die for periods of time, are resurrected, solid relationships are built, and when the agreement finally comes it can be very gratifying to watch and see your work turn into actual dollars.

SG: What is the future for The Orchard?

JP: The Orchard's core competency is in its ability to efficiently ingest and deliver content on a large scale. All related business areas, for example, marketing, new technology development, publishing, and so forth, are planets that circle around the same sun. We will continue to develop our ingestion and delivery capabilities, simultaneously seeking out new opportunities that allow us to leverage our core business, thus creating new and expanded services as well as dollars for our clients.

Chapter 21

How a Music Publisher and Indie Label Adapt to a Digital Music World

Interview with Alisa Coleman, Senior VP of ABKCO Music and Records

Alisa Coleman is senior vice president of ABKCO Music & Records, one of the world's leading entertainment companies. It is home to critical catalog assets that include compositions and recordings by Sam Cooke, the Rolling Stones, Bobby Womack, the Animals, and the Kinks as well as the Cameo-Parkway masters by such artists as Chubby Checker, Bobby Rydell, the Orlons, Dee Dee Sharp, ? & the Mysterians, and many more. The soundtrack division continues to market and release major-motion-picture soundtracks, which in the past have included Alexandre Desplat's Oscar-nominated score for Wes Anderson's *Fantastic Mr. Fox* and the Edgar Wright blockbuster *Scott Pilgrim vs. the World*. ABKCO (www.abkco.com) is active on many fronts, including the release of critically lauded compilations and reissues from its catalog, film and commercial placement of its master recordings, and music-publishing properties in all media. It is engaged in ongoing catalog research and development, ensuring its continuing role as an innovator in the entertainment field.

SG: You oversee global licensing for ABKCO. Besides dealing with my requests for the use of music in documentaries and concerts, what does that job entail?

AC: ABKCO is an entertainment company that owns not only compositions and master recordings, but films, images, videos, name and likeness rights, and brandmarks. Part of my job at ABKCO is to license our intellectual property for a wide variety of projects, including motion pictures, television, advertising, consumer goods, apparel, and a host of digital and new-media products and services. Our catalog includes the works of such artists as Sam Cooke, the Rolling Stones, Bobby Womack, and Chubby Checker, as well as films and videos by these artists, including the Grammy award–winning documentary *Sam Cooke: Legend*. I invest quite a bit of time in the areas of business development, asset management, and brand building. We are always looking to identify new opportunities and innovative business partnerships that can produce an outcome consistent with our objectives of maximizing revenue, enhancing our brand, and growing our catalog of assets. In the global-licensing marketplace, where the demand for content is robust, to say the least, it is important for ABKCO to source new opportunities that not only make sense financially, but facilitate the artistic relevance and timelessness of our property.

SG: You are also executive in charge of soundtrack releases. Can you give me some examples, perhaps, of your most successful soundtrack, and your most recent?

AC: We established our soundtrack division at ABKCO several years ago with the objective of leveraging our experience and success in synchronization licensing, digital marketing, new-media exploitation, and retail distribution. There are many reasons why we are interested in a soundtrack project —if the film includes at least one of our songs, our relationship with certain studios, music supervisors, writers, and directors, as well as the overall profitability of the project. Each soundtrack is viewed as a partnership, and while in many cases our relationships start with the music supervisors, we are ultimately dealing with the producers and/or studios. The partnership concept allows us to be open in creating a variety of financial ways in which our partners can participate in the soundtrack (royalty or profit sharing). Our objective is to help create a careful blend of the music used in the film to provide the consumer with an auditory experience that mimics the significant portions of the film. In preparing the release, we negotiate with third-party record labels and artists to ensure that all objectives are maintained, as well as maximizing the financial benefits. The releases with our songs in them include Wes Anderson's *The Darjeeling Limited* and the 2010 Academy Award–nominated *Fantastic Mr. Fox,* the director's first animated feature, based on Roald Dahl's book, as well as soundtracks to *Scott Pilgrim vs. the World* and *Middle Men,* and the soundtrack to the first season of the hit Showtime series *Californication.* We have also released the scores to *Men Who Stare at Goats* and *Percy Jackson & the Olympians,* as well as *Scott Pilgrim* (by Nigel Godrich) and the video game for *Scott Pilgrim* (Anamanaguchi). If you intend to judge the success of a soundtrack project by sales alone, then you will surely be disappointed. Success can be measured in a number of ways besides sales: chart positioning, awards, and the exposure of our overall catalog to different demographics.

SG: Whom do you use to distribute your physical and Internet-based sales?

AC: ABKCO uses several major distribution companies to bring our products to market (each of which provides access to different niche or territorial markets). We have a fully integrated sales and marketing staff in-house that coordinates with our distributors and deals directly with each individual retailer and e-tailer. Although our distributors have outstanding relationships with buyers, we have found it's important for us to also retain our direct relationships and utilize all of the resources offered by our distributors. With a decrease in the physical locations in which products are sold, you have to be able to reach consumers everywhere they're connected, especially through mobile and app-based devices. Our relationship with digital companies (whether with the assistance of our distributors or directly) is the key to this exploitation. Making our music available for licenses for a variety of Internet applications also expands our sales potential. It's no surprise that some of the biggest affiliates to iTunes are music apps like Tap Tap and Guitar Hero, and our associations with their products have helped to generate an increase in awareness and in sales on our recordings.

SG: Which works better for you financially in terms of margin and in terms of net income—sales of hard copies, or downloads?

AC: Many people, including artists, would have you believe that record companies make more money on the digital side, since they do not have to print booklets, manufacture CDs, or ship product. This is simply not the case. Consumers demand better deals for digital product, whether lower price points or increased content (perceived value added). We are constantly challenging ourselves to find better ways to increase our income while providing more content to consumers. At this time, it means providing consumers with deluxe digital editions of releases with content that is not available elsewhere at an equal or lower cost than the physical product. More content means more costs for licensing/royalties (both compositions and masters), which in turn offsets some of the perceived increased margin on digital product. It should be noted that the industry is at this time also using the value-added concept with physical product by including T-shirts, shopping bags, and/or other limited edition items to give consumers added incentives to buy. In the case of *Scott Pilgrim vs. the World,* the director of the film asked us to include an additional three tracks in the soundtrack that were recorded by Beck during the making of the film. We decided to issue a deluxe digital version with a preorder video incentive (for a limited period of time) to help generate interest in the music, which we hoped would in turn translate into increased sales. Our regular digital edition with nineteen tracks initially sold through iTunes at $11.99 (the physical release with the same tracks retails for $15.98 and could be found at a sale price at $11.00). While the price to the consumer for the deluxe edition was $15.98 (a mere $4.00 more than the regular digital version), our costs increased in fees to our distributor, master and publishing royalties for the additional three tracks, upfront artwork costs for the deluxe booklet and preorder video incentive. Additionally, all of the royaltors on the project benefited from the uplifted price due to an increase across the board in their royalty payment, which, in actuality, slightly reduced ABKCO's profit margin on this product. Does this make good business sense? The simple answer is yes . . . by releasing this product we accomplished several objectives—we received more real estate on iTunes, thereby making our product more visible (two products instead of one); preorder sales led to chart placement; the slight reduction in the profit margin was offset by a larger number of download/sales; and most importantly, we kept our partners and the director happy. We look forward to working with him on his next project.

SG: Who does the marketing and promotion for the soundtracks?

AC: ABKCO does the initial legwork for marketing and promotion in-house, but we outsource larger projects to individual firms that specialize in reaching different consumers through varied media. We are in a unique position to leverage our skills from the catalog arena with soundtracks, given our successful track record on our recorded catalog releases. Soundtracks have several opportunities to be marketed alongside the film. Since the window between the theatrical release and video distribution is ever shrinking, we have to develop a comprehensive plan to support marketing, which extends well beyond the television exploitation of the film in markets worldwide. We approach each project differently and work with marketers to reach each film's target demographic through a variety of means, including live performances and social media. We have gathered SMS information during a promotional giveaway and then remarketed to consumers with SMS messages on day of release. However, we have found that our most valuable tool is the relationships we cultivate with the artists to enlist their help in reaching their fan base by utilizing their Twitter, Facebook, websites, and so forth.

SG: Let's talk more about ABKCO. We know that it is a publishing company, and that's how you and I interface—I request licenses from you for my clients' projects all the time. But ABKCO also produces soundtracks. How else is ABKCO different from a traditional music publisher?

AC: As I mentioned previously, as a music publisher and full-service intellectual-property content provider, ABKCO owns and controls musical compositions and master recordings as well as copyrights, cinematic films, graphic and photo images, video footage, name and likeness rights, and several brandmarks. In addition, ABKCO is also a full-service record company, which includes manufacturing, marketing, promotion, and sales (recent releases include the award-winning anniversary box set edition of the Rolling Stones' "Get Yer Ya-Ya's Out!"). Over the years, we have released hundreds of bestselling albums and singles and diverse films, such as Alejandro Jodorowsky's *El Topo* and *The Holy Mountain*. ABKCO also has a film-production company, and we have several projects under development, including a biopic of Sam Cooke.

SG: Let me ask some broad questions now. You've been in the music business your whole career. What do you see as the major changes in the synchronization licensing, and how has digital technology changed things?

AC: Technology, especially digital technology, has influenced all media licensing and not just the music business. When I first started in the industry, synchronization licensing was relatively narrow in scope, especially in the way it was implemented. Television and motion-picture licenses, for example, were originally limited in media and sometimes in term and territory. Audiovisual licenses for home use were just beginning. Over the years, however, as a result of the ubiquitous nature of technology products and services, licensees have moved to expand the rights they request, such as the right to incorporate future technologies. This has led to incremental licenses, which generated significant income for music publishers and other copyright holders. As licensing continues to be dynamic, it has morphed into all-media perpetual licenses being written. At ABKCO we look at synchronization opportunities as a starting point to expand the reach and range of our catalog. We use digital technologies to ensure that a use of a song on a television show or in a commercial is marketed on several fronts—a commercial use could cause us to market a digital relaunch of the original single or a music video. We cross-monitor all synchronization uses with SoundScan reports and have found that invariably, they directly affect the sales of our recorded music product.

SG: What do you consider to be the most important function of a music publisher?

AC: Aside from income generation and collection, in my experience the most important function of a music publisher is to protect and preserve the copyright worldwide for the benefit of the creator (the writer), which includes exposing the copyright in a manner that will not take away from its value or meaning. For example, we always receive a large number of requests for the use of the song "A CHANGE IS GONNA COME," written by Sam Cooke. Our policy requires that each request is subject to a high level of scrutiny to ensure that the song is not used in a manner that would otherwise defame the copyright. One such performance included a subtle lyric change in the first verse that ultimately changed the meaning of the song. This request was denied. Additionally, music publishers must continually revitalize their catalogs by obtaining covers to expose their works to new generations, whether through audio recordings, video games, television, or sampling.

SG: I know that you studied the music business in college. Would you recommend students study the business as you did, and if so, what kind of courses should they take?

AC: There are some objectives I feel very strongly that all music business majors should achieve: as part of their core curriculum they should be required to study music, not just the business of music—they should know how to read music, tempo, and so on and know the history of the music (not just the history of Gregorian chant, but current music history and trends); they should take finance courses (since the music business is based on the exchange of money and deal making); and they should complete at least one internship.

SG: Whether or not they studied music business in school, what advice or recommendations would you have for young people looking for jobs in the business, and given the downturn in income from the record business, and the massive layoffs at the major labels, do you think that a career in the music business is a wise decision?

AC: While some people may just wander into the music business, most have a passion for music. If you have such a passion, you should pursue it—wise not does enter the equation. There will always be jobs in this industry, —and someone will have to fill them—you should just ensure that you are the best qualified and most well educated for these jobs. Young people should be open to exploring all aspects of the music industry before making a determination on a niche area for employment. They should join as many professional organizations related to the industry (whether music publishing or recorded music) and attend as many networking events as possible. Additionally, once you have a job in the business, you should continue to educate yourself by attending professional-organization events. Our business is constantly changing. Beyond 2010, additional technology will be developed to alter how music will be made, listened to, shared, and enjoyed in years to come—and the platforms it will be delivered on. The best advice I could offer anyone is to pursue their passion, and if they choose a career in the music business they should be prepared to work long hours, to learn as much as they can from the people around them, and to bring their creativity and individuality to work with them every day.

Chapter 22
The Changing Role of the Manager in Today's Music Business

Interview with Ari Martin, Nettwerk Management

Ari Martin is a leading figure in artist management today, currently serving as vice president of Nettwerk Management. Under the umbrella of Nettwerk Music Group, Nettwerk Management is responsible for managing the careers of Sarah McLachlan, Jamiroquai, Dido, Brand New, and Guster, among others. In this interview, Ari provides his insight on the traditional role of the manager in establishing and sustaining an artist's career, how this role has changed over the past ten years, and advice for how to get connected.

SG: Ari, can you give a thumbnail sketch of your career and how you got into the management business?

AM: I didn't set out to be a manager. I went to law school with the intent of becoming an entertainment attorney. I interned at entertainment law firms and in major-label business-affairs departments and discovered that I preferred the creative and business aspects of music rather than the legal side. So although I got my degree and passed the bar, instead of practicing law I looked for any job I could find at a label. I ended up at Epic Records in the scheduling and production department. It was very administrative, focusing on the manufacturing and shipping areas. I was fortunate in that the scheduling department reported to marketing and I was eventually trained as a product manager. I later moved over to Arista Records and worked with Sarah McLachlan. Through Sarah, I got to know the staff at Nettwerk and was eventually hired by them to start a New York office.

SG: Who are some of Nettwerk's clients?

AM: Sarah McLachlan, Dido, Guster, Katherine Jenkins.

SG: What are the basic role and functions of a manager?

AM: Basically, the manager's role is to represent the artist in all aspects of their business. I like to think of the manager as the mirror image of the artist, in that the artist handles music and creative issues, while the manager handles everything else—which is not to say that the manager can't be creative and the artist can't contribute to marketing and business issues, but generally there's a pretty clear business/creative division. The primary function of a manager is to recognize and identify the artists' vision and to determine the best way to convey that vision to the outside world or bring it to market.

To put that into more concrete terms, the manager will develop the overall marketing plan and career strategy, set goals, and bring together and coordinate the necessary components. This could mean securing a record deal, finding an agent, finding a producer, hiring independent marketing companies, creating corporate branding relationships, or any combination of these or other elements. The manager is then constantly communicating with everyone involved and monitoring the progress of the project.

SG: How has that role changed in the last ten years as major labels have lost a lot of money, shed massive number of employees, and dropped many artists?

AM: The biggest overall change in the practice of artist management is the increasing pressure on managers to provide services that were traditionally the exclusive role of the labels. The labels have reduced their commitment to long-term artist development. That's nothing new, but the ongoing reductions of budgets and manpower are compounding the problem. So, over the last few years, managers have placed more emphasis on plugging any gaps in the marketing plan that the labels may be neglecting. Of course, good managers have always been active in marketing, but it was more about leveraging relationships and seeking opportunities. Those functions are still important, but now management companies are going to the lengths of setting up in-house departments covering radio promotion, new media, publicity, tour marketing, and other traditional label services. The latest iteration of this development is the case where the manager goes a step further by creating a "virtual label." This is most common (and most effective) when directed toward an established artist with a sizable fan base, but it can also be done at the grassroots level. The obvious advantage is the ability to retain master rights and to earn more income with fewer sales. The manager produces a marketing plan and budget, arranges for distribution, and builds a team of independent marketing and promotion services to work the project. The manager takes on the role of quarterback, ensuring that all the moving parts are operating in a smooth and productive fashion. Ultimately, these changes I'm describing result in more work and responsibility for the manager. But with that comes a greater degree of control over the fate of the artist—a very worthwhile tradeoff.

SG: Does an artist need a label?

AM: The answer to this question depends on the artist's goals. If it's a pop, country, or urban act in need of commercial radio and mainstream media attention, that artist requires the resources of a major. An independent act with modest expectations has more flexibility. The key is to be self-sustaining—this is most commonly found in grassroots touring acts that are part of a thriving musical scene. They build fans by touring and through word of mouth, and can communicate, market, and sell product to their fans with DIY tools that are readily available to any artist. In between is a gray area where each act needs to assess their definition of success, the audience they're trying to reach, and the resources or funding required to reach them.

SG: Does a manager's role in the artist's professional life vary according to the type of music? For instance, would a manager for a rock band such as Coldplay have the same duties as the manager of a rap act such as 50 Cent?

AM: I couldn't comment on those acts in particular, but generally the answer is yes and no. Different genres will emphasize different methods, but there's always a certain degree of overlap. For example, a rock band might build an audience through touring, while a rap act might depend more on mix tapes and features with other artists. On the other hand, they could both focus on blogs/press, online marketing, and commercial radio. So managers in different genres might differ somewhat in the specific parts of the business they focus on, but the overall role of career guidance is the same.

SG: If a manager has more responsibility, should he get more than the traditional 15 to 20 percent?

AM: Possibly, if the manager is handling matters beyond the traditional manager duties. For example, if the manager is also acting as business manager, attorney, or label head for the artist, it might be appropriate to commission a larger percentage. Also, if the manager is investing his or her own money into the project, that would definitely warrant a larger percentage or some other form of nontraditional arrangement. Those are some instances where the percentages might go beyond the norm, but every situation is different.

SG: What are the basic terms of a management contract?

AM: It varies, but typically the manager agrees to advise the client in all aspects of their career in exchange for a percentage of the artist's revenue. The percentage can be gross or net, depending on the rate and type of revenue stream. The agreement is in place for a specified term.

SG: Do you ever go on verbal agreements? If not, do you know any successful managers who don't have written agreements?

AM: We have in the past, but recently we've tried to have written contracts whenever possible.

SG: Are there any advantages for the artist or the manager in not having a written agreement?

AM: I can't think of any advantage for the manager. On the artist side, I suppose they'd see the freedom as an advantage, but if it's a successful artist and they decide to leave the manager, they'd have to negotiate some kind of mutually beneficial separation agreement or they'll probably wind up in court. It really benefits both sides to have a written agreement so that everyone knows what to expect.

SG: What kind of acts is Nettwerk looking for?

AM: That's hard to answer, because each manager at Nettwerk has his or her own preferences.

SG: How do you get a good manager?

AM: The stock answer is to keep developing on your own until a good manager finds you. But for those who are a bit more impatient, I'd suggest that they research the managers they're interested in and just e-mail them. In the old days you could send a press kit, but it would probably end up in a pile somewhere. But nowadays everyone has time to click on a link and listen long enough to decide if they want to know more.

Chapter 23

The Changing Role of the Manager in Today's Music Business, Part 2

Interview with Ed Arrendell, Manager of Wynton Marsalis

As founder and president of the Management Ark, Inc., Ed Arrendell has earned a reputation as a deal-oriented manager. He negotiated terms for Apple's video iPod commercial released during the 2006 Super Bowl and most recently arranged the Metropolitan Opera's first live broadcast in Abu Dhabi. Ed's experience covers the spectrum, from record deals, film score, book, and music-publishing deals to international tours, sponsorships, and corporate events. His long-term client Wynton Marsalis's significant success includes nine Grammy awards and the Pulitzer Prize for Music. Ed has worked with a diverse client group including Kevin Eubanks, Cassandra Wilson, James Ingram, BeBe Winans, and the band assembled by Sting to launch his solo career with players Branford Marsalis, Omar Hakim, Darryl Jones, and Kenny Kirkland. Ed is a graduate of the Harvard Business School and has worked in venture capital and strategic planning.

SG: How did you get started in the music business?

EA: I never considered a career in the music industry prior to meeting Wynton Marsalis. Wynton was living in New York, I was living in Boston, and we met in Seattle. At the time I had a management consulting practice in strategic and financial planning and was in Seattle working on a turnaround for a venture capital client. After work one night I went to hear Wynton at Parnell's Jazz Club, and we started talking after the show. He was frustrated with the business because, among other things, it didn't make sense to him that his net was such a small fraction of his gross. Like many artists, he didn't realize that the music-industry compensation game (royalty and commission structures) places the artist last in line. Initially, I started helping by restructuring agreements to better serve his interests rather than the "industry agenda." At some point, Wynton asked me if I would take over his management. I admired his commitment to his craft and his tradition. It felt like something I was supposed to do, so I bought out his previous manager's contract and got busy. In 1982, everyone in the record business thought Wynton was on the wrong path and would have limited potential unless he agreed to play instrumental pop music. He wanted to play jazz, but the industry was selling fusion, so we encountered tremendous resistance. Initially, I found many aspects of working in the music business unpleasant, with far too many challenging personalities with elephant-sized egos. Over the years, however, we've developed some very rich relationships.

Other artists that I've worked with include Branford Marsalis, Kenny Kirkland, Kevin Eubanks, Nicholas Payton, Cassandra Wilson, BeBe Winans, and James Ingram. I negotiated the contracts for the band that Sting hired to launch his solo career with the recordings *Nothing Like the Sun* and *Dream of the Blue Turtles,* and the documentary *Bring on the Night.* With Branford Marsalis, Kenny Kirkland, Darryl Jones, and Omar Hakim, that band was one of the most talented in rock-and-roll history. Most recently, I arranged the Metropolitan Opera's first live broadcast in Abu Dhabi.

SG: What is the role of the manager?

EA: A manager's role is to develop and implement a plan that will enable an artist to achieve his objectives, identify new outlets for the artist's talents, and ensure that the artist is the primary financial beneficiary and owner of his/her intellectual property.

Some of the specifics include securing and negotiating a recording contract; developing recording budgets; managing the record production process; hiring producers and engineers as needed; developing and implementing a marketing plan for each record release; engaging a publicist and implementing a publicity plan; engaging the right booking agent; creating and implementing a global tour plan; developing and implementing a social-media strategy; doing corporate sponsorship deals, book and music publishing deals; identifying career-advancement moves; coordinating all of the elements above to distinguish the artist from their peers; and providing lifestyle guidance. It's a big job.

SG: What accounts for artistic success?

EA: The primary ingredients for artistic success are superior talent and vision. There's a lot of good talent in the world, but people aren't looking for good, they're looking for great. There needs to be something within you that stands out and sets you apart from the pack. Artists also need a long-term vision of how to create themselves and connect to the world. Some artists fade after a record or two. They may have talent but lack vision. It also helps to have good instincts about people, because you'll need to attract a team of competent people to help implement your vision.

SG: What are the ingredients for a healthy artist–management relationship?

EA: The ingredients essential for a healthy long-term artist–management relationship are trust and competency. I can't emphasize enough the value of trust. An artist that trusts his or her manager becomes free to create and doesn't have to divert energy to other matters. Creative capital is a finite resource. Artists with poor managers can experience energy drains from spending too much time minding noncreative aspects of their careers. Competency is equally important. A manager has to be able to get the job done, build the career, bring deals to the table, manage relationships, and make the artist stand out.

Managers constantly make decisions that have a major impact on their clients' lives. It's a serious business with tremendous responsibility that requires well-developed skills. I recommend acquiring several years' work experience in marketing, strategic planning, or deal structuring before trying to manage an artist's career. Social media is also a skill set with growing import. Do not hire your best friend who's working at Subway to manage your career.

SG: Mistakes for new artists to avoid?

EA: One of the most common mistakes that new artists make is to focus on money too early. New artists should focus on exposure, not money. It doesn't make sense to pay an artist that nobody knows big bucks. If, however, you get enough exposure to build an audience, you'll develop the leverage to be paid well. I recently presented an opportunity to perform in South Africa to an artist who is unknown there. The offer included several thousand dollars plus round-trip business-class airfare for the artist and his band. He turned down the offer because the promoter wouldn't agree to send him first-class and include an extra-business class ticket for the artist's personal assistant (at a cost of approximately $5,000). I'm willing to bet anyone that this artist will continue to be unknown. Go for exposure, build your audience, take every opportunity to play, and don't worry about money.

It's also wise to keep the same friends you had before becoming a celebrity. Celebrity often attracts false friendship. Build new friendships carefully and thoughtfully. In the record business, "I love you, dawg" means "We made a bunch of money from you this year!"

SG: Do you see the music business making a comeback?

EA: The digital revolution has disrupted the music business and changed the manager's role significantly. Record companies, radio, and a strong publicist were once the primary marketing engines for artists. In today's fragmented business environment, much more energy and imagination is required to reach and engage your fans. I expect the long-term rewards of digital distribution, social networking, and direct-to-consumer marketing to far outweigh the short-term revenue declines. Today there are many more ways for artists to connect with their fans and for people to discover music.

SG: How can a new artist find a good manager?

EA: Best way to find manager is to build a strong following and develop a reputation for putting on a great show. Managers are interested in talent that's "happening." If you're special, we'll find you. You can also try connecting with an artist who has a good career and ask him/her to introduce you to their manager.

SG: Should all managers have written agreements?

EA: A contract is a good idea, as it eliminates ambiguities. I've worked both with and without contracts. When I've used contracts, I've had to create my own agreement because I've been unable to find an attorney who will give me an agreement that's fair for the artist. I'm constantly being told what type of "protection" I need. The best way for a manager to protect his interests is to do a great job, not to sign an artist to onerous terms. There are artists, however, who are just greedy and will try not to pay a manager after he's cut a good deal, so a management contract should have some teeth in it . . . just not too long.

SG: What is most rewarding?

EA: The most rewarding part of the job is the nonprofit work that we do. There are a lot of dedicated people who work hard to provide valuable services to folks in need. Supporting charitable causes is tremendously gratifying.

Chapter 24
The Changing Role of A&R

Interview with Michael Caplan, CEO of One Haven Music and Former Senior VP at Epic

Music-industry veteran Michael Caplan has worked with artists like the Allman Brothers, G. Love & Special Sauce, Tower of Power, and Stevie Ray Vaughn.

SG: Michael, can you give us a thumbnail description of your career at Sony, where I was an attorney for ten years? I don't think our paths crossed, but I think they kind of segregated the lawyers from the A&R people.

MC: Yeah. Sure, I'll do that, and then I'll actually take you into the present. I was a nice Jewish boy meant to be either a lawyer or a doctor. And I was fortunate to be able work at a record store called Cutler's in New Haven, Connecticut, my hometown, which was on Yale's campus. And it was the classic mom-and-pop store, and still exists. It was great, it was half classical and half pop—it actually had a line drawn down the middle, and the classical guys had to wear suits and we had to wear jeans and T-shirts. But I decided in 1968 I could be a lawyer after I read Clive Davis's biography and started on the path of going to college and law school. But after three weeks of law school, I dropped out. I figured I would leave it to you, Steve.

SG: Just three weeks?

MC: Three weeks was all it took. And the day that the first Devo album came out, *Are We Not Men? We Are Devo!,* I dropped out and went to go work at a record store in Boston called Strawberry's, which I didn't know at the time was owned by the infamous Morris Levy. I worked my way up to store manager, then got a job working for Polygram doing merchandising and inventory, moved into sales, and then they had a layoff post–*Saturday Night Fever,* so I went back to work for Morris, and this time I was operations manager of the chain. I learned a lot—we developed the whole concept of playlists in stores and the lightboxes outside and made some great inroads in co-op advertising. In 1981 I went to go work for then CBS Records, doing local promotion in Hartford, and it was my job to get records played on the radio. Got promoted to New York in 1983, to do national A&R promotion, album-oriented rock. And I went into A&R pretty much the same year and did that at what was CBS/Epic Records, which then morphed into Sony, for twenty years. I left in 2003 and started Or Music, an independent record label, where I was president, and we signed

Los Lonely Boys and Matisyahu. I made the mistake of partnering a little too closely with Sony in what was called upstreaming, and they put me out of business in 2005.

SG: Sony put you out of business?

MC: Yeah. It was basically like they withheld my money. They kept saying, Michael, you need to come back to work, you need to come back to work with us. In a classic case of "better the devil you know," I did go back to work there in 2006. And I did that for a year, and then I started a new company, which I now head as CEO. I also started a publishing company, also called One Haven Music, in conjunction with BMG.

SG: Who are some of your artists?

MC: Butch Walker, Young Veins, Railroad Earth, Greg Nice, and working on a couple now that I can't announce that are more seasoned professionals. And on the publishing side, I signed a publishing deal with Bill Laswell for his catalog. I also just signed an artist on both the record and the publishing side named Kina Grannis, who I think is going to be very big. We're working in the studio right now.

SG: So explain to us what an A&R guy does, and how does an A&R guy morph into a record label and a publishing company?

MC: Well, *A&R* stands for artist and repertoire, and it's basically the person at the record company that's charged with finding the artists and then sort of guiding them through the process of making the first record, introducing them to the vision of the company. And it's a pretty likely job to ultimately morph into owning your own label, since it's about identifying the talent, and that is, of course, the primary concern of any record company.

SG: How has the function of A&R people changed in the last twenty years?

MC: The role of A&R has changed a lot because of the Internet. Back when I first started doing it, you'd hear about a band in Butte, Montana, and then you'd have to make your way out there. And now, pretty much, you have ready access to everything on the Internet. So those days of having to be in the club at two a.m. and not having any idea of who or what you're going to see, those days are gone. The flow of information is a lot quicker. People make the mistake of thinking that A&R pretty much says whether an act is good or bad. Even lawyers can do that. That is purely a matter of opinion. To me, classic A&R was created by guys like Ahmet Ertegun, Jerry Wexler, and John Hammond, who were about taking an artist, finding them in a very raw state, and then working with them to hone their craft. Nowadays you pretty much find things readymade, because now people can make their own first records at home. And that is certainly one way my job has changed; I no longer get to participate, pretty much, in making that first record. It's the second record I have to help with, because as I said, and as you know, it used to be that it took hundreds of thousands of dollars to make a record, but now anybody can make a record in their home. So the function has changed, and lots of people think they can do it.

Also, it used to be that you needed a major label to do those budgets of hundreds of thousands of dollars, and now you don't. Now anybody can be a record label. Anybody can get the music up on iTunes or through CD Baby, or get their own distribution. It still requires money to market it, because people are able to get on the Internet and access millions of things, but what is going to draw their attention to any one given thing? Things still need to be marketed. . . . But in terms of starting a record company, it's a very easy thing to do these days. To be successful, it's as difficult as it ever was, if not more difficult.

SG: The record business has fallen on tough times in the last ten years, and the major labels have been especially hard hit. How has this affected A&R as a career choice?

MC: The business is decidedly smaller, and obviously the Internet has again leveled the playing field, but also basically made music free. It's kind of hard to compete with free. And I really think largely it's our fault, and when I say "our," I mean the collective business of the major labels. We made our consumer hate us. And you show people something like MTV's *Cribs* and artists making a gazillion dollars and people who view that stuff don't realize that 99 percent of artists barely make a subsistence living and that what they see on those "celebutard" shows are really the exception rather than the rule. And you sue your customer [for illegal downloading], and you put the original Napster out of business instead of warming up to it. Basically, we've created a situation where people don't feel guilty about stealing music. There's a snowball effect, unfortunately, and what's going to happen is the next Bruce Springsteen is going to decide to become a technologist instead of becoming a recording artist, because there's not going to be any money to be made in the field. We're victims of our own doing, unfortunately.

SG: I agree that suing your own customers was not a good idea. But in regard to Napster, I recently interviewed Ted Cohen, who was senior VP at EMI, but before that, Ted was a consultant for Napster. This is what he had to say—before Napster came to the table, they lobbied Congress to try to change the copyright law to make Napster exempt so they wouldn't have to pay anything, and when that failed they came back to the table, and according to Ted they offered one billion dollars, but only one billion, and no royalty. So according to Ted Cohen, the record labels got an offer that they had to refuse because they were making fourteen billion, and if they accepted the one billion from Napster, their income would have declined to a fraction of what it was.

MC: Perhaps that offer could have been negotiated. Beyond that, being at a major label at the time, I will tell you that they were not accepting of the fact that digital was coming. I'll never forget when I got the first Diamond Rio MP3 player, 32 MB, you know, played music for a half hour and the battery lasted forty-five minutes, and I remember taking it to the head of Sony Music and saying, "Your life is about to change forever." And he looked at it and said to me, "People will never buy CDs over the Internet." He couldn't even fathom an Amazon CD physical business, let alone digital delivery. The problem was that the people that were running the major labels were making so much money, and it was illusory, too, because the reason the business was going up was because the consumer was buying his old records again, but on CD. The labels were so interested in preserving the status quo that all they would try to do was stamp out the technology.

It's sad, because you look at the analogy of what happened in the movie business, which was successfully able to move the consumer from a VHS to a DVD because it was better quality. And you couldn't even record at first to a DVD. And we as a business didn't bother to tell people, look, when you do MP3s at 128 kilobytes, you're at a tenth of the quality of a CD. All we did was try to stamp it out. We didn't even bother to tell or teach the consumer that it was an inferior format. So back to your original question, which was about the Napster offer, I'm sure that no one even bothered to investigate it. You know, it's not like Napster were good guys. But if the record companies and retailers had embraced the technology, we could have owned it.

SG: As you know, the majors have laid off a large part of their staff, particularly the A&R departments. How do the labels discover new talent?

MC: The major labels exist to deal with the American Idols, the Susan Boyles, the America's Next Great Talent, or taking things like Lady Gaga and spending millions of dollars on it. In a lot of cases now they're looking at what the independent labels are doing, and then at a certain point buying them out. . . . They're looking increasingly at independent labels to help provide their farm teams.

SG: Would you say that the majors are now depending on major producer artists like Akon, who brought Lady Gaga to Interscope, and Usher, who found Justin Bieber, to bring in new talent?

MC: Yeah, but you know, look, that's always been the case—in terms of where I'm looking for talent, the number-one place is artists that I admire and asking them what they like. G. Love brought me Jack Johnson. I didn't sign him, ultimately, because at the time I was pushing on G. to take his artistry to the next level. It's always a great source—you don't necessarily need to send an A&R guy out to San Francisco to see an act, you can find out about these acts—I just signed Kina Grannis. She's got three million people signed up to her YouTube channel, [and] I'd have to be an idiot to think that only my opinion counts.

SG: Have major-label signing decreased?

MC: It's definitely been cut down in proportion to the way the business has been cut down.

SG: When I was at Sony from the mid- to late 1990s to the early 2000s, the average record-deal advance was a quarter to a half a million dollars. Are the deals less rich now?

MC: Certainly. It used to be that hundreds of thousands of dollars would be de rigueur, but now there's a great disparity where you'll still have artists signed for a million bucks or something crazy, but you know this is obviously fewer and far between. But on the lower end, it's much more under six figures. I mean, I personally wouldn't sign an artist for more than $75,000 down, no matter what.

SG: Are you doing 360 deals, and sharing in income from other sources than selling records?

MC: No, I would say I don't do 360. I think this was invented by labels who decided, "You know, I'm doing a terrible job on your records and we're not making any money. So let me screw up the rest of your business." It wasn't really born of a very pure place. That being said, I'm not doing 360 but I might do 120 or 180—for example, I did a deal with a jam band who does very well live. They do about a million and a half a year, but they haven't really sold that many records, and I've made a record with them that I think is ten times better than anything they've ever made. So I made a deal with them where if the record sells a certain amount beyond which they normally sell, I will participate in the touring income, because the record will have a knock-on effect on that, as well.

SG: So if you help them become successful, you share in that success, but only if you help.

MC: Right, I'm certainly not doing the 360-or-else. Again, I don't think it was born of a very righteous place, you know.

SG: Right, and again, in at the outset of the 360 deal, it was we'll just take 20 to 25 percent of everything because we're giving you a big advance, and because we can.

MC: Yeah, and like I said, it was because we screwed up our own business and now we want to screw up your business, as well.

SG: Well, let's talk about how an artist can make it today. It's common to hear they have to achieve significant success before they get signed with a major, but if you look at the charts, the top ten of everything, R&B, or hip-hop, or pop, or even country, it's still major record labels that represent or at least distribute these artists. And if that's true, how do you get a deal with a major these days if they're signing so few acts?

MC: Well, first, of all that stuff is changing. Basically what you're talking about is radio, which is still the biggest factor in terms of making an artist get into the top ten. It used to be that radio was 85 percent of a factor in selling a record, and you know, now it's probably 40 percent. It's still the biggest way for a record to happen. But I think the deterioration of radio is just going to be accelerated even further and the Internet will become a much bigger factor than it already is. There are different kinds of acts that can gain from success before they come to a record company's attention. Now, Lady Gaga, let's use her as an example. She played a lot of gigs and a lot of people were like, "Boy, *that's* a strange girl," but she didn't really get much headway before she had a major deal. But there are many artists now that are able through a combination of Facebook, Myspace, Twitter, and all that stuff to get something going.

SG: Arcade Fire comes to mind.

MC: Well, yeah. Kina Grannis, the artist I recently signed, is making a great living. She's got three million subscribers on YouTube, she sold out her very first tour out on Twitter, just off of Twitter. I mean, she played Highline Ballroom in New York City, seven hundred people. So you are able to do some stuff by yourself. It depends on the kind of artist you are; if you're a country artist, or Top 40 artist, then obviously it's a lot more difficult.

SG: The Highline Ballroom is obviously not Madison Square Garden.

MC: No, but to be able to play it on your first gig is pretty damn amazing. But Top 40 artists, again, like the Lady Gagas, the Susan Boyles, you can't start that stuff by yourself, and that's where the major labels have the leg up.

SG: Well, is your goal to get artists like Kina signed to a major, or are she and you happy with where you are?

MC: While Kina sold ten thousand records out of her own bedroom, I certainly think I can do a better job than that. She needs to be marketed and positioned in the few stores that are left and she needs some radio attention, some press attention. I think I can bring her far beyond that.

SG: So you're going to bring her to the next level, and then in the future you don't necessarily think in terms of signing her with a major.

MC: I don't. But at a certain point if I think that she's got a song that can go Top 40 and go all the way, I might look for strategic partners. And if that includes a major label, so be it.

SG: Do you have specific advice on how artists should approach either majors or, for instance, Michael Caplan? Do they have to achieve a certain amount of success before *you* would take a look?

MC: *[Laughs.]* It definitely helps. Otherwise, you have to just hope that I chance upon you. You know, I like what I like, and whether it's three Mexican brothers or a Hasidic reggae rapper, those things I find defy logic. But it certainly helps to take yourself as far as you can on your own—if you're a rock band making a name in your hometown or in your own local region, doing the social-networking thing, it's something, for sure. You know, I encourage everybody do the Facebook, do the Myspace, do the Twitter, and, you know, get as far as you can on your own.

SG: Does it matter whether somebody you know and trust presents an artist to you?

MC: Absolutely. Absolutely people that I trust in my network. Certainly.

SG: Would you have any specific advice to new artists besides looking good and sounding great?

MC: Don't take anything for granted, and work as hard as you possibly can. Nobody else will, you know—you are your own best advocate. And don't just sit there and think, "I'm great, someone's going to find me." Work as hard as you can, and do as much as you can by yourself.

SG: And finally, how do people find out more about what you're up to now?

MC: You can go to my website—Onehavenmusic.com—and if you want me to hear some music, you could submit it through there. We have a SoundCloud account, and as soon as I can figure it out, I'm going to start listening to it!

SG: Well, just hire a twenty-year-old or younger and they'll figure it out for you.

Chapter 25

How to Make It in Today's Music Business

An Interview with Don Passman, Author of
All You Need to Know About the Music Business

Don Passman is a leading entertainment lawyer who has handled legal affairs for such artists as R.E.M. and Janet Jackson. Don is the author of *All You Need to Know About the Music Business*, which has sold hundreds of thousands of copies over the last eighteen years. I sat down with Don to ask him some questions about his views on the future of the music business, and how independent or new artists can break into the business using the Internet and new marketing tools.

SG: *All You Need to Know About the Music Business* is a great guide. Everything from deals with managers, to how to pick lawyers, and it includes a great overview of music publishing. Plus, it gives the broad strokes and the fine points in artist recording agreements. It even deals with new laws and contracts pertaining to digital distribution. But I read in your website that without a doubt, and I quote, "The biggest change in the music business since the last edition of this book is the advent of the so-called 360 deal." Tell us about 360 deals and whether you are for them or against them.

DP: Well, 360 deals are the trim that the record companies have adapted that says that they can, in essence, because they no longer make money just in the recording business, ask for a percentage of income in other areas of the artist's life, such as touring, merchandising, publishing, endorsement, things like that.

SG: Now, why should a record company deserve a greater piece of all the artist's revenues?

DP: Well, whether they deserve it or not, it's a reality. And the companies are all doing it. So if you are wanting to sign with a major company or even most of the independents these days, unless you've got an enormous amount of leverage, you're gonna have to do it. The argument, why they do it, is to say, "We're the only ones who are really spending money to build your career. You get an enormous benefit because of the money we spend and the marketing we do, and therefore we should share in your success."

SG: If you're the artist's advocate, would you try to negotiate for additional advances against additional sources of income that the labels want to share in, or at least want the labels to demonstrate that they are actually going to do something to help you sell merchandise or promote your concerts?

DP: Well, their answer to that will that they help you sell merchandise and promote concerts because they are building a career and an image for you, and without the marketing and the money they put into you, you wouldn't have any career in either merchandising or in touring. They gave up the pretense of actually helping with that quite a while ago. It's now just simply, "This is the deal, if you'd like to make it or not."

SG: They've let go of many people; there are fewer staffers to perform those functions.

DP: Correct, now some companies take what they call active 360 rights, meaning they actually take the merchandising rights and then turn it over to a subsidiary to manufacture the merchandise, but a lot of them are just doing what they call passive rights, meaning they have a right to a piece of the income without doing anything.

SG: Including publishing.

DP: Yes.

SG: Give us a few bullet points on the new elements of the seventh edition of your book, and why people who have the sixth should buy the seventh.

DP: Well, this is probably the most extensive update I've ever done of the book, just because so much has changed in the last three years. The 360 deals we talked about were just barely mentioned in the sixth edition. The Copyright Royalty Board has come down with some key decisions regarding digital delivery of music. There's new customs that are beginning to settle in, in terms of streaming and user-generated content, ringtones, digital downloads. And then, of course, as I always do in each of the editions, I update the figures and the trends of normal record publishing and recorded music deals.

SG: I would like to ask you a couple of practical questions that I have to deal with all the time. Lawyers—when do you need one? How do you find a good one? How much will it cost? And most importantly, what if you don't have a lot of money?

DP: Lawyers in the music business can come in quite early if they like your music. A lot of them will help shop it. So you can come to a lawyer when you've got some recorded demos and actually have them help you get a deal. The way you find one is there's a lot of techniques, which are set out in my book. But essentially, do some research—there are a number of websites that include lists of music lawyers. And there are other ways to access lawyers, including bar association referrals. After that, it's a matter of checking them out. If you find somebody you like, ask for references from other people who have worked with them. In terms of the money, some of the younger lawyers will charge a relatively small amount upfront and then take a percentage, and they'll roll the dice with you.

SG: What about money? Say you are approached by a manager or small label and you want to hire a lawyer to review the contract but you have no money.

DP: Well, that's tricky. I mean, if you find a lawyer that believes in your music or sometimes on the basis of the fact that a label is interested, you can get a lawyer to go roll the dice with you. Again, some of them will work with you on a percentage and take a chance.

SG: Well, what I think sometimes works, but tell me if you agree or disagree, is if the manager really likes you and believes he can help you become successful and thereby help himself get 15 to20 percent, do you think it's an appropriate approach for the artist to ask the manager to cover the cost of securing a lawyer to review the agreement?

DP: You know, there are occasions when managers will put up some money for an artist early on. I think it's gotten rarer and rarer today, unfortunately. But as the old expression goes, "It never hurts to ask."

SG: Talking about managers. I went to a CMJ panel recently during the conference,[1] and one of the seminars had four or five managers on the panel. And I was shocked to hear these managers say that they're better off if they don't have written deals, as it engenders more trust.

DP: Well, there are some problems, particularly in California, in enforcing management contracts, but I do know that a lot of the top managers do not have written contracts. And their theory, which I admire them for, is that the artist needs me just as much, or more, than I need them. If they're not happy, they can go. If I'm not happy, I can go. And by the way, a lot of those people have been with their managers for—twenty to thirty years.

SG: I recently did an interview with jazz artist Jon Batiste, who has a deal with the management wing of Blue Note nightclub, and that deal is verbal, which I think is refreshing. And the reason Jon went with them is because another manager, a fairly prominent one, wanted a six-year written agreement. So he found a good manager that is willing to work with him based on trust. But I think a verbal deal generally favors the artist rather than the manager.

DP: I think that's probably right, but on the other hand, it makes for a good relationship. There are certainly legitimate managers that want a written agreement, and I talk about how to protect yourself when you're making one of those deals in my book.

---

1. CMJ: www.cmj.com/marathon

SG: Let's explore recent changes in the business. I left Sony in 2002, and already the fortunes of the record companies were declining. According to the RIAA, sales of prerecorded music hit their peak in 1999 at around 14.5 billion dollars and have dropped more than half over the last ten years. Is the record business in as much trouble as those figures would indicate?

DP: Yes, the record business is in very serious distress. CD sales are dropping; the rise in digital is coming nowhere near making it up. And there is not, as of today, any new technology that's a clear view of how the future is going to turn things around. I personally believe it will turn around, but at the moment we are in a downward trend.

SG: Let's discuss how the major labels have handled the digital revolution. There is a lot of criticism that they didn't cooperate with the Internet for too long. What have the major labels done right and wrong?

DP: Well, in the rearview mirror, there's no question that they have made a lot of mistakes in the past. And by the way, it wasn't just the record companies. The publishers and the artists were not so in favor of these things, either. Nobody foresaw what was going to happen or how bad it was going to get, but they have definitely made mistakes that, had we been able to rewrite history, we might have done differently. On the other hand, the piracy genie is out of the bottle, and it's not going to get put back in so easily. I think that the future only gets brighter when we come up with something, which we can't get delivered today, that is more appealing and reasonably priced than the pirates.

SG: Spotify has gotten a lot of attention—it's an advertiser-supported service that's free to users, offers millions of tracks, and is wildly popular. It exists only in Europe, and reportedly the labels have asked too much money for it to launch in the United States. Do you think the labels will cooperate with Spotify so that they can launch in the U.S.?

DP: I think Spotify will launch in the U.S. in some fashion. And I think the labels are getting more malleable as their business model erodes. The main fear that everyone has in these situations is are they are going to give away too much forever, and both sides therefore are very cautious about the kind of deals they want to make, which is one of the reasons why things are going so slowly. And one of the reasons also is that the new businesses haven't taken off in part. I mean, there are a lot of reasons for that, I think, but part of it is the deals are expensive because the record companies and the publishers are afraid they are going to give away their music too cheaply and be stuck with that forever.

SG: Well, some say if they don't allow these new business models to emerge, they will be digging themselves deeper into a hole that they will not be able to climb out of.

DP: I totally agree. If you strangle the baby in the crib it'll never grow up, and if I ruled the world I would be licensing music to anything that seems credible and possible on a short-term basis to see whether it works. And if it works, then we revisit what the licensing is going to cost.

SG: I have a couple of theories for your consideration. In terms of being an independent artist or a new artist, people say, "Well, you know record sales are way down, you might as well give it away to promote the concerts you're doing, because the real money is in touring." But it seems to me that there may be even less money in live shows and touring now than before. For instance, I heard a manager say yesterday that "if you're not a headliner at a festival, it's still good promotion," implying that only the headliners make real money. What do you think?

DP: Well, I think there's less money but not necessarily for those reasons. I think there's less money because the economy's not in very good shape. And therefore people are going to fewer concerts and they are willing to pay less for the ticket prices, which shrinks the market. It's been true for years that until you got a good-sized draw, you couldn't make much money on the road. It's just too expensive to be out there. So there's never been huge money in touring until you get up into the really higher levels or if you go the absolute opposite, which is you're a small band touring very minimally in a very limited area and with very few expenses and you can make some money. But the real money is in the headliners, you know, for the last twenty-some-odd years.

SG: For many years the path to success was to get out there, perform in front of some audiences, get a buzz, and then get signed to a major label and get your half a million dollars. Of course, after recording expenses and what you have to pay your managers, lawyers, and business agents, it's more like $50,000, but that was still the Holy Grail. And now, since the majors are signing fewer and fewer artists, the question is, for those who are new artists and may never be signed to major labels because of cutbacks, can they realistically expect to make a decent living from their music?

DP: Well, you know the odds of anybody making a decent living in the music business are unfortunately a bit of a long shot, because you are dealing with that artistic and creative palette. On the other hand, as I said earlier, if you develop a local following, get good at marketing yourself, keep your expenses down, you could make a decent living at it. If you want to break free at it, that becomes an entirely different equation.

SG: Well, let's talk about breaking through. You know, there are eight million bands on Myspace by some estimates. And another statistic is that although there were over 100,000 releases in 2009 of new albums (both digital and plastic versions), only 10,000 sold more than 1,000 units, and only 1,000 sold more than 10,000 units, which are pretty startling stats! What is the key factor in becoming a successful artist?

DP: I think it's a combination. I think that you can have great talent and if nobody knows about it, you won't do very well. You can also be moderately talented and market yourself extremely well and have a very long, healthy career. So I think you need both. Given the mix between the two of them, I think passion and drive probably trump talent, to be blunt. All the superstars I've known have had a burning desire to be at the top and been willing to walk through walls to get there, and regardless of whether they might be the most talented musicians or not, if they've got that drive and passion and are willing to do whatever it takes to get it, they usually get there.

SG: Celine Dion comes to mind to me, because she had such passion to make a success, and Mariah Carey. But you know, they had the machine behind them. Millions and millions of dollars in marketing and independent promotion and very expensive videos. How do you do without that?

DP: Well, it's interesting and, I think, the great trend in the business that the young bands are figuring it out faster than the labels. The young bands now are starting to figure out how to directly connect with their fans. They do this by building a mailing list when they do gigs. They'll give away a pen or a sticker or something if you sign their mailing list, and then they stay in touch with their fans. They'll send them tweets, they'll e-mail pictures, they'll just develop a relationship with the fans, grow their audience organically, and then start to build a buzz from the ground up.

SG: I interviewed Jill Sobule, who is successful singer-songwriter. But she was dropped by two major labels. On her own she created a website to raise money for her next record. And it was like, "Give me $20 dollars and I'll send you the CD when it comes out. Or give me $50 and I'll autograph it, or give me $100 and you get extra free tickets to my shows. Or give me $5,000 and I'll come to your house. Or give me $10,000 and I'll let you perform on the record!" And it worked. She got $80,000, and she only asked for $75,000. Is that kind of a business model other artists can use?

DP: Yes, in fact, I think there are a couple artists who have done that and it seems that if you've got a fan base, that seems to work pretty well.

SG: Right, if you keep in touch with the fans and create personal relationships though the web, you can tap into that. Let me give you one more theory about the future of the business. I think the business may be coming full circle. In the beginning of the modern recording business, we're talking about the 1940s though the early 1960s, it was about entrepreneurs like Berry Gordy and Ahmet Ertegun. Gordy created Motown and found the Jacksons, Stevie Wonder, the Supremes. Ahmet discovered Ray Charles, Aretha Franklin. These music men recorded their artists, sold as many records as they could, and promoted them the best way they knew how, all without the aid of a major corporation. But when multinational companies such as Warner and Sony discovered that they could make a lot of money selling records, they ate up all these little labels and entrepreneurs, and at that point we got the Celine Dions and the Ricky Martins, for better or worse. I think the future of the music business will go back to the Berry Gordy and Ahmet Ertegun model, and it will about entrepreneurs with great ears and a business sense, and they will be the essential core team, but instead of a big company, they'll have a new marketing and distribution tool, and that'll be the Internet. What do you think?

DP: I absolutely agree with you. I think we're already seeing it. I'd say we're going back to that era in the sense that we're going away from albums and we're heading back to singles, which was the business model back in the 1950s and 1960s, when these entrepreneurs were able to get a hold of the business. One of the great things about the changes I see coming is exactly that. We're going to see more innovative music, more interesting music. The problem, of course, is that now the access to the marketplace is so easy, everybody can do it, as you say. There are millions of artists on Myspace, so getting through the noise is the challenge in this market. But again, if you start small, if you do these marketing techniques that are being developed by the younger bands, I think there's a real opportunity to do it, grow it, and certainly a number of them are going to break through.

Chapter 26
Indie-Label Perspective

Interview with Rich Bengloff, President of A2IM:
American Association of Independent Music

Rich Bengloff is the president of A2IM, an organization of independent music labels that promotes business opportunity and provides advocacy and representation, as well as networking opportunities for the independent label community. In this interview, Rich describes the role of A2IM in the independent music community and how independents are holding their own in an industry that was once dominated by major music companies.

SG: Tell us about A2IM, its history, goals, and membership.

RB: The American Association of Independent Music (A2IM, www.a2im.org) is a nonprofit trade organization fighting for and protecting the rights of the independent-music-label community. A2IM was formed by the independent-music community in the fall of 2004 via meetings organized by a small group of music-label activists. The first A2IM president, Don Rose (formerly of Ryko), was brought in to lead the organization, and A2IM was formally incorporated in June 2005. A2IM is an organization made up of independent music labels that have banded together to form a central voice advocating for the health of the independent-music sector. Our membership includes 253 music labels of varying sizes and genres, many owned by artists like Alison Brown and Garry West, Burning Spear, Brett Gurewitz of Epitaph/Anti/Hellcat, the Hanson brothers, Joan Jett, Carole King, Moe, the Skaggs Family, Gillian Welch, and so on. Many of our label members are also located outside of the traditional New York, Nashville, Southern California music centers, including Mountain Apple in Hawaii, Barsuk in Seattle, Kill Rock Stars in Portland, Six Degrees in San Francisco, Basin Street in New Orleans, Saddle Creek in Omaha, RhymeSayers in Minneapolis, Red House in St. Paul, Alligator in Chicago, Righteous Babe in Buffalo, and YepRoc in the Carolinas, and many members are true "brands," like Century Media for metal or Alligator for the Blues. In addition to our label members, A2IM has 114 associate members (those who work with, depend upon, or support independent music). A2IM's mission statement is to obtain tangible economic gains for its members via advocacy, commerce opportunities, and member services, including education, most notably the Independent Music Label roadmap and resulting A2IM committee reports. Examples include the A2IM New Media Committee white papers on e-mail marketing, direct-to-fan commerce, and social networks. A2IM is hard at work every day to improve the business of independent music companies.

SG: What are the principal differences and similarities between A2IM and the other trade group representing labels, that is, the Recording Industry Association of America, aside from the fact that the major labels are not members of A2IM? I ask this because my understanding is that RIAA represents indie labels as well as majors. So why do the indies need their own trade group?

RB: The RIAA represents the four major label companies (EMI Music, Sony Music, Universal Music, and Warner Music). As A2IM also represents labels who invest in the creation of music, there are many times that A2IM, as well as the artist–creator community organizations, find themselves on the same side of an issue. An example would be the current campaign to have Congress enact a Performance Right Act to pay sound-recording owners royalties when the AM/FM plays music. As A2IM's mission is to ensure access and fair treatment for our members, there are areas, such as A2IM's support of net neutrality and against the previously proposed orphan works legislation, [where our positions] differ from [those] of the RIAA. As noted earlier, education and functioning as an extra employee to assist members with questions are other functions performed by A2IM that are not a primary functions performed for its members by the RIAA. A2IM is one of over 20 independent-music-label organizations that are members of the Worldwide Independent Network (WIN).

SG: Exactly what does "indie" mean—do you include labels that are distributed by the majors, or only labels that distribute themselves? What about labels that have their own management team, such as Mute, but which are owned by a major (in Mute's case, EMI)?

RB: The A2IM board votes on all member applications, and the A2IM board's definition of an independent label is based upon control/ownership of music masters, not based upon who distributes the music under a distribution agreement of limited duration. In many cases, music labels have direct relationships and self-distribute to certain services such as iTunes, Amazon MP3, and some of the steaming services, all of which are becoming a higher percentage of music-label revenues. Labels owned by a major, like Mute used to be, are not eligible to be members of A2IM, although Mute recently had a recent change in ownership and now would be eligible.

SG: Given your definitions, what proportion of income from recorded music is earned by the "indie" world versus the majors?

RB: Based upon ownership of masters, independents had over 30 percent overall Nielsen SoundScan market share of 2009 recorded-music sales, including almost 40 percent of digital recorded-music sales.

SG: I think there were over 100,000 records released last year in the United States alone; what proportion of those records would you say were released by indie labels or unsigned artists?

RB: The vast majority would have been independent releases, with independent music labels probably 80–90 percent of label releases using older 2008 SoundScan statistics from a member.

SG: By the way, these days any artist can become a "label" by making a record on their Mac and calling TuneCore to place their record on iTunes. What are your criteria for joining A2IM—would you consider such an artist a "label," or do you require labels to have more than one artist?

RB: As noted above, we have a number of artist-owned labels, and some of them, Moe on Fatboy Records, Carole King on Rockingale Records, Gillian Welch and Dave Rawlings on Acony Records, and so on are labels with only one or two artists on their roster. These, of course, are substantial artists with established careers. A2IM sees a label as an entity that supports artists with the infrastructure needed for their careers, be it promotion, publicity, marketing, tour support, and so on. As noted previously, the A2IM board votes on membership, and membership is generally open to all labels that wish to join and learn/contribute as a member of our community.

SG: Part of A2IM's mission is to represent the independent sector's interests in government and legislative matters. What would you say the most important legislative issue(s) have been in the last several years, and how was A2IM involved?

RB: The most important issue for independents is access, and A2IM, via its participation on the SoundExchange board, was instrumental in helping SoundExchange reach a consensus ensuring that the rates set by the Copyright Royalty Board in 2007 were revised for a number of services, including pureplay webcasting services like Slacker and Pandora, to ensure that they stay in business, as they play a much higher percentage of independent music. On all issues, A2IM is able to lend a voice on behalf of the independent-music middle class, representing small businesspeople across the United States and not just L.A., Nashville, and New York.

SG: What are the issues that are currently percolating?

RB: There is a laundry list, but two issues currently stand out. The first is net neutrality and the ability to get equal access to consumers for marketing and promotion as well as commerce. The second issue, which is related, is getting the assistance of Internet service providers (ISPs), both broadband and mobile, to fight piracy, as is currently happening in Europe. The combination of these two issues needs to be sorted out to ensure an environment to support music creation and investment to be able to move forward.

SG: In the past decade we have seen a precipitous decline in income from record sales. It's down by around half of what it was in 1999 in the United States, and the decline has been even steeper around the world. First of all, why do you think we have suffered such a decline?

RB: The reason for the drop in recorded-music sales is first because consumers have changed their consumption patterns and are no longer concerned with ownership of music as long as they are able to access the music, via streaming, when they wish to listen via on-demand services, many of which are free to access. Satellite services like Sirius/XM were insignificant ten years ago and now reach over 19.5 million people paying a average of over $10 a month, Pandora reaches a web audience of over 19 million people, as well, and so on. In addition, other entertainment sources, like games and other applications, now compete for the consumer's time in their 168-hour week. The second reason for the drop is acquisition of music via P2P at no cost or via ripping and burning CDs purchased by others, as CD burners became standard PC equipment a decade-plus ago. The P2P problem needs to be addressed via working with ISPs and via government legislative intervention.

SG: We all know that the decline in income from recorded music has greatly hurt big-label companies, as they had the most to lose, but has the decline hurt the indie labels as much?

RB: The indie-label market share percentages have grown over the past decade, but it's a higher percentage of a shrinking pie, so indies are feeling distress, as well, especially since indies have much lower economies of scale. That said, the independent-music-label community has always been populated by people for whom music resonates in their lives and who historically have, for the most part, made less money than their major-label counterparts. That work ethic, making music we love, continues to be part of the indie-music compensation

SG: What is the future of indie labels and the recording business in general? Are you optimistic?

RB: I believe the indie music labels' ability to adapt to the evolving music marketplace is a plus, but without fundamental changes to ensure legal consumer access to music, we all face an uncertain future. Recent government announcements by the current presidential administration, including Victoria Espinel, U.S. intellectual property enforcement coordinator, and Vice President Joe Biden, coupled with the pending introduction in the Senate of the Online Infringement and Counterfeiting Act, S-3804," sponsored by sixteen Democratic and Republican senators (including the bulk of the Judiciary Committee), make me optimistic for government assistance and the overall future of the music business as we adapt to the new consumer-consumption models.

Chapter 27
Are Record Labels Still Necessary?

T he next two interviews, in this chapter and the one following, both address the issue of whether record labels are still needed but provide nearly opposite points of view.

Interview with Bruce Iglauer, President and Founder, Alligator Records

Bruce Iglauer is the president and founder of Alligator Records, the largest contemporary-blues label in the world. Bruce founded the independent Chicago-based label in 1971 at the age of twenty-three, operating it by himself from a one-room apartment. Now Alligator's catalog contains over 250 releases, more than 100 of which were produced or coproduced by Bruce himself, including albums by Hound Dog Taylor, Albert Collins, Koko Taylor, and Shemekia Copeland. Twenty-six of the albums he's produced have been nominated for Grammy awards, with one winner. Bruce is also a member of the board of A2IM and codirector of the Blues Community Foundation, which is dedicated to supporting blues music education.

SG: Bruce, you recently published an editorial in *Billboard* magazine titled "Labels Are Here to Stay." What inspired you to write the commentary for *Billboard,* and what are the basic points you wanted to make?

BI: I wrote the commentary for *Billboard* because I was asked to—it was for their independent-labels issue, and I sit on the board, as you said, for what we call A2IM, the American Association of Independent Music, which is an organization of independent labels and companies, that works with them and serves them. I was asked by the executive director if I would run my mouth on paper.

SG: Do you think that labels are still necessary, and if so, why?

BI: Yes, for artists who have careers in this business and who want to concentrate on making their music and not upon trying to become businesspeople. Having that kind of support that is available on a label is the only way to go. You could make a record on your own, that's the easy part, but getting anybody to notice that that record exists, getting people to listen to it, getting them to say something about it publicly, and getting them to invest money in your career, that is tough.

SG: You wrote that "the aggressive, committed, independent labels have immediate connections, and do-it-yourself artists just don't." But aren't these media connections largely obsolete now that many magazines are failing and commercial radio just plays Top 40? Can't any band submit their music to blogs and online magazines and distribute the music themselves?

BI: Yes, they can submit, and yes, they can distribute to the extent that they can make the music available. There is a difference between making music available and promoting and marketing music. For the most part, the skills that are involved in promoting and marketing music are ones that you learn over a long period of time. There are fewer publications, and the media has moved a little more to being online. But the reality is that the average do-it-yourselfer, for example, can't reach the music editor of *USA Today*. That person is not going to take the do-it-yourselfer's call. With regard to commercial radio, yes, playlists are not as good as they have been at certain times in the past. But commercial radio still is the number-one way that people find out about music, and this is shown in surveys and polls over and over again. Reaching commercial radio is very difficult for anybody, including the majors. But again, the do-it-yourselfer may end up getting a track or two on a local-interest kind of show or new-release kind of show. But the do-it-yourselfer is not going to get into regular rotation on a radio station. It's hard for labels to get anything in regular rotation on a commercial radio station. But people learning about music is mostly about their hearing the music over and over again, and for music to lock into our brains and get its little hooks in there. We can't forget the words to "I Get Around" by the Beach Boys, no matter how much we want to. You're going to hear it over and over again. That's the function of radio. And nonterrestrial radio, which I listen to, for the most part doesn't give that kind of rotation, even if they're committed to music.

SG: In his book *Ripped: How the Wired Generation Revolutionized Music,* Greg Kot points out that although there is more recorded music being produced than ever before (over 100,000 albums were released last year in the United States alone), there is very little great music. But he argues that if you can do great music in the age of the Internet, you can't help but be successful, because your fans will find you. The Arctic Monkeys, for instance, had a huge following on the web even before they were signed. What say you to Greg Kot?

BI: In the history of the arts in general and in the marketing of the arts in general, we can say with a good deal of sureness that quality doesn't always rise to the top. And the good stuff doesn't always get seen and doesn't always get heard, and how many great authors and great playwrights and great poets and great painters died in obscurity? Now you can say, "Yes, the Internet makes their work available," but it doesn't bring a mass of public attention to it by virtue of it being available. The difference between having your recording on CD Baby or The Orchard or even having it available through iTunes, and having a team market it and make the public aware of it, is a huge difference. I absolutely don't believe that quality rises to the top. Lack of quality has risen to the top many times, and those of us who sit down and listen to the average hit or commercial radio station would probably argue that lack of quality rises to the top way more than quality does.

SG: Let's talk about how to make money in the record business. Here is the philosophy of Trent Reznor of Nine Inch Nails:

> Forget thinking you're going to make any real money from record sales. Make your records cheaply, but great, and give it away. As an artist you want as many people as possible to hear you and word of mouth is the only true marketing that matters.

Now, he does have an ancillary point, which is that once you create a fan base by being "great" and giving your music away, then you should start selling other stuff, such as special packages or limited editions signed by hand. He also advises making downloads available that include high-resolution versions that you can give away with these premiums, and sell T-shirts, sell buttons, posters, whatever. He argues that music is free, whether you want to believe that or not—every piece of music you can think of is available free right away, a click away. So you need to use the records to sell your fans something else.

BI: As far as his model, I don't disagree with it . . . if you control your own masters, if you control your own publishing, if you own all the rights, and if you have the money. To be able to make your own recordings in a quality version and put together these premium packages and produce merch that you can market and set up a quality website that's going to do all these things for you. And in the case of Trent Reznor, if someone already knows who you are because the old version of the record business put you out in front of the public, and implemented your potential following discovering you existed, became the bridge that carried you across, then yes, you can do this. There is nothing wrong with giving away anything you want. I could give away my car tomorrow. The question is, "Is there a demand?" In the case of my car, there definitely isn't. At any rate, I don't think there's anything wrong with what Trent says, I just don't think it's a way you can launch a career.

SG: So what you're saying is if you already famous, like Nine Inch Nails, or for that matter Radiohead, and you can afford to make premium packages, this could be a good model.

BI: What has happened in the course of pushing the do-it-yourself world is that we forget that many, many creative artists who are now successful did not bankroll their own careers. I work, and have worked, my whole career with artists who have often virtually nothing. With artists with very little formal education, with artists who come out of the poorest communities of the country, with artists who are lucky to own an amp and a guitar, much less a vehicle to put a band in, and have no idea and no capitalization for getting the rest of this done. The do-it-yourself rock world has for the most part, although there are exceptions, become a world of middle-class and upper-middle-class people. Kids who can rehearse in Daddy's garage 'cause Daddy has a garage and because there is a daddy and who can make a down payment on a van. And who basically can invest part of their lives in trying to build a music career because there is another way that they know there will be some food on the table. And so this do-it-yourself world tends to eliminate those in the bottom third of economic brackets in this country who can't make their own records, who can't set up websites, who can't make premium packages, who can't go on the road and sleep in the van or a hotel. So there is this sort of economic segregation that's gone out, that nobody talks about because the indie rock world is a world of people who are, to a great extent, entitled, educated, and supported by their families.

SG: Another distinction is the kind of music we're talking about; a singer-songwriter doesn't need a great deal of resources to make a record, but I've been working with a band that does complex world/soul/R&B music, which requires great musicians and producers. They needed $50,000 to complete their next record, and it took them two yours to finance and complete it.

BI: Yes, and you can make records for studio bills in the relatively low thousands of dollars. But I work with a lot of artists who can't put up or get together a few thousand dollars, much less $50,000.

SG: Talking about money, you recently wrote in your blog that at Alligator, about $1 in every $4 that comes in the door is paid out to an artists and songwriters. Now, that's a lot more generous than the normal record deal. How do you make that work?

BI: As far as how we do it, the answer is we have pretty tight belts here. Our high-rise building is three stories, and we don't do things in an extravagant manner. Also, our company is not based on trying to create hits, and one of the ways independents have survived for so many years is by setting their sights on what they can do rather than what they can't do.

SG: Let's turn our attention to the impact technology has made on the business: How has Alligator adapted to the digital world?

BI: With difficulty. For forty years of my life, I got used to the way things used to be, and adapting has been hard. I would be perfectly happy in the world of physical goods and no Internet distribution whatsoever. We've tried to change with the times. I developed the website Alligator.com and started selling online in the mid-1990s. I read about various technologies and I thought, "This Internet thing sounds kind of cool, and it wouldn't be too hard to set up a website, so I think I'll do it. I'll just apply for the name Alligator.com," and it was available. We mostly sell physical goods, as well as lots of merchandise from Alligator.com, because of our demographic. For us, our more youth-oriented artists like Eric Lindell or JJ Grey & Mofro might sell 30–35 percent of their music as downloads. But for most of our blues artists, the numbers are much closer to 10 percent, and the remainder is physical goods. Now, obviously the whole music industry has shrunk dramatically over the last ten years. The fact that this started when illegal Napster started is no coincidence. The numbers I saw in *Billboard* recently were that the industry worldwide now generates about 48 percent of the dollars that were generated in 1999. That's a number that I believe. My company is smaller than it was in 1999, significantly so, both in sales and in staff. So right now, up until the latest economic downturn, we were making a modest profit, which is fine, because getting me rich is not the goal of Alligator. I'll settle for getting along. With the latest economic downturn and the further shrinkage, things are really tough this year.

SG: Has illegal file sharing hurt small labels like yours as much as the majors?

BI: What happened when illegal downloading started was it ran record stores right out of business. A perfect example is Record Service in Champaign, Illinois, which was right next to the University of Illinois campus—it existed for I believe twenty-five years. It was a thriving, deep-catalog, customer-friendly store with reasonable prices, obviously pretty much rock-oriented, as you'd expect from being next to a campus. They lost 25 percent of their business, and in one year it folded. And that means that not only are they no longer selling Sony and EMI and Warner products, they're no longer selling Alligator products, 'cause they no longer exist.

Downloading killed retailers, and the sad thing about that is that record retailers were not only a place where sales were made, they were a place where discoveries were made. And one of the problems with Internet marketing, with iTunes, and with the other legal downloaders is there is almost no easy way to discover the existence of other music. There isn't the excited clerk to turn you on to some music that he or she knows you'll like 'cause you've been a regular customer in the store. There isn't the experience of standing by the bin and reading liner notes, which I used to do as a kid for hours at a time because I could only afford one LP maybe a month. So I would invest ten hours of liner-notes reading to make that $5 or $3.50 decision. That kind of discovery is gone. The system won't support it, and that's truly a shame, because a lot of musicians just aren't getting heard and not getting a chance, and I don't know how to solve that problem at all. I know the problem; I don't know the solution.

SG: One solution the labels have come up with is the 360 deal—taking revenues from other revenue streams besides record sales. What is your point of view concerning 360 deals?

BI: Well, it's an interesting model and there are a number of questions. You're an attorney, and you may be able to answer them better than I. But obviously if you're going to ask an artist to become that artist's business entity and have that artist working for you, or working for a business entity that you the label and the artist are co-running, then you better be offering some kind of reward to the artist greater than somewhere between $1 and $2 royalty on an album sale (which is kind of industry standard). In that case, you'd better be prepared to invest significantly in the artist. That means laying out dollars against potential future income.

The problem with the 360 deal is an example of my artist giving my company 10 percent of their gross live performance fee because I fronted them $25–50,000. A lot of my artists, and a huge number of artists in other fields of music, don't make enough money in live performance, so either they can't afford to give out 10 percent of their fee or would never be able to pay me back my money. Most musicians in this country who are professional musicians are making in the low hundreds of dollars for their performances, not in the many thousands of dollars for their performances.

And in specialized music, which I tend to record, for somebody to be making $1,000 a night in a club, out of which they're paying four or five guys or women, their transportation, their hotel, their insurance if they have it (good luck), there's nothing left. I know people who are professional musicians, who make their living as musicians, and can't afford to have one sick day in their entire working lives, because they can't afford to lose that one day's worth of income.

SG: I think that the most important factor is if the record company is looking for a piece of merchandising or performance, then they have to be actively involved in securing gigs or helping make the T-shirts.

BI: Well, certainly that's true. When I started Alligator, there was an interesting model and the model was the Capricorn label, which you may remember; it had the Allman Brothers and a number of southern rock acts—Phil Walden's company. And they had an in-house booking agency . . . they were sort of doing a proto-360 deal back in the early 1970s. In fact, I was involved when I started my company—no one wanted to book my artists, so I became the booking agent. I also became the roadie, the guy who sold the LPs at the gig; I was often the publisher, and the press guy, and everything else. Because I had artists who had no idea how to get a gig out of town. You know, I told you, I worked with a lot of artists who had very little formal education and no connections at all. So I did kind of a 360 deal, except I wasn't smart enough to take a piece of the gig money except for taking a small booking commission. I'm certain that if I put my mind to it I could do the math so I could arrange it so that we could "split" with the artist, and the artist would make absolutely nothing.

SG: Perhaps a 360 deal would make more sense if the artist got a bigger piece of record royalties than a standard deal, but they receive only their usual 10–15 percent. Do you think that's fair?

BI: Well, one of the problems the labels have and do-it-yourselfers don't is do-it-yourselfers only have to deal with the economics of their individual recording. When you're running a label and you have a catalog and you haven't made all perfect business decisions, some of your recordings have lost money, and somehow you have to make up for those losses, or the bad employee, or you bought too big a building or whatever. You have to make up for those with the profit of the successful recording. So when artists look and say, "Well, how could something sell in the store for $18 or for $9.99 online and I'm getting a buck or a buck and a half, why aren't I getting a bigger piece of that?" and part of the answer is it costs a lot of money to make that sale, and part of the answer is because somehow we have to cover for our other [expenses]. So in a sense you, the success, are paying for the failure.

SG: Tell us about the American Association of Independent Music. First, what exactly is an "indie" label?

BI: The definition of *independent* has changed, at least in our minds, in this industry. It used to be that an independent was a label that came though what we're calling independent distributors.

Distributors that were not owned by or part of major-label conglomerates. But these days, almost all the distributors who distribute independently owned labels are in fact entities like RED, ADA, and Caroline that are owned or partially owned by international corporations that also have their own labels. So part of the role of A2IM is to have the industry redefine what constitutes an independent as defined by ownership, which means that it doesn't matter who does distribution, which could change tomorrow, it matters who actually owns the corporation that's producing the music. And if you count by that, you go from a little under 20 percent of the music in this country being independent to somewhere in the mid-30s. Which is important, because if you look closely you discover that the independent community, if you define it that way, is as big as any major and bigger than some of them.

SG: What makes Alligator an indie, and who do you use for distribution?

BI: For many, many years we were the classic independent. We had a group of distributors all around the country. At one time we had over twenty distributors in the United States alone, plus international distributors. As the independent world shrank, as we figured out how to ship quickly all over the country, and as the role of distributors in getting radio play and press sort of ceased, then we went with a smaller and smaller number of distributors, and eventually, we decided we only needed one national distributor. And we made a deal in 2000 with Ryko Distribution, which was part of the same company that owned Ryko the label. A couple of years ago, Ryko Distribution was bought by WEA but maintained itself as an independent entity within WEA. That is, we didn't deal with anybody from WEA at all, we dealt only with Ryko, our contract was with Ryko, all the marketing, all the sales were done though Ryko; WEA simply did the physical fulfillment of shipping CDs to stores and collecting money on Ryko's behalf. Recently, because of the downturn in the economy, WEA decided to roll Ryko into ADA, which is the Alternative Distribution Alliance, which was their other independent distributor that they owned. So now we're with ADA, but still Alligator is 100 percent owned by me. ADA does marketing for us, they do sales for us, and through WEA they do collections for us. They have nothing to say about who we sign, about what kind of business deals we make, or give any direction whatsoever to what we do artistically or as a business decision. To get back to the definition of *independent,* just because ADA is owned by WEA doesn't mean that Alligator is somehow not an independent label.

SG: As you know, RIAA has announced that it would stop going after people who download music from P2P. What is your point of view?

BI: I got married late in life, and I married into grandchildren, and I remember when original illegal Napster started and I was explaining to my grandchildren why this was in fact stealing. And they didn't understand. They just thought, "Oh, this music is available, we can do this. There is nothing wrong. Our friends do it, it's fine." So in terms of my reaction, and I'm not speaking in terms or A2IM but only for myself, my reaction is if we remind the public that stealing is stealing, then at least they can stop giving these stupid rationalizations for why the music should be free and understand that they are stealing. Do I think that Jammie Thomas in particular should pay over a million dollars because she had some illegal files on her computer? Of course not, and she won't, because it will either be appealed or she'll declare personal bankruptcy—but how do you make the point? I don't know the answer, I just think that at this point the public chooses not to learn that P2P is theft. By any definition, it's theft.

[*Author's note: See Chapter 10 for a summary of the case against Jammie Thomas.*]

SG: If people buy a computer including a CD burner and pay at least $50 a month for high-speed Internet, perhaps they feel entitled to download music without paying an additional fee. This raises the argument that there should be a royalty imposed on the people who are making money from free music—the Internet service providers. What do you think about that idea?

BI: The way I've understood the idea is not to tax the ISPs, but to use them essentially as collection agents. But it's still a can of worms. It feels good, but how do you figure out what the ISP should be charging its customers; are we expecting the ISPs to fingerprint or use fingerprint technology to identify what files are being submitted? How will the ISPs know if the files are legal or illegal? And then what's a fair way of charging their users, and then what's a fair way of distributing the money that they might collect? It's very difficult. I don't believe that that means it shouldn't be explored.

Beyond that, of course, the ISPs are extremely resistant and are powerful. They are parts of very powerful corporations. You know, the entertainment industry, even including the music and television industries, is relatively small compared to other industries in this country, and the protection of its copyrights is not at this point sort of a national priority or an international priority. As far as taxing or putting some type of fee on hardware makers, I just haven't seen it been floated and taken very seriously.

SG: Often the copyright law is shaped by political and economic influence, and that's how the ISPs got a safe harbor under the DMCA—immunity for carrying illicit sites including music. This brings me to a similar issue. For years, the broadcasters have avoided paying for the performance of recorded music. Do you think that the Performance Rights Act, which would make the radio stations pay labels and artists for the first time, has a shot of passage?

BI: A2IM has been a very strong supporter of this legislation, and actually I myself have been to Washington to support it. Fighting the National Association of Broadcasters is really tough, and politicians are completely scared of them. They're scared that they may be denied airtime or scared that they will have the broadcasters become their enemies. Nonetheless, more and more, there seems to be a grassroots understanding of the fairness of this in two ways. First because the Digital Millennium Copyright Act makes the digital broadcasters, the webcasters, the satellite-radio services and a number of other services pay the copyright holders and the artists as well as the songwriters and publishers for music they're webcasting. And if you're going to have a level playing field—if Sirius XM is going to compete against Clear Channel—then you can't have a fee, a royalty that Sirius XM has to pay, and Clear Channel doesn't. It's antitrust, and my understanding is that you're making an unlevel playing field.

SG: SoundExchange, which represents the labels and the artists for the purpose of Internet radio (they negotiate the rates), recently made a deal that "pureplay" webcasters (those that make money exclusively from advertising rather than selling goods or services) such as Pandora and Last.fm would pay 25 percent of revenues to them. The reason that this is good news is because a couple of years ago, the Copyright Royalty Tribunal handed down rates that were so high that those services probably would have had to go out of business.

BI: Well, this settlement has been strongly supported by the A2IM. One of the reasons is that webcasters have tended to play a larger proportion of independent music than is even our market share by the definition of market share I gave you earlier. Pandora, I've been told, plays over 40 percent independent music, so that level of exposure, along with a royalty, is pretty great for us. Yes, I like the Pandora service; obviously I like it better if they're going to be paying for the music that is in fact the basis for their having a business at all. I didn't want them to go out of business; I actually testified before the Copyright Tribunal on the subject of the economics of independent labels. I didn't ever suggest what was a fair royalty rate for anybody. I just talked about how we make our money and how we spend our money, because they had heard mostly from majors, and in fact John Simson, who is the head of SoundExchange, has become quite a dear personal friend and is a guy who is absolutely dedicated to fairness for musicians and for copyright holders. They put a huge amount of effort into locating the correct rights holders, especially heirs of musicians. I give them great respect for the efforts they put in to try to make sure every dollar and every penny is correctly distributed. So I'm very happy about this settlement, which as I understand supersedes or eradicates the Copyright Tribunal finding.

SG: Well, we've covered a range of issues. Given huge declines and the continued prevalence of file sharing, will the recording business, as we have known it, survive?

BI: The problem is, of course, that if the business continues to implode, part of what will happen is that artists will suffer. Music may get recorded, but the difference between getting recorded and getting heard, as I said earlier, is huge. And I don't think that the multinationals can survive in their present form. Their overheads are simply too high. But I think the majors will have to combine their forces if they're going to survive, and in fact they have in a lot of places. Just to give you a physical-goods example, in Scandinavia all of the majors use the same physical fulfillment center. The same warehouse, the same trucks, the same shipping, the same billing. I wouldn't be surprised to see at least one more conglomeration of majors. The media has been talking about it for years, and I wouldn't be surprised to see EMI get sucked up by somebody else. It is, after all, the Beatles catalog. You'd think that would be worth something, wouldn't you? The question is whether they can shrink and still be majors. Whatever you want to say about music being available online, and people reading blogs instead of magazines or newspapers, the reality is that the vast majority of people are impacted by a very small amount of media. Some of us who are more inquisitive may read a hundred bloggers, but the vast majority of people still hear the network news or look at the front page of a newspaper or read a review in one of the well-circulated publications. But that's going to be the case for a long time. And it's especially going to be the case that people are still going to learn about new music from commercial radio that plays the same small number of songs over and over again. And as long as that exists, it's going to need powerhouse record labels to beat down the doors to try to get those commercial record stations to pay attention. Now, ask me again in ten years and I may give you a better answer.

SG: Well, there may be fewer future U2s and Coldplays and Mariah Careys, but there may be a world, and I think this is what Greg Kot envisions, where artists such as some of your artists can make a better living because of the Internet. Let's hope. But let's end the conversation on that hopeful note and also allow you to give a plug. What's coming next for Alligator Records?

BI: Next up is our debut record by an artist named Tommy Castro, who's based on the West Coast. Tommy's been with a number of labels in the past and built a following the old-fashioned way by playing about 150 to 200 live dates a year and just being terrific live and has a very devoted family and following. His bestselling albums have sold in the 50,000 range in the United States. Which in my field of music is a very nice number.

Chapter 28

Are Record Labels Still Necessary? (A Futurist's POV)

Interview with Greg Kot, Music Critic at the *Chicago Tribune* and Author of *Ripped: How the Wired Generation Revolutionized Music*

Since 1990, author Greg Kot has been music critic at the *Chicago Tribune* and a regular contributor to *Rolling Stone* magazine. With Jim DeRogatis, Greg cohosts a rock-and-roll talk show titled *Sound Opinions* on Chicago Public Radio. Greg's biography of Wilco, *Learning How to Die,* was published in 2004, and *Ripped* was published in 2009 by Simon and Schuster.

SG: The basic thesis of *Ripped* seems to be, and I quote, "A decade ago the vast majority of mainstream music was funneled though a handful of media conglomerates. *Ripped* tells the story of how the laptop generation created a new grassroots music industry with fans and the bands rather than the corporations in charge. In this new world bands aren't just music makers, but self-contained multimedia businesspeople." Greg, can you tell us why and how these changes occurred?

GK: Technology came along which enabled fans and artists to level the playing field. The whole notion of record companies, and then record companies that became these multinational conglomerates, skewed the way people were hearing music by the late 1990s. The pipeline for new music to get out to the public had really become narrow. You had to work with one of these big record companies, who in turn had to work with one of the big radio stations, who were working with one of two big concert promoters in this country. So you had a lot of power concentrated in a very few number of places, and very little new music was getting out there. A very select few artists were getting promoted. The industry was based on blockbuster albums. If you didn't sell at least a couple million albums, you weren't considered worth promoting. When the Internet came along and enabled people to communicate directly with each other about the music they loved, and to communicate directly with the bands making that music, it changed that whole scheme of how new music got out there.

SG: Well, you also wrote that fans aren't just consumers, but distributors and even collaborators. What did you mean by this?

GK: The whole idea that the Internet has promoted is this idea of intimacy with the creators. Before, there was this large number of middle men between the creators and the fans, and the fans were essentially a marketing demographic. They were a faceless mass of people who bought a product from a massive corporation. And what has happened now is that fans really do feel invested in the artist, because they are able to communicate directly with them though websites, through e-mails, and though message boards. They are getting music directly from the artists. In the case of Radiohead, Nine Inch Nails, all the way down to someone like Jill Sobule. You've got these artists who are at all levels able to communicate directly to fans, and the fans feel directly invested in these artists. They don't feel like they're dealing with a corporation and they're being sold a widget. They realize, this music has meaning and it's being made by a real person that I can talk with, and communicate with, and I feel like I'm involved in their career in some way. Bands even take it a step further by having fans remix their music or create videos for it. In Jill Sobule's case, investing and becoming investors. That's critical, and it's changed the dynamic of the relationship where it's now not only just a corporation selling to a consumer, but an artist collaborating with their most ardent fans—and that's critical.

SG: I read the chapter on Death Cab for Cutie just yesterday, and it seemed like they had the personal relationship with the fans even before they had a website, just because the fans would talk to each other about the band on the Internet.

GK: The band was startled by this. The members of Death Cab for Cutie were of the generation just before the Napster era. They went to college in the early/mid-1990s, so they missed that boat a little bit. They were out there just like any other independent band with no promotion behind them. They were slogging from town to town playing for six people, but they noticed in their second or third tour that their audiences were getting bigger. Quite a bit bigger than their record sales had seemed to reflect, and they were wondering, "Well, wait a minute, how do you guys know about us?" and the fans said "Well, we're trading—I was sent your MP3 file with your music by a friend of mine," and they're going, "What's an MP3 file?" They vaguely knew about this stuff, but the fans were distributing their music for them and getting the word out about the band. Soon enough they were coming to towns, and there were audiences there singing their songs back to them. They were making a better living than they thought they would be able to do. This is because the fans were out there promoting their music for them.

SG: Right, but according to the book, their really big break came when their music was featured on a TV show.

GK: That was further along in their career. They were at the cusp where somebody who was programming a TV show would think, "Hey, this is a cool band, they're on my radar screen, I want to license some of their music." It was a twofold thing here. It was an opportunity for the band on this new show, this relatively new show, *The O.C.,* which didn't have a huge budget. And Death Cab being a relatively unknown band still at the same time wasn't going to demand a whole lot of money to get the music licensed. The show became a cult hit, especially among high school students and college students. The manager of the band told me a very interesting story. He said "that to have the music on the TV show was one thing, but then there was the whole notion of, OK, you've heard this great song, now how do you get it?" If this had happened five or ten years earlier, someone would have said "Ah, that's a cool song," and then they would have to spend a couple months searching around for it, figuring out who was that band, how do they get that song, and where do they buy it. Now, with the Internet, a lot of fans were able to sign on right away to *The O.C.* website, and there it was. Listed who this band was, what that song was that they played, and the fans were able to instantly get that gratification of finding out who that band was and being able to purchase the music. The manager said "it was an interesting consonance of the old media, TV, combining with the new media to create a phenomenon."

SG: The liner notes in the book state, "Greg Kot masterfully chronicles this story of how we went from $17.99 to $0 in less than a decade." Now, this is a pretty provocative statement! Should artists give away their records and rely on money from performance, merchandising, or licensing for TV shows like *The O.C.*?

GK: Nobody wants to see giving away music happen. The larger point here is that no matter what I think about it, it's going to happen anyway. I think we have to get around this idea that any intellectual property that can be digitized can be instantly copied and sent around the world no matter what we do about it. So the notion of being able to control it is really slipping away from any creative person, whether it's a musician, a writer, a movie maker. You have to be prepared that eventually your creative work is going to get out there into the world. And you will not be able to control how it's distributed. Most of it will be given away, yes. And rather than moan about it, rather than complain about it, say, "Well, wait a minute, one of the biggest obstacles to being recognized for creativity is actually having your work heard or seen by someone." With the Internet you've got this incredible tool for being able to distribute your music, sometimes in ways you couldn't have even imagined. Figure out a way to exploit the fact that more people than ever are listening to music or are watching film or reading a book. Let's figure out a way to make that economic model work, and there *are* other ways to make it work. The twentieth-century rules can't apply to what is going on now in the twenty-first century. We're talking about a completely different way of consuming music and yes, free is going to be a big part of that. Let's not resist that, let's figure out a way to make that work in favor of the artist so the artist can get compensated.

SG: Well, let's talk about compensation and the role of the labels. In Death Cab's case, they actually left their small label after *The O.C.,* even though they were selling hundreds of thousands of units, and signed with Atlantic, a major record company, in the hope of reaching a broader audience. Do you think that's still necessary if an independent artist has success on an indie label or by themselves, that it's still necessary to sign with a major in order to reach a worldwide audience?

GK: I talked with the Death Cab guys about this, and they said at the time they signed the deal with Atlantic they felt the physical product was still an important part. An important enough part of what they did and how music was distributed. They felt they needed a bigger label that could get that physical product out into the world in a bigger way. And their issue wasn't so much with Barsuk Records—that was their independent label—but it was more of "how are we going to get this record out not only in America but in Europe," where they had these multiple licensing deals with different small, little labels. They wanted to consolidate that all under one roof. And their belief in 2005 was that yes, the physical product still matters, it's still a big part of how our fans want this music. Five years later, you're looking at that and saying, "You know what, if they were doing that deal now would they necessarily need to have signed with Atlantic, could they have not have done this thought their own website?" There are still certain costs and marketing costs associated with manufacturing, distributing, marketing, publicizing, selling physical product that, you know, there is no one better equipped to do that than a well-run record label. So there is certainly a lot of merit to signing with a label when it comes to the physical product. When you're talking about digital stuff, it's much more practical for an artist to, not necessarily do it on their own, but certainly with a much smaller management team around them. It doesn't have to be the traditional big label, it doesn't have to be a midsized label, it can be a very small team of dedicated businesspeople who are beholden to the band. Who love the band but are maybe a little bit more business-oriented. Know how to set up a website, know how to set up distribution channels for digital product, and know the ins and outs to licensing and booking tours. So what I'm envisioning is a shift away from these bigger labels, which were the by-products of the twentieth-century business, until a much more flexible, agile record label emerges. This type is run by people who are invested in a few bands and can help them distribute digital product around the world.

SG: Let's talk about the role of small labels. Bruce Iglauer, president of a blues label named Alligator, wrote a commentary in a recent edition of *Billboard* that implied even though recording costs have declined, and the Internet has made it possible to reach a worldwide audience to promote and sell their music, record labels are still necessary. He points out that there were over 100,000 new album releases in the United States alone (including digital titles) last year, and less than 10,000 sold more than 1,000 units. He argues that aggressive indie labels have done what do-it-yourself artists can't do on their own, build immediate connections and marketing savvy that leads to music sales. Do you disagree with Bruce?

GK: There is no doubt that on a certain scale a record label makes perfect sense for an artist as a vehicle for getting music out there. Talking about major artists, they need major muscle behind them to sort of keep that superstar status going. I would argue that if you're a new artist right now and you haven't established an audience for yourself, and you're depending on a record label to do that for you, it's the worst thing you could possibly do. If you're in a position of strength, and you've already established an audience, and if you have a huge worldwide audience, you're Madonna, you're U2, you're Radiohead, you're Prince, it makes sense to get in bed with a big label and say, "Hey, let's make lots of money together." But in the case of a new artist, it's absolutely deadly to say, "Oh, I'm going to let these guys build my audience for me." First of all, they're going to take a lot of your money away, out of your pocket. You're going to be able to distribute, you're going to be able to do a lot more on your own on a smaller level. The key for a lot of bands that are artists is that they want that instant hit, they want that instant fame, they want that instant money. When Bruce talks about the low success rate of most artists, most of those albums probably suck. It comes right down to the fact they don't deserve to sell a lot of copies. Not everybody is destined to be a success. Rule number one is "You gotta be good"; if you're good, you're gonna find your audience sooner or later. The biggest mistake that a lot of new artists make is this empty promise of I'm the greatest and I'm going to be the one that sells a million copies of my debut album and if I don't get that it's a huge disappointment. Patience and perseverance go hand in hand with talent. You've got the talent, you've got the goods, you've got the music. If you're patient and you persevere, your work is going to get recognized, it will get out there. The Internet is incredibly difficult at keeping a secret. If you're good, word is going to get out there really fast. So maybe bands need to start looking at themselves a little harder and say, "Well, maybe this making music isn't what I'm really good at. Maybe there is something else I can do." The people that are good, who are making good music, in the age of the Internet are going to find it almost impossible not to have some kind of success at some kind of level.

SG: In *Ripped* you write about Prince, Death Cab, and Radiohead, but all these bands first established themselves with the help of labels. Can you give us examples of artists who are successful without first being marketed and distributed by a label?

GK: There have been a number of artists in the last few years where you've seen success before they were even signed to anything. In fact, they built their audience before they got the deal. You know, Lily Allen being a great example in the UK of someone who put their songs up on their Myspace page and built an audience for herself before her first record even came out. Her record company wasn't really interested in rushing her record out there, and the next thing you know she was a hit and they realized, "Wait a minute, maybe we oughta get her record out." The Arctic Monkeys, another band in the UK that was very successful in building an audience through its website. They had a following coming out to their shows and singing their songs. They were a hit band before they signed a record deal. What I was saying earlier about this whole notion of "being good," if you're good, people are going to find out about it. And there is so much music out there, but at the same time there is so little great music. The great artists do stand out, and they will be talked about. There are countless examples like that of bands who have developed followings through the Internet. One of the key things for that is it's not necessarily a following, where it's gonna be on the national or international radar screen. It's not going to be to the extent of "Wow, that's the next big thing, there's the next Beatles." No, it's more about the kind of small community-based regional success where a band can have a reasonable chance of making a modest living at playing its music. The possibility of a true artist middle class emerging after all of this is the one other thing that's been really lacking in the music business for the last fifteen years. Because it has become either you make a lot of money, or you don't make any money at all. It's a have-or-have-not situation, and the people who actually make money are in the top 5 or 10 percent. Ninety percent of the bands fail. They lose their deals, they don't make money on their record sales, and they drop out. Now we have a situation where if a band perseveres, remains patient, and are good, they're going to do just fine. They may not make multimillions of dollars, but there's a real possibility of making $50,000 to $80,000 a year playing music. For a lot of musicians, that's a perfectly acceptable level of living. You don't have to be Mariah Carey and sell forty million units.

SG: Unless you want to make $80 million.

GK: Everyone would like to make $80 million, but very few people are in a position to do that. Very few people are interested in doing the things Mariah Carey has to do in order to sell those kind of units. It's an illogical goal for most of the people who get into music. It's the mentality that everyone has to be Mariah Carey. That is what ruined the music industry. As a result, a lot of promising and talented artists were shunned off into the margins and were kind of lost.

SG: I do recall receiving dozens of drop notices at Sony if they sold less than 100,000 units. Our offices were littered with them.

GK: For example, if a band sells 70–80,000 copies, that's enough to sustain a label like the Chicago label Thrill Jockey. If Bruce Iglauer of Alligator sold 80,000 copies of an album by one of his artists, that would make his year. It's ridiculous that the economics became so skewed that a record that sells as much as 80,000 copies could be deemed a failure.

SG: One of the things that I like about the new music business is that digital tools have made recording much more affordable, and an artist can actually produce and market and distribute themselves without letting another party take 90 percent of their income.

GK: A lot of these complaints about "Oh my god, I'm not going to make any money on record sales." Well, when did you make money on record sales when you're a recording artist? About a 5 to 10 percent success rate, where fewer than 10 percent of the artists signed to these big labels were actually making money off their record sales. Relatively few people made money off record sales in the past fifty years except for the record companies.

The point being, how can whatever comes down the road to replace that be any worse. You weren't making money on record sales in the past, or if you were, it was such a modest amount, it certainly wasn't enough to make a living. Now the model has changed, the ability to not only keep more of that money has changed, because you're able to use that as a way of promoting other things you do as an artist, the rest of you—the whole idea of licensing, merchandising, touring, and all these other aspects of who an artist is—using the recorded music as sort of a promotional tool for that, and that's where the idea for innovation really is intriguing. How do you use the Internet for that sort of thing? Keep your recording costs at a modest level but yet get music out there that is intriguing, that's interesting, that draws people into your fold. So that when you do come to town and play a show, they want to come out and see you, and they're talking about your music. That's where the future of the music industry lies. That's where the possibilities are endless for how artists can use self-release through the Internet as a tool for promoting everything that they do and sustaining a career. Whereas in the past it was, "I'm recording this music, but I'm not really participating in anything else, I'm kind of just going out there and I'm kind of working for this big label and they're keeping most of the money and I'm never seeing any money." And then the label gets tired of you and says, well, you're not making enough, and then you're dropped, and then what do you do? Your career is over.

SG: I agree the game has changed, especially for powerful artists like Prince. He now enters into one-off agreements with majors and keeps most of the money.

GK: It's really smart. He understood; he'd been in the game long enough to realize how it was played, and he realized that control of your master recordings was absolutely critical, that short-term deals were critical. He turned the tables and is basically using the old system to his advantage, whereas in the past Prince clearly felt like the system was using him.

SG: Talking about the system, let's talk about the future of the big labels for a moment. First let me ask you about that lawsuit that just came down with Jammie Thomas. You wrote about it in *Ripped,* but the book came out a little too early to capture the last step of her trials with the RIAA, and she was ultimately found liable for over a million dollars in damages for downloading twenty-four songs from Kazaa. Now, the big labels argue that this will have a positive impact, that people will think twice about using peer-to-peer and trading music online for free. Do you agree?

GK: No, because they've been suing people for five years, and in fact at the end of last year they basically gave up. They realized they weren't making any impact at all on peer-to-peer file sharing. For every legitimate download in the country, there are forty illegitimate downloads. The Jammie Thomas trial is a residue of the era when they were still suing people. She got her retrial, so as a result the trial went into this year. The verdict was ridiculous. Look at what that jury awarded in punitive damages to the record label, $80,000 per song. How that value was ascribed to those songs is beyond belief. It had something to do with the fact that she was such a poor witness, and they do believe she was lying to them. Frankly, it was not the best example of the kind of case you would like to see. . . . You didn't want to use this as your test case, because frankly she was not a particularly strong witness. But at the same time, if anything, the verdict, instead of scaring people, just outraged them even more. It made them realize, you know what, these people are completely off their rocker if they think this is a fair verdict. If you apply the standards that were applied to Jammie Thomas to the entire American population, you'd have about 50 percent of the U.S. population considered criminals. It is the way that people are accessing and distributing music right now. And most people don't think they're doing anything wrong. Think about Lars Ulrich of Metallica making a hundred copies of his first EP on cassette and passing it around to his friends and saying, "Hey, listen to this, this is cool." There are clearly people who are going to abuse that. They are going to take music and they are going to say, "Hey, it's free music. I'm just going to keep this. I like it and I'm going to keep it." But there are people who were turned on to Metallica at the time, and they kept that cassette and they made ten copies for their friends. And they came out to see the show, and when Metallica released their next record, they bought it. That's how you build a fan base, and the same is true now. A lot of what's going on now with peer-to-peer file sharing is simply people turning on other people to new music and saying, "Hey, listen to this, I really liked this song." So no, people might not necessarily buy that song, because they've gotten it from a friend. But they've just found out about a new band, and it's crossed their radar screen, and if the band is really, really good, there is no reason why that should hurt the band. Someone says, "Hey, this is amazing, and I really love this piece of music." The next time the band puts something out, they're gonna want a piece of it, they're gonna want to get it, they're going to want to see the band, they're going to want to learn more about the band. I don't see how that's a bad thing.

SG: Well, in terms of the major labels, they've suffered massive declines in revenues, but they're still huge players in the recording industry. For instance, the week before Michael Jackson's untimely death, Sony only sold 10,000 units of his albums, and the week after his death, they sold over 400,000. So it seems like Sony will have a future, if only to distribute Michael Jackson albums. Is that going to be the role of the major labels, or do you see any other role for them except peddlers of catalog?

GK: Catalog has been sustaining record labels for a lot longer than the last year or so. Think about the 1990s, the CD era, some of the bestselling albums of the decade were of material that was recorded in the 1960s. So it isn't surprising for these big labels to continue making money off of what they've done in the past, and the Michael Jackson episode is a great example of that. It was an interesting story, because not only was he selling a lot of units, but he was selling a lot of CDs. People were going back and buying CDs, and you're going to see another surge in CD sales when the Beatles catalog is reissued yet again on compact disc and remastered in the fall. There is this whole notion that because some new technology comes along, it's going to kill off everything that preceded it. It's only going to enhance everything else that goes around it. Who knew we would be seeing a real resurgence in vinyl sales right now? Ten years ago, vinyl was dead, and nobody cared. You're seeing kids going out and buying vinyl now because it's a cool thing, it's a cool artifact to have. Again, the new technology, if nothing else, is actually increasing the appetite that people have for music, and if the record companies could get around the idea that this is actually a good thing, let's put all that brain power and all that money we have into figuring out ways to exploit this instead of crushing it and making it go away. I think everybody could be pretty happy and actually even make money off the new system. It's taken ten years and the music industry still hasn't come up with any viable plan for how to deal with this new reality. And that's what's really disturbing, and they have no one to blame but themselves for that situation.

SG: Would you have any recommendations for Sony, Warner, Universal, and EMI?

GK: These multinationals need to get together, they need to come to the table, they've got this incredible resource, which is their back catalog. They've got all this amazing music, basically every recorded piece of music that is available. If they could create a one-stop shopping source for all of that recorded music, make it available in beautiful, high-quality digital downloads where the bit rate is very high, the sound quality is first rate, there's no viruses, you can get anything you imagine with a simple touch of a button, you would have people lining up around the world for that service.

SG: Isn't that iTunes, Greg?

GK: iTunes doesn't have nearly the availability. One of the reasons that the peer-to-peer networks are still thriving in the iTunes age is that they have much more music available than iTunes does. iTunes still has vast numbers of major bands, major artists, major pieces of music that are not available, not in service.

SG: Why do you think that is? Why do you think they withhold the deep catalogs?

GK: It's not so much the labels sometimes, it's the artists sometimes who don't want to get involved, either. They see this as kind of a "Who's making the money here," and once again, it's not the artists. iTunes is making the money, the labels are making the money, but the artists really aren't making the money. If they did create a superstore with every piece of recorded music available, pooling their resources, making it really easy. A one-click kind of thing, make it feel free, make it either subscriber based or advertiser based, or some kind of system where there is a fee of some sort on the Internet connection or on the PC or on the downloading device, but make it feel reasonable and give them access to everything. And don't put restrictions on how it's used. I think you'd make a lot of money off that. You'd make a lot of money off that, and people will flock to it. If you make it simple, make it accessible, respect the intelligence of your audience, realize they not only want the new hot stuff from Lil' Wayne but they want these obscure tracks from German art rock bands of the early 1970s. Put all that stuff on there because it's all available, it all could be available.

SG: It's all available anyway.

GK: The heads of these corporations have to realize the only way they're going to survive is to come together and pool their resources. They can succeed, because they do have an incredible amount of resources available to them. But right now they're too busy squabbling, and still trying to fight this nasty Internet thing instead of embracing it. They really haven't fully embraced it, and until that day happens, they're just going to get killed. Their business is going to slowly drain away, and it's really kind of sad to watch. Because as much as people say, "You're against the major labels," there was a time when the major labels did a lot of good things and put out some wonderful music, and created some wonderful relationships between fans and artists. But right now they've just created so much ill will that people look at them and say they've deserved to die, there's no reason for them being around.

SG: Well, all I can say is I hope they're listening. Greg, can people listen to your radio show Sound Opinions on the Internet?

GK: Absolutely—it's available at www.soundopinions.org, and we stream the show, it's available for download, podcast, it's readily available anywhere, anytime you want to listen to it.

Chapter 29
New Business Models

Interview with John Buckman, President and Founder of Magnatune.com

Magnatune is a website that offers streaming radio in various genres including alt rock, classical, electronica, rock, hip-hop, jazz and blues, new age, and world. But unlike other Internet radio services, Magnatune also offers subscriptions to users for interactive streaming and downloads. Finally, Magnatune makes available its music for licensing in movies, TV, and commercials.

SG: You say in your website you are a label but you are not evil. What makes you not evil?

JB: The major labels have typically engaged in two behaviors that I think are "evil":

1. Attacking the consumer: whether they are trying to make a personal CD backup, rip CDs to their computer, or make personal YouTube videos that have music in them, the major labels consistently alienate their customers with their actions.
2. Destroying musicians: major-label record deals are notorious for their entangling muscians in unfair deals, locking up their careers, and usually simply not paying.

Magnatune behaves in ways we think avoid this kind of behavior:

1. Befriending the consumer: we consistently choose pro-customer policies, from Creative Commons licensing of our purchased music, to "share our music with three friends," perfect-audio-quality WAVs, and more.
2. Helping musicians: besides paying 50 percent of gross revenue to musicians, our musician contracts are also nonexclusive, allowing the musicians to pursue the directions they choose.

SG: When I originally interviewed you for the first edition of my book in 2004, you were an online record company with a licensing component. Now you are an Internet radio site married to a subscription service, although you kept licensing. Why did you switch your business model?

JB: We found that people are mostly tired of having to spend time shopping music websites, to decide which one or two albums they want to buy. This is one reason piracy is so popular: it reduces the work. Our all-you-can-eat membership plan was growing 20 percent monthly at the same time that our download sales were decreasing 30 percent yearly. Clearly, our fan base liked the all-you-can-eat offering, so we decided to focus 100 percent on it.

SG: You charge $15 a month for your subscription service, which is kind of expensive compared to Napster and Rhapsody, which are $5 and $10, respectively. But you write in your website that members "get to listen to everything on the Magnatune web site, without any commercials, and anything you want to download you can do so as if you had paid for it." Does that mean I can download everything on the site and keep it permanently even if I stop paying my subscription fee? And if so, what would motivate people to keep on paying the $15 per month?

JB: Magnatune members have unlimited access to all our music: they can download, stream, play it on their iPhone, whatever they like. And, since we are anti-DRM, they absolutely can keep the files if they choose to cancel their membership.

We release four new albums every week, and with over ten thousand songs in the catalog, most people find it more convenient to keep their membership than to spend tons of time figuring out which albums they want to download and canceling immediately.

We find that approximately 20 percent of members cancel within ninety days, which, if you invert that percentage, means that 80 percent choose to remain members, in order to keep getting access to new albums, as well as downloading albums as they discover then.

SG: Your website states, "Please do not put your downloads on a peer-to-peer network such as LimeWire." If people can own the records after downloading them, why do you discourage them to share it on P2P? Do you think that P2P cannibalizes additional memberships?

JB: We don't think that the current P2P companies are ethical businesses: they clearly make money by promoting copyright violation. We don't want to promote P2P companies, nor have any business dealings with them.

Furthermore, yes, we do think that if all of Magnatune's music were easily available on P2P networks, it would cannibalize our membership offering.

SG: I noticed that your deal with the artists is quite fair. According to the website, the following provisions apply:

▶ **Nonexclusive license:** you're giving us a license to sell your music, but you can sign agreements with others. This means you can sell your own CDs at concerts, as well as sign with another label.
▶ **Contract is limited to music you submit:** our contract extends only to the music you submit to us. There is no future obligation to send us your music.

- ▶ **50/50 gross revenue split on music:** our main sources of revenue are our download memberships and licensing. We split the amount we collect 50/50 with you. Note that most record companies split the profits: we split what we receive, no deductions.
- ▶ **Twice-yearly payment:** we pay your royalties at least twice a year (in early July and early January). If your royalties are less than $100, we hold on to them until they reach at least $100.
- ▶ **Transparent bookkeeping**: as a Magnatune musician, you can view every sale of your music in detail. What they paid, who they are, and what VISA or PayPal charged us are all available to you. We provide reports in HTML, Acrobat PDF, Text and as a spreadsheet download. Your royalty is calculated by taking 50% of the money we collect for your music.

But what about licensing? Do the artists have to give you specific permission to license their work?

JB: Musicians receive 50 percent of gross revenue, no matter how their music was used to obtain revenue. That means 50 percent of licensing, 50 percent of membership fees (prorated based on what each member listened to).

SG: What about commercials? Does the artist have to specifically approve a request by, say, a toothpaste company for use of music in a commercial?

JB: Artists give us a blanket permission to pursue business opportunities with their music, without our needing to seek further permission from them. We avoid licensing our music to porn and politics, but other areas (such as a toothpaste commercial) are fine. If a musician has a problem with this, we're not the right service for them. Our main goal is finding money for their music.

SG: Who sets the price? For instance, if a low-budget movie producer wants to use some music, who negotiates the fee?

JB: We set the price based on what our competition is charging, and we also frequently negotiate special fees based on quantity purchases or specific uses.

SG: You make all the music on your site subject to a Creative Commons license. According to your site:

This means that the music you get as a member can be shared with your friends, can be remixed, backed up, copied to all your computers, and used in your own non-commercial projects (such as YouTube Videos or Podcasts.) If you'd like to use our music in your non-commercial work, please join as a member, download the music you like, and have fun! If your use of our music is for commercial purposes, please buy a license online.

Why do you use Creative Commons?

JB: We use a Creative Commons license on our music because we think that people who pay for our music are the honest ones, and we want to reward their honesty by adding value to the music where we can. The Creative Commons license allows Magnatune members to, for instance, make noncommercial YouTube videos that use our music. This makes our music "more valuable" to our customers, and hence they are more likely to continue to pay us.

SG: Will you ever deal with the majors, and if not, why not?

JB: We are not a distribution service for other record labels: we pick our own music and deal directly with musicians. There are ethical reasons for this (see "we are not evil"), but it also makes good business, because the person creating the good we sell (the musician) is well paid in this relationship, with no middlemen, and thus motivated to work with us. Furthermore, working directly with musicians simplifies the legal issues and makes it possible for us to offer straightforward online music licensing.

SG: What's next for Magnatune?

JB: We're launching a new business called "MoodMixes," which will be providing music for restaurants and shops.

SG: How will the service be different than other background-music services?

JB: The music will be entirely Internet delivered, and we'll be making eight-hour mixes matched to the establishments' opening hours (no repeated music) and moods (softer during busy times).

Chapter 30
Music Videos in Today's Music Business

Interview with Camille Yorrick, Former VP of Video Sony Music

Camille is a recording-industry veteran, having served as VP at Sony Music and consultant at Interscope Records.

SG: Camille, you rose through the ranks at Sony to become a VP in the late 1990s and mid-2000s. Can you give us a thumbnail sketch of your career at Sony? When did you start, at what level, and how did you become a VP?

CY: My journey in the music business began as a director's assistant in the late 1980s with choreographer/director Diane Martel. Diane Martel went on to become one of the most prolific music video directors of the early 1990s and continues today. She began working with Mariah Carey when Mariah was just starting out. I was on the set of one Mariah's music videos with Diane when I met Lee Rolontz, who was head of the video-production department at Columbia then. Lee saw something in me and offered me a full-time job as a coordinator in her office at Columbia.

After a year as a coordinator, Lee decided to leave her post as head of video production for other pursuits. Joanne Gardner came in to replace Lee and promoted me right away. I was really fortunate to be working with people who believed in me. The first video I commissioned was the Fugees' "Fu-Gee-La." This was the first single from an album that went on to sell over twenty million copies. After that, I just continued to grow in the department. Becoming a VP took four years, a lot of hard work, and long hours. I did a lot of classic videos as part of that team. I worked on Lauryn Hill, Destiny's Child, Nas. We broke a lot of artists. It was an amazing experience.

SG: You left Sony around 2007—what changes did you see from when you began until the time you left?

CY: By 2007, the music business was definitely going through a lot of growing pains. The digital era and payola scandals had done a lot of damage to the infrastructure of the record companies. The feeling of enthusiasm was greatly diminished. Music, as a business, was suddenly a shrinking industry. We were spending less on videos . . . people were more unsure in general about where it was all going. Most of my mentors were gone . . . people like Joanne Gardner and Don Ienner. I was not confident in the road ahead at Sony. It felt like the right time to step out.

SG: Given the fact that the business is down from around $15 billion in 1999 to only $6 billion in 2010, do you think big record companies like Sony have a future? What do you think, and what do you hear from artists?

CY: I think music, as a business, will always be around, though I think the "business" part of it will continue to transform. Big companies now have less employees, less artists . . . but if an artist wants an international presence in the marketplace, big companies are still the most surefire way to make it happen. For younger, developing artists, a big company is not important. There are so many success stories about new artists taking a grassroots approach to getting their music out . . . through the Internet, live shows, licensing, et cetera.

SG: When I was at Sony from 1991 to 2001, we made approximately a hundred videos a year, just at Columbia Records. How many were they making when you left?

CK: Wow, hard to say . . . maybe forty to fifty per year as a department, but the number was shrinking rapidly.

SG: The average budget in the 1990s was around $125,000 to $150,000, with the budgets well beyond that for superstars like Pearl Jam and Bruce Springsteen, and Michael Jackson videos started at $500,000 and were often more than a million dollars! Are those days over? What is the average budget now?

CK: The average budget today is lower in general, but there is often an extreme range between budgets for emerging artists and your global superstars. We've moved into a time where an investment in a big video for an artist, that is expected to sell globally, can pay off. I don't feel like there are hard-and-fast rules . . . it just depends. The audience is still there.

SG: I work with Pitchfork TV, the alternative rock/video website. They are making short concert videos for only hundreds of dollars. They look grainy and handmade, but Pitchfork's young audience loves them. What do you think of these kind of "guerilla" videos?

CK: I think there is room for all kinds of visual expression, when it comes to music. It should be celebrated. Just think, everyone can be a filmmaker in today's culture. Technology makes that possible. I can see that kind of grassroots spirit all over the business today.

SG: Should all new artists run out and get flips or a good video camera and start shooting their songs and using YouTube or Vimeo to get attention?

CK: I don't think there is one approach that will work for everyone. At the end of the day, there needs to be something real there to get people's attention. A good song . . . a great artist . . . people need to grab on to something. There is a whole lot of clutter out there.

SG: Tell us what the major window was for videos when you started at Sony, and what the major windows are now. Also would you say that YouTube is as important, or more important, than MTV?

CK: At the height of the business, MTV's TRL show [*Total Request Live*] was everything. Every big artist wanted to be on that show to premiere their videos. MTV was very different then . . . there were videos on all day, and MTV showed a lot more respect to videos as an art form. I'm not sure if you remember in the 1990s MTV had something called "Buzz Clips." That was a special title MTV used to give to videos they thought broke some new ground in terms of the visual interpretation of music. These "Buzz Clips" would get extra spins. This kind of attention would be hard to imagine in today's MTV/music business. YouTube is like a visual jukebox . . . it's overwhelming . . . but do I think it's as important as MTV, absolutely! More important? That's a more complicated question. MTV was the birthplace of mass video consumption. YouTube is an extension of that.

SG: After you left Sony, you went to Interscope. Tell us what your major role was there. Specifically, didn't you work on VEVO?

CK: I started my own company, when I left Sony, and was doing some consulting. An opportunity came up at Interscope, and the major caveat was that they were spearheading the launch of VEVO. I thought the idea of labels taking control of the digital marketplace for music videos was solid. There was also a lot of expectation that labels would be able to produce artist-related content for VEVO . . . the music business's own "network," in a sense. That was interesting to me. The process of launching VEVO had some unexpected challenges, and I'm not sure what the current goals are for it, besides a hub for music videos and behind-the-scenes pieces. It's definitely a good place to see popular videos.

SG: Now you're completely free. Tell us about some of your current projects. For instance, didn't you recently produce a video of a festival in Fort Greene?

CK: Yes. I still have my own company, and I've been working with Fort Greene Festival, as well as other clients. I just finished producing a concert film and TV special with Beyoncé. I'm fortunate that I'm able to mix it up a bit. I'm still a very visual person and still love working with music and artists.

SG: Are you doing it like we did in the old days, that is, spending a lot of money to produce a glossy product? Or have they cut back on the budgets?

CK: The music-video budgets have been cut way back in general. They are still being made . . . but with new technology . . . you don't have to spend as much, and labels don't want to spend as much. There are still a few marquis international artists that may get bigger budgets . . . but they are few and far between.

SG: What makes for a great music video?

CK: A great representation of the song and artist . . . something that can get people's attention and drive them to watch it over and over again.

SG: What's next for Camille Yorrick? Do you want to go back to the majors, or do you want to stay independent, and why?

CK: The majors? I'm very interested to see where all of that goes. I'm treading some new ground for myself, which I'm enjoying. I'm wise enough to never say "never," but I know what feels "unlikely."

SG: Since this interview—and by the way, we're going to include a transcription of this episode in the third edition of my book—is for music-business professionals, as well as artists, what advice would you have to somebody trying to break into the business now? Specifically, since a lot of career paths in a lot of major labels have dried up, would you still recommend trying to get a job with a major, or are there other new opportunities that you would suggest?

CK: I think the majors are still a great training ground. My experience there was invaluable. The music "business" is so unique, in that you get experience in corporate America . . . which is the basis of industry in this country . . . .but you're still working with a product that makes people happy. People will always love and want music.

Chapter 31
Challenges Facing Digital Music Entrepreneurs

Interview with Steve Masur, Digital Media Attorney, and Moses Avalon, Author of *Confessions of a Music Producer*

Steve Masur is a founder and senior partner of MasurLaw, a law firm focusing on digital media and entertainment, corporate finance, and intellectual property. He is a member of the executive board of the International Association of Entertainment Lawyers and is editor of *Collective Licensing at the ISP Level* (IAEL 2010).

Moses Avalon is author of *Confessions of a Record Producer: How to Survive the Scams and Shams of the Music Business* (fourth ed, Hal Leonard 2009) and *Secrets of Negotiating a Record Contract* (Hal Leonard 2010). Avalon currently runs a music-consulting service that offers workshops and contract analysis to artists, managers, producers, and labels. He is also a sought-after speaker for his expertise on issues facing the music business and maintains a popular blog and newsletter at www.mosesavalon.com/mosesblog.

I asked Steve Masur a series of questions. What follows are Steve's thoughtful responses to these questions, followed by Moses's responses to Steve's comments.

SG: What are the greatest challenges facing new digital-music startups, and have the major labels impeded the growth of legitimate alternatives to free music?

SM: The major labels are still asking for advances, but now, instead of the advances being their primary business model, they serve the purpose of weeding out the better business opportunities from the mass of underfunded, underresearched, or otherwise unrealistic ones. Also, the majors now see more clearly the value of having a market of sustainable and even successful online, mobile, and cloud-based music services. This has made them more collaborative in their approach. However, they still face significant challenges.

The first challenge is that consumer confusion over music-distribution technologies has inhibited music promotion and eroded demand for recorded music. A smaller percentage of the population identify themselves as hardcore music fans, and the typical person on the street is now less identified with their music than in previous eras. Radio has become more generic, fewer people listen to radio, and from an empirical perspective, nothing else has fully replaced radio as a solid way to identify new music choices (although there are great alternatives in this race, like Shazam, Pandora, and MOG). Furthermore, this downward new-music-exposure spiral is increasing as declining sales of recorded music further limits promotion budgets, and new music is even harder for the typical person to hear about. Quixotically, the countertrend is that because of the Internet, music you already know about has never been easier to find, and more people than ever before listen to music on mobile devices. To my mind, this spells only one thing; unrealized economic opportunity.

The second challenge is that consumer adoption of new paid digital-music services is not growing quickly enough. To my mind, changing this does not take rocket science, it takes promotion. During previous format changes, there was a huge amount of promotion beckoning consumers to adopt the new formats. Equipment manufacturers extolled the virtues of LPs over 78s and 45s. CD players were relentlessly pushed into hands, homes, and finally into cars. Music marketers made you feel compelled to change over your entire record collection into the new format and buy more music on the new format. But now, despite the freely available, already ubiquitous standard formats of MP3 and others, the only music service you regularly see promoted on TV and billboards is iTunes. And it's the only massively successful one. Furthermore, after nearly ten years in existence, Shazam made it onto an iPhone commercial, and a Super Bowl commercial, and now everyone knows about Shazam and it's one of the most successful apps. Yes, Steve Jobs is brilliant and he is the Henry Ford of our time, but in many regards, he is just doing what's obvious, promoting Apple's products well. My perusal of the numbers reveals that these services are competing pretty damned well with "free," at least when measured on the basis of money made per download, so the promotion is definitely worth the money.

The third set of challenges surrounds the law that evolved around music's previous distribution models. This law has created populations of stakeholders who have a legal right to collect part of the proceeds from music sold but who play little or no role in selling the music they control. Furthermore, these people are insulated from the real market by the record labels, which must pay them. So in many cases, these stakeholders are the reason that wholesale prices for music are so high, and the record labels take the rap for their unwillingness to budge on price. This upward price pressure is then passed on to the digital music services, which then can't make enough of a legal margin to properly promote their service and make a modest profit. This is the position in which music services promoting plain old downloads and streams find themselves. Woe unto the entrepreneur who comes up with a truly new and novel way to market, promote, and sell recorded music. He or she must overcome a poisonous, complicated, and ultimately highly expensive nettle of legal issues. If they fail to get deals done and are sued on any of the many bases available to the stakeholders, a judge who chooses not to ignore the precedent must rule in favor of the stakeholders. Even when the labels want to license music to these people, they can't, because of their agreements with the stakeholders. In short, the stakeholders are protected by the law at the expense of the market, and the recorded-music industry as a whole continues to decrease in size. Any entrepreneur who does a proper due diligence will ultimately reach these conclusions. As a result, prudent entrepreneurs choose other available businesses with fewer problems, so recorded music continues to attract only the most passionate about music, or most disdainful of the law.

Last, but possibly not least, it is actually still possible to download music for free, and the paid download services have still failed to sufficiently differentiate themselves to be perceived as better than the free services, even if they actually are. I think the cure for this is good promotion of these new services, and overcoming the technical problems that make it difficult for the normal consumer to use them in all the places they like to listen to music.

MA: Wow, Steve has said a mouthful of truth here. And I agree with most of it, but rather than pat each other on the back, which doesn't benefit the readers of this book, I'm going to take a Socratic approach and comment only on the parts that I disagree with, or sort of disagree with.

The second-to-last paragraph of his reply may be one of the best summaries of the difficult business dynamic faced in the music space that I've ever read. It's balanced and states the issues clearly. But I have a different take on a few nuances, and perhaps if he reads this, Steve may agree with me, and change some of his overall views. I will repeat certain sections of his answer and then give my comments.

"**SM:** This upward price pressure is then passed on to the digital music services, which then can't make enough of a legal margin to properly promote their service and make a modest profit."

MA: Well, I would agree with that were it not for the many business plans I've seen and vetted for labels and investors on so-called new models. I see about ten a year. Most are reinventing the wheel; they are merely record companies, but with a new twist. They all still revolve around signing artists and exploiting exclusive rights to masters. But the point that makes this worth disagreeing with is the salary and bonus schedules I've seen in these plans. Not a single one has a CEO making less than $150,000 a year, and not a single one has executive overhead that is costing the venture capitalists less than $1 million a year. Now, it's hard to cry a river for a guy who says, "These damn labels are charging too much—if I give them what they want I'll go broke," and the same guy wants $150K a year for an untried startup. And if you try to tell these guys that they should defer a salary for the first three years, they will have no part of it. They want to get paid for their genius now. Which sends the little voice in my head saying, these guys are not really in the music-innovation business. They are in the get-the-money-now business. But even if they agree to defer, their investors won't let them. VC guys know most of these ventures fail, and so they won't get excited about anything that defers a large salary. They want the CEO to be incentivized to make the plan work, not walk away because they are not getting paid anyway. And so we have a conundrum. There are no business plans where the so-called innovators are willing to work strictly off a back end, because either their VC backers will not allow it, or the executives themselves won't allow it. High overhead means you need to make big profits. Therefore, for the venture to make a profit, the licensing fees must be lower than is reasonable.

My suggestion is if you want to innovate in an industry that has been doing well for over half a century, expect to have to prove yourself BEORE you get paid. That goes for the VC folks, as well.

"**SM:** In short, the stakeholders are protected by the law at the expense of the market."

MA: Not sure I buy this, and after reading my response, my guess is that Steve wouldn't, either. The market is created by the "stakeholders," and the principal stakeholders are the labels. If they want to destroy it or recreate it, it's theirs to do that. This comment is born out of what has become the copyright vs. copyleft argument. The question boils down to this: who should have more power over how a work is sold and distributed, the creators of a work, or the people who buy it? Clearly, the law as it's written now says the creators should have a limited monopoly on how their work is distributed. These are copyrightists. The copyleftists feel the other way, that once a work is created, the public should get to decide its fate. A comment like the one above (if I read it right) betrays a copyleftist agenda. It suggests that the market should control how much people pay for music, if anything. I don't think commerce would function well like that under our current laws and justice system.

"SM: But now, despite the freely available, already ubiquitous standard formats of MP3 and others, the only music service you regularly see promoted on TV and billboards is iTunes. And the only massively successful one is iTunes."

MA: Well, one reason people are shy about getting into this space is that so far there is only one "success" story, and even iTunes has stated publicly that they are barely profitable. This is with a licensing model that retains over 30 percent of revenues from sales. iTunes is 30–70 partners with the labels, and they still cannot make a lot of money. So how is a startup supposed to make a go of it with a deal that will never be as sweetheart as iTunes'? A more fair statement would be this: so far NO ONE has come up with a method that satisfies both content creators/holders and retail vendors, including iTunes.

"SM: Radio has become more generic, few people listen to the radio, and from an empirical perspective, nothing else has really fully replaced radio as a solid way to identify new music choices."

MA: Here I can flatly disagree, but asking the question, how does anyone know there are less people listening to the radio? Who says? From where are we starting our survey—2008? Sure, maybe if you start your survey at 2006–7 you can make that statement, but I don't see how you can say it if you begin your survey at anything before 1999. Every car sold in the United States has a radio. Car production has just about doubled in the United States since 1999. That means twice as many radios are in use. That does not even include the many types of devices that have AM/FM tuners incorporated into them, like many MP3 players, or broadcast apps for smart phones. If I had to guess, I think I'd be on firm ground by saying that there are probably three times as many FM radios in use today as there were a decade ago. How can you make the leap from that type of empirical data to "less people are listening to the radio"? Where's the data that backs that up? Are we to presume that car manufactures got it all wrong, and they are making radios that people are NOT using?

SG: Are there examples of business models that could have been good for the business but that the labels decided to block?

SM: In my opinion, the biggest missed opportunity in the music business was the failure of the first Napster. Yes, it's true that it was very difficult and expensive throughout the 1990s to get licenses for digital-music services, and this remains true today. But I watched in disbelief as the major labels blocked the development of the most efficient music-distribution service ever to exist. I thought that Napster would continue free for a few months, maybe a year at the outside, and then the labels would license them. You would have to pay for downloads, and that would be it. I just couldn't believe that they would not want to take over and control this technology, and take advantage of the cost savings and increased margins to be gained migrating off of physical distribution. I think they adhered too closely to an analyst report telling them that most of the money was being made from physical delivery, and I think they might actually have believed they might be able to stop this technology from existing using the law.

MA: And then I couldn't believe Napster refused to present *any* viable business model that included paying rights holders. I believe that Napster could have presented almost any business model that paid rights holders, no matter how tenuous, and the courts might have upheld their right to continue developing the business. But to just say, "Hell, no, we won't pay, and we don't believe we should have to," this was unbelievable, and impossible for the courts to uphold. This was the match that set off the burning of the library of Alexandria that put us in the dark ages from which we are still trying to emerge today. If Napster had been legally licensed, unauthorized peer-to-peer would have survived, yes, but they might have stayed on the margins and may not have gained the foothold and massive penetration that they did. Ultimately, a centrally served database such as Napster is technologically the better way to go, because you can do a lot more to guarantee quality of experience, as the cloud-based services are proving today.

[*Author's note: See Ted Cohen's interview, included in Part IV, in which he tells the story of how Napster offered a billion dollars to the labels but WITHOUT a royalty or any share in Napster's income.*]

MA: So, this is interesting, because the Ted Cohen YouTube video makes the opposite case of the one made in the initial part of Steve's answer. He tells of an arrogant bunch of piss ants who thought they would change copyright law, not one that wanted to work with labels on normal business terms. Napster only offered $1 million (not $1 billion, as Ted said in his interview with you), for all rights two years after they drew first blood. It was intended as a joke. A paltry sum that no label in their right mind would accept. I've said all I have to say on this subject in my blog and in the book *Million Dollar Mistakes*. Here's the link to my blog:http://www.mosesavalon.com/mosesblog/http://www.mosesavalon.com/mosesblog/major-labels-and-the-internet-what-really-went-wrong-at-that-party-in-1999/

SG: What has made Spotify so popular in European countries in which it has been allowed to launch?

SM: Spotify is popular because it works well. I have had the opportunity to demo it to music lovers here in the United States. I have yet to find one who does not become addicted to the ability to call up and instantly play any song or band of which you can think. I've had friends report back that they spent entire days listening to Uriah Heep, Gentle Giant, Chico Science, obscure Nigerian rock or New York acid jazz that they might have found difficult to find any other way. Centrally serving music from the cloud, with catching of your most frequently played songs, so you can hear them when your connection cuts out, is the way to go. I've been pushing cloud-based streaming and download services since MusicStream, which was the first one I saw that integrated a music service with social networking and playlist sharing. I really do believe that the more music you expose to people, the more music they will want, and the faster the industry will grow. However, there is a lot of work to do around developing new business models and pricing plans. These must be developed through experimentation, not guesswork. The longer rights holders deny digital-music distribution companies the ability to experiment with different pricing plans, promotions, and product offerings, the longer it will take for new music products to be created and for real money to be made. Although I would never condone or support stealing money from artists and rights holders, there are some excellent lessons to be learned from the short-lived success of AllofMP3. com regarding effective pricing and viral promotion. A lot of users signed up, and a lot of money was made. The only thing that was missing was paying the rights holders. Rights holders should get deals done with digital-music companies and support experimentation with different pricing plans and payment structures. This is the future of the recorded-music business.

SG: What are the chances that the labels will allow Spotify to launch in the United States?

SM: I don't know, ask the labels. Spotify is one competitor in a crowded field of great music services. If I were the labels, I would lower advances, license all of these services on a revenue share, and let the services spend their money on promoting themselves to consumers. The digital distribution horse is out of the barn. What these services are really doing is expanding the number of people who pay for digital music, not the number of people who use it. That's already a huge number.

SG: Why are the majors tolerating it in Europe?

SM: I have no idea. Ask the majors. But for you, Steve, I'm going to go out on a limb here and offer suggestions based on culture and technology that I can't back up with numbers.

The European market is very different than the U.S. and Canadian market. First, people listen to different music, and it means something different to them. The governments in Europe support music much more aggressively than we do, and European music tastes are broader. Europeans adopted playlists over albums earlier than we did. Furthermore, in Europe, mobile digital signal delivery standards were strictly controlled, so most digital delivery to mobile phones uses similar standards. As a result, it is easier and less expensive to roll out digital services to European mobile users, and Europeans have long experienced a much wider range of digital services delivered directly to their mobile phones. As a result, there is less of a learning curve to using these services and integrating them into their daily lives, so widespread adoption can happen more quickly there than here. Finally, and most importantly, Europe is smaller, and more densely populated, so digital signal penetration is almost completely ubiquitous in Europe. As a result, a digital stream delivered to a mobile phone in Europe is much less likely to drop out than it is here.

MA: I don't have any germane comments about Spotify. It may not even be in business in a year, so why devote page space to it?

SG: Do you agree with Universal's lawsuit against Grooveshark?

SM: Universal has the right under existing law to bring these claims, and Grooveshark has the right to defend against them. Grooveshark is an example of the dynamic I described above. It is a new way to market and sell music, run by people who are highly passionate about their music, which the law has left exposed to claims by stakeholders.

MasurLaw advised Grooveshark for a few months during its earliest days. At that time, we advised them that it might be possible (not necessarily legal, but possible) to experiment with new ways to sell music to people, even without having obtained the rights, then hold the money in escrow to use as a budget to cut deals with the rights holders to pay them their share of the proceeds. We came up with this idea because bitter past experience had taught us that we would not be able to obtain the rights on behalf of Grooveshark, without having already demonstrated "traction," or tangible proof of a working business model. We also advised them that for an unknown startup company, any PR is good PR, and that getting sued by a large international conglomerate corporation might be a good, cheap, and effective way to promote their service to a large number of people. Unfortunately, we no longer represent them and don't know the particulars of the case, but we hope they use the opportunity that Universal has given them to its fullest advantage, sell more music, and help grow the recorded-music industry.

MA: This is a half truth at best. I consulted ad hoc for Grooveshark. Here's what I can say. The majors offered Grooveshark a onetime licensing agreement of somewhere between $4 and $7 million. A very reasonable fee, all things considered. Grooveshark didn't want to pay it. They thought it was high. I was told their attorneys were advising them that they could beat the labels in court if push came to shove. Their entire mentality was a holdout from the Napster era of doing business with the majors, which is, we'll do it our way and let them try to stop us. UNI is doing just that. They will win, and Grooveshark and its investors will never accept responsibility for their actions. I've had talks with people very high up on both sides. I didn't think the fee was excessive, but I was willing to try to get Grooveshark a better deal. Grooveshark was interested in my services, but they wanted me to work off a back-end fee; I would be paid a percentage that was the difference between what the majors offered and what I could get them down to. This model would have compromised my integrity in being an artists'-rights advocate and my judgment as to what was fair to both sides. I passed.

My experience with Grooveshark is they echo and embody the very reason that tech folk and content folk just do not get along: both feel entitled to their points of view. The difference being that content has about one hundred years of legal precedent on their side; the tech folk have lots and lots and lots of new and very arrogant VC money. My suspicion, based on how immaturely some of these "information should be free" startups respond to reasonable negotiations is that much of their money comes from inheritance and/or dealings that did not require the acknowledgment of the creative work of others. The tech people just don't seem to "get" the copyright concept, until it applies to their trademarks and software. They just don't think writing a great song or making a great recording is all that hard compared to writing code for a social-media platform. In my view, that's why they thumb their nose at the music space.

SG: LimeWire lost in court and now face a determination on damages that may exceed a billion dollars. Do they deserve it?

SM: During the days of horse-drawn carriages, traffic accidents were rarely fatal and superhighways were not necessary. The law that applies to copyrightable material today developed during an era of physical distribution. The relevance of these laws to an inexpensive, nearly instantaneous means of distribution should be examined more carefully, and with an open mind to doing things differently.

LimeWire is an example of a new way to market and sell music, and its business model has already been proven to make money. I'm just not sure it makes enough money to pay rights holders at the rates they require and the law allows. We would have loved the opportunity to work with LimeWire on developing new legal business models. I personally pitched them on this many times. They have a big installed base and a great brand name. In my opinion there is still a good opportunity here.

MA: Yes, I agree with Steve, if things were different, they wouldn't be the same. If the law didn't require LimeWire to pay for rights, then they would not have to pay labels/artists. But the law does require it. The fact that you may invent a new widget that sells an old product in a new way does not mean that you get to trample on the law, the rights of creators, and an infrastructure that presently feeds thousands of people. To ignore that is selfish and immature. That's what these guys were. They wanted to be geekstars. Now they are unemployable and un-investable.

SG: As sales of CDs have dropped precipitously, so has income from recorded music, and digital has not picked up the slack. It's been estimated that 90 percent of music downloads are unauthorized. Can authorized music ever catch up with "free"?

SM: Absolutely. If you provide good value and promote well, people will pay money. Value competes quite well with free. With music services, you can compete with free on convenience and ease of use, safety, quality of service, stability and longevity (trust), availability on a wide variety of devices, or through music-recognition or social-media services. Pandora, iTunes, and Spotify all prove that people will pay money for value. We're just in the early days, and there is a lot of work left to do. In New York, we have clean, good-tasting, efficiently delivered water available for free all over the city, yet people still buy it in plastic-leaching bottles delivered by trucks that burn petroleum. There is a lesson in this for the recorded-music business; promote your product well, and people will buy it, even if they can get it for free.

Also, you can't compare CD sales to digital distribution. Digital distribution of music is a completely different business requiring completely different business practices. The winners in the old game are rarely the winners in the new game, unless they are very smart and agile. To extend my previous analogy, during the nineteenth century, there were a great many makers of horse-drawn carriages, many of which were custom-build shops. The advent of automobiles and mass production changed things a great deal, and very few of the carriage makers survived. A company called Superior Coach survived by continuing its custom builds, and building ambulances, hearses, and other special-use vehicles. But the real winners were new companies that did things differently. Similarly, everything about the value chain of digital music services is different, and they must do things completely differently. You can still buy a Faith Hill cassette tape at a Little America truck stop on the outskirts of Evanston, Wyoming. This is a completely different sale then selling a Ke$ha CD at the Best Buy in downtown Evanston, Coldplay on iTunes, or DangerMau5 on Beatport.

MA: This is excerpted from my new book, *100 Answers to 50 Questions About the Music Business*. First, it's pure hyperbole that CD sales are going into the abyss. Will they eventually go the way of the dinosaurs? Vinyl made a comeback. So who really knows?

Regardless, it is also something of a myth that major labels make most of their profit from CD sales. They have not since about 1992. Sure, they make lots of income, but income is not profit. The biggest profit center for labels is the licensing of masters to film and television (and recently to new stuff like iTunes, Spotify, Pandora, etc.) The cost to license content is zero, leaving a 100 percent profit margin. Labels get a call from a film producer or director or Internet-service developer who wants a hit song in their movie, or a blanket license for a catalog. The cash register starts a-ringing. Think of the Black Sabbath song "Iron Man" in the movie *Iron Man*. What do you think Paramount paid for that license? Coupla bucks?

This does not mean that labels don't care if CDs sell. CDs and LPs were once the mainstay of label income, but when licensing began to boom in the late 1970s, record companies began to see the "disc" (the LP and later the CD) as something other than the final product. A philosophy that would mature over the next ten years, but which was kept secret from most major-label employees, who were told that CD sales were everything. Meanwhile, higher-ups knew otherwise.

To them, the final product was the six-figure movie license, and the disc was relegated to being a way of recouping the research and development costs of the catalog. In other words, labels need to invest in new artists in order to build catalog that they can someday license for $1,000 on the penny. To do that, they need to spend money on creating and promoting new recordings. They need to make new hits. To recoup the cost of the development, they have the disc (and to some degree, the download).

Automakers recoup about 10 cents from derivative products for every dollar they invest in the R&D of a new car, even in good times. Sometimes it takes ten years to pay back the costs of a new model. Other industries don't fare much better. This is why the music business is so friggin' profitable. R&D is recouped at a ratio of about 1:2 with physical sales, then the hits are licensed for profits of about 10,000:1.

That's why labels can afford a 30 percent drop in CD sales spread out over five years and can still afford to pay senior execs six-figure bonuses each year. Their profit is not grounded in CD sales at all. One *Iron Man*–type license a year pays the salaries of an entire executive team. And major labels do hundreds of such licenses each year. If CD sales are down, it simply means their R&D takes a hit that year and that they cannot spend as much money on new artist development the next year, or they have to fire a few midlevel executives until sales recover. Which history shows they always do.

Does a 30 percent drop in CD sales have any negative impact on the business overall? Maybe and probably, but it's not as catastrophic as the tech-biased media would have you think, nor as bad as labels would have us believe. But it is a great excuse to clean house of a few overpaid executives, renegotiate legal bills, drop a few barely recouped acts, and whine to Congress that we need new legislation to protect us from rampant Internet theft.

Major labels, like most big conglomerates, exaggerate to everyone equally to serve their best interests. To artists they say, "You didn't sell enough," to their staff they cry poverty in the form of a pink slip, and to the government they scream "theft." And the band plays on.

SG: Are mobile subscriptions the answer—making "free" music part of your monthly mobile fee? Is this happening already?

SM: Mobile subscriptions are one answer of a great many. There is a lot of marketing and experimentation left to do. A lot of Americans don't even know what a streaming music service is, or why they would want it, for the same reason they didn't know in 1972 that they would want the level of cable TV they now have. In 1972, or even in 1985, they also would not have been willing to pay so much for it. It is very early days for digital music services. We have to work hard, be patient with the difficulty people have adopting new ways of doing things, and sell good services that provide good value.

MA: I think it's a viable answer in Europe and other parts of the world, but not for the United States. We in the U S of friggin' A like to own things. iTunes make you feel like you own something, but that illusion will be shattered if and when a major label does not renew their licensing agreement with them and suddenly an entire catalog disappears from the store and then, with your next update, from your personal iTunes library. In the United States we like to own stuff. So the idea of paying monthly for a virtual record collection will work for some, but not most in the U.S.

SG: "Free" music is not free at all. ISPs make fortunes from people who need high-speed Internet to get "free," and people spend small fortunes on computers, MP3 players, et cetera so they can hear "free" music. Is the answer to the woes of the recording business to put a levy on the ISPs and makers of the devices that allow people to "steal" music?

SM: I don't think so. ISP licensing is at best a "mop up" that cleans up the Internet's free uses of marginal value the same way that ASCAP, BMI, and SESAC performance licenses mop up the money that would otherwise be left on the table in bars and restaurants nationwide and around the world. I don't think there is any single answer to the woes of the music business. First, we have to find great music that people feel compelled to buy just because it is good. Then we have to create new music services that are easy to use and promote them well. After addressing these fundamentals, we have to retrofit our law to work better with the new distribution paradigms. As part of this process, yes, we can consider new ideas for how to mop up payment for uses that are not otherwise addressed by the market. I edited the 2010 International Association of Entertainment Lawyers' book *Collective Licensing at the ISP Level.* This book focuses not on whether ISP licensing is a good idea, but whether it is possible, and how to do it, from the perspective of experts in twenty-two countries. That's because I strongly believe we should stop talking about what's good or bad and instead talk about what might work, and build it.

MA: Many smart people are in favor of this model and I would be, too, if someone could show me exactly how this money will end up in the pockets of artists and songwriters. So far, no one has. Sure, there will be collection agents, but these will use the same pooling systems that have failed us for years. The top people get the majority of the cash. Like ASCAP and BMI. Then there are the large administration fees. These are the real winners of this model, and if you look closely at some of the strongest proponents of it, you'll see they are jockeying for this administrative position. Blanket fees have hardly put a dime in the pockets of artists when they were applied to "blank media" or digital tape recorders. Will they work here? I'd like to believe they could, but I just don't see it yet.

SG: What is the next big thing?

SM: Hopefully, a lot of great new music will be the next big thing. After that, music labels and the stakeholders they have to pay, working hand-in-hand with digital distribution services, promoters, and artists to promote music sales, increase demand, and provide good value to consumers at a fair price. That's what I want. But what do I really think is the next big thing? Disintermediation; or put another way, a lot of entitled people making a lot less money than they used to. That's what seems to be going around in America today.

MA: I believe that we are perched on the verge of an essential change in the way music interposes in our world. Pop music is an art form but has become a gentrified neighborhood. Good artists and executives are still moving there, yes, but not the Picassos, Mozarts, or Einsteins. In truth, most artists I know who are successful do not think they are advancing the medium to a new level with their latest release. They don't have to record the next *Sergeant Pepper's* to be happy. Nor do labels want them to, now that singles are more compatible with the net-based buying habits. This is probably no big revelation, but it does paint a huge sign on the wall that says, "Pop is a dying art form."

Music's power vanguard was the early 1960s through the late 1970s. During that almost thirty-year span, music rallied people and ultimately influenced foreign policy. It showed the world what three chords and a voice can do. Unfortunately, the conditions that existed then are absent today. Mainly, portable broadcast radio as a means to experience music. Back then, your favorite song was something you could hear in the background of just about any indoor or outdoor commercial space. This made music both ubiquitous and harmonious, meaning you knew that when you were hearing a socially relevant song, so were thousands of others—at exactly the same time. That was the power of radio. It unified us at a time when the draft was in effect and the youth of American were politicized.

Conversely, today, we still have things to get political about, but thanks to MP3 devices and "smart radio" apps, music is now so very much an *individual* experience rather than a group one. While Internet technology may be revitalizing the money side of music, iThings have been the most significant assassin to pop's ability to be a cultural leader. We hardly turn to public forums like radio for something new, and we will never again be able to sneakily thumb through a date's record collection to get a read on their tastes or politics. Now you'll need a password to hack into their hard drive or smart phone.

Yep, just about the only time music is uniting us face-to-face is, on the rare occasion, at concerts. And, according to studies, we are going to fewer and fewer of those, as well. Every day we are becoming more disconnected from music as a *social* experience and moving closer to it being a mere commodity. Pop is becoming more ethereal, more virtual, and shrinking in stature. So much so that for a few years in the early 2000s, many people thought that they had a "right" to *free* music because music's new virtual format felt free. Sure, stealing a CD from a record store was an obvious crime, but sharing a file? C'mon. How can that be illegal?

In music's next incarnation, the form will be decided probably not by its creators but by its fans. Some person sitting in front of a screen IM-ing his BFF will be hit by inspiration. Someone out there reading this, maybe you, must say to him or herself, no, I'm not going to write yet another three-minute song with a verse, chorus, verse structure, not because I'm not good at it, and not because I don't think I have what it takes to make it a hit, but because the world simply does not need another one. What the world needs is for that person's unique talent for communicating to be channeled into coming up with something so different that when you first hear or see it you cannot instantly figure out *how* it will make money. You may not even recognize it as a traditional form of pop music.

But until that day arrives, we will still be making and selling the same product that we know, over and over again. We'll find more clever ways to monetize it and repackage it. But it will only be some new version of the same old thing. The days of the three-minute pop hit are past. We can build on it. We can remold it, but we must accept pop music's destiny as a powerful medium that, like the printing press and cave drawings, is an artifact of society's youth. We need the *next* group experience. (And I don't mean Twitter.)

It's time for something new.

It's time for something new.

It's time for something *new.*

Acknowledgments

I would like to express my appreciation to those who helped me with their expertise, insights, and encouragement, including Moses Avalon, Aziza, Ray Beckerman, Esq, Corey D. Boddie, Esq., Paul Brandes, Jan Bridge, Powell Burns, Wallace Collins, Esq., Amy Dadow (my muse), Ralph De Palma, Esq., Jessica Ellison, Eric de Fontenay, Zouheir Faraj, Ricky Gordon (aka "Dirty Red"), Kyra La Rock, Eric Kline, Xocoa and Yaakov Love, Margot B, Steve Masur, Esq., Greg McBowman, Deborah Newman, Marty Novare, Esq., Daniella Ohad, John Paige, Esq., Paul Resnikoff, Barron Rachman, David Sanders, Charles Sanders, Esq., John Simson, Esq., Ed Steinberg, Jennifer Sullivan, Peter Thall, Esq., Ashford Tucker, Esq., Fred von Lohmann, Esq., and Jana Vejmelka, Esq.

Special thanks to Dan Coleman, the producer of my Internet radio show on the future of the music business at MyRealBroadcast.com. Some of the interviews in this book were originally produced for that series. Also special thanks to Kristi Zimmerman for her transcription services and John Cerullo, my publisher, for taking on this edition, and my literary agent, Andrew Stuart.

Finally, I would like to acknowledge my great mentor and partner, Eric Kulberg of Universal Media.

Index

A2IM. *See* American Association of Independent Music

AAC, 175

ABKCO, 246, 248–49

Ableton Live, 153

Abu Dhabi, 256

AC/DC, 129

Acony Records, 275

ACPA. *See* Anticybersquatting Consumer Protection Act

Acrobat PDF, 298

ACTA. *See* Anti-Counterfeiting Trade Agreement

ACUM, 13

ADA (Alternative Distribution Alliance), 182, 283

admin deals, 9, 84

Adobe, 171

ad-supported streaming, 221, 228, 236

advances, 17–18

advertisement, 28, 45
  clearing music for, 99–100
  co-op, 259
  Grokster, 124
  history of, 94–95
  iPod, 94–95
  iTunes and, 92, 96
  licenses in, 96–98
  music promotion, 95–96
  on Myspace, 160
  Pandora, 69–70
  radio and, 61
  revenues, 224, 234
  revenue sharing, 133
  StreamCast, 124
  webcasting, 64, 285
  YouTube, 76, 223

advertising-supported services, 78

A&E, 90

AEPI, 13

Aerosmith, 41, 46, 95, 113, 116

AFofM (American Federation of Musicians), xix, 68, 142

AFTRA (American Federation of Television and Radio Artists), xix, 16, 68, 142

aggregators, 168

AHRA. *See* Audio Home Recording Act

Airplay, 85

AKM, 13

Akon, 262

album sales, xv

Alexa Internet rankings, 155

Allen, Harry, xxxii

Allen, Lily, 291

Allen, Woody, 201

Alligator, 273, 280, 283, 286, 290

Allman Brothers, 259, 282

AllofMP3.com, 309

"All the Right Moves" (One Republic), 92

All You Need to Know About the Music Business (Passman), 51, 266

Alpha Rev, 191

Alternative Distribution Alliance. *See* ADA

Amazon, 60, 79, 116, 177, 205, 237–38, 244, 261
  Honor System, 134
  music sales, xiii

American Association of Independent Music (A2IM), xv, 138, 273, 282, 284–85

American Federation of Musicians. *See* AFofM

American Federation of Television and Radio Artists. *See* AFTRA

American Idiot, 100

American Idol, 262

American Society of Composers, Authors, and Publishers. *See* ASCAP

Amplify.com, 227

A&M Records, Inc. vs. Napster, Inc., 121

Anamanaguchi, 247

Anderson, Chris, xxxiii

Anderson, Wes, 246

Android, xxii, 60, 172

Andy Warhol Museum, 216

the Animals, 246

Anti, 273

Anti-Counterfeiting Trade Agreement (ACTA), 150

Anticybersquatting Consumer Protection Act (ACPA), 47

antipiracy laws, 15n3

AOL Radio, 60, 62

"Apologize" (One Republic), 92

Apple, 29, 95, 109, 305

apps, 172–74

   native, 174

APRA, 13

A&R, 187, 192

   changing role of, 259–65

Arcade Fire, xxxiv, 165–66, 238, 264

archived programming, 68

the Arctic Monkeys, 278, 291

Area, 187

Are We Not Men? We Are Devo! (Devo), 259

Arista Records, LLC, et al. vs. Launch Media, Inc., 67

Arista Records, LLC, et al. vs. Lime Group, 143–44

ARPANET, 229

Arrendell, Ed, 255–58

Artemis Records, 181, 201, 203

Artistdirect.com, 133

artists

   apps for, 172–74

   business models for, xxxi–xxxii

   business practices, 15–19

   digital technology and, xxv

   Facebook for, 156

   goals of, xvi

   management and, 256–57

   new opportunities for, xxxi

   signing, xvii

   web-savvy, xvii

ASCAP (American Society of Composers, Authors, and Publishers), 130, 132, 175, 224, 241

   AT&T and, 24

   Creative Commons and, 32

   database, 8, 101–2

   Non-Interactive Services, 74

   public performance and, 82–84, 111

   revenues, 14

   role of, 12–15, 57–58, 73–75, 81, 99, 313–14

Atlantic Records, 186, 187, 188, 190, 202

"Atomic Dog" (Clinton), 36

Atreyu, 191

AT&T, 24, 139, 148

attribution no derivatives, 28

attribution noncommercial, 28

attribution noncommercial no derivatives, 28

attribution noncommercial share alike, 28

attribution share alike, 28

audio compilations

   masters and, 86

   songs on, 85–86

Audio Home Recording Act (AHRA), 55, 129

Auto-Tune, 242

Avalon, Moses, 304–15

Azoff, Irving, 187

baby bands, 97, 103

backup musicians, 16

backup vocalists, 16, 142

Bad Boy Records, 205

Baha Men, 181

Baker, Meredith, 139

Baker, Roy Thomas, 153

Bandcamp, xxxi, 154, 167, 175–76

bandwidth levies, 134

Barry, Hank, 229

Barsuk, Records, 290

Basin Street, 273

Batiste, Jon, 268
Bat Out of Hell (Meat Loaf), 42
Bayh, Evan, xxiii
the Beach Boys, 49–50, 278
the Beastie Boys, 29
the Beatles, 129*n*2, 215, 285
Beatport, 312
Beckerman, Ray, 146
Bee Gees, 104
Bell Canada, 244
Bengloff, Rich, 273–76
Berlin, Irving, 13
Berman, Jay, xix
Berne Convention, 46
Bertelsmann AG, 133, 229
Best Buy, 233, 236, 312
BET, xxiv
Bette Midler vs. Ford Motor Company, 99
Better Than Ezra, 182
Beyoncé, 302
Biden, Joe, 276
Bieber, Justin, 163, 223, 240, 262
Big Beat, 187
BigChampagne, 119, 128, 129, 131, 134, 220, 237
Big Machine Records, 186
Billboard, xxxiv, 96, 105, 127, 177, 277, 280, 290
Bing, 172
BitTorrent, xxi, xxiv, xxx, 127, 128, 129, 140
Blackberry, 60
Black Eyed Peas, 161, 220
Black Label Society, 182
Black Sabbath, 187, 312
blanket licenses, 132–33
blog, xxi, xxxi, 62, 154, 183, 188, 304
    approaching, 166–67
    overview of, 166, 278, 280, 285
    popularity of, 208
    starting, 168
    as tastemakers, 165–66
bloggers, 166, 167
"Blowin' in the Wind" (Dylan), 8
Blue Note Records, 8
Blues Community Foundation, 277
Blue Suede Groove, 181

Blunt, James, 188
BMG, xxvii, 125
BMI (Broadcast Music Incorporated), 32, 132, 175, 224, 241
    database, 8, 101–2
    revenues, 14
    role of, 12–15, 57–58, 73–75, 81, 99, 313–14
B.o.B., 188
Bolton, Michael, 35, 36
Bono, 209
The Book of Ice, 219
Boombox Project, 219
Bootsy's Rubber Band, 43
Borchetta, Scott, 186
Bowie, David, 209
Boyle, Susan, 262, 264
BPI. *See* British Phonographic Industry
Brandenburg, Karlheinz, 229
branding, 97
Brand New, 251
Braun, Scooter, 163
breach-of-contract claim, 48
Breaking Benjamin, 191
"Bridge over Troubled Water" (Simon), 108
Bridgeport Music, Inc. vs. Dimension Films, 26
Bridgeport Music, Inc. vs. UMG, 36
Bridge Ratings, 52
Bright Tunes Music vs. Harrisongs Music, 38*n*1
British Parliament, 6
British Phonographic Industry (BPI), 127*n*1
Broadcast Music Incorporated. *See* BMI
broad rights, 87, 93, 103
Broadway, 100–101
Brooklyn Vegan, 231
Brother Records, Inc. vs. Jardine, 49
Brown, Alison, 273
browser, 169
Bruno Mars, 188, 220
Buckman, John, 296–99
Bug, 208
Buick, 95
Burger King, 94
Burning Spear, 273
Butler, Win, 166

buyouts, 87–88
Buzz Clips, 302
Byrne, David, 29, 30

cable shows, 92–93
Cadillac, 95
California Years, 204, 205
Cansei de Ser Sexy, 94–95, 163
Cape Farewell, 219
Capitol Records, 164, 196
Capitol vs. Thomas-Rassett, 146–47
Caplan, Michael, 259–65
Capricorn, 282
Carey, Mariah, xxv, 125, 162, 271, 286, 300
Caroline Distribution, 195, 283
Carpenter, Mary Chapin, xix
Carver, Jason, 173
cascading style sheet (CSS), 169, 171
cassettes, xxix
Castro, Tommy, 286
catalog songs, 96
Cavallo, Bob, 191
CBS Radio, 61
CBS Records, xxiv, 187, 259
CD (compact disc), xxix, 114, 116, 134, 178
    copying, 56, 57, 70, 276, 296
    distributing, 81, 176–77, 205, 283
    mechanical royalties, 111, 179
    rootkit disaster and, 121
    sales, 207, 261–62, 294, 312
    sales declines, xxvi, 19, 221, 311
    singles, xxix
CD Baby, xviii, xxxi, 176, 278
    payment from, 178
Cee Lo, 188
censorship, xxiv
Century Media, 273
Chang, Jeff, 216
Charles, Ray, 271
Cher, 22
Chevrolet, 94
Chicago Tribune, 287
the Chiffons, 38n1
Chipmunks, 104
Chubby Checker, 246

Chuck D, 29, 31, 216
Citadel, 62
Citibank, xxvii
Clarida, Robert, 34
clearance, 88
    for advertising, 99–100
    copyright, 101–3, 101–5
    masters, 89, 91
    professionals, 108
Clear Channel, 61, 64, 284
Cliff, Jimmy, 173
Clinton, George, 36, 39
Clooney, George, 208
cloud-based music service, xxii
cloud-based streaming, 309
Clueless, 201, 208
Clyburn, Mignon, 139
CMT. *See* Country Music Television
Cohen, Ted, 121n1, 227–34, 246, 261, 308
COICA. *See* Combating Online Infringement
    Counterfeits Act
Coke, 94
Coldplay, 19, 253, 286, 312
Coleman, Alisa, 246–50
Collective Licensing at the ISP Level (Masur), 130,
    304, 314
Collins, Albert, 277
Collins, Bootsy, 43
Columbia Law School, 34, 36
Columbia Records, xxxii, 17
Combating Online Infringement Counterfeits Act
    (COICA), xxi–xxii, xxiii–xxiv
Comcast, 139, 148
Comcast vs. FCC, 140
commercial radio, 95, 186, 195, 252–53, 278–79
commercial webcasters, 69–72
compact disc. *See* CD
compulsory license, 10, 66
    individual, 133
    uses not covered by, 11
comScore, xxxiii
Confessions of a Music Producer (Avalon), 304
Constitutional Council of France, 149
consumer electronics industry, 120–21
content ID, 135, 136n1

contributory infringement, xxii, 122
controlled composition clauses, 18
Cooke, Sam, 246, 249–50
cool, 183–84
co-op advertising, 259
Copeland, Shemekia, 277
Copps, Michael, 139
co-pub deals, 9, 84
copying, 56, 57, 70, 276, 296
copyleftism, 307
Copyright Act, 5, 12, 22, 23, 73, 80, 110. *See also*
    Digital Millennium Copyright Act
  importance of, 7
  on publication, 21
  section 104A, 21
  section 107, 24
  section 114, 91
  section 115, 57, 110
  section 118, 91
copyright duration, 21–23
copyright law, 5–7, 106, 284
  clearance, 101–5
  defined, 5
  infringement of, 20
  origins of, 6
  RIAA and, 66
  rights protected by, 6
  works protected by, 5–6
Copyright Law Deskbook (Clarida), 34
Copyright Office, 20, 86
copyright registration, 19–21
Copyright Royalty Board (CRB), 69, 78, 110, 111,
    267, 275
Copyright Royalty Tribunal, 59, 82, 285
corporate copyright, 22
Corporation for Public Broadcasting, 72–73, 91
Cote, Denise, 111
Country Music Television (CMT), 235
Court of Appeals, 26
Cowan Liebowitz & Latman, 34
CRB. *See* Copyright Royalty Board
Creative Commons, 6*n*1, 27–28, 296, 298–99
  ASCAP and, 32
  attribution noncommercial, 28
  attribution noncommercial no derivatives, 28

attribution noncommercial share alike, 28
  attribution share alike, 28
Creative Suite, 171
credit card companies, xxiii
Cribs, 261
the Cribs, 173
Cronin, Charles, 36
cross-pollination strategies, 159–60
CSS. *See* cascading style sheet
Cyrus, Miley, 191

Dahl, Roald, 247
Dance Dance Revolution, 112
Danceteria, 187
DangerMau5, 312
Darjeeling Limited, 247
Davis, Clive, 259
Davis, Miles, 53
Death Cab for Cutie, 92, 188, 288–90
Death Magnetic (Metallica), 114
the Decemberists, 161
Deep Purple, 49
DeRogatis, Jim, 287
Derr, Tom, 181
Desplat, Alexandre, 246
Destiny's Child, 300
Detica, 131
Deutsch, Sarah, 232
Devo, 259
Diamond Rio, 261
Dido, 251
digital audio workstations, 153
digital distribution, xxv, 312
Digital Media Association (DiMA), 69
Digital Millennium Copyright Act (DMCA), xx,
    135, 137, 148, 233, 284
  application of, 59
  notifying, 37
  P2P and, 125
  public performance and, 66–68
  safe harbor provision, xxii, 128
  section 104, 82
  webcasting and, 56–57
digital music business history, 119–26
digital music law, 55–59

digital music services, 81–84

digital patronage, 134

Digital Performance Right in Sound Recordings Act, xx, 56, 66

digital phonorecord deliveries (DPDs), 57, 110

Digital Rights Management (DRM), xxxi, 77, 125, 170, 210

digital technology, xv
  artists and, xxv
  growth projections, 63
  impact of, xxv
  major labels and, xxv

DiMA. *See* Digital Media Association

Dion, Celine, xxv, 214, 242, 271

Disney, 186–87, 191–94

Disqus, 162

distribution, 244–45
  CDs, 81, 176–77, 205, 283
  digital, xxv, 312

District of Columbia, 110

DIY approach (do-it-yourself), xxxi–xxxii, xxxii–xxxiii, 192, 203, 278, 279

DJ Spooky, 216–19

DMCA. *See* Digital Millennium Copyright Act

documentaries, 25, 90–91, 106

Dodge, 95

"Dog Days Are Over" (Glee Cast), 220

do-it-yourself. *See* DIY approach

domain names, 47, 169

downloads, xxviii, 76–84
  growth of, xxvii
  iTunes, 57, 78, 113
  public performance compared to, 81–82
  publisher payment from, 81
  services, 78
  stores, 76–77
  tethered, 57–59

"Do You Wanna Dance" (Midler), 98

DPDs. *See* digital phonorecord deliveries

Dragonforce, 113

dramatic works, 15

Dream of the Blue Turtles, 256

Dreamweaver, 171

DRM. *See* Digital Rights Management

Dropbox, xxx

DrumMania, 112

Duckworth, Cara, 144

Durban, Dick, xxiii

DVD, xxix, xxxiv, 70, 104, 177, 182, 262
  instructional video, 89

Dylan, Bob, 8, 95, 162

the Eagles, xxxiii, xxxiv, 240

Earle, Steve, 181

Ebb, Fred, 11

e-commerce, 170

Edison Research report, 64, 143

Ed Sullivan Show, 89

educational webcasting, 72

8-bit Rebellion, 173

Elbo.ws, 168

Electra vs. Perez, 147

Electronic Arts, 113

Electronic Frontier Foundation, 120, 132, 145

Elektra, 188

Elliott, Alan, xviii

El Topo, 249

EMI, xxii, xxxi, 7, 125, 194–97, 209, 232, 261, 274, 281, 285

EMI Label Services, 194–97

Eminem, 31
  lawsuit again Universal, 79–80

eMusic, 77, 133, 244

Eno, Brian, 216

Entercom, 62

Entertainment Law & Finance, 101–5

Epic Records, 251

Epitaph, 273

Ertegun, Ahmet, 260, 271

Escape Media, 136

Espinel, Victoria, 276

Estefan, Gloria, 108

Eubanks, Kevin, 255, 256

Eurhythmics, 113

European Union, 148

exclusive deals, 9

exclusive rights, 306

exclusivity, 16–17

Expelled (film), 25
Extravaganza, 201

Fabulous, 207
Facebook, 61, 154–55, 162, 168, 183, 204–5, 264
    for artists, 156
    benefits of, 157
    fan pages, 156
Factory Records, 187
Fairport Convention, 187
fair use, 24, 26
    classic, 50*n*9
Fanning, Shawn, xxi, 121*n*1, 227–34
Fantastic Mr. Fox, 246–47
Fatboy Record, 275
Faxon, Roger, 232
F.B.T. Productions, LLC vs. Aftermath Records, 79
FCC, 138–39
Federal Appeals Court, 140
Federal Circuit Court, 82
Federal Court of Appeals, 110
Federal Trade Commission, 121
Feist, 95
festival licenses, 94
50 Cent, 195, 253
file-sharing services, xxx. *See also* P2P
    legalizing, 128–32
Fine Art of Sampling Contest, 29
"Firework" (Perry), 220
First City, 187
FLAC, 175
Flash, 170, 171
Fleetwood Mac, 211
Fleischer, Joe, 134
Folk's Songs (Watts), xxxii
Ford, 98, 232
Ford, Henry, 305
Fort Greene Festival, 302
Fox Network, 235
Frank, Jay, 235–43
Franken, Al, 138–39
Franklin, Aretha, 94
Fraunhofer Institute, 229
Free Culture (Lessig), 6*n*1

free music, 129–30, 313
"Freeway of Love" (Franklin), 94
French National Assembly, 148
Frito-Lay, 99
FrontPage, 171
FTP, 229
Fueled by Ramen, 188
"Fu-Gee-La" (Fugees), 300
the Fugees, 300
Funeral (Arcade Fire), 165–66
Future Hit DNA (Frank), 237

G. Love and Special Sauce, 259, 262
GarageBand, 29
Gardner, Joanne, 300, 301
Garland, Eric, 119, 134, 220–27, 229, 236, 238
GEMA, 13
Genachowski, Julius, 138
Gershwin, George, 11, 238
Gershwin, Ira, 11
Gertner, Nancy, 147
"Get Down Tonight" (KC and the Sunshine Band), 96
"Get Yer Ya-Ya's Out!" (Rolling Stones), 249
"Ghetto Symphony," 108
Giant Records, 187
Glass, Daniel, 181
Glee Cast, 220
Go Daddy, 47
Godrich, Nigel, 247
Goets, Thomas, 29–32
Goldberg, Danny, 201
Goldman Sachs, 40
Gomez, Selena, 191
"Goody Goody," 108
Google, xxi–xxii, 137–38, 162, 168, 218, 222
Google Buzz, 217
Google Docs, xxii
Google Maps, 139
Google Talk, 217
Gordon, Steve, xvi, xix, xxxiv, 101–5, 106
Gordy, Berry, 271
Gorton, Mark, 144
Gossip Girl, 92
Grace Potter and the Nocturnals, 191

Grand Theft Auto, 112, 115
Grannis, Kina, 260, 262, 264
Grateful Dead, 41, 46
Graves, Matt, 158*n*3
Greenwald, Julie, 187
"Grenade" (Bruno Mars), 220
Grey's Anatomy, 92
Griffin, Jim, 131
Groffman, Elliot, 19
Grokster, xxx, 121–24, 144
    advertisement, 124
Grooveshark, 136–38
    Universal and, 310
"Groovin'", 98
GS1U.S., 177
Guitar Freaks, 112
Guitar Hero, 112–13, 247
G-Unit, 195
Gurewitz, Brett, 273
Guster, 251

HADOPI, 148, 149, 150
Hakim, Omar, 255
Haley, Nick, 94–95, 163
Hall, Richard Melville. *See* Moby
Halo, 116
Hammond, John, 260
Happiness Index, 217
Harmonix, 113, 115
Harp, Jessica, 173
Harris, Michael, 194–97
Harrison, George, 35, 38, 38*n*1, 129*n*2
Harry Fox Agency (HFA), 10–11, 58, 81, 85–86, 102
Harvard Business School, 255
hashtags, 160
Hatch, Orrin, xxii, xxiii
HBO, 92
Hellcat, 273
Hello Music, 230
Hertz, Ken, 202
"He's So Fine," 35, 38, 38*n*1
"Hey, Soul Sister" (Glee Cast), 220
HFA. *See* Harry Fox Agency
Highline Ballroom, 264
Hill, Faith, 41

Hill, Lauryn, 162, 300
The Hills, 92
hit songs, 235–43
Hollywood Records, 186–87, 191–94
The Holy Mountain, 249
home recording, xxv
home video, 86–88
"Hotel California" (Eagles), 240
Hot Tuna, 187
Hound Dog Taylor, 277
Howling at the Moon (Yetnikoff), 119
HTML, 170, 171
Hype Machine, 231
Hypem.com, 168
hyperlink, 170

Ienner, Don, 301
IFPI. *See* International Federation of the
       Phonographic Industry
"I Get Around" (Beach Boys), 278
Iggy Pop, 95
Iglauer, Bruce, 277–86, 290, 292
"I Got a Feeling," 163
"I Kissed a Girl" (Sobule), 201, 203
Ilberman, Mel, 126
iLike, xxxi, 172
"I'll Be There" (Jacksons), 108
"Imagine" (Lennon), 25
imeem, 138
Imogen Heap, 161
IMRO, 13
independent movies, 102–3, 213
indie labels, 209–15, 246–50, 276
    RIAA and, 274
individual compulsory licenses, 133
individual song deal, 9
Infinity Radio, 64
infringement
    contributory, xxii, 122
    copyright law, 20
    vicarious, xxii
Ingram, James, 255, 256
injunctions, 104
In Rainbows (Radiohead), xxxiii
instructional videos, 89

Intellectual Property Rights Distribution Fund, 68
Intellectual Property Rights Enforcement Directive, 148, 149
interactive press kits, xix
interactive streaming, 15, 58–59, 76–84
interactive-subscription services, 78
interactive webcasting, 105
Internal Revenue Code, 72
International Association of Entertainment Lawyers, 130, 314
International Federation of the Phonographic Industry (IFPI), xxvii
Internet, xv, 105
    jargon, 169–70
    piracy and, xxii
    radio, xxxi
Internet Corporation of Assigned Names and Numbers, xxiii, 47
Internet radio. *See* webcasting
Internet Service Providers (ISPs), xxii, xxx, 120, 284
    licensing, 313
Internet Underground Music Archive, 133, 229
Interscope Records, xxxiii, 262, 300
IODA, 137
Iovine, Jimmy, 231
iPad, xxx, 60, 128
iPhone, 60, 76, 126, 128, 172, 218, 228, 305
iPod, xxx, 61, 76, 126, 128, 163, 228
    advertisements, 94–95
IPRS, 13
Iron Man, 312–13
"Iron Man" (Black Sabbath), 312
Island Def Jam Music Group, 163
Isley Brothers, 35, 36
ISPs. *See* Internet Service Providers
Israelite, David, 14, 83, 110, 142
Issa, xxxiii
It Takes a Nation of Millions (Public Enemy), 217
iTunes, xxxii, 27, 62, 133, 295, 311–13
    advertising and, 92, 96
    affiliates, 247
    availability on, 295
    birth of, 126
    downloading from, 57, 78, 113
    music sales, xxiii, xxvii, 43, 79–80, 112, 116, 248

Orchard and, 244, 278
    promotion of, 305, 307
    ringtones, 109
    software, 176
    store, 37, 60, 76, 138, 146–47, 177–80, 183, 188, 192, 205, 223, 225–28, 237, 240, 261, 274–75, 278, 281

Jackson, Janet, 232, 266, 301
Jackson, Joe, 202
Jackson, Michael, xxv, 119, 162, 294
the Jacksons, 108
Jagger, Mick, 102
Jaguar, 95, 96
Jamiroquai, 251
Jardine, Al, 49
JASRAC, 13, 87
Java, 170
Jenkins, Katherine, 251
Jersey Boys, 100
Jett, Joan, 273
Jillsnextrecord.com, 204
jingles, 94, 97, 100
JJ Grey & Mofro, 280
Jobs, Steve, 126, 128, 305
Jodorowsky, Alejandro, 249
Joel, Billy, 162
John, Elton, 68
John Butler Trio, 173
John Doe lawsuits, 144
Johnson, Jack, 262
Jomanda, 187
Jonas Brothers, 191
Jones, Darryl, 255
Jones, Norah, 8
Jordan, Jason, 191
JPEG, 170
Just Dance, 114
"Just the Way You Are" (Bruno Mars), 220

Kadence, 173
Kahne, David, 191
Kallman, Craig, 187–97
Kander, John, 11
Karr, Rick, 153

Kassbaum vs. Steppenwolf Productions, Inc., 49
Kazaa, xxx, 122, 125, 146, 147, 221, 224, 293
KC and the Sunshine Band, 96
Keating, Zoe, 176
Keller, Daphne, 216
Kemp, Tara, 187
Kern, Jerome, 13
Kesha, 220, 240, 312
Kickstarter, xxxi
Kid Rock, 129, 188
Kiewl, Tony, 95–96
Kill Rock Stars, 273
Kilpatrick Townsend & Stockton LLP, 40
Kinect, 114
King, Carole, 273, 275
the Kinks, 246
Kirkland, Kenny, 255, 256
Kiss, 41
Kittie, 181
Kot, Greg, 92, 278, 286–95
Kristofferson, Kris, 209
Krumper, Michael, 181
Kulash, Damian, 164
Kurupt, 181
Kwun, Michael S., 136

labels, 16. *See also specific labels*
    advances in, 17–18
    artists signed by, xvii
    business practices, 15–19
    consumer electronics industry vs., 120–21
    controlled composition clauses, 18
    fans vs., 124–25
    indie, 209–15, 246–50, 276
    LimeWire vs., 143–44
    major, xxv, xxvi–xxx, 186–97, 274
    master rights, 18
    need for, 277–86
    P2P vs., 121–22
    pay from, 79
    royalties in, 17–18
    technology vs., 121
    as venture capitalists, xvi
    virtual, 252
Lack, Andy, 222

Lady Antebellum, 161
Lady Gaga, 92, 115, 163, 223, 231, 237, 262–64
Last.fm, xxxi, 143, 237, 239, 246
    customizing, 60–62, 67
    growth of, 172, 223, 285
    promotion on, 154, 167, 175
Laswell, Bill, 260
LAUNCHcast, 67, 70, 70n2
Law and Order, 207
Leahy, Patrick, xxii, xxiii, 140, 142
Learning How to Die (Kot), 287
Led Zeppelin, 95, 240
Lefsetz, Bob, 214, 224
Legends, 85
Lennon, John, 10, 25
Lennon, Julian, 25
Lennon, Sean, 25
Lennon, Yoko Ono, 25, 129n2
Lennon vs. Premise Media Corp., 25
Les Nubians, 189
Lessig, Lawrence, 6n1, 22, 27, 28
Levy, Morris, 259
Librarian of Congress, 110
licenses, 85–106
    in advertising, 96–98
    blanket, 132–33
    compulsory, 10, 11, 66, 133
    fees, 96–97
    festival, 94
    individual compulsory, 133
    ISPs, 313
    masters, 18, 57, 109, 116, 248, 312
    master use, 15–16, 89
    for new media, 107–16
    Noncommercial Sampling, 30
    nonexclusive, 297
    parameters, 115–16
    practical tips for, 101–5
    radio, 66, 97–98
    Sampling Plus, 30–31
    songs, 109–11
    statutory, xx, 10, 56–57, 66–68, 127–29, 133, 141
    synch, 89
    video games, 111–15
    voluntary collective, 132

Lil' Wayne, 295
LimeWire, xxx, 124, 128, 221, 297, 311
    labels vs., 143–44
Lindell, Eric, 280
Linkin Park, 173
Liquid Audio, 227
Live365.com, 60, 62
Live Nation, xxxiii
Logic, 153
Lohmann, Fred von, 145
looped programming, 68
Lord, Rob, 229
Lory, Dave, xv
Los Angeles Time, xxiv
Los Lonely Boys, 260
Lovato, Demi, 191
Love, Mike, 50
LoveCat Music, 92
"Love Is a Wonderful Thing," 35, 36
LPs, xxix, 312
Ludwig Museum, 216
Luini, Jon, 229
Lykke Li, 188
Lynch, David, 212

"Macarena," 104
Macbook Air, 96
Macromedia, 171
made for hire, 22
Madison Square Garden, 264
Madonna, xxxiii, 41, 231, 290
Magnatude, 296, 297–98
mainstream success, 186–97
major labels, 186–97, 274
    digital technology and, xxv
    extinction of, 194–97
    suffering of, xxvi–xxx
Mallette, Pattie, 163
managers, 251–58
    artists and, 256–57
Manilow, Barry, 182
Mars, 187
Marsalis, Branford, 255, 256
Marsalis, Wynton, 226, 255–58
Martel, Diane, 300

Martin, Ari, 251–54
Mary Poppins, 35
MasterCard, xxiii
masters
    audio compilations and, 86
    clearing, 89, 91
    control of, 100, 274, 279
    copyrighted, 7–9, 21–22, 195
    defined, 6
    exclusive rights to, 306
    licensing, 18, 57, 109, 116, 248, 312
    ownership, xxxii, xxxiii, 140
    rights to, 18, 306
mastertones, 109
master use license, 15–16, 89
Masur, Steve, 130, 304–15
Matisyahu, 260
MCA, 201
McCartney, Jesse, 191
McCartney, Paul, xxxiii, 10, 41, 129*n*2
McDowell, Robert, 139
McLachlan, Sarah, 251
MCPS, 87
MCSC, 13
Meadowlands, 12
Meat Loaf, 42
mechanical rights, 9
mechanical royalties, 8
    CD, 111, 179
Mediafire, xxx
media tariffs, 13
Men Who Stare at Goats, 247
Mercer, Johnny, 108
Mercury Lounge, 166
Merge Records, 165
Merlin, xv
Metallica, 113, 114, 293
Metropolitan Opera, 256
"Mexican Pharmacy" (Sobule), 204
MFN. *See* most favored nations
MGM vs. Grokster, 122, 123–24
Michael, George, 17
Michaelson, Ingrid, 173
Mickey Mouse Protection Act. *See* Sonny Bono
        Term Extension Act

microcasters, 71

Microsoft, 94, 114, 171

Midler, Bette, 98

Miller, Mitch, 119

Miller, Paul. *See* DJ Spooky

Million Dollar Mistakes (Avalon), 308

minimum use, 26

Mission of Burma, 209

MIT Press, 216–17

mobile music, xxvii

mobile phones, 309

Mobile Roadie, 172

mobile subscriptions, 313

Moby, 206, 209–15, 216

Modtones, 109

Moe, 273, 275

MOG, 228

MoodMixes, 299

Moredock, Isaac, 136

morning media activities, *65*

Morpheus, 122, 123

Morris, Doug, 187

most favored nations (MFN), 86, 88–89, 91, 94, 104

motion pictures, 93–94

   independent, 102–3

Motown, 108, 271

Mottola, Tommy, 126

Mountain Apple, 273

"Moving Digital Britain Forward," 131

Mozart, 107, 187

MP3 players, xxx

MP3s, xxv, 77, 111, 116, 175, 307

MP3Tunes.com, xxii

MTV, xxiv, 162–63, 302

Murdoch, Rupert, 160

musical theatre, 100–101

Music First Coalition, 141

"Music Is My Hot, Hot Sex" (Cansei de Ser Sexy), 94–95, 163

music lawyers, 51–54, 267–68

   fees, 52–53

   shopping, 53–54

MusicNet, 125–26

music sales

   albums, xv

Amazon, xiii

   CDs, xvi, 19, 207, 221, 261–62, 294, 311, 312

   RIAA on, xvi

   shrinkage of, xvi

   in 2009, xxviii

   Wal-Mart, xiii

MusicStream, 309

music supervisor, 105

Mute, 211

"My Fair Lady" (Byrne), 30

Myspace, 61, 154, 270, 272

   advertisements on, 160

   death of, 160–62, 183

   friends on, 225

   popularity of, 138, 155, 188–89, 204–5, 212, 214

   promotion through, 230

   redesign, 161

   sound quality on, 174–75

   usefulness of, 167–68, 263–64

Mysto, 163

"My Sweet Lord" (Harrison), 38*n*1

NAB. *See* National Association of Broadcasters

Naim, Yael, 96

Napster, xxvii, xxx, 124, 128, 244

   blanket licenses and, 132–33

   failure of, 308

   impact of, 221, 224

   litigation against, 121–22, 133

   new, 76, 78–80, 83, 225, 297

   offer made by, 227–34, 261–62, 308

   original, xxi, 261, 280, 283

Nas, 300

Nathonson, Matt, 196

National Association of Broadcasters (NAB), 140, 141, 284

National Music Publishers' Association, 10, 14, 83, 110, 142

National Public Radio (NPR), 60–61, 72, 142, 230

native apps, 174

N'Dour, Youssou, 242

Nesson, Charles, 147

Netflix, 233

net receipts, xxxii

Nettwerk Management, 251–54

network neutrality, 138–40, 275

network shows, 92–93

Network Solutions, 47

new media, 107–16

New Music Seminar, xv, xvii, 187, 222, 230

New Order, 209

New School, 171

"New Soul" (Naim), 96

"New York, New York," 11, 15

New York Times, 166, 224

Next Big Sound, 237

Ne-Yo, 163

Nice, Greg, 260

Nickelodeon, 207

Nielsen, 172

"Night and Day" (Porter), 8

Nike, 94

Nimmer, David, 23*n*4

Nine Inch Nails, xxxiii, 41, 288

99 Records, 187

Nintendo, 113

Ninth Circuit Court of Appeals, 99, 122

Noncommercial Sampling license, 30

non-commercial webcasting, 72

nonexclusive license, 297

non-pureplay, 69–70

Nothing Like the Sun, 256

"Now Get Busy," 30

NPD Group, 111

NPR. *See* National Public Radio

'N Sync, 164

NYU Tisch School of the Arts, xxxiv

Obama, Barrack, xxiv

The O.C., 92, 288–89

Ogg, 175

OK Go, xxxiv, 164

on-demand streaming, 60, 87, 137, 276

One Haven Music, 259, 265

One Music, 142*n*5

Online Infringement and Counterfeiting Act, 276

online marketing, 176–80, 181–85

online presence, 168–69

online tipping, 134

"Only Girl (in the World)" (Rihanna), 220

Open Reach, 130

Oppenheim, Matt, 145

The Orchard, 244, 278

Orlons, 246

Or Music, 259

ownership, xxxii

P2P (person-to-person), xxx, 132, 276, 297

DMCA and, 125

labels vs., 121–22

subscriptions, 133

Page, Will, 130

paid prioritization, 139

Palin, Sarah, 204

Palladium, 187

Palm OS, 60, 228

Pandora, xxxi, 60–62, 67, 143, 172, 230, 246

advertising, 69–70

cost management, 240–41

growth of, 228, 236, 239, 275–76, 285

tagging system, 175

Paracadute, 164

Paramore, 188

Pascal, Jason, 244–45

passive participation, 19

Passman, Don, 34, 51–54, 232, 266–72

Patent and Trademark Office (PTO), 41, 44

Patsavas, Alexandra, 92

Patterson, Jeff, 229

payola, 141, 300

PayPal, 179–80, 205, 298

Payton, Nicholas, 256

PBS, 17, 106

Pearl Jam, 162, 301

penny rate, 87

Percy Jackson & the Olympians, 247

Performing Rights Act, 140, 142, 284

performing-rights organizations (PRO), 12*n*2, 13, 132

income of, 14–15

Perri, Christina, 188

Perry, Katy, 197, 220

person-to-person. *See* P2P

Peters, Marybeth, 110

phones. *See also* Android; iPhone

mobile, 309
    smart, 309
phonorecords, 11
    defined, 6
PI. *See* preliminary injunction
Pink, 220
piracy, 275, 297
    Internet and, xxii
PirateBay, xxiv
Pirate Bay Act. *See* Combating Online Infringement
        Counterfeits Act
Pitchfork, 40, 231, 301
Pitman plant, xxv
Pizzi, 163
Plain White T's, 191
Plan B, 188
Playstation 3, 113
Pop, Iggy, 95
Porter, Cole, 8, 238
Post, Mike, 207
Potter, Grace, 191
PowerPoint, xxxiv
PPD. *See* publisher's price to dealers
preliminary injunction (PI), 38
Presley, Elvis, 85, 89, 101, 106
press kits, interactive, xix
Pressplay, 125–26
"Pretty Woman," 24
Prince, xxxiii, 211, 290, 293
private copying, 56, 57, 70, 276, 296
PRO. *See* performing-rights organizations
Project Playlist, 62
promotion
    advertisement, 95–96
    on iTunes, 305, 307
    on Last.fm, 154, 167, 175
    on Myspace, 230
    on radio, 192–94
    on YouTube, 157
promotional use, 90–91
property, 50
ProTools, 153
PRS, 13
Psychostick, 184
PTO. *See* Patent and Trademark Office

Public Announcement, 36, 39, 216
publication
    Copyright Act, 21
    definition, 22
public broadcast stations, 91
public domain, 21, 86, 107
Public Enemy, 209
publicists, 206
public performance, 7
    ASCAP and, 82–84, 111
    DMCA and, 66–68
    downloading compared to, 81–82
    ringtones as, 111
    songwriters and, 12
public performance rights, 12–15, 16, 56, 73
    radio and, 140–44, 284
publishers, 7–8
    digital music services and, 81–84
    writers and, 84
publisher's price to dealers (PPD), 87
Puente, Tito, 108
Pulitzer Prize, 255
Pump It Up, 112
pureplay, 69–70

Queen, 153
? and the Mysterians, 246
Quicktime, 170
Qwest, 139

radio, 7–8, 12, 56–57, 194, 214. *See also* webcasting
    advertising and, 61
    commercial, 95, 186, 195, 252–53, 278–79
    exposure and, 304–5
    importance of, 143–44
    licenses in, 66, 97–98
    marketing and, 263
    popularity of, 307
    promotion, 192–94
    public performance rights act and, 140–44, 284
    satellite, 67, 73, 110
    Top 40, 186
    traditional, 143–44
Radiohead, xxxiii–xxxiv, 288, 290
Raekwon, 196

Railroad Earth, 260
"Raise Your Glass" (Pink), 220
RAO, 13
Rap Attack (Toop), 216
Rapidshare, xxx, 233
the Rapture, 31
Rawlings, Dave, 275
Rdio, 244
RealPlayer, 170
recorded music, 89, 91, 98
recording agreements
    advances, 17–18
    duration, 17
    exclusivity in, 16–17
    options, 17
    recoupment in, 18
recording companies. *See* labels
Recording Industry Association of America. *See*
        RIAA
Record Service, 281
recoups, 8, 203
    in recording agreements, 18
RED, 283
RedOctane, 112
Reed, Lou, 209
Reich, Steve, 216
R.E.M., 41, 266
Resnikoff, Paul, 161–62
retweets, 159
ReverbNation, 230
"Revolution" (Beatles), 94
Rezende, Ana, 95
Reznor, Trent, xxxiii, 279
Rhapsody, xxvii, 58, 177, 225, 230
    costs of, 227–28, 297
    growth of, 60, 244
    interactivity of, 76
    pay from, 79, 80, 83
Rhino, 182, 186
RhymeSayers, 273
RIAA (Recording Industry Association of America),
        xv, xvi, xix, xxvi, xxx, 283
    copyright law and, 66
    indie labels and, 274
    lawsuits, 56, 123–25, 144–47

on ringtones, 110
on sales, 269
on service revenue, 83
tactics, 148
webcasting and, 68
RIAA vs. Tenenbaum, 147
Righteous Babe, 273
Rihanna, 220
ringtones, 24, 108–11
    iTunes and, 109
    public performance and, 111
    RIAA on, 110
RioBORG, 227
Ripped (Kot), 92, 278, 287, 293
Robertson, Michael, xxii
Robischon, Noah, 116
Rock Band, 113
Rockingale Records, 275
Rock Ridge Music, 181–85
Rogers, 244
the Rolling Stones, 92, 94, 102–3, 108, 215, 246, 249
roll-over payment, 87, 103
Rolontz, Lee, 300
rootkit disaster, 121
Rose, Don, 273
Rosen, Hilary, 230
Rosenthal-Newsom, Tracy, 115
Roxio, 122*n*2
Royal Caribbean, 95
royalties, xxxii, 17–18
    mechanical, 8, 111, 179
    from subscription services, 80–81
Rubberband, 43
Rube Goldberg machine, 164
Rumer, 188
Rundgren, Todd, 202
Rush, 113
Rydell, Bobby, 246
Ryko Distribution, 283

SABAM, 13
SACEM, 13, 131
SACM, 13
Saddle Creek, 273
sampling, 26, 30–31

Sampling Plus license, 30–31
SAMRO, 13
satellite radio, xxx, 67, 73, 110
"Satisfaction," 102, 108
Saturday Night Live, 204
Scandinavia, 285
Schneider, Michael, 173–74
Schumer, Charles, xxiii
SCMS. *See* Serial Copy Management System
Scott Pilgrim vs. the World, 246, 248
screensavers, xix
scrobbling, 61
SDMI. *See* Secure Digital Music Initiative
"Secrets" (One Republic), 92
Secrets of Negotiating a Record Contract (Avalon), 304
Secure Digital Music Initiative (SDMI), 120
sellouts, 95
Senate Judiciary Committee, xxiv
Serial Copy Management System (SCMS), 55
service revenue, 83
SESAC (Society of European Stage Authors & Composers), 32, 132, 175, 241
    database, 8, 101–2
    role of, 12–15, 57–58, 73–75, 81, 99, 313–14
Sessions at West 54th, 17
Sexton, Cynthia, 114
SGAE, 13
Sharp, Dee Dee, 246
Shazam, 305
Sherman, Cary, 124, 144
"Shut Up and Let Me Go" (Ting Tings), 96
SIAE, 13
Siberry, Jane, xxxiii
SICAM, 13
Silverman, Tom, xv–xvii, xxi, xxxi, 119, 127–28, 222, 229
Simon, Paul, 53, 108
Simson, John, xx
Sinatra, Frank, 15, 68, 101, 238
Sirius XM, 67, 73, 276, 284
Sister Hazel, 183
Sivers, Derek, xvii, xviii, 176–77
Six Degrees, 273
Six Feet Under, 92

Sixth Circuit, 26
Skaggs Family, 273
Skype, 61
Slacker, 62, 172, 228, 275
Slash, 195, 196, 209
smart phones, *173*
smashTheTONES, 109
Smithsonian Folkways Recordings, 101
Snoop Dogg, 108
Sobule, Jill, 201–8, 271, 288
SOCAN, 13
social networks, 143, 153–54
    aggregators, 162–63
    online presence and, 154
Society of European Stage Authors & Composers. *See* SESAC
songs
    on audio compilations, 85–86
    hit, 235–43
    licensing, 109–11
songwriters, 7–9
    public performance and, 12
Sonny Bono Term Extension Act, 22
Sony ATV, 108, 125, 126, 211
Sony Betamax case, 122
Sony Music, xix, xxv, xxvii, xxxi, 7, 17, 53, 106, 141, 186, 269, 274, 281, 294, 300, 301
"So Sick" (Ne-Yo), 163
So So Def, 163
sound-alikes, 98–99
SoundCloud, 154, 167, 174–75, 265
SoundExchange, xv, 68–69, 70*n*3, 72, 128, 175, 241, 275, 285
    rates paid to, 69–73
Sound Opinions, 287, 295
sound recordings, defined, 6
SoundScan, 177, 191, 220, 274
soundtracks, 116, 246–50
Sound Unbound, 216
Sousa, John Philip, 13
Souter, David H., 123, 124
Spears, Britney, xxxiv
Special Rider Music, 8
Spielberg, Steven, 11
Spiewak, Jason, 181–85

Spinner, 95

SpiralFrog, 138

Spitzer, Eliot, 141

Spotify, 136–38, 221, 228, 233, 244, 269, 309

Springsteen, Bruce, xxv, 12, 114, 162, 211, 261, 301

"Stairway to Heaven" (Led Zeppelin), 240

Stalin, Joseph, 25

standard fees, 96

Stanton, Louis L., 135

Starbucks, 231

Starbucks' Hear Music, xxxiv

"Start Me Up" (Rolling Stones), 94

State Farm, 164

Statute of Queen Anne, 6

statutory licensing, xx, 10, 56–57, 127–29, 133, 141
    webcasting and, 66–68

Stein, Ben, 25

Steppenwolf, 49

Stewart, Dave, 113

Sting, 95, 255, 256

Stipe, Michael, 209

Stone, Joss, 113

Stones in Road (Carpenter), xix

"Stop and Stare" (One Republic), 92

"Strangers in the Night," 96

StreamCast, 124

streaming, 42–44, 62, 64, 69, 165, 313
    ad-supported, 221, 228, 236
    cloud-based, 309
    costs of, 240–41
    interactive, 15, 58–59, 76–84
    on-demand, 60, 87, 137, 276
    reporting, 72, 176

Stuart, Thomas, 43

Stuart vs. Collins, 43

Sub Pop, 41

subscription services
    royalties from, 80–81
    strategies, 158–59
    tethered downloads and, 82–83

success, 220–26

"Suicide & Redemption" (Metallica), 114

Sunenblick vs. Harrell, 43

Super Bowl, 226, 305

Superior Coach, 312

"Supermodel" (Sobule), 208

Supreme Court, 24

the Supremes, 271

Swift, Taylor, 173, 186, 237

synch fee, 90

synch license, 89

synchronization, 8
    rights, 11–12

TAG Strategic, 227

Taj Mahal, 187

Tap Tap Revenge, 172, 247

Target, 236

Taylor, Koko, 277

Tel Aviv University, 127

television programs, 90–93
    cable shows, 92–93
    foreign, 90
    network shows, 92–93
    public broadcasting, 9

templates, 171

Tenenbaum, Joel, 145, 147

territory, 98

tethered downloading, 57–59, 76–84
    subscription services and, 82–83

Thall, Peter, 34, 53

theft, 34–40

"They Can't Take That Away from Me" (Gershwins), 11

Things Here Are Different, 201

third-party rights, 178

This Is Your Brain on Music, 239

Thomas, Jammie, 145, 146, 283, 293

Thompson Records, 209

360 deal, 18–19, 263, 281

three-strikes law, 148–50

Thrill Jockey, 292

"Through the Fire and Flames" (Dragonforce), 113

Thumbplay, 244

T.I., 188

"Tik Tok" (Kesha), 240

"The Time (Dirty Bit)" (Black Eyed Peas), 220

Ting Tings, 96

TLDs. *See* top-level domain names

Toop, David, 216

Top 40 radio, 186, 188
top-level domain names (TLDs), 48
Topspin, 230
Total Request Live, 302
Tower of Power, 259
Tower Records, xxvii, 236
Toyota, 205
trademarks, 40–51
    application process, 43–46
    federal registration, 42–43
    protectable forms of, 41–42
    quasi-protectable, 41–42
    strongest, 45*n*5
    zones of protection, 42, 45
traditional radio, 143–44
transmissions, 12
transparency, 226
Trigg, James, 40
Tucker, Ashford, 40
TuneCore, xxxi, 176, 178, 230, 275
the Tunnel, 187
TVT, 245
TweetDeck, 162
Twitter, 154–55, 158, 162, 168, 183, 212, 225, 264
    cross-pollination strategies, 159
2 Live Crew, 24

U2, 286, 290
UBC, 13
UCLA, 36
Ulrich, Lars, 293
Ultimate Chart, 220, 222, 224, 238
Ultimate Love Songs Collection, 85
Ultimate Rock Collection, 85
UMG vs. Grooveshark, 136–37
Uniform Domain-Name Dispute Resolution Policy
        (UDRP), 47
United States vs. ASCAP, 82, 111
Universal, xxxi, 7, 125, 231
    Eminem's lawsuit against, 79–80
    Grooveshark and, 310
Universal Music Group, 101, 108, 137, 274
University of Georgia School of Law, 40
Uptown Records, 43
URL, 170

U.S. vs. ASCAP, 24
USA Today, 278
Usher, 262
Ustream, 162–63, 164–65, 226

Vale, Jerry, 119
Valentino, Bobby, 196
Vanguard Records, 196
Van Halen, 113
Vanuata Pacifica Foundation, 216–17
Van Zandt, Little Steven, 114
Vasquez, Richard, 187
Vaughn, Stevie Ray, 259
venture capitalism, xvi, 306
Verizon, 111, 139, 148, 232
Verizon Navigator, 139
The Very Best of Elvis Presley, 85
VEVO, 302
VH1, xxiv
Viacom, xxiv, 61, 113
Viacom vs. YouTube, 135–36
vicarious infringement, xxii
Victoria's Secret, 95
video, xxix, 102, 157, 162–73, 249, 300–303
    home, 86–88
    instructional, 89
    wedding, 89–90
video games, 111–15
Vimeo, 157
vinyl, xxix, 9, 86, 178, 191, 209, 210, 294, 312
Vinyl Mania, 187
viral, 162–65
Virgin, xxvii
virtual labels, 252
VISA, 298
Visa, xxiii
Vision Critical, 61
Voinovich, George, xxiii
Volkswagen, 95
voluntary collective licensing, 132

Wait for Me (Moby), 209, 214
Waits, Tom, 99
Waits vs. Frito-Lay, 99
Walden, Phil, 282

Walker, Butch, 260
Wall Street Journal, 139
Wal-Mart, xvii, 37, 77, 236
   music sales, xiii
Walton, Gertrude, 145
Warner, xxxi, 7, 78, 125, 231, 281
Warner Brothers, xxxiii
Warner/Chappell, 108
Warner Music Group, 141, 274
Watts, Jeff, xxxii
We Are Hunted, 168
Web 2.0, 170
webcasting, xxx, 15, 57–75, 275, 284. *See also*
    specific services
   advertising, 64, 285
   commercial, 69–72
   current rates payable by, 74–75
   defined, 60, 83
   DMCA and, 56–57
   educational, 72
   growth projections, *63*
   importance of, 62–64
   interactive, 105
   non-commercial, 72
   payment for, 142
   RIAA on, 68
   statutory license and, 67–68
websites, 107
   design, 169
   hosting, 169
   making, 168–72
wedding videos, 89–90
Weezer, 41
Welch, Gillian, 273
"We R Who We R" (Kesha), 220
West, Garry, 273
Wexler, Jerry, 260
"What's My Name" (Rihanna), 220
What They Never Told You About the Music Business
   (Thall), 53
White Vans, 130
"Wicked Game," 96
Wilco, 95

Will.I.Am, 242
Wilson, Cassandra, 255, 256
WIN. *See* Worldwide Independent Network
Winans, BeBe, 255, 256
Windows 95, 94
Windows Media Player, 77, 170
Wired (magazine), xxxiii, 29
Womack, Bobby, 246
Wonder ,Stevie, 271
Wood, Kimba, 144
work-for-hire, 23, 94
"Working Man" (Rush), 113
Worldwide Independent Network (WIN), 274
Wright, Edgar, 246
writer's share, 7, 84

Xbox 360, 114
Xbox Live, 172

Yahoo! Music, 62, 143
YepRoc, 273
Yetnikoff, Walter, 119
Yorke, Thom, xxxiii
Yorrick, Camille, 300
Young MC, 115
the Young Rascals, 98
Young Veins, 260
YouTube, 62, 95, 189, 212, 262, 302
   advertisements on, 76, 223
   going viral on, 162–65
   growth of, 143, 155, 160, 162, 223–26
   lawsuits against, 135–36
   promotion on, 157
   relevance of, 183–84

Zafiris, Christina, 181
ZAIKS, 13
Zenith Optimedia, 64
Zevon, Warren, 181, 207
Zingy, 109
zones of protection, 42, 45
Zuckerberg, Mark, 155
Zune, 95, 172

About the Author and Editors

Author: Steve Gordon is an entertainment attorney, writer, and consultant based in New York City specializing in the production, distribution, and financing of music, television, documentaries, feature films, and digital entertainment projects. Steve also operates a music-clearance service for producers, filmmakers, and labels who use music in documentaries, television programs, compilations, advertising campaigns, motion pictures, and online-based projects. Steve's clients include artists, independent music and TV producers, and digital-entertainment entrepreneurs, as well as major labels and multinational entertainment corporations. He is the recipient of two Fulbright Scholarships: in 2007 to present a series of lectures at Boconni University in Milan, Italy, and another in 2010 to teach a course based on this book at Recanati, the graduate school of business at Tel Aviv University, Israel.

Steve also served as a business-affairs executive and attorney at Sony Music for a decade and previously worked as an attorney for Atlantic and Elektra records as well as for the performing-rights organization SESAC and for Dino de Laurentiis, a Hollywood studio. He is a graduate of New York University Law School. For published articles, his podcast and videos, upcoming speaking engagements, client list, and contact information, see www.stevegordonlaw.com.

Editor: Robert W. Clarida, Esq., Partner, Cowan, Liebowitz & Latman; author of the treatise *Copyright Law Deskbook* (BNA, 2009); and numerous articles, including bimonthly columns in the *New York Law Journal;* adjunct faculty, Columbia University School of Law; editor, *Journal of the Copyright Society of the USA;* PhD in music composition, State University of New York; and former assistant professor of music at Dartmouth College. Bob is a graduate of Columbia University Law School.

Technical editor: Natalie Noyes, Esq., Film and TV Department, Matador Records, Beggars Group. Natalie is a graduate of the University of Michigan and the University of Connecticut School of Law.